HM Prepare for Class

HM Improve Your Grade

HM ACE the Test

Do you find the marginal callouts useful?

#	Answer		Number of Responses	Percentage
1	Strongly agree		166	38.16%
2	Agree		207	47.59%
3	Somewhat agree		55	12.64%
4	Disagree		7	1.61%
	TOTAL:		435	100.00%

Mean: 1.777 Mean Percentile: 80.57% Standard Deviation: 0.723

"I like that the key terms are given at the beginning of the chapter. It helps to know what is important while reading. I also like that the key definitions are put in the margins. It makes it easier for reviewing and studying."

—Joe Hoff, student at University of Wisconsin–LaCrosse

human relations The study of *why* our beliefs, attitudes, and behaviors sometimes cause relationship problems in our personal lives and in work-related situations.

total person The combination of characteristics that make up the whole person.

organizational culture The collection of shared values, beliefs, rituals, stories, and myths that foster a feeling of community among organizational members.

scientific management The systematic study of a job to break it down into its smallest movements to increase efficiency.

KEY TERMS

communication *p. 18*
conflict resolution *p. 21*
Hawthorne studies *p. 15*
human relations *p. 4*
informal organization *p. 16*
motivation *p. 19*
organizational culture *p. 11*
scientific management *p. 15*
self-acceptance *p. 19*
self-awareness *p. 19*
self-disclosure *p. 20*
total person *p. 9*
trust *p. 19*

HM **Prepare for Class**
Chapter Glossary

Improve Your Grade
Flashcards
Hangman
Crossword Puzzle

"The test preppers within the chapter seem to be a hit with the students. That way they could stop and review while the information was still fresh."

—Malika Blakely, Professor at Georgia State University

Do you find the test prepper useful?

#	Answer		Number of Responses	Percentage
1	Strongly agree		163	38.08%
2	Agree		194	45.33%
3	Somewhat agree		65	15.19%
4	Disagree		6	1.40%
	TOTAL:		428	100.00%

Mean: 1.799 Mean Percentile: 80.02% Standard Deviation: 0.741

Data in barcharts from student survey at San Francisco State University.

Human Relations

Principles and Practices

STUDENT ACHIEVEMENT SERIES

Human Relations

Principles and Practices

Barry L. Reece
Virginia Polytechnic Institute and State University

Rhonda Brandt
Ozarks Technical Community College

Houghton Mifflin Company
Boston New York

Vice President, Executive Publisher: George Hoffman
Executive Sponsoring Editor: Lise Johnson
Senior Marketing Manager: Nicole Hamm
Senior Development Editor: Julia Perez
Senior Project Editor: Nancy Blodget
Art and Design Manager: Jill Haber
Cover Design Director: Tony Saizon
Senior Photo Editor: Jennifer Meyer Dare
Senior Composition Buyer: Chuck Dutton
New Title Project Manager: Susan Peltier
Marketing Assistant: Lauren Foye

Cover Photo: © PunchStock / BrandXpictures

Printed in the U.S.A.

Library of Congress control number: 2007938070

Instructor's edition:
ISBN 13: 978-0-618-97612-6
ISBN 10: 0-618-97612-4

For orders, use student text ISBNs:
ISBN 13: 978-0-618-97599-0
ISBN 10: 0-618-97599-3

1 2 3 4 5 6 7 8 9 – EB – 12 11 10 09 08

Brief Contents

Contents

About the Authors

Student Achievement Series: Human Relations represents a compilation of more than thirty years of research by authors Barry Reece and Rhonda Brandt. Their combined years of postsecondary teaching experience and on-site consulting with business, industry, and educational institutions provide the basis for their real-world approach to human relations skill building. With their diverse backgrounds, they work together to consistently offer their readers up-to-date information and advice in this best-selling text.

Barry L. Reece is a professor at Virginia Polytechnic Institute and State University. He received his Ed.D. from the University of Nebraska. Dr. Reece has been actively involved in teaching, research, consulting, and designing training programs throughout his career. He has conducted more than 500 workshops and seminars devoted to leadership, human relations, communications, sales, customer service, and small business operations. He has received the Excellence in Teaching Award for classroom teaching at Virginia Tech and the Trainer of the Year Award presented by the Valleys of Virginia Chapter of the American Society for Training and Development. Dr. Reece has contributed to numerous journals and is author or coauthor of thirty-two books. He has served as a consultant to Lowe's Companies, Inc., Wachovia Corporation, WLR Foods, Kinney Shoe Corporation, and numerous other profit and not-for-profit organizations.

Rhonda Brandt teaches interpersonal and business communications, human resources management, and various related courses in the Business and Marketing Division of Ozarks Technical Community College in Springfield, Missouri. She received her bachelor's degree in business education with vocational certification from the University of Northern Iowa and a master's degree in Practical Arts and Vocational/Technical Education from the University of Missouri. She has served as a faculty member at Hawkeye Community College and Administrative Support Department Chair at Springfield College. Ms. Brandt is currently serving as Executive Director of the International Association of Online Teachers (*www.online-teachers.org*), an organization dedicated to providing teachers from all disciplines the opportunity to enhance their professional credentials and online teaching opportunities, while at the same time providing educational institutions access to experienced and credentialed faculty. Rhonda continues to conduct workshops and seminars for teachers, small businesses, and large corporations throughout the nation, just as she has done for more than twenty-five years.

Preface

Interpersonal and communication skills, the ability to work effectively within a team, and personal ethics and integrity are the attributes that are ranked highest by those who make hiring and promotion decisions today. We have seen the evolution of a work environment that is characterized by greater cultural diversity, more work performed by teams, and greater awareness that quality relationships are just as important as quality products in our global economy.

The importance of human relations can be summarized in one concise law of personal and organizational success: All work is done through relationships. Employees are more productive when they have the ability to develop effective relationships with their boss, fellow workers, customers, and clients. Organizations are increasingly using relationship-building strategies to develop customer loyalty.

● Major Strengths

Human Relations—Principles and Practices builds on strengths that have been enthusiastically praised by instructors and students.

- The **"total person" approach** to human relations has been expanded and enriched in this edition. We continue to believe that human behavior at work and in our private lives is influenced by many interdependent traits such as emotional balance, self-awareness, integrity, self-esteem, physical fitness, and healthy spirituality.
- The text provides the reader with an overview of the **seven major themes of effective human relations**: Communication, Self-Awareness, Self-Acceptance, Motivation, Trust, Self-Disclosure, and Conflict Resolution. These broad themes serve as the foundation for contemporary human relations courses and training programs.
- A hallmark of this text is the use of many **real-world examples** of human relations issues and practices. These examples build the reader's interest and promote understanding of major topics and concepts. Many of the organizations cited in this text have been recognized by the authors of *The 100 Best Companies to Work For, The 100 Best Corporate Citizens, 100 Best Companies for Working Mothers,* and *America's 50 Best Companies for Minorities.*

◆ The *Student Achievement Series:* A Team Approach: Built by Professors and Students, for Professors and Students

Over the past three years Houghton Mifflin has conducted research and focus groups with a diverse cross-section of professors and students from across the country to create the first textbook series that truly reflects what professors and students want and need in an educational product. Everything we have learned has been applied to create and build a brand-new educational experience and product model, from the ground up, for our two very important customer bases.

Student Achievement Series: Human Relations—Principles and Practices is based on extensive professor and student feedback and is specifically designed to meet the teaching needs of today's instructors as well as the learning, study, and assessment goals of today's students. Professors and students have been involved with every key decision regarding this new product development model and learning system—from content structure, to design, to packaging, to the title of the textbook, and even to marketing and messaging. Professors have also played an integral role as content advisors through their reviews, creative ideas, and contributions to this new textbook.

▼ WHAT STUDENTS TOLD US

Working closely with students has been both rewarding and enlightening. Their honest and candid feedback and their practical and creative ideas have helped us to develop an educational learning model like no other on the market today. Students have told us many things. While price is important to them, they are just as interested in having a textbook that reflects the way they actually learn and study. As with other consumer purchases and decisions they make, they want a textbook that is of true value to them. *Student Achievement Series: Human Relations* accomplishes both of their primary goals: It provides them with a price-conscious textbook, and it presents the concepts in a way that pleases them.

Today's students are busy individuals. They go to school, they work, some have families, they have a wide variety of interests, and they are involved in many activities. They take their education very seriously. Their main goal is to master the materials so they can perform well in class, get a good grade, graduate, land a good job, and be successful.

Different students learn in different ways; some learn best by reading, some are more visually oriented, and some learn best by doing through practice and assessment. While students learn in different ways, almost all students told us the same things regarding what they want their textbook to "look like." The ideal textbook for students gets to the point quickly; is easy to understand and read; has fewer and/or shorter chapters; has pedagogical materials designed to reinforce key concepts; has a strong supporting website for quizzing, testing, and assessment of materials; is cost conscious; and provides them with real value for their dollar.

■ TAKING WHAT PROFESSORS AND STUDENTS TOLD US TO CREATE: *Student Achievement Series: Human Relations*

Student Achievement Series: Human Relations provides exactly what students want and need pedagogically in an educational product. While other textbooks on the market include some of these features, the *Student Achievement Series* is the first textbook to fully incorporate all of these cornerstones, as well as to introduce innovative new learning methods and study processes that completely meet the wishes of today's students. It does this by:

- Being concise and to the point.
- Presenting more content in bulleted or more succinct formats.

- Highlighting and boldfacing key concepts and information.
- Organizing content in more bite-size and chunked-up formats.
- Providing a system for immediate reinforcement and assessment of materials throughout the chapter.
- Creating a design that is open, user-friendly, and interesting for today's students.
- Developing a supporting and integrated Web component that focuses on quizzing and assessment of key concepts.
- Eliminating or reducing traditional chapter components that students view as superficial.
- Creating a product that is easier for students to read and study.
- Providing students with a price-conscious product.

★ PROFESSORS AND STUDENTS: WE COULDN'T HAVE DONE IT WITHOUT YOU

We are very grateful to all the students across the country who participated in one form or another in helping us to create and build the first educational product pedagogically designed specifically for them and their learning and educational goals. Working with these students was an honor, as well as a lot of fun, for all of us at Houghton Mifflin. We sincerely appreciate their honesty, candor, creativeness, and interest in helping us to develop a better learning experience. We also appreciate their willingness to meet with us for lengthy periods of time and to allow us to videotape them and use some of their excellent quotes. We wish them much success as they complete their college education, begin their careers, and go about their daily lives.

STUDENT PARTICIPANTS

Acosta, Pricilla, *University of Texas at Brownsville*
Adamec, Christopher J., *Indiana University, Bloomington*
Aiken, Katie, *Miami University*
Albert, Chris, *California State University, Sacramento*
Allen, Laura, *Carroll College*
Araujo, Javier H., *University of Texas at Brownsville*
Arreola, Jose, *University of Texas at Brownsville*
Back, Hillary, *James Madison University*
Baker, Elaine, *Iowa Lakes Community College*
Barrett, O'Neil, *Borough of Manhattan Community College*
Barron, Joe, *Providence College*
Beal, Laura, *Miami University*
Belle, JaLisha Elaine, *Adrian College, MI*
Beverly, Carolyn, *Southwest Tennessee Community College*
Bis, Ryan, *Boston University*
Boyd, Shawn, *Southwest Tennessee Community College*
Brantley, Gerius, *Florida Atlantic University*
Brewster, Angie, *Boston College*
Brez, Cyleigh, *Miami University*
Bruss, Joy, *Carroll College*
Buchholz, Mike, *James Madison University*
Butters, Amy, *Carroll College*
Calvo, Veronica, *Keiser College*
Campbell, Jessy, *James Madison University*
Chester, Elaine, *Columbus Technical College*
Chimento, Kristin, *Miami University*
Coker, Nadine, *Columbus Technical College*
Collins, Shayla, *Southwest Tennessee Community College*
Connolly, Catie, *Anna Marie College*
Cooper, Angelique, *DePaul University*
Cooper, Jolinda, *Beaufort County Community College*
Counihan, Mallory, *James Madison University*
Day, Brian, *Georgia State University*

Delaney-Winn, Adam, *Tufts University*
Denton, Justin, *California State University, Sacramento*
DiSerio, Stephanie, *Miami University*
Diz, Rita, *Lehman College*
Dolcemascolo, Christine, *California State University, Sacramento*
Dolehide, Maggie, *Miami University*
Dripps, Matthew, *Miami University*
Duran, Gabriel, *Florida International University*
Ebron, Clara, *Beaufort County Community College*
Espinoza, Giovanni, *Hunter College*
Fahrenbach, Tanya, *Benedictine University*
Fargo, Sarah Louise, *Indiana University, Bloomington*
Faridi, Muneeza, *Georgia State University*
Fischer, Christina, *University of Illinois at Chicago*
Fisher, Emily Katherine, *Indiana University, Bloomington*
Fleming, Linda, *Columbus Technical College*
Frazier, Sharita, *Georgia State University*
Gabri, Holli, *Adrian College, MI*
Gagnon, Danielle, *Boston University*
Gamez, Iris, *University of Texas at Brownsville*
Garza, Brenda, *University of Texas at Brownsville*
Gillispie, Renata, *Southwest Tennessee Community College*
Glater, Paulina, *DePaul University*
Gonzalez, Donna, *Florida International University*
Goulet, Michelle, *Carroll College*
Greenbaum, Barry, *Cooper Union*
Griffis, Jill, *Carroll College*
Hall, Rachel, *Miami University*
Harris, Emma, *Miami University*
Hawkins, Roy, *Southwest Tennessee Community College*
Hightower, Kendra, *Southwest Tennessee Community College*
Hill, Erika, *University of Florida*
Hoff, Joe, *University of Wisconsin–LaCrosse*
Hooser, Ginny, *Western Illinois University*
Huang, Jin, *Georgia State University*
Janko, Matt, *University of Massachusetts–Amherst*
Johnson, Peggy, *Iowa Lakes Community College*
Johnson, Stella, *Columbus Technical College*
Keltner, Travis, *Boston College*
Khan, Javed, *University of Central Florida*
Knowles, Mary, *University of Central Florida*
Konigsberg, Matthew, *Baruch University*
Kozeibayeva, Leila, *Indiana University, Bloomington*
Krouse, Molly, *James Madison University*
Kuhnlenz, Fritz, *Boston University*
Lambalot, Lindsey, *Northeastern University*
Lanier, Mary, *Southwest Tennessee Community College*
Largent, Thomas, *Adrian College, MI*
Lawrence, Lucy, *Beaufort County Community College*
Lee, Cheng, *University of Wisconsin–LaCrosse*
Lippi, Steven, *Boston College*
Long, Crystal, *Iowa Lakes Community College*
Lopez, Henry, *Florida International University*
Ly, Bryant, *Georgia State University*
Lynch, Jessie, *Miami University*
Mancia, Mario, *Georgia State University*
Marcous, Michael, *University of Central Florida*
Marith, Sarah, *Boston University*
Marshall, Nichole, *Columbus Technical College*
Mavros, Nichelina, *Fordham University*
McLean, Chad, *California State University, Sacramento*
McNamara, Meghan, *California State University, Sacramento*
Medina, Jose A., *University of Texas at Brownsville*
Michalos, Marika, *City College of New York*
Miller, Evan, *Parsons School of Design*
Monzon, Fernando, *Miami Dade College*
Moore, Donald, *Beaufort County Community College*
Nitka, Matt, *University of Wisconsin–LaCrosse*
Noormohammad, Rehan, *Northeastern Illinois University*
Offinger, Caitlin, *Amherst College*
Ortiz, Laura, *University of Texas at Brownsville*
Paredes, Idalia, *University of Texas at Brownsville*
Paruin, John, *Adrian College, MI*
Queen, Durrell, *University of New York*
Randall, William, *Southwest Tennessee Community College*
Rayski, Adrienne, *Baruch University*
Rederstorf, Melonie, *Adrian College, MI*
Ringel, Kevin, *Northwestern University*
Rodriguez, Juan F., *University of Texas at Brownsville*
Rodriguez, Uadira, *University of Texas at Brownsville*
Rosenwinkel, Wendy, *Iowa Lakes Community College*
Royster, Megan, *Indiana University, Bloomington*
Savery, Alison, *Tufts University*
Schaffner, Laura, *Miami University*
Schiller, Raquel, *University of Central Florida*
Schlutal, Aubrey, *James Madison University*
Silgvero, Jesus Javier, *University of Texas at Brownsville*
Silva, Miriam, *University of Texas at Brownsville*
Simkovi, Jordan, *Northwestern University*
Smith, Christine, *James Madison University*
Smith, Everrett, *Southwest Tennessee Community College*
Smith, Karl, *Western Illinois University*
Smith, Letesha, *Southwest Tennessee Community College*
Staley, Ahmad, *Columbus Technical College*

Stenzler, Michael, *University of Central Florida*
Stondal, Adam, *Adrian College, MI*
Teekah, Karissa, *Lehman College*
Thermitus, Patrick, *Bentley College*
Thurmon, Lorie, *Beaufort County Community College*
Toft, Gregory, *Baruch University*
Tolles, Rebecca, *Miami University*
Tran, Vivi, *University of Central Florida*
Trzyzewski, Sam, *Boston University*
Uribe, Vanessa, *Florida International University*
Vayda, Kristin, *Miami University*
Werner, Michael, *Baruch University*
Wesley, Adrian, *Southwest Tennessee Community College*
White, Robert, *DePaul University*
Williams, Jen, *Carroll College*
Williams, LaTonya, *Southwest Tennessee Community College*
Wong, Helen, *Hunter College*
Yusuf, Aliyah, *Lehman College*
Zittericsch, Steve, *Iowa Lakes Community College*
525 Students in MKTG 431: Principles of Marketing, San Francisco State University

We are equally grateful to all the professors across the country who participated in the development and creation of this new textbook through content reviews, advisory boards, and/or focus group work regarding the new pedagogical learning system. As always, professors provided us with invaluable information, ideas, and suggestions that consistently helped to strengthen our final product. We owe them great thanks and wish them much success in and out of their classrooms.

PROFESSOR PARTICIPANTS AND REVIEWERS

Blakely, Malika, *Georgia State University*
Boeckelman, Keith, *Western Illinois University*
Brown, Paula E., *Northern Illinois University*
Calhoun, Cynthia, *Southwest Tennessee Community College*
Eliason, Robert, *James Madison University*
Fine, Terri Susan, *University of Central Florida*
Fisher, Bruce, *Elmhurst College*
Fox, Mark, *Indiana University South Bend*
Hensley, Kermelle, *Columbus Technical College*
Hladik, Paula, *Waubonsie Community College*
Nalder, Kimberly Love, *California State University, Sacramento*
McConnel, Lisa, *Oklahoma State University*
Meyer, Judith, *Beaufort County Community College*
Peterson, Suzanne, *Arizona State University*
Petkus, Donald A., *Indiana University, Bloomington*
Schacherer, Aileen, *Iowa Lakes Community College*
Schultz, Debbie, *Carroll College*
Silver, Gerald, *Purdue University–Calumet*
Thannert, Nancy, *Robert Morris College*
Thomas, Ron, *Oakton Community College*
Thompson, Kenneth, *DePaul University*
Weeks, Benjamin, *St. Xavier University*

✱ ORGANIZATION OF THE TEXT

The nine chapters in *Human Relations—Principles and Practices* provide the reader with an in-depth presentation of the **seven major themes of effective human relations**. Chapter 1 begins with an overview of the nature, purpose, and importance of human relations and concludes with a description of each major theme. These themes are interrelated and therefore discussed in more than one chapter. For example, the various dimensions of the **communications** theme are discussed in Chapters 2 and 8. **Self-disclosure** is also discussed in these chapters. Chapter 3 focuses on **self-acceptance**, a guiding force in our lives. Chapter 4 explains how personal values influence ethical choices. The material in this chapter and Chapter 8 helps the reader understand the fundamentals of **conflict resolution**. Self-assessment activities, strategically placed throughout the text, contribute to increased **self-awareness**. The themes of **trust** and **motivation** (self and others) surface in selected chapters.

CHAPTER LEARNING ACTIVITIES

A major goal of this text is to help students develop new behavior patterns. At the end of each chapter are several learning activities that can result in dramatic performance improvement. These activities will help students make the changes they want in their life.

- A carefully designed **role-play application** exercise. These role plays are very "user-friendly" and are designed to reinforce key chapter concepts.
- A **Career Corner** learning activity. Through its inviting question-and-answer format, students can obtain answers to important work-related questions.
- **Application exercises**. A variety of learning activities help students improve and internalize their human relations skills.
- **Self-assessment instruments**. These online assessments provide multiple opportunities to complete self-assessment activities and then reflect on the results.

AN EFFECTIVE TEACHING AND LEARNING PACKAGE

FOR INSTRUCTORS:

Online Instructor's Resource Manual (Rhonda Brandt, Ozarks Technical Community College). This resource includes detailed teaching notes for each chapter, suggested responses to end-of-chapter questions and exercises, and additional application exercises. This manual is available on the HMTesting and course management platforms (BlackBoard/WebCT).

Digital Test Bank (Tricia Penno, University of Dayton). The Test Bank includes over 500 questions. Each question is identified by its corresponding learning objective, estimated level of difficulty, page number, and question type (knowledge, understanding, or application). This test bank is available on the HMTesting and course management platforms (BlackBoard/WebCT).

DVD. An expanded video program accompanies the text. Each chapter has its own video designed to illustrate the concepts discussed in the chapter by applying the discussion of the text to real-world case examples. The segments are designed to be shown in the classroom to generate discussion. The video guide for instructors can be found on the Instructor Website and course management platforms (BlackBoard/WebCT).

HMTesting Instructor CD. This CD-ROM contains electronic Test Bank items. Through a partnership with the Brownstone Research Group, HM Testing—now powered by *Diploma*®—provides instructors with all the tools they need to create, author/edit, customize, and deliver multiple types of tests. Instructors can import questions directly from the test bank, create their own questions, or edit existing algorithmic questions, all within *Diploma*'s powerful electronic platform.

HM Management Space™ Instructor Website. This text-based instructor website offers valuable resources including basic and premium PowerPoint slides, downloadable Instructor's Resource Manual files, a video guide, classroom response system content, and much more.

HM Management Space™ BlackBoard®/WebCT®. This online course management system, powered by BlackBoard, contains Instructor Resource Manual files, test bank pools, a video guide, classroom response system content, video segments, quizzes, discussion threads, basic and premium PowerPoint slides, audio chapter summaries and quizzes (MP3s), *Interactive Skills Self-Assessments,* homework, and much more.

FOR STUDENTS:

HM Management Space™ Student Website. This text-specific student website offers non-passkey-protected content such as ACE practice tests, audio glossary terms, career snapshots, outlines, summaries, glossaries (chapter-based and complete), and much more. Content behind the passkey includes ACE+ quizzes, Flashcards, Interactive Games, Interactive Assessments, and Audio Chapter Reviews.

THE SEARCH FOR WISDOM

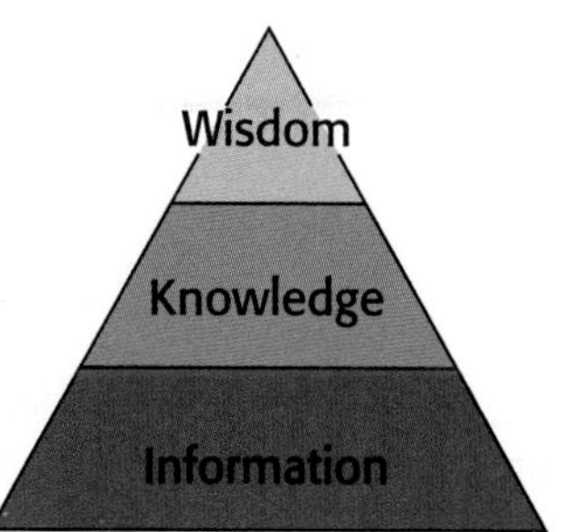

The search for what is true, right, or lasting has become more difficult because we live in the midst of an information explosion. The Internet is an excellent source of mass information, but it is seldom the source of wisdom. Television often reduces complicated ideas to a sound bite. Books continue to be one of the best sources of knowledge. Many new books, and several classics, were used as references for the *Student Achievement Series: Human Relations.* A sample of the books we used to prepare this edition follows:

How Full Is Your Bucket? by Tom Rath and Donald O. Clifton
A Whole New Mind by Daniel H. Pink
Now Discover Your Strengths by Marcus Buckingham and Donald O. Clifton
The Success Principles by Jack Canfield
The Leadership Challenge by James M. Kouzes and Barry Z. Posner
The Sedona Method by Hale Dwoskin
The Art of Happiness by the Dalai Lama and Howard C. Culter
Be Your Own Brand by David McNally and Karl D. Speak
Civility—Manners, Morals, and the Etiquette of Democracy by Stephen L. Carter
Complete Business Etiquette Handbook by Barbara Pachter and Marjorie Brody
Creative Visualization by Shakti Gawain
Do What You Love . . . The Money Will Follow by Marsha Sinetar

Emotional Intelligence by Daniel Goleman
Empires of the Mind by Denis Waitley
The Four Agreements by Don Miquel Ruiz
Getting to Yes by Roger Fisher and William Ury
How to Control Your Anxiety Before It Controls You by Albert Ellis
How to Win Friends and Influence People by Dale Carnegie
The Human Side of Enterprise by Douglas McGregor
I'm OK—You're OK by Thomas Harris
Minding the Body, Mending the Mind by Joan Borysenko
Multiculture Manners—New Rules of Etiquette for a Changing Society by Norine Dresser
The 100 Absolutely Unbreakable Laws of Business Success by Brian Tracy
1001 Ways to Reward Employees by Bob Nelson
The Power of 5 by Harold H. Bloomfield and Robert K. Cooper
Psycho-Cybernetics by Maxwell Maltz
Re-Engineering the Corporation by Michael Hammer and James Champy
Self-Matters: Creating Your Life from the Inside Out by Phillip C. McGraw
The 7 Habits of Highly Effective People by Stephen Covey
The 17 Essential Qualities of a Team Player by John C. Maxwell
The Situational Leader by Paul Hersey
The Six Pillars of Self-Esteem by Nathaniel Branden
Spectacular Teamwork by Robert R. Blake, Jane Srygley Mouton, and Robert L. Allen
Working with Emotional Intelligence by Daniel Goleman
You Just Don't Understand: Women and Men in Conversation by Deborah Tannen

Acknowledgments

Many people have made contributions to *Human Relations—Principles and Practices.* Throughout the years the text has been strengthened as a result of numerous helpful comments and recommendations. We extend special appreciation to the following reviewers and advisors who have provided valuable input for this and prior editions:

Aldrich, James, *North Dakota State School of Science*
Amnotte, Thom, *Eastern Maine Technical College*
Ashbacker, Garland, *Kirkwood Community College*
Avila, Sue, *South Hills Business School*
Banks, Shirley, *Marshall University*
Barry, Rhonda, *American Institute of Commerce*
Borgen, C. Winston, *Sacramento Community College*
Bowerman, Jane, *University of Oklahoma*
Bowers, Jayne P., *Central Carolina Technical College*
Capps, Charles, *Sam Houston State University*
Carter, Lawrence, *Jamestown Community College*
Chew, Cathy, *Orange County Community College*
Cicero, John P., *Shasta College*
Cowden, Anne C., *California State University, Sacramento*
Dzik, Michael, *North Dakota State School of Science*
Elias, John, *University of Missouri*
Feldman, Marilee, *Kirkwood Community College*
Fernsted, Mike, *Bryant & Stratton Business Institute*
Fewins, Dave, *Neosho County Community College*
Flowers, Dean, *Waukesha County Technical College*
Gann, Jill P., *Ann Arundel Community College*
Garrett, M. Camille, *Tarrant County Junior College*
Greene, Roberta, *Central Piedmont Community College*
Hall, Ralph, *Community College of Southern Nevada*
Hanna-Jones, Sally, *Hocking Technical College*
Hansen, Daryl, *Metropolitan Community College*
Hayes, Carolyn K., *Polk Community College*
Heinsius, John J., *Modesto Junior College*
Hiatt, Stephen, *Catawba College*

Hickman, Jan, *Westwood College*
Hill, Larry, *San Jacinto College—Central*
Hurd, Bill, *Lowe's Companies, Inc.*
Jeanis, Dorothy, *Fresno City College*
Katz, Marlene, *Canada College*
Kegel, Robert, Jr., *Cypress College*
Kelley, Karl N., *North Central College*
Kennedy, Vance A., *College of Mateo*
Leonard, Kristina, *Westwood College*
Lineweaver, Deborah, *New River Community College*
Lloyd, Thomas W., *Westmoreland County Community College*
Loomis, Jerry, *Fox Valley Technical College*
Lynch, Roger, *Inver Hills Community College*
Mann, Edward C., *The University of Southern Mississippi*
Martin, Paul, *Aims Community College*
McReynolds, James K., *South Dakota School of Mines and Technology*
Moorhead, Russ, *Des Moines Area Community College*
Mueller, Marilyn, *Simpson College*
Napier, Erv J., *Kent State University*
Ollhoff, Barbara, *Waukesha County Technical College*
Palumbo, Leonard L., *Northern Virginia Community College*
Patton, James, *Mississippi State University*
Paulson, C. Richard, *Mankato State University*
Peralta, Naomi W., *The Institute of Financial Education*
Price, William, *Virginia Polytechnic Institute and State University*
Pritchett, Shirley, *Northeast Texas Community College*
Pulliam, Linda, *Pulliam Associates, Chapel Hill, NC*
Reece, Lynne, *Alternative Services*
Reed, Jack C., *University of Northern Iowa*
Richards, Lynn, *Johnson County Community College*
Sartawi, Khaled, *Fort Valley State University*
Schaden, Robert, *Schoolcraft College*
Shannon, Mary R., *Wenatchie Valley College*
Shatto, J. Douglas, *Muskingum Area Technical College*
Smith, Marilee, *Kirkwood Community College*
Stallings, Camille, *Pima Community College*
Stearns, Lori, *Minnesota West Community Technical College*
Stewart, Cindy, *Des Moines Area Community College*
Tavallali, Rahmat O., *Wooster Business College*
Tavlin, Jane, *Delgado Community College*
Thakur, V. S., *Community College of Rhode Island*
Truesdale, Linda, *Midlands Technical College*
Turner, Wendy Bletz, *New River Community College*
Wayner, Marc, *Hocking Technical College*
West, Tom, *Des Moines Area Community College*
Whipple, Steven, *St. Cloud Technical College*
Worley, Burl, *Allan Hancock College*

We would also like to thank Tricia Penno of the University of Dayton for her assistance in revising the test items and PowerPoints and Paul Mallete for preparing MP3 summaries and quizzes for the student website, ACE quizzes, and Quizzes and Classroom Response System Content.

Over 200 business organizations, government agencies, and nonprofit institutions provided us with the real-world examples that appear throughout the text. We are grateful to organizations that allowed us to conduct interviews, observe workplace environments, and use special photographs and materials.

The partnership with Houghton Mifflin, which has spanned nearly three decades, has been very rewarding. Several members of the Houghton Mifflin College Division staff have made important contributions to this project. Sincere appreciation is extended to Julia Perez, who has worked conscientiously on the text from the planning stage to completion of the book. We also offer sincere thanks to other key contributors: George Hoffman, Lise Johnson, Stacy Shearer, and Nicole Hamm.

Barry L. Reece
Rhonda Brandt

Human Relations

Principles and Practices

1 Introduction to Human Relations

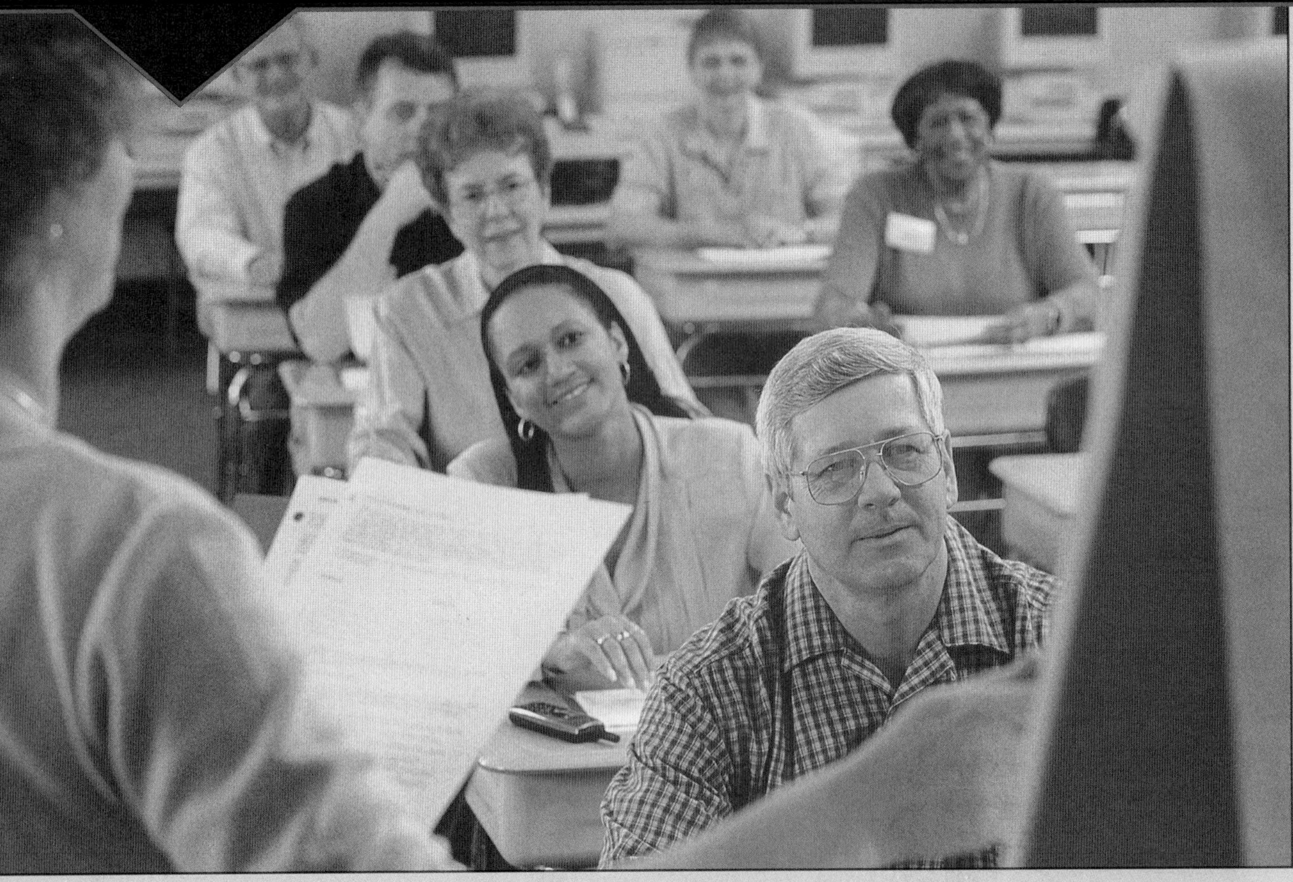

The job market has become a place of churning dislocation caused by corporate mergers, business closings, downsizings and the outsourcing of many jobs to foreign countries. Very often, workers who lose their jobs must return to the classroom to acquire new skills.

1 *Explain the nature, purpose, and importance of human relations in an organizational setting.*

2 *Identify major developments in the workplace that have given new importance to human relations.*

3 *Identify major forces influencing human behavior at work.*

4 *Understand the historical development of the human relations movement.*

"No matter what we do, we do it with people . . . people make it all happen."

—Harry E. Chambers

Chapter Outline

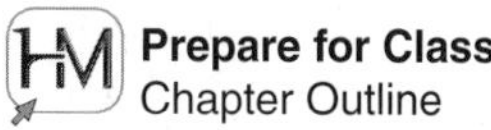

5 *Identify seven basic themes that serve as the foundation for effective human relations.*

A Career of Self-Development

Fred Harp has a clear memory of the advice given to him by his uncle. He told Mr. Harp to "get a job and stay with it." Mr. Harp has tried to follow that advice. After graduating from North Bend High School in North Bend, Oregon, he set his sights on a career in the timber industry and started work at a nearby plywood mill. Nine months later the mill closed, and he was out of work. Changing environmental laws, which reduced the amount of timber available for logging, had a major impact on Oregon's timber industry.

Next Mr. Harp found a job in the paper industry, a traditional source of good jobs in Oregon. Four years later the mill closed during a slump created by excess factory capacity and stronger global competition.

Mr. Harp concluded that old-line industries such as timber and paper were a thing of the past. He decided his future lay in electronics. Oregon's economic planners were busy recruiting high-tech manufacturers, and he wanted to work in that growing

KEY TERMS

communication *p. 18*
conflict resolution *p. 21*
Hawthorne studies *p. 15*
human relations *p. 4*
informal organization *p. 16*
motivation *p. 19*
organizational culture *p. 11*
scientific management *p. 15*
self-acceptance *p. 19*
self-awareness *p. 19*
self-disclosure *p. 20*
total person *p. 9*
trust *p. 19*

Prepare for Class
Chapter Glossary

Improve Your Grade
Flashcards
Hangman
Crossword Puzzle

industry. Soon he began working in a large compact-disc plant opened by Sony Corporation. He enjoyed Sony's team culture and the training programs that prepared workers for advancement. As demand for high-tech workers increased, Mr. Harp quit his job at Sony and took a better-paying job at a nearby HMT Technology disc-drive plant. A few years later, he and most of his coworkers were given pink slips. The company was bought by Komag Incorporated, and all U.S. production jobs were moved to Malaysia.

After losing yet another job, Mr. Harp decided to return to the classroom. The electric power industry was very healthy in Oregon, so he enrolled in a thirteen-month course in energy management. Unfortunately, by the time he graduated the demand for power in Oregon had declined sharply, and he was not able to find work. Today Mr. Harp works for the Lane County facilities-maintenance department. He is hoping this job will not disappear.[1]

The career path followed by Fred Harp reminds us that today's labor market is characterized by a great deal of uncertainty. The old *social contract* between employer and employee was based on the notion of lifetime employment. The new social contract emphasizes personal responsibility for self-development. Today's employers expect employees to assume greater responsibility for increasing their value. Self-development is a major theme of this text.

THE NATURE, PURPOSE, AND IMPORTANCE OF HUMAN RELATIONS

1 *Explain the nature, purpose, and importance of human relations in an organizational setting.*

Each year *Fortune* magazine publishes a list of the 100 best companies to work for in America. The list always includes a variety of small and large companies representing such diverse industries as health care, retailing, finance, manufacturing, and hospitality. Job seekers study the list carefully because these are the companies where morale is high and relationships are characterized by a high level of trust and teamwork. These companies provide a strong foundation for employees to focus on their necessary self-development, therefore enhancing a positive peer-to-peer working environment. America's best companies realize that all work is done through relationships. This chapter focuses on the nature of human relations, its development, and its importance to the achievement of individual and organizational goals.

Human Relations Defined

human relations The study of *why* our beliefs, attitudes, and behaviors sometimes cause relationship problems in our personal lives and in work-related situations.

The term **human relations** in its broadest sense covers all types of interactions among people—their conflicts, cooperative efforts, and group relationships. It is the study of *why* our beliefs, attitudes, and behaviors sometimes cause relationship problems in our personal lives and in work-related situations. The study of human relations emphasizes the analysis of human behavior, prevention strategies, resolution of behavioral problems, and self-development.

Human Relations in the Age of Information

The restructuring of America from an industrial economy to an information economy has had a profound impact on human relationships. Living in an age in which the effective exchange of information is the *foundation* of most economic transactions means making major life adjustments. Many people feel a sense of frustration because they must cope with a glut of information that arrives faster than they can process it. The age of information has spawned the information technology revolution, and many workers experience stress as they try to keep up with ever changing technology.

Increased reliance on information technology often comes at a price—less human contact. Sources of connection away from work are also being trimmed way back. Unfortunately, a human-contact deficiency weakens the spirit, the mind, and the body.[2] To thrive, indeed to just survive, we need warm-hearted contact with other people.

Jeff Danziger, Cartoon Arts International/CWS

The authors of *The Social Life of Information* describe another price we pay for living in the age of information. A great number of people are focusing on information so intently that they miss the very things that provide valuable balance and perspective. Neglecting the cues and clues that lie outside the tight focus on information can limit our effectiveness. Think about written proposals negotiated on the Internet and signed by electronic signature. Such transactions lack the essence of a face-to-face meeting: a firm handshake and a straight look in the eye. Today's knowledge worker needs to take more account of people and a little less of information.[3]

THE IMPORTANCE OF INTERPERSONAL SKILLS

2 *Identify major developments in the workplace that have given new importance to human relations.*

One of the most significant developments in the age of information has been the increased importance of interpersonal skills in almost every type of work setting. Technical ability is not enough to achieve career success. Studies indicate that communication and interpersonal skills are highly rated by nearly all employers who are hiring new employees. They want to know how new hires will treat coworkers and customers, how they speak and listen at meetings, and how well they extend the minor courtesies that enhance relationships. Your people skills will often make the difference in how high you rise in the organization.[4]

Several important developments in the workplace have given new importance to human relations. Each of the following developments provides support for human relations in the workplace.

- *The labor market has become a place of churning dislocation caused by the heavy volume of mergers, acquisitions, business closings, bankruptcies, downsizings, and outsourcing of jobs to foreign countries.* Layoffs in America, which often exceed 200,000 workers per month, have many negative consequences. Large numbers of companies are attempting to deal with serious problems of low morale and mistrust of management caused by years of upheaval and

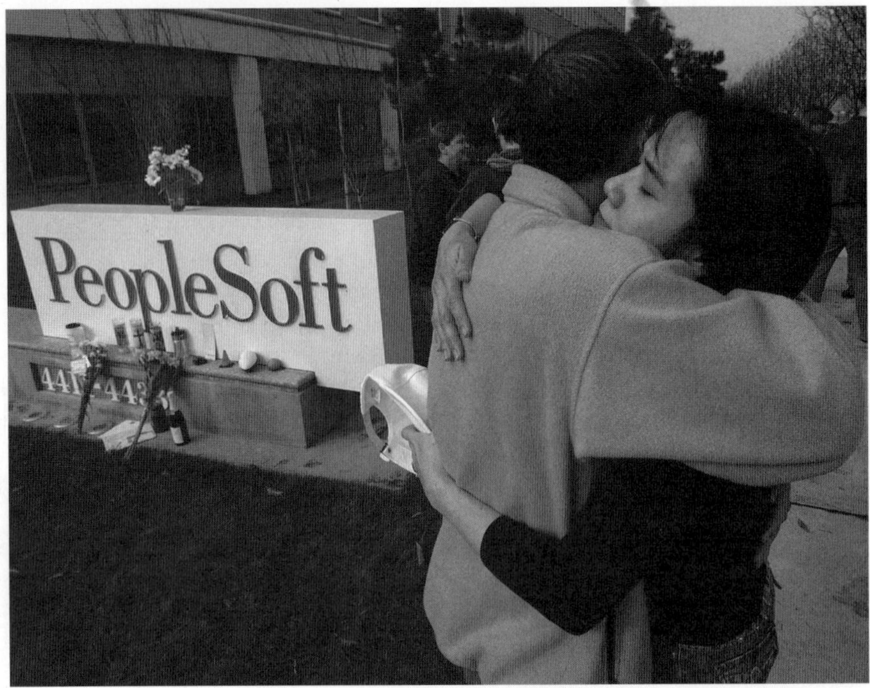

Soon after Oracle completed a $10.3 billion takeover of rival PeopleSoft, 5,000 employee layoff notices were delivered to workers. Most of the affected employees worked for PeopleSoft. These two PeopleSoft employees attempt to console each other.

restructuring. Employees who remain after a company reduces its ranks also suffer; they often feel demoralized, overworked, and fearful that in the next round of cuts they will be targeted.[5]

- *Changing work patterns create new opportunities and new challenges.* The Bureau of Labor Statistics reports that about 30 percent of the U.S. work force is made up of self-employed, temporary, and part-time workers. In recent years we have seen the creation of a phenomenon called *Free Agent Nation,* the growth of self-employed workers who are engaged in consulting and contract work. About 16 million people are now "soloists." Strong demand for temps has surfaced in such diverse fields as medical services, banking, heavy manufacturing, and computers. Many temps land full-time jobs after proving themselves in temporary positions.[6]

- *Organizations are increasingly oriented toward service to clients, patients, and customers.* We live in a service economy where relationships are often more important than products. Restaurants, hospitals, banks, public utilities, colleges, airlines, and retail stores all must now gain and retain the patronage of their clients and customers. In any service-type firm, there are thousands of "moments of truth," those critical incidents in which customers come into contact with the organization and form their impressions of its quality and service.

  In the new economy almost every source of organizational success—technology, financial structure, and competitive strategy—can be copied in an amazingly short period of time.[7] However, making customers the center of the company culture can take years.

TOTAL PERSON INSIGHT

Harry E. Chambers Author, ***The Bad Attitude Survival Guide***

"No matter what we do, we do it with people. People create the technology. People implement the technology. People make it all happen. People ultimately use whatever it is we create. No matter how small your organization or how technical its process, it takes people to be successful."

- *Workplace incivility is increasingly a threat to employee relationships.* A popular business magazine featured a cover story entitled "The Death of Civility."[8] The author describes an epidemic of coarse and obnoxious behavior that weakens worker relationships. At a team meeting, a member's cell phone rings several times and is finally answered. As the person talks loudly on the phone, the rest of the team members wait. An employee routinely brushes his teeth at the drinking fountain, and the boss takes three phone calls during an important meeting with an employee. Stephen L. Carter, author of *Civility,* believes that rudeness, insensitivity, and disrespect are the result of people believing in "me" rather than "we." He says civility is the sum of many sacrifices we are called on to make for the sake of living and working together.[9]

- *Many companies are organizing their workers into teams in which each employee plays a part.* Organizations eager to improve quality, improve job satisfaction, increase worker participation in decision making and problem solving, and improve customer service are turning to teams.

  Although some organizations have successfully harnessed the power of teams, others have encountered problems. One barrier to productivity is the employee who lacks the skills needed to be a team member. In making the transition to a team environment, team members need skills in group decision making, leadership, conflict resolution, and communications.[10]

- *Diversity has become a prominent characteristic of today's work force.* A number of trends have contributed to greater work force diversity. Throughout the past two decades, participation in the labor force by Asian Americans, African Americans, and Hispanics has increased; labor force participation by adult women has risen to a record 60 percent; the employment door for people with physical or mental impairments has opened wider; and larger numbers of young workers are working with members of the expanding 50-plus age group. Within this heterogeneous work force we will find a multitude of values, expectations, and work habits. There is a need to develop increased tolerance for persons who differ in age, gender, race, physical traits, and sexual orientation. The major aspects of work force diversity are discussed in Chapter 7.

- *Growing income inequality has generated a climate of resentment and distrust.* Most measures of income and wage distribution indicate that the wage gap continues to exist. The top 20 percent of American families on average earn about $10 for every dollar earned by the bottom 20 percent. About 37 million people live in poverty, and over 45 million do not have health insurance.[11]

Scientists are finding that socioeconomic status—our relative status influenced by income, job, education, and other factors—impacts our physical and mental health. Most agree that psychological factors such as pessimism, stress, and shame are burdens of low social class.[12]

These developments represent trends that will no doubt continue for many years. Many other developments have also had an unsettling impact on the U.S. work force in recent years. In 2001 the economy was jarred by the collapse of several hundred dot.com companies. The World Trade Center terrorist attack on September 11, 2001, crippled the airline and aerospace industries. In 2002 public trust in the corporate establishment was shaken by a wave of corporate scandals that involved Enron, Tyco, Merrill Lynch, Arthur Andersen, WorldCom, and many other companies.

It is safe to say that no line of work, organization, or industry will enjoy immunity from these developments. Today's employee must be adaptable and flexible to achieve success within a climate of change and uncertainty.

The Challenge of Human Relations

To develop and apply the wide range of human skills needed in today's workplace can be extremely challenging. You will be working with clients, customers, patients, and other workers who vary greatly in age, work background, communications style, values, cultural background, gender, and work ethic.

Human relations is further complicated by the fact that we must manage three types of relationships (see Figure 1.1).

- *Manage relationship with self.* Many people carry around a set of ideas and feelings about themselves that are quite negative and in most cases quite inaccurate. People who have negative feelings about their abilities and accomplishments and who engage in constant self-criticism must struggle to maintain a

FIGURE 1.1

Major Relationship Management Challenges

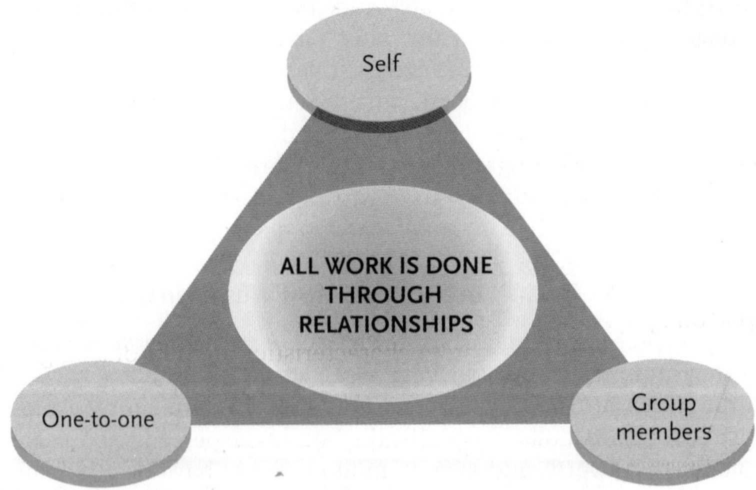

TOTAL PERSON INSIGHT

Daniel Goleman Author, ***Working with Emotional Intelligence***

"The rules for work are changing, and we're all being judged, whether we know it or not, by a new yardstick—not just how smart we are and what technical skills we have, which employers see as givens, but increasingly by how well we handle ourselves and one another."

good relationship with themselves. The importance of high self-esteem is addressed in Chapter 3.

- *Manage one-to-one relationships.* People in the health care field, sales, food service, and a host of other occupations face this challenge many times each day. In some cases, racial, age, or gender bias serves as a barrier to good human relations. Communication style bias is another common barrier to effective one-to-one relationships.
- *Manage relationships with members of a group.* As already noted, many workers are assigned to a team on either a full-time or a part-time basis. Lack of cooperation among team members can result in quality problems or a slowdown in production.

The Influence of the Behavioral Sciences

The field of human relations draws on the behavioral sciences—psychology, sociology, and anthropology. Basically, these sciences focus on the *why* of human behavior. Psychology attempts to find out why *individuals* act as they do, and sociology and anthropology concentrate primarily on *group* dynamics and social interaction. Human relations differs from the behavioral sciences in one important respect. Although also interested in the why of human behavior, human relations goes further and looks at what can be done to anticipate problems, resolve them, or even prevent them from happening. In other words, this field emphasizes knowledge that can be *applied* in practical ways to problems of interpersonal relations at work or in our personal life.

Human Relations and the "Total Person"

The material in this book focuses on human relations as the study of *how people satisfy both personal and work-related needs.* We believe, as do most authors in the field of human relations, that such human traits as physical fitness, emotional control, self-awareness, self-esteem, and values orientation are interdependent. Although some organizations may occasionally wish they could employ only a person's physical strength or creative powers, all that can be employed is the **total person**. A person's separate characteristics are part of a single system making up that whole person. Work life is not totally separate from home life, and emotional conditions are not separate from physical conditions. The quality of one's work, for example, is often related to physical fitness or one's ability to cope with the stress created by family problems.

total person The combination of characteristics that make up the whole person.

Many organizations are beginning to recognize that when the whole person is improved, significant benefits accrue to the firm. These organizations are establishing employee development programs that address the total person, not just the employee skills needed to perform the job. At 3M Corporation employees attend lunchtime seminars on financial planning, parenting, and other topics that help them achieve work/life balance. J. Rolfe Davis Insurance Company offers employees an on-site Weight Watchers class and a "Strides for Pride" walking program.[13]

The Need for a Supportive Environment

Lee Iacocca, the man who was credited with helping Chrysler Corporation avoid bankruptcy, said that all business operations can be reduced to *people, product,* and *profit.* He believed that people come first. Iacocca understood that people are at the heart of every form of quality improvement.

Some managers do not believe that total person development, job enrichment, motivation techniques, or career development strategies help increase productivity or strengthen worker commitment to the job. It is true that when such practices are tried without full commitment or without full management support, there is a good chance they will fail. Such failures often have a demoralizing effect on employees and management alike.

A basic assumption of this book is that human relations, when applied in a positive and supportive environment, can help individuals achieve greater personal satisfaction from their careers and help increase an organization's productivity and efficiency.

TEST PREPPER 1.1, 1.2

ANSWERS CAN BE FOUND ON P. 237

True or False?

F 1. The age of information has increased human contact in the workplace.

F 2. Strong technical ability should guarantee success in today's sophisticated economy.

Multiple Choice

____ 3. Companies such as the Container Store and SAS Institute are at the top of *Fortune*'s 100 best companies to work for because:
- a. they emphasize open communication, employee loyalty, and meaningful work.
- b. they have employee turnover in the 40–50 percent range.
- c. their employees have the best technical skills.
- d. they have the best company benefits.

____ 4. One of the main differences between human relations and the behavioral sciences is that:
- a. the behavioral sciences are oriented more toward application than is the field of human relations.
- b. the field of human relations attempts to anticipate, resolve, and even prevent problems.
- c. the behavioral sciences are less interested in the reasons for human behavior than is the field of human relations.
- d. the field of human relations focuses exclusively on the workplace.

____ 5. Recent developments that have increased the importance of human relations in the workplace include:
- a. general higher morale among today's workers.
- b. more leisure time than ever.
- c. changing work patterns that are creating new opportunities and new challenges.
- d. workers who can expect to work for fewer employers than ever before.

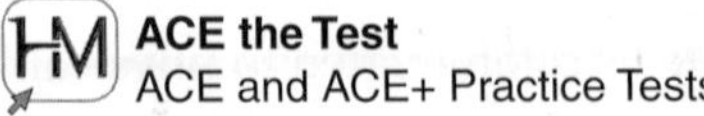

The Forces Influencing Behavior at Work

3 *Identify major forces influencing human behavior at work.*

A major purpose of this text is to increase your knowledge of factors that influence human behavior in a variety of work settings. An understanding of human behavior at work begins with a review of the six major forces that affect every employee, regardless of the size of the organization. As Figure 1.2 indicates, these are organizational culture, supervisory-management influence, work group influence, job influence, personal characteristics of the worker, and family influence.

Organizational Culture

Every organization, whether a manufacturing plant, retail store, hospital, or government agency, has its own unique culture. The **organizational culture** is the collection of shared values, beliefs, rituals, stories, and myths that foster a feeling of community among organizational members.[14] The culture of an organization is, in most cases, the reflection of the deeply held values and behaviors of a small

organizational culture The collection of shared values, beliefs, rituals, stories, and myths that foster a feeling of community among organizational members.

Improve Your Grade
Audio Glossary

FIGURE 1.2

Major Forces Influencing Worker Behavior

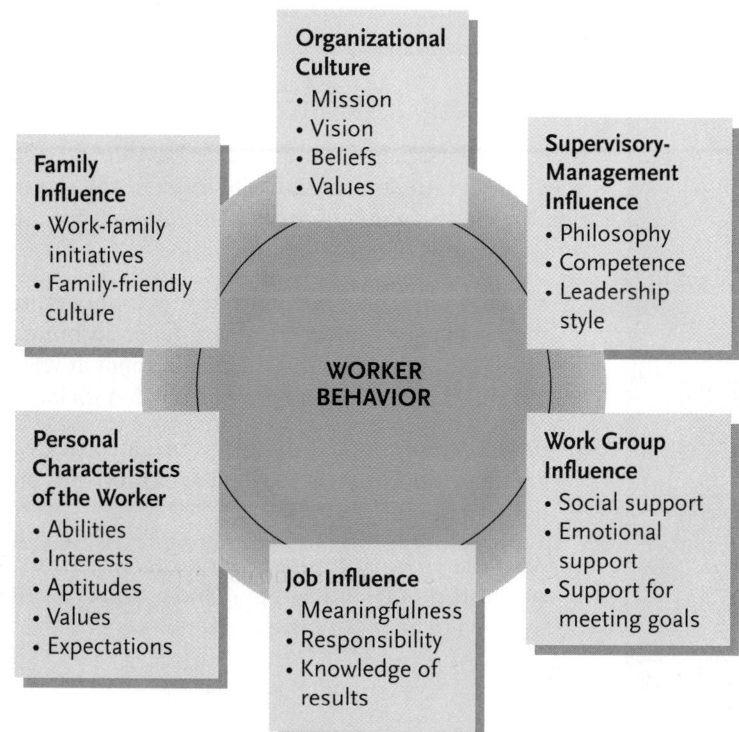

group of individuals. In a large organization, the chief executive officer (CEO) and a handful of senior executives will shape the culture. In a small company, the culture may flow from the values held by the founder.[15]

HM **Improve Your Grade** Career Snapshot

- Enron Corporation, the second-largest company in U.S. history to file for bankruptcy, maintained a corporate culture that pushed everything to the limits: business practices, laws, and personal behavior. This culture drove Enron to dizzying growth, but it eventually collapsed under the weight of greed, deception, and corruption.[16]
- By contrast, eBay, the auction website company, has developed a culture that emphasizes customer service and a loyal work force. The culture is based on two principles: "We believe people are basically good" and "We believe everyone has something to contribute."[17]

Many employees are fired or choose to quit their jobs because they are a poor fit with the corporate culture. It's a good idea to carefully study the organizational culture of a company before accepting employment there.

Supervisory-Management Influence

Supervisory-management personnel are in a key position to influence employee behavior. It is no exaggeration to say that supervisors and managers are the spokespersons for the organization. Their philosophy, competence, and leadership style establish the organization's image in the eyes of employees. Each employee develops certain perceptions about the organization's concern for his or her welfare. These perceptions, in turn, influence such important factors as productivity, customer relations, safety consciousness, and loyalty to the firm.

Maria Benjamin, Wegmans Food Markets employee, offers a cookie to a young customer. Wegmans is usually ranked near the top of Fortune *magazine's list of 100 best companies to work for. This Rochester-based chain is beloved by its employees and customers.*

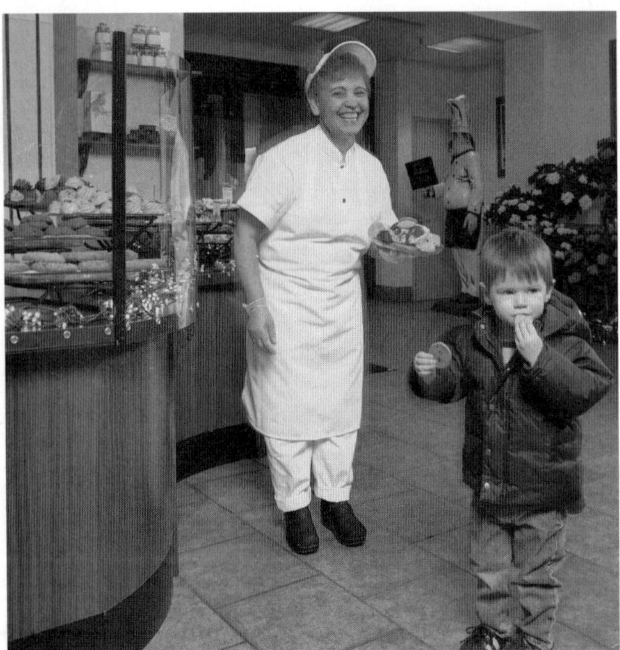

Work Group Influence

In recent years, behavioral scientists have devoted considerable research to determining the influence of group affiliation on the individual worker. This research has identified three functions of group membership.

- *Social needs.* When employees feel more connected to their colleagues at work, they are generally more productive.[18] Many people find the hours spent at work enjoyable because coworkers provide needed social support.
- *Emotional support.* The work group can provide coworkers the support needed to deal with pressures and problems on or off the job.
- *Assistance in solving problems and meeting goals.* A cohesive work group lends support and provides the resources we need to be productive workers.

Job Influence

Work in modern societies does more than fulfill economic needs. When we find meaning and fulfillment in our jobs, we become more complete as human beings.[19] As one organizational consultant noted, work has taken center stage in the lives of most people: "We spend most of our waking hours doing our jobs, thinking about work, and getting to and from our workplaces. When we feel good about our work, we tend to feel good about our lives. When we find our work unsatisfying and unrewarding, we don't feel good."[20] Unfortunately, many people hold jobs that do not make them feel good. Many workers perceive their jobs to be meaningless and boring. Some workers experience frustration because they are powerless to influence their working conditions.

Personal Characteristics of the Worker

Every worker brings to the job a combination of abilities, interests, aptitudes, values, and expectations. Worker behavior on the job is most frequently a reflection of how well the work environment accommodates the unique characteristics of each worker. For more than half a century, work researchers and theorists have attempted to define the ideal working conditions that would maximize worker productivity. These efforts have met with some success, but unanswered questions remain.

Identifying the ideal work environment for today's work force is difficult. A single parent may greatly value a flexible work schedule and child care. The recipient of a new business degree may seek a position with a new high-tech firm, hoping to make a lot of money in a hurry. Other workers may desire more leisure time.

Coming into the workplace today is a new generation of workers with value systems and expectations about work that often differ from those of the previous generation. Today's better-educated and better-informed workers value identity and achievement. They also have a heightened sense of their rights.

Family Influence

A majority of undergraduates name balancing work and personal life as their top career goal.[21] Most people want time for family, friends, and leisure pursuits. However, finding employers who truly support work/life balance can be difficult, especially during a slowing economy.

The new economy is a 24/7 economy. When businesses operate twenty-four hours a day, seven days a week, the result is often a culture of relentless overwork. In many cases workers must live with on-call-all-the-time work schedules.

The number of dual-income families has doubled since 1950. Both parents have jobs in 63 percent of married-couple homes. When both partners are working long hours, it is more difficult to stay committed to a good life together. Marital distress often has a negative impact on organizational productivity.

Many organizations have found that family problems are often linked to employee problems such as tardiness, absenteeism, and turnover. The discovery has led many companies to develop work-family programs and policies that help employees juggle the demands of children, spouses, and elderly parents.[22]

TEST PREPPER 1.3

ANSWERS CAN BE FOUND ON P. 237

True or False?

T 1. Employees develop perceptions about an organization's concern for their welfare based on the philosophy, competence, and leadership styles of their managers.

F 2. Identifying the ideal workplace for today's worker is relatively easy. Most workers want the same thing—more pay.

Multiple Choice

____ 3. The organizational culture at Enron Corporation, prior to filing for bankruptcy:
- a. emphasized customer relations and repeat business.
- b. flowed from the board of directors and major stockholders.
- c. pushed everything to the limit: business practices, laws, and personal behavior.
- d. fostered a feeling of community among employees.

____ 4. When Cinda's husband developed cancer, her coworkers gathered around her and her family. They provided food, transportation, and other daily necessities for her children so that Cinda could be with her husband during his treatment. Cinda's coworkers were providing:
- a. help with her social needs.
- b. goal-setting behavior.
- c. emotional support.
- d. personal structure and values.

____ 5. One way in which employers are coping with family influences on human relations is by providing:
- a. increased penalties for absenteeism, tardiness, and turnover.
- b. work-family programs and policies.
- c. substance abuse counseling for employees.
- d. retraining for laid-off workers.

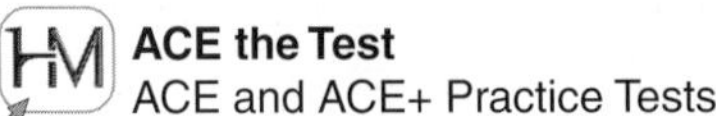

THE DEVELOPMENT OF THE HUMAN RELATIONS MOVEMENT

4 *Understand the historical development of the human relations movement.*

The early attempts to improve productivity in manufacturing focused mainly on trying to improve such things as plant layout and mechanical processes. But over time, there was more interest in redefining the nature of work and perceiving workers as complex human beings. This change reflected a shift in values from a concern with *things* to a greater concern for *people.* In this section we briefly examine a few major developments that influenced the human relations movement.

The Impact of the Industrial Revolution

The Industrial Revolution marked a shift from home-based, handcrafted processes to large-scale factory production. Prior to the Industrial Revolution, most work was performed by individual craftworkers or members of craft guilds. Generally, each worker saw a project through from start to finish. Skills such as tailoring, carpentry, and shoemaking took a long time to perfect and were often a source of pride to an individual or a community. Under this system, however, output was limited.

TOTAL PERSON INSIGHT

James Baughman Director of Management Development, **General Electric Co.**

"You can only get so much more productivity out of reorganization and automation. Where you really get productivity leaps is in the minds and hearts of people."

The Industrial Revolution had a profound effect on the nature of work and the role of the worker. Previously, an individual tailor could make only a few items of clothing in a week's time; factories could now make hundreds. However, the early industrial plants were not very efficient because there was very little uniformity in the way tasks were performed. It was this problem that set the stage for research by a man who changed work forever.

Taylor's Scientific Management

In 1874 Frederick W. Taylor obtained a job as an apprentice in a machine shop. He rose to the position of foreman, and in this role he became aware of the inefficiency and waste throughout the plant. In most cases workers were left on their own to determine how to do their jobs. Taylor began to systematically study each job and break it down into its smallest movements. He discovered ways to reduce the number of motions and get rid of time-wasting efforts. Workers willing to follow Taylor's instruction found that their productivity soared.[23]

Frederick W. Taylor started the **scientific management** movement, and his ideas continue to influence the workplace today. Critics of Taylor's approach say that the specialized tasks workers perform often require manual skills but very little or no thinking. It's fair to say that Taylor's ideas gave workers the means to work more efficiently, but they left decisions about how the work should be done to foremen and supervisors.[24]

scientific management The systematic study of a job to break it down into its smallest movements to increase efficiency.

Mayo's Hawthorne Studies

Elton Mayo and his colleagues accidentally discovered part of the answer to variations in worker performance while conducting research in the mid-1920s at the Hawthorne Western Electric plant, located near Chicago. Their original goal was to study the effect of illumination, ventilation, and fatigue on production workers in the plant. Their research, known as the **Hawthorne studies**, became a sweeping investigation into the role of human relations in group and individual productivity. These studies also gave rise to the profession of industrial psychology by legitimizing the human factor as an element in business operations.[25] After three years of experimenting with lighting and other physical aspects of work, Mayo made two important discoveries:

Hawthorne studies An investigation into the role of human relations in group and individual productivity.

1. All the attention focused on workers who participated in the research made them feel more important. For the first time, they were getting feedback on their job performance. In addition, test conditions allowed them greater freedom from supervisory control. Under these circumstances, morale and motivation increased and productivity rose.

informal organization A network of relationships created by the interaction of workers on the job.

Improve Your Grade
Audio Glossary

2. Mayo found that the interaction of workers on the job created a network of relationships called an **informal organization**. This organization exerted considerable influence on workers' performance.

Although some observers have criticized the Hawthorne studies for flawed research methodology,[26] this research can be credited with helping change the way management viewed workers.

From the Great Depression to the New Millennium

During the Great Depression, interest in human relations research waned as other ways of humanizing the workplace gained momentum. During that period, unions increased their militant campaigns to organize workers and force employers to pay attention to such issues as working conditions, higher pay, shorter hours, and protection for child laborers.

After World War II and during the years of postwar economic expansion, interest in the human relations field increased. Countless papers and research studies on worker efficiency, group dynamics, organization, and motivational methods were published. Douglas McGregor, in his classic book *The Human Side of Enterprise,* argued that how well an organization performs is directly proportional to its ability to tap human potential.[27] Abraham Maslow, a noted psychologist, devised a "hierarchy of needs," stating that people satisfied their needs in a particular order. Later, Frederick Herzberg proposed an important theory of employee motivation based on satisfaction. Each theory had considerable influence on the study of motivation.

Since the 1950s, theories and concepts regarding human behavior have focused more and more on an understanding of human interaction. Eric Berne in the 1960s

HUMAN RELATIONS IN ACTION

Big-Book Blockbusters

Each year between 4,000 and 5,000 new books claiming to be about business are published. Here is a list of four heavyweights:

- ***The One Minute Manager*** by Kenneth Blanchard and Spencer Johnson. (Published in 1982 and still making bestseller lists.)
- ***Reengineering the Corporation*** by Michael Hammer and James Champy. (A *BusinessWeek* reviewer said, "May well be the best-written book for the managerial masses since *In Search of Excellence.*")
- ***Built to Last*** by Jim Collins. (According to *USA Today,* it's "one of the most eye-opening business studies since *In Search of Excellence.*")
- ***In Search of Excellence*** by Tom Peters and Robert Waterman. (Described by the *Wall Street Journal* as "one of those rare books on management that are both consistently thought provoking and fun to read.")

revolutionized the way people think about interpersonal communication when he introduced transactional analysis, with its "Parent-Adult-Child" model. At about the same time, Carl Rogers published his work on personality development, interpersonal communication, and group dynamics. In the early 1980s, William Ouchi introduced the Theory Z style of management, which is based on the belief that worker involvement is the key to increased productivity.

There is no doubt that management consultants Tom Peters and Robert Waterman also influenced management thinking regarding the importance of people in organizations. Their best-selling book *In Search of Excellence,* published in 1982, describes eight attributes of excellence found in America's best-run companies. One of these attributes, "productivity through people," emphasizes that excellent companies treat the worker as the root source of quality and productivity. The editors of *Fast Company* magazine say that *In Search of Excellence* "fired the starting gun in the race to the New Economy."[28]

We have provided you with no more than a brief glimpse of selected developments in the human relations movement. Space does not permit a review of the hundreds of theorists and practitioners who have influenced human relations in the workplace. However, in the remaining chapters, we do introduce the views of other influential thinkers and authors.

TEST PREPPER 1.4

ANSWERS CAN BE FOUND ON P. 237

True or False?

____ 1. Taylor's scientific management gave workers the power to develop their own work processes and increased their input into the management of the organization.

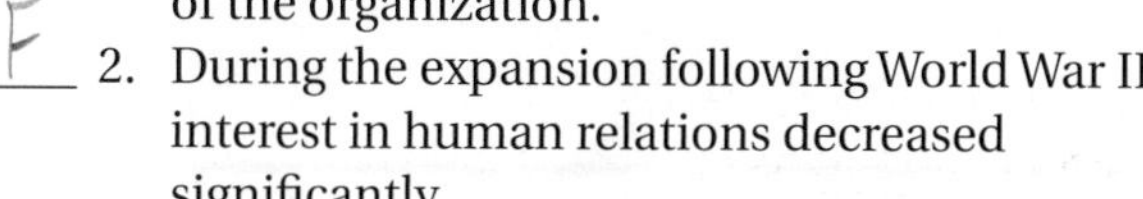

____ 2. During the expansion following World War II, interest in human relations decreased significantly.

Multiple Choice

____ 3. In the Hawthorne studies, Elton Mayo discovered that workers interact on the job to create:

a. an informal organization.
b. highly skilled work teams.
c. fatigue.
d. the most productive work procedures.

____ 4. During the late 1940s and throughout the 1950s, American management theorists focused on:

a. abuses of child laborers.
b. scientific management.
c. better pay and working conditions.
d. group dynamics and motivational methods.

____ 5. Taylor's scientific management helped organizations to:

a. understand the importance of teamwork.
b. understand the value of communication in the workplace.
c. standardize work processes and increase efficiency.
d. create wellness programs to increase employee health and productivity.

HM **ACE the Test**
ACE and ACE+ Practice Tests

MAJOR THEMES IN HUMAN RELATIONS

5 *Identify seven basic themes that serve as the foundation for effective human relations.*

Seven broad themes emerge from the study of human relations. They are communication, self-awareness, self-acceptance, motivation, trust, self-disclosure, and conflict resolution. These themes reflect the current concern in human relations with the twin goals of (1) personal growth and development and (2) the achievement of organizational objectives. To some degree, these themes are interrelated (see Figure 1.3), and most are discussed in more than one chapter of this book.

Communication

communication The means by which we come to an understanding of ourselves and others.

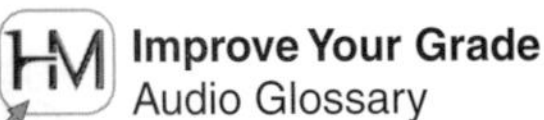

It is not an exaggeration to describe communication as the "heart and soul" of human relations. **Communication** is the means by which we come to an understanding of ourselves and others. To grow and develop as persons, we must develop the awareness and the skills necessary to communicate effectively. Communication is the *human* connection. That is why the subject is covered in more than one section of this book. In Chapter 2 we explore the fundamentals of both personal and organizational communication. It is these fundamentals that provide the foundation for all efforts to improve communication. Suggestions on how to improve communication will appear in other chapters.

FIGURE 1.3
Major Themes in Human Relations

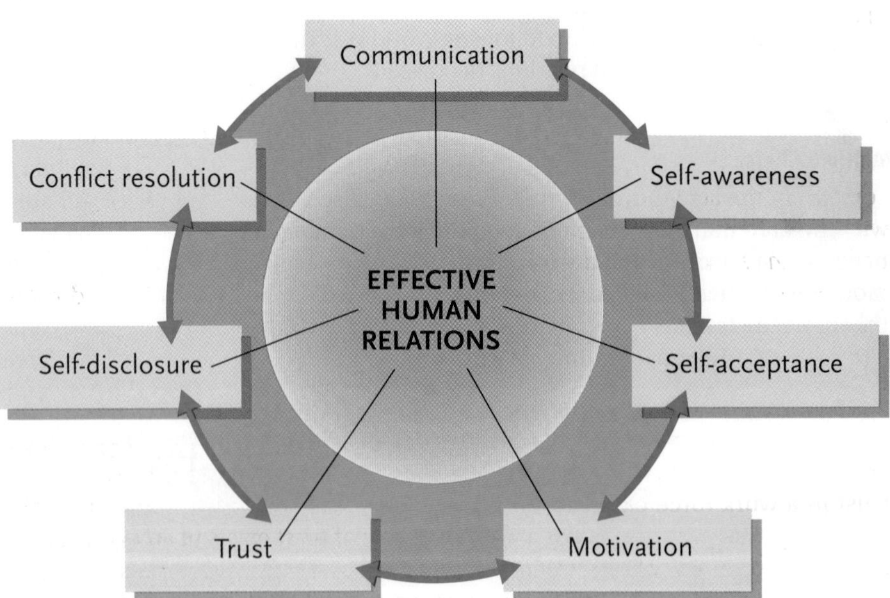

Self-Awareness

One of the most important ways to develop improved relationships with others is to develop a better understanding of ourselves. With increased **self-awareness** comes a greater understanding of how our behavior influences others. Stephen Covey, author of *The Seven Habits of Highly Effective People,* says that self-awareness enables us to stand apart and examine the way we "see" ourselves, as well as to see other people.[29]

self-awareness An understanding of ourselves and how our behavior influences others.

The importance of self-awareness is being recognized by an increasing number of authors, trainers, and educators. Daniel Goleman, author of the best-selling book *Emotional Intelligence,* has given us new insights into the importance of self-awareness. Goleman says IQ accounts for only about 20 percent of a person's success in life. The rest, he says, you can credit to "emotional intelligence." Of all the elements that make up emotional intelligence, Goleman asserts, self-awareness is the most important. He notes that a deficit in self-awareness can be damaging to one's personal relationships and career.[30]

Self-Acceptance

The degree to which you like and accept yourself is the degree to which you can genuinely like and accept other people. **Self-acceptance** is the foundation of successful interaction with others. In a work setting, people with positive self-concepts tend to cope better with change, accept responsibility more readily, tolerate differences, and generally work well as team members. A negative self-concept, however, can create barriers to good interpersonal relations. Self-acceptance is crucial not only for building relationships with others but also for setting and achieving goals. The more you believe you can do, the more you are likely to accomplish. Chapter 3 explains why high self-esteem (complete self-acceptance) is essential for effective human relations. That chapter also helps you identify ways to achieve greater self-acceptance.

self-acceptance The degree to which you like and accept yourself.

Motivation

Most people who engage in the study of **motivation** seek answers to two questions: "How do I motivate myself?" and "How do I motivate others?" If you are really committed to achieving peak performance, you must motivate yourself from within.[31] Inner drives for excellence can be very powerful. To motivate others, you need to understand time-proven, well-researched theories and well-established motivation strategies. Chapter 4 will help you identify the priorities and values that motivate you.

motivation Inner drive for excellence.

HM **Improve Your Grade**
Audio Glossary

Trust

Trust is the building block of all successful relationships with coworkers, customers, family members, and friends. There is compelling evidence that low levels of trust in a work force can lead to reduced productivity, stifled innovation, high stress, and slow decision making.[32] When a lack of trust exists in an organization, a decline in the flow of information almost always results. Employees communicate less information to their supervisors, express opinions reluctantly, and avoid

trust Trust exists when we firmly rely on the integrity, ability, and character of a person or organization.

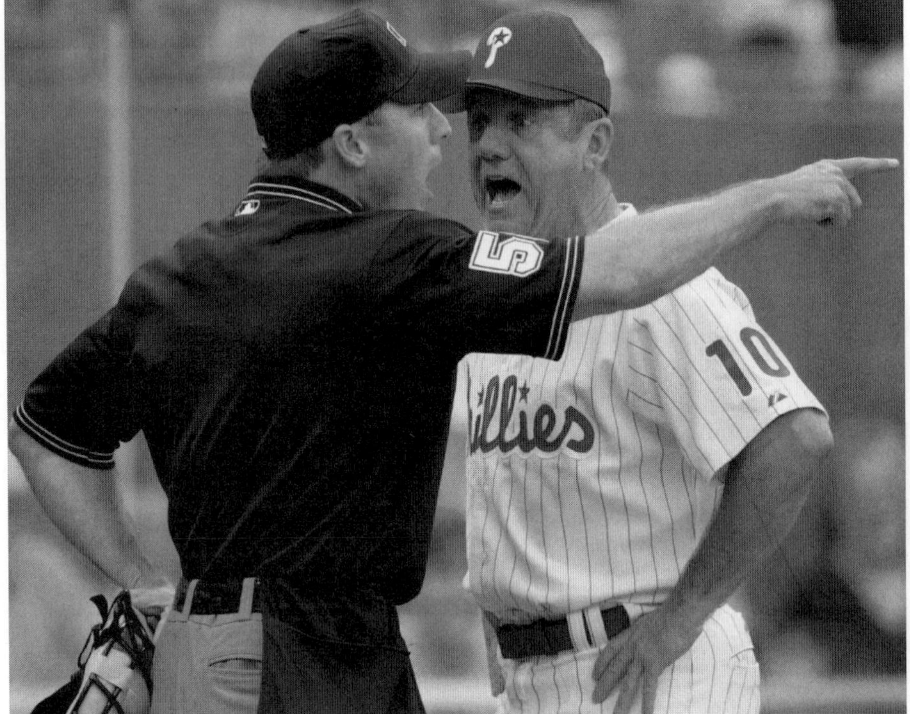

Conflict at work is quite common, so the ability to anticipate or resolve disagreements can be an invaluable skill. Stressful conditions at work or at home often create or magnify problems.

discussions. Cooperation, so necessary in a modern work setting, deteriorates. When a climate of trust is present, frank discussion of problems and a free exchange of ideas and information are more likely to take place.

Self-Disclosure

self-disclosure Sharing information about yourself with others.

Self-disclosure and trust are two halves of a whole. The more open you are with people, the more trust you build up. The more trust there is in a relationship, the safer you feel to disclose who you are. Self-disclosure is also part of good communication and helps eliminate unnecessary guessing games. Managers who let their subordinates know what is expected of them help those employees fulfill their responsibilities. Chapter 2 emphasizes the need of individuals to verbalize the thoughts and feelings they carry within them and provides many practical suggestions on how to use constructive self-disclosure.

Conflict Resolution

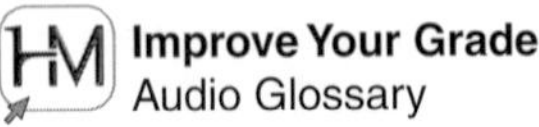

Improve Your Grade
Audio Glossary

Conflict in one form or another surfaces almost daily in the lives of many workers. You may experience conflict during a commute to work when a careless driver cuts you off at a freeway exit ramp. If your job includes supervisory-management responsibilities, you will spend a great deal of time in **conflict resolution**, attempting to resolve conflicts among members of your staff. As a team member, you may assume the role of mediator when other team members clash. Conflict also surfaces when working parents attempt to balance the demands of both work and family. Stressful conditions at home often interfere with work performance, and on-the-job pressures create or magnify problems at home.[33] The ability to anticipate or resolve conflict can be an invaluable skill. Chapter 8 provides several valuable suggestions on how conflict can be resolved effectively.

conflict resolution Attempting to resolve conflicts among coworkers or members of a team.

TEST PREPPER 1.5

ANSWERS CAN BE FOUND ON P. 237

True or False?

T 1. Lack of trust in an organization typically leads to reduced communication.

Multiple Choice

____ 2. The "heart and soul" of human relations is:
   a. conflict resolution.
   b. motivation.
   c. self-disclosure.
   d. communication.

____ 3. Author Daniel Goleman's major premise is that:
   a. emotional intelligence is more crucial to life success than is IQ.
   b. self-acceptance must precede self-awareness.
   c. no matter how self-aware one is, one cannot succeed without self-acceptance.
   d. motivation is the key to communication.

____ 4. As she learns more about the workers she supervises, Pearl, the new supervisor of the packaging department, gradually opens up to them. This demonstrates the relationship between:
   a. motivation and self-awareness.
   b. conflict resolution and trust.
   c. self-acceptance and communication.
   d. trust and self-disclosure.

____ 5. Susan seems insecure and reserved with others in the workplace. Many of her coworkers see her as aloof. Susan should try to improve in the area(s) of:
   a. motivation.
   b. trust and self-disclosure.
   c. self-acceptance.
   d. self-disclosure.

HM **ACE the Test**
ACE and ACE+ Practice Tests

Improve Your Grade
Learning Objectives Review
Audio Chapter Review
Audio Chapter Quiz

LEARNING OBJECTIVES REVIEW

1 *Explain the nature, purpose, and importance of human relations in an organizational setting.*

- Human relations is the study of why our beliefs, attitudes, and behaviors sometimes cause relationship problems in our personal and work lives.
- It covers three types of interactions among people—their conflicts, cooperative efforts, and group relationships.
- Human relations, when applied in a positive and supportive environment, can help increase an organization's productivity and efficiency.

2 *Identify major developments in the workplace that have given new importance to human relations.*

- The restructuring of America from an industrial economy to an information economy has had profound implications for the study of human relations.
- Developments in the workplace that increase the importance of human relations:
  - churning dislocation in the labor market
  - changing work patterns
  - the need for higher service standards
  - increasing workplace incivility
  - greater reliance on team-based structures
  - work force diversity
  - growing income inequality

3 *Identify major forces influencing human behavior at work.*

- These forces include:
  - organizational culture
  - supervisory-management influence
  - work group influence
  - job influence
  - personal characteristics of the worker
  - family influence

4 *Understand the historical development of the human relations movement.*

- Early attempts to improve productivity in manufacturing focused on such things as plant layout and mechanical processes. With the passing of time there was more interest in redefining the nature of work and perceiving workers as complex human beings.
- Two landmarks in the study of motivation and worker needs are:
  - Frederick Taylor's work in scientific management (focusing in improving production processes to increase productivity)
  - Elton Mayo's Hawthorne studies (focusing on the informal organization)
- Later research by Douglas McGregor, Frederick Herzberg, Carl Rogers, William Ouchi, and others contributed greatly to our understanding of how to achieve productivity through people.

5 *Identify seven basic themes that serve as the foundation for effective human relations.*

- Seven major themes emerge from a study of human relations:
  - communication
  - self-awareness
  - self-acceptance
  - motivation
  - trust
  - self-disclosure
  - conflict resolution
- These themes reflect the current concern in human relations with personal growth and satisfaction of organization objectives.

Career Corner

Q: The daily newspapers and television news shows are constantly reporting on mergers, business closings, and downsizing efforts. With so much uncertainty in the job market, how can I best prepare for a career?

A: You are already doing one thing that is very important—keeping an eye on labor market trends. During a period of rapid change and less job security, you must continuously study workplace trends and assess your career preparation. Louis S. Richman, in a *Fortune* magazine article entitled "How to Get Ahead in America," said, "Climbing in your career calls for being clear about your personal goals, learning how to add value, and developing skills you can take anywhere." Richard Bolles, author of the best-selling job-hunting book *What Color Is Your Parachute?*, says you must do a systematic inventory of the transferable skills that you already possess. Then identify the skills that you still need to develop. Keep in mind that today's employers demand more, so be prepared to add value to the company from day one. Search for your employer's toughest problems and make yourself part of the solutions.

The skills you can take anywhere are those transferable skills required by a wide range of employers. These are important because there are no jobs for life. Be prepared to work for several organizations, and anticipate changing careers.

Applying What You Have Learned

1. Throughout this book you will be given many opportunities to engage in self-assessment activities. Self-assessment involves taking a careful look at the human relations skills you need to be well rounded and thoroughly prepared for success in your work life and fulfillment in your personal life. To assess your human relations skills, complete the self-assessment exercise for Chapters 2 through 9 at **college.hmco.com/pic/reeceSAS**. These assessment exercises will provide you with increased awareness of your strengths and a better understanding of those abilities you may want to improve.
2. In his book *The Success Principles,* Jack Canfield describes fifty principles that will increase your confidence, help you tackle daily challenges, and teach you how to realize your ambitions. Number one on his list is "Take 100% responsibility for your life." This includes the quality of your relationships, your health and fitness, your income, your career success—everything! He says most of us have been conditioned to blame events outside of our life for those parts of our life we dislike. Reflect on your life up to this point and identify situations in which you blamed someone or something else for your failure to achieve a goal or improve in some area. Do you see any situations in which you felt justified in blaming others or refused to take risks?[34]
3. The seven broad themes that emerge from the study of human relations were discussed in this chapter. Although these themes are interrelated, there is value in examining each one separately before reading the rest of the book. Review the description of each theme and then answer these questions:

   a. When you take into consideration the human relations problems that you have observed or experienced at work, school, and home, which themes represent the most important areas of study? Explain your answer.
   b. In which of these areas do you feel the greatest need for improvement? Why?

Improve Your Grade
Self-Assessment Exercise

ROLE-PLAY EXERCISE

The college you attend offers career counseling, job placement assistance, and help finding summer internships. You plan to meet with a career counselor and seek help finding a summer internship with a well-established company. You will be meeting with a class member, who will assume the role of career counselor. The purpose of this meeting is to give the counselor some basic information about your career plans and the type of company you would like to work for. Prior to the meeting, prepare a written outline of information you plan to present during the meeting. The outline should focus on answers to the following questions:

- What type of work would be most meaningful?
- What type of organizational culture would be most appealing to you?
- What do you find to be the basic rewards of work?

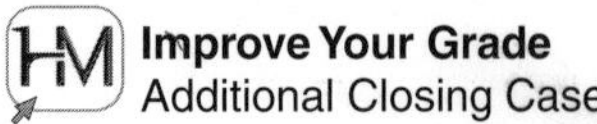

CASE 1.1

Challenges in the New Economy

At the beginning of the new millennium, a growing number of social researchers, economists, and consultants tried to predict what the world of work would be like in the years ahead. We pay close attention to these and to even more recent forecasts because work is a central part of our identities. As one writer has noted, our working life—in a few short decades—adds up to life itself. Work can also be one of the major fulfillments in life. What will the new economy be like from a worker's viewpoint? Here are three predictions:

- *In the new economy, everyone is an entrepreneur.* This is the view expressed by Thomas Petzinger, Jr., author and former columnist for the *Wall Street Journal.* He reports on factories where shop floor employees handle customer service calls and create new ways to solve customer problems. At UPS the drivers are the eyes and ears of the sales force. They help identify new customers and help solve customer service problems. Many bank tellers are actively involved in sales and service activities.[35] Today the term *intrapreneur* is used to describe an employee who takes personal "hands-on responsibility" for developing ideas, products, or processes. To become an intrapreneur in a corporate setting often means using your creativity more often, taking some risks, and moving beyond your job description. The new economy will give many workers an opportunity to take more responsibility for their work.

- *The new economy features the art of the relaunch.* How often will you change jobs during your lifetime? Five times? Ten? Fifteen? The new economy offers more career options, more challenges, and more uncertainty. Chances are, you will need to relaunch your career several times. Molly Higgins held a career track job in the human resources department of a large company. When she discovered that in the entire department there wasn't a single position she aspired to, it was time to relaunch her career. In recent years, thousands of people joined the ranks of new dot.com companies, only to lose their jobs in a matter of weeks or months. One analyst says that changing jobs will require using your learning skills and applying the skills you have already learned.[36]
- *In the new economy, getting a job may be easier than getting a life.* We have, in recent years, seen an increase in the standard of living. The price we pay for a bigger home, a nicer automobile, or a vacation in Italy is often a more demanding work life. Some people choose to work harder in order to acquire more "things." In some cases, corporate downsizing has left fewer people to do the same amount of work. Working more hours and working harder during those hours can result in greater stress, a breakdown in family life, and a decrease in leisure time.[37]

Questions

1. Would you feel comfortable assuming the duties of an entrepreneur within an existing company, or would you rather start your own business?
2. You are likely to relaunch yourself several times during the years ahead. Does the prospect of several relaunches seem frightening to you, or do you look forward to the challenge?
3. What steps would you take to achieve better work/life balance?

Resources on the Web

Prepare for Class, Improve Your Grade, and ACE the Test. Student Achievement Series resources include:

ACE and ACE+ Practice Tests	Chapter Glossaries	Audio Glossaries
Audio Chapter Quizzes	Chapter Outlines	Internet Insights
Audio Chapter Reviews	Crossword Puzzles	Self-Assessment Exercises
Learning Objective Reviews	Hangman Games	Additional Closing Cases
Career Snapshots	Flashcards	

To access these learning and study tools, go to **college.hmco.com/pic/reeceSAS**.

HM ManagementSPACE

2 Improving Personal and Organizational Communications

Over 3000 patients were potentially exposed to hydraulic fluid during surgeries at Duke hospitals. They may have had contact with improperly cleaned surgical instruments.

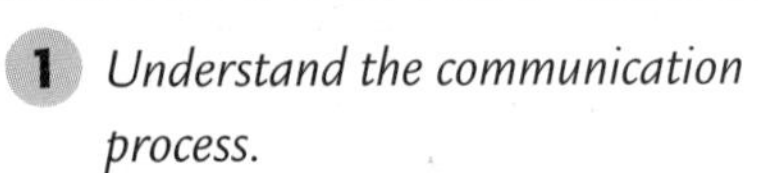

1 *Understand the communication process.*

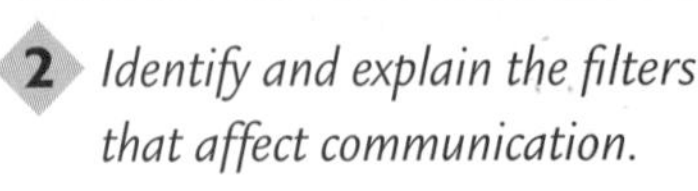

2 *Identify and explain the filters that affect communication.*

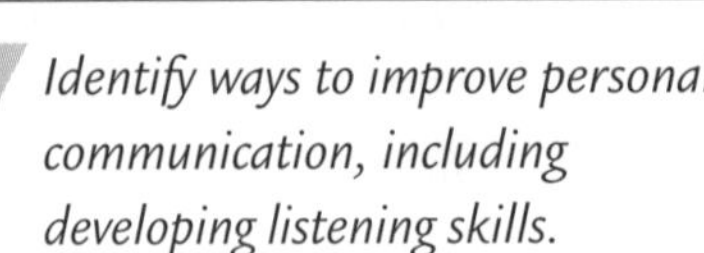

3 *Identify ways to improve personal communication, including developing listening skills.*

"Many skills are valuable at work, but one skill is essential: the ability to communicate."

—Eric Maisel, Author, *20 Communication Tips @ Work*

Chapter Outline

- **The Communication Process**
  - Impersonal Versus Interpersonal Communication
  - Sender–Message–Receiver–Feedback
- **Communication Filters**
  - Semantics
  - Language and Cultural Barriers
  - Emotions
  - Attitudes
  - Role Expectations
  - Gender-Specific Focus
  - Nonverbal Messages
  - Who Is Responsible for Effective Communication?
- **How to Improve Personal Communication**
  - Send Clear Messages
  - Develop Effective Listening Skills
  - Use Constructive Self-Disclosure
- **Communicating via Technology**
  - Voice Mail
  - E-mail

HM **Prepare for Class**
Chapter Outline

4 *Learn how to effectively communicate through technology.*

Unhealthy Communication

Workers employed by Automatic Elevator, a Durham, North Carolina, company, performed routine maintenance on the elevators at two Duke University Health System hospitals. Following the completion of their service, employees of Automatic Elevator emptied used petroleum-based hydraulic fluid into several empty detergent drums. Duke employees discovered the drums, assumed they were surplus stock, and returned them to the original vendor, Cardinal Health, a hospital-supply company. Employees at Cardinal Health failed to detect the contents of the detergent drums and delivered the drums to two Duke hospitals. Later, Duke University Health System administrators found that the used hydraulic fluid was piped into the instrument cleaning systems at both hospitals.

Duke administrators were slow to notify the nearly 3,800 surgical patients who may have had contact with the improperly cleaned surgical instruments. Many of these patients reported

KEY TERMS

Prepare for Class
Chapter Glossary

Improve Your Grade
Flashcards
Hangman
Crossword Puzzle

suffering infections, poor healing, achy joints, weight loss, and extreme fatigue during the months following their surgery. Some of these patients, feeling that Duke should have made more information available sooner, have hired lawyers.[1]

Ineffective communication can negatively influence the lives of many people. In this case, literally thousands of people were affected because someone "failed to communicate." As you reflect on this situation, think about all the frontline employees who were in a position to prevent this crisis.

Effective communication can play a critical role in every aspect of the modern organization. In one form or another, it is the key to improving customer service, resolving conflict, creating productive work teams, improving employee morale, and achieving many other goals. Communication is also the key to effective personal relationships and career success.

THE COMMUNICATION PROCESS

1 *Understand the communication process.*

Most people take communication for granted. When they write, speak, or listen to others, they assume that the message given or received is being understood. In reality, messages are often misunderstood because they are incomplete or because different people interpret messages in different ways. The diversity of today's work force calls for a greater understanding of how to communicate effectively, through technology or face to face, with people from different cultures, countries, and lifestyles. Yet even though people and communication methods may be diverse, the basic communication process remains the same.

Impersonal Versus Interpersonal Communication

impersonal communication A one-way process that transfers basic information such as instructions, policies, and financial data.

In a typical organization the types of communication used to exchange information can be placed on a continuum ranging from "impersonal" on one end to "interpersonal" on the other.[2] **Impersonal communication** is a one-way process that transfers basic information such as instructions, policies, and financial data. Generally, organizations use this information-delivery process when they use electronic bulletin boards or memos as quick, easy ways to "get the word out." Their effectiveness is somewhat limited because there is little, if any, possibility for the person receiving the information to clarify vague or confusing information.

interpersonal communication The exchange of information between two or more people

Interpersonal communication is the exchange of information between two or more people. Such words as *share, discuss, argue,* and *interact* refer to this form of two-way communication. Interpersonal communication can take place in meetings, over the phone, in face-to-face interviews, or even during classroom discussions between instructors and students. If interpersonal communication is to be effective, some type of feedback, or response, from the person receiving the information is necessary. When this exchange happens, those involved can determine whether the information has been understood in the way intended. This is one of the reasons that some managers still prefer person-to-person meetings and telephone calls instead of e-mail. The speed of technology can be invaluable when it

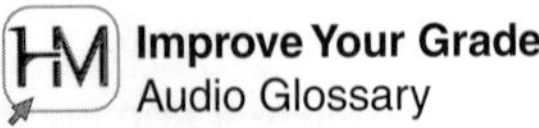
Improve Your Grade
Audio Glossary

TOTAL PERSON INSIGHT

Eric Maisel Author, ***20 Communication Tips @ Work***

"Many skills are valuable at work, but one skill is essential: the ability to communicate. Whether you are presenting your ideas at a committee meeting, dashing off fifteen e-mails in a row, chatting with a coworker at a copy machine, evaluating an employee, or closing a deal over the phone, what you are doing is communicating. These exchanges are the backbone and the life blood of every organization and every relationship."

comes to impersonal information giving, but it cannot replace the two-way, interpersonal communication process when feedback and discussion are necessary.

Sender–Message–Receiver–Feedback

Effective communication is a continuous loop that involves a sender, a message, a receiver, and **feedback** that clarifies the message.[3] To illustrate, suppose your friend phones from your neighborhood convenience store and asks for directions to your home. You give your friend the appropriate street names, intersections, and compass directions so that he can drive to your door without getting lost. When your friend repeats his understanding of your directions, you clarify any misunderstandings, and he drives directly to your home. A simplified diagram of this communication process would look like Figure 2.1.

feedback A reply or return of information that confirms the understanding of a message.

Now suppose you are late for an appointment, and the plumber you had requested three days ago calls you from her cell phone and asks directions to your house. She explains that she has gotten lost in this neighborhood before, and it is obvious that English is her second language. The communication process becomes much more complicated, as shown in Figure 2.2. As your message travels from you to your plumber, it must pass through several "filters," each of which can alter the way your message is understood. Most communications flow through this complex process.

FIGURE 2.1

Diagram of Simple Communication Process

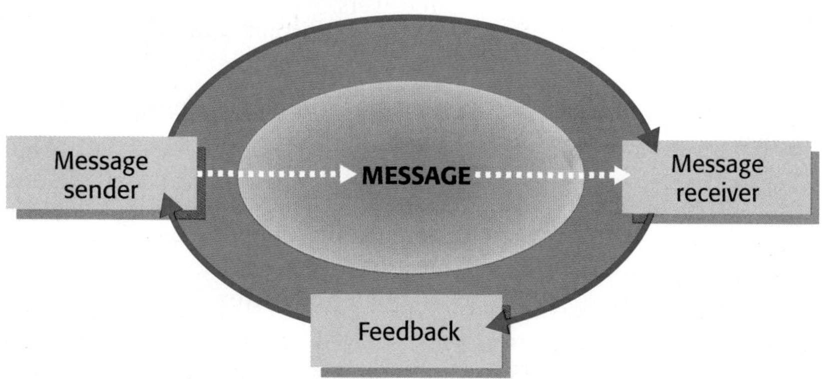

FIGURE 2.2

Diagram of More Complex Communication Process

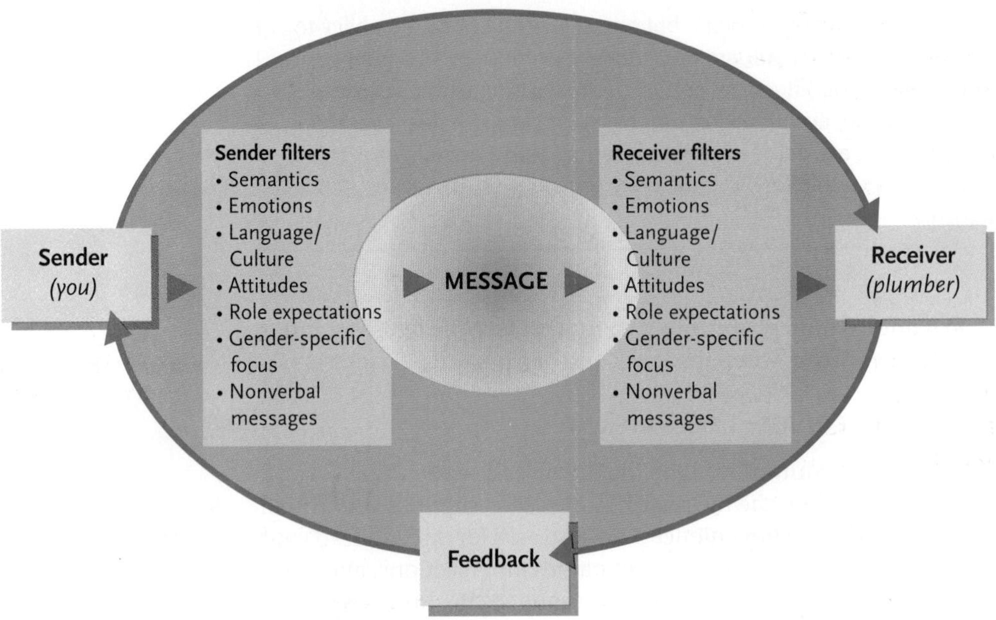

TEST PREPPER 2.1

ANSWERS CAN BE FOUND ON P. 237

True or False?

F 1. Interpersonal communication typically includes no possibility for feedback in the exchange.

T 2. Most communication processes are complicated by flowing through a variety of filters that influence the way a message is understood.

Multiple Choice

a 3. Which of the following is appropriate content for an impersonal communication?
   a. Company policy manuals
   b. Performance evaluations
   c. Layoff notices
   d. Complex instructions for using new office software

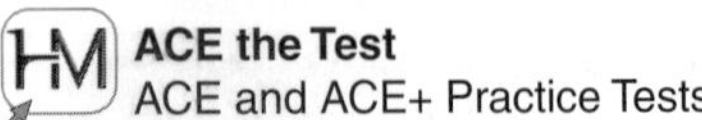

C 4. Andie and Zane discuss new lunch options in the company cafeteria in Andie's office. Which of the following statements best describes their discussion, using the simple model of the communication process?
   a. Andie is the sender, and Zane is the receiver.
   b. Neither Andie nor Zane is a sender, but both are receivers.
   c. Both Andie and Zane are senders and receivers.
   d. Neither Andie nor Zane is a receiver, but both are senders.

C 5. Interpersonal communication can be described as:
   a. one-way.
   b. transferring basic information such as instructions or financial policies.
   c. sharing or discussing.
   d. of limited effectiveness.

COMMUNICATION FILTERS

2 *Identify and explain the filters that affect communication.*

Messages are sent—and feedback is received—through a variety of filters that can distort the intended message. (See Figure 2.2.) When people are influenced by one or more of these filters, their perception of the message may be totally different from what the sender was attempting to communicate. Both sender and receiver must be keenly aware of these possible distortions so that they can intercept any miscommunication.

Semantics

We often assume that the words we use mean the same things to others, but this assumption can create problems. **Semantics** is the study of the relationship between a word and its meaning(s). Words have associated meanings and usages. We can easily understand what words like *typewriter, computer,* or *envelope* mean. But more abstract terms, such as *job satisfaction, downsizing,* or *internal customers,* have less precise meanings and will be used and interpreted by different people in different ways. The more abstract the term, the less likely it is that people will agree on its meaning.

semantics The study of the relationship between a word and its meaning(s).

- When Enron wanted to cover up questionable business practices, employees developed some creative accounting jargon. One report included the following sentence: "Enron entered into share settled costless collar arrangements. . . . The transactions resulted in noncash increases to noncurrent assets and equity."[4]
- Corporate employees often use important-sounding jargon that is almost incomprehensible. Better Communications, a firm that teaches writing skills to employers, clipped this statement from a memo circulated at a *Fortune* 500 company: "Added value is the keystone to exponentially accelerating profit curves."[5]
- Every industry has its own jargon that can be confusing to those outside that industry. The same is true for young people entering the work force who have communicated extensively via Internet chat rooms. They often assume that their Internet jargon, or cyberlingo, is understood by everyone. Cyberlingo is a feature of the online culture that crosses race, gender, and geography, as this language is accepted and understood by young people all over the world. However, when cyberlingo is used in the mainstream of communication within organizations, it can be confusing to those who are unfamiliar with "words" such as *FAQ* (frequently asked questions), *GMTA* (great minds think alike), *IMHO* (in my humble opinion), and *OTOH* (on the other hand).[6]

Language and Cultural Barriers

When organizations throughout the world connect to the Internet, the people within those organizations must be ready, willing, and able to communicate in a multilingual, multicultural working environment. Although English is the dominant language in the global marketplace, everyone must adjust his or her communication style to accommodate the needs of those whose first language is not

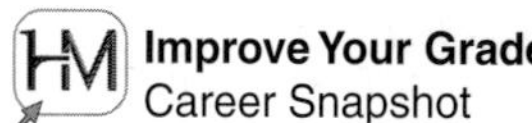

These Indian employees work at Gecis, an international call center based in Gurgaon. In order to answer calls from outside of India, they must learn foreign accents and be prepared to help customers solve a wide range of technical problems.

English. Keep in mind how muddled a message might get when it is translated from one language to another in the mind of the receiver. To avoid the damage this filter might cause, avoid using industry-specific jargon or culture-specific slang.

The needs of a multicultural work force are getting more attention today because of globalization and employers' growing support for cultural diversity among their workers. The culture in which we are raised strongly influences our values, beliefs, expressions, and behaviors. It also influences the way we interpret the values, beliefs, expressions, and behaviors of others.

When the sender and receiver understand each other's cultural background, both should make the effort to adjust and improve their messages accordingly.

- People living in the United States, Canada, Europe, Israel, or Australia usually prefer direct-approach communication; they tend to say more or less exactly what they mean. Their cultures value clarity, fluency, and brevity in communication.
- Many people from Asia, Arab countries, and much of Africa prefer a more indirect style of communication and therefore value harmony, subtlety, sensitivity, and tact more than brevity. They try hard to connect with their listeners.[7]

Emotions

Strong emotions can either prevent people from hearing what a speaker has to say or make them too susceptible to the speaker's point of view. If they become angry or allow themselves to be carried away by the speaker's eloquence, they may "think" with their emotions and make decisions or take action they regret later. They have shifted their attention from the content of the message to their feelings about it.

You may have had the experience of your spouse or parent angrily demanding to know why you forgot to run an errand. If you allow someone else's anger to trigger your own, the conversation may quickly deteriorate into an argument. The real issue—what happened and what is to be done about it—is lost in the shouting match. Detaching yourself from another's feelings and responding to the content of the message are often difficult. It is hard to realize that another person's emotional response is more likely about fear or frustration than it is about you as an individual. Yet many jobs require that employees remain calm and courteous regardless of a customer's emotional state. Emotional control is discussed in Chapter 8.

Attitudes

Attitudes can be a barrier to communication in much the same way as emotions. The receiver may have a negative attitude toward the sender's voice, accent, gestures, mannerisms, dress, or delivery. These negative attitudes create resistance to the message and can lead to a breakdown in communication. Perhaps the listener has an established attitude about the speaker's topic. For example, a person who is strongly opposed to abortion will most likely find it difficult to listen with objectivity to a pro-choice speaker. Keep in mind, however, that an overly positive attitude can also be a barrier to communication. When biased in favor of the message, the listener may not effectively evaluate the speaker's information. More is said about the power of attitudes in Chapter 5.

Role Expectations

Role expectations influence how people expect themselves, and others, to act on the basis of the roles they play, such as boss, customer, or subordinate. These expectations can distort communication in two ways.

1. If people identify others too closely with their roles, they may discount what the other person has to say: "It's just the boss again, saying the same old thing." A variation of this distortion occurs when we do not allow others to change their roles and take on new ones. This often happens to employees who are promoted from within the ranks of an organization to management positions. Others may still see "old Chuck" from accounting rather than the new department head.
2. Role expectations can affect good communication when people use their roles to alter the way they relate to others. This is often referred to as "position power." For example, managers may expect employees to accept what they say simply because of the authority invested in the position. Employees are not allowed to question the manager's decisions or make suggestions of their own, and communication becomes one-way information giving.

Gender-Specific Focus

Gender roles learned throughout childhood can influence the way men and women communicate. After all, boys and girls do grow up in different worlds, and they are conditioned to approach communication in different ways. Girls are socialized as children to believe that talking holds relationships together. As adults, women use conversation to seek and give confirmation and support and to reach a consensus with others. Boys are socialized to maintain their relationships primarily through their activities. As a result, men are more likely to perceive conversation as a form of competition during which they must negotiate to gain the upper hand and protect themselves from being put down.[8]

Nonverbal Messages

nonverbal messages "Messages without words" or "silent messages" that are communicated through facial expressions, voice tone, gestures, appearance, and posture.

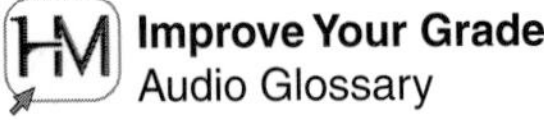

When we attempt to communicate with another person, we use both verbal and nonverbal communication. **Nonverbal messages** are "messages without words" or "silent messages." These are the messages (other than spoken or written words) we communicate through facial expressions, voice tone, gestures, appearance, posture, and other nonverbal means. Research indicates that our nonverbal messages have much more impact than verbal messages. The late Peter Drucker, author of numerous management books, said, "The important thing in communication is to hear what isn't being said."[9] He recognized that when someone else is speaking, your understanding of what is said depends very heavily on what you see.

Some people will walk into a meeting with their shoulders slumped forward and head down. They will slouch in their chair, lean their chin on the palm of their hand, play with a pencil or paperclip on the table, or clutch their arms across their chest. Others will walk into the room with chin held high and shoulders back, sit straight in their chairs, and lean slightly forward with both arms "open" to whoever is speaking during the meetings. Experts agree that the words you say during a meeting, no matter how powerful, are often forgotten or disregarded unless your nonverbal presence commands respect.[10] This chapter limits its discussion to the form of nonverbal communication commonly referred to as "body language." Physical appearance, another powerful form of nonverbal communication, is discussed in Chapter 6.

Many of us could communicate more clearly, more accurately, and more credibly if we became more conscious of our body language. We can learn to strengthen our communications by making sure our words and our body language are consistent. When our verbal and nonverbal messages match, we give the impression that we can be trusted and that what we are saying reflects what we truly believe. But when our body language contradicts our words, we are often unknowingly changing the message we are sending. If a manager says to an employee, "I am very interested in your problem," but then begins to look at her watch and fidget with objects on her desk, the employee will most likely believe the nonverbal rather than the verbal message.

You can improve your communication by monitoring the nonverbal messages you send through your eye contact, facial expressions, gestures, and personal space.

Eye Contact

Eyes transmit more information than any other part of the body. Because eye contact is so revealing, people generally observe some unwritten rules about looking at others. People who hold direct eye contact for only a few seconds, or avoid eye contact altogether, risk communicating indifference. However, a direct, prolonged stare between strangers is usually considered impolite, even potentially aggressive or hostile. Continuous eye contact is especially offensive in Asian and Latin American countries. As a general rule, when you are communicating in a business setting, your eyes should meet the other person's about 60 to 70 percent of the time. This timing is an effective alternative to continuous eye contact.

Facial Expressions

If you want to identify the inner feelings of another person, watch facial expressions closely. A frown or a smile will communicate a great deal. We have all encountered a "look of surprise" or a "look that could kill." Most of our observations are very accurate. However, facial expressions can be intentionally manipulated. When a person is truly happy, the muscles used for smiling are involuntarily controlled by the body's limbic system. When you force a smile, the cerebral cortex (under voluntary control) activates and the person appears to have a "fake" look when he or she smiles. That is why actors often recall a past emotional experience to produce the emotional state they want.[11] If we are able to accurately assess the facial expressions of others and draw conclusions accordingly, we can be sure that others are doing the same to us.

Gestures

Gestures send messages to people about how you are reacting to them and to the situation in which you find yourself. They often add an element that is perceived as a lively speaking style that keeps the attention of others. In some cultures, if you fail to gesture, you may be perceived as boring and stiff.[12] Be aware that some gestures that may be common in one culture may have dramatically different meaning to people from another culture. The examples in Figure 2.3 illustrate how the same gesture can have very different meanings.

FIGURE 2.3

Same Sign, Different Meanings

Source: Atlanta Committee for Olympic Games, by Sam Ward, *USA Today.* Taken from Ben Brown, "Atlanta Out to Mind Its Manners," *USA Today,* March 14, 1996, p. 7c. Copyright © 1996 *USA Today.* Reprinted with permission.

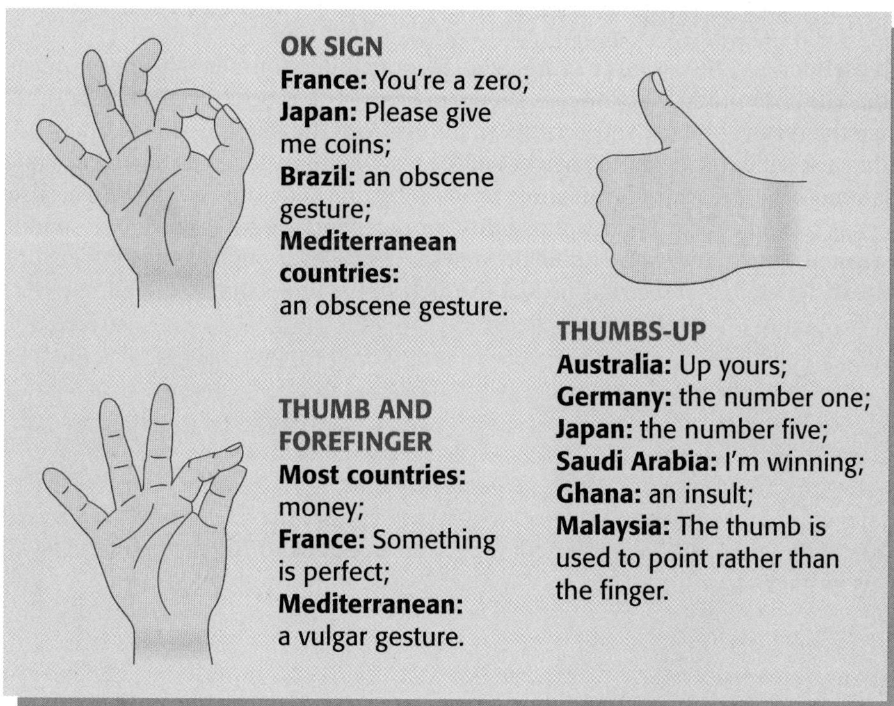

OK SIGN
France: You're a zero;
Japan: Please give me coins;
Brazil: an obscene gesture;
Mediterranean countries: an obscene gesture.
THUMBS-UP
Australia: Up yours;
Germany: the number one;
Japan: the number five;
Saudi Arabia: I'm winning;
Ghana: an insult;
Malaysia: The thumb is used to point rather than the finger.
THUMB AND FOREFINGER
Most countries: money;
France: Something is perfect;
Mediterranean: a vulgar gesture.

Personal Space

Research conducted by Edward Hall provides evidence that people use the space around them to define relationships. It is possible to make others uncomfortable by standing too close to them or too far away from them. A customer may feel uncomfortable if a salesperson stands too close. A job applicant may feel uncomfortable if the interviewer maintains a distance of several feet. Hall identified four "zones" of comfortable distances that help us understand this nonverbal effect on others:[13]

1. *Intimate distance* includes touching to approximately 18 inches from another person. Most people will respond with defensiveness when strangers intrude into this territory.
2. *Personal distance* ranges from 18 inches to 4 feet. This distance is usually reserved for people we feel close to, such as spouses or close friends.
3. *Social distance* is 4 to 12 feet and is used for most business meetings and impersonal social gatherings. Business can be conducted with a minimum of emotional involvement.
4. *Public distance,* which usually involves one-way communication from a speaker to an audience, is 12 to 15 feet.

Hall's research involved the culture of only the United States and should prove helpful to those from other cultures who are attempting to communicate better with Americans. Americans should realize that the distances Hall describes may be different when they are attempting to effectively communicate with those from another culture. For example, Asians are accustomed to close contact. Watch for signals of discomfort, such as leg swinging, foot or finger tapping, and gaze aversion, caused by invading the other person's space.[14]

Who Is Responsible for Effective Communication?

The sender and the receiver share *equal* responsibility for effective communication. The communication loop, as shown in Figure 2.2, is not complete if the message the receiver hears, and acts upon, differs from the one the sender intended. When the sender accepts 100 percent of the responsibility for sending a clear, concise message, the communication process begins. But the receiver must also accept 100 percent of the responsibility for receiving the message as the sender intended. Ideally, receivers should provide senders with enough feedback to ensure that an accurate message has passed through all the filters that might alter it.

Test Prepper 2.2

Answers can be found on p. 237

Multiple Choice

____ 1. Zelda, a native of Katmandu, speaks Hindi more slowly than her coworkers, whose first language is Hindi. She also assumes that the meaning of a Hindi word is its dictionary definition and does not readily understand connotations and colloquialisms. Which of the obstacles to good communication affects Zelda most?

a. Role expectations
b. Language and cultural barriers
c. Attitudes
d. Gender-specific focus

____ 2. "Did you finish the monthly report yet?" asks Jenna of her coworker, Phil. "No," he replies through clenched teeth, as he looks down at his desk. Which of the following probably has the greatest impact on Jenna?

a. Phil's nonverbal message
b. Phil's semantics
c. Phil's gender-specific focus
d. Phil's culturally based meaning

ACE the Test
ACE and ACE+ Practice Tests

____ 3. Hakeem is dismayed to discover that he offended coworkers by standing 2 feet away from them during business conversations. In the United States, what distance would have been more appropriate?

a. 12 to 18 inches
b. 15 to 20 feet
c. 25 to 100 feet
d. 4 to 12 feet

____ 4. If a manager says to an employee, "You don't need to know why. I expect you to do this because I told you so," which communication filter is being displayed?

a. Emotions
b. Role expectations
c. Nonverbal messages
d. Semantics

____ 5. If Casey's manager says, "Good job!" but simultaneously frowns, Casey will likely believe

a. that Casey's manager is unhappy with Casey's performance.
b. that Casey's manager is pleased with Casey's performance.
c. that there is something wrong with Casey's manager.
d. that Casey's manager is trying to trick Casey.

How to Improve Personal Communication

Identify ways to improve personal communication, including developing listening skills.

Now that you understand the communication process and the various filters messages must pass through, you can begin to take the necessary steps to improve your own personal communication skills.

Send Clear Messages

Send clear, concise messages with as little influence from filters as possible so that you can avoid being misunderstood. A new employee stood before the paper shredder in her new office. An administrative assistant noticed her confused look and asked if she needed some help. "Yes, thank you. How does this thing work?" "It's simple," said the assistant and took the thick report from the new employee and fed it through the shredder. "I see," she said, "but how many copies will it make?" This kind of miscommunication could easily have been avoided if both parties had followed these simple rules:

- *Use clear, concise language.* Avoid slang, jargon, or complex, industry-specific semantics that the receiver might not understand. Tailor your messages to your receivers by using words and concepts they understand.
- *Use repetition.* When possible, use parallel channels of communication. For example, by sending an e-mail and making a phone call, you not only gain the receiver's attention through dialogue but also make sure there is a written record in case specific details need to be recalled.
- *Use appropriate timing.* An important memo or e-mail may get no attention simply because it is competing with more pressing problems facing the receiver. When you need someone's cooperation, be acutely aware of his or her schedule and workload so that you can avoid causing any inconvenience or frustration. Timing the delivery of your message will help ensure that it is accepted and acted on.
- *Consider the receiver's preferences.* Some people prefer to receive information via e-mail, and others prefer telephone calls or face-to-face contact. Monitor and discover the preferences of those you communicate with on a regular basis, and adjust your communications with them accordingly.

Develop Effective Listening Skills

We may be born with the ability to hear, but we have to learn how to listen. We may think we are good listeners, but the truth is that most people don't listen at all. Too often we simply speak and then think about what we are going to say next, rather than concentrating on what the other person is trying to say. For example:

- At Hewlett-Packard, employees take listening courses in which they listen, mirror back what they heard, and then elaborate on what it meant. Participants learn that two customers might say similar things, but their messages might have totally different meanings because they have had their own unique experiences that influence their messages. Two employees experiencing a similar frustration at work may take their concerns to management for corrective action. Yet each employee has a unique perspective on the problem, and both need to be heard before management can take effective, appropriate action.

TOTAL PERSON INSIGHT

Ken Johnson Author (www.listen.org/quotations/quotes_effective.html)

"Listening effectively to others can be the most fundamental and powerful communication tool of all. When someone is willing to stop talking or thinking and begin truly listening to others, all of their interactions become easier, and communication problems are all but eliminated."

HUMAN RELATIONS IN ACTION

Career Advice

A recent college graduate wrote to Anne Fisher, career advice columnist for *Fortune* magazine, and asked: "I just graduated from Yale and am about to start my first real job, and I'm curious about something. If you had to pass along just one piece of advice on which to build a career, what would it be?"

Anne answered, "I've always liked Albert Einstein's dictum: 'If A equals success, then the formula is A = X + Y + Z. X is work. Y is play. And Z is, Keep your mouth shut.' Or as my dad used to say, 'Nobody ever learns anything while they're talking.' If you make it a habit to listen more than you speak, you can't go too far wrong."

- Effective listening can often evoke creative, "out-of-the-box" ideas. An engineer at Hewlett-Packard took his listening-skills training seriously and started "coffee talks" in his department every Friday afternoon to improve the listening skills among his coworkers. The resulting lively conversations generated new ideas that stimulated the creation of new products that led to millions of dollars in profits.[15]
- A well-known furniture company delivered hundreds of desks to its customers, but many of the desks arrived damaged and unusable because of inadequate packaging. The company's crate builder estimated that one desk model alone was returned twenty times per month. The company lost hundreds of thousands of dollars when it had to replace the damaged desks. Why didn't the company identify this problem earlier? Senior managers simply did not listen to the concerns from the packaging department or from their customers. They took action only after a customer called complaining that the same desk was ruined twice.[16]

Active Listening

Active listening is fueled by curiosity and requires your complete concentration on what you are hearing, body language that exhibits your listening attitude, and feedback as to what you think the speaker is trying to tell you. In some cases a simple statement such as "Please tell me more about that" will help you become an active listener. Susan Scott, author of *Fierce Conversations,* offers this advice: "Dig for full understanding. Use paraphrasing and perception checks; don't be satisfied with what's on the surface."[17] When you become an active listener, you will make fewer mistakes, learn new information, and build stronger relationships.

active listening Listening that involves complete concentration on what one is hearing, body language that exhibits a listening attitude, and feedback as to what one thinks the speaker is trying to say.

If you would like to pursue additional resources to help you become a better listener, access the information available through the International Listening Association at www.listen.org. In addition, carefully examine Table 2.1, Active Listening Skills, and make every effort to implement its recommendations when you are interacting with others. You may be surprised by the impact you can make.

Critical Listening

To add depth to your active listening skills, consider honing your critical listening skills. **Critical listening** is the attempt to see the topic of discussion from the

critical listening The attempt to see the topic of discussion from the speaker's point of view and to consider how the speaker's perception of the situation may be different from one's own.

TABLE 2.1

Active Listening Skills

1. **Develop a listening attitude.** Regard the speaker as worthy of your respect and attention. Drop your expectations as to what you are going to hear or would like to hear. Maintain good eye contact and lean slightly forward. Don't rush the speaker. Be patient and refrain from planning what to say in response until the speaker has finished talking.
2. **Give the speaker your full attention.** This is not easy because the messages you hear are often spoken at a much slower rate than you are able to absorb them. This allows your mind to roam. Your senses are constantly receiving extraneous information that may divert your attention. To stay focused, you may want to take notes, if it is appropriate to do so.
3. **Clarify by asking questions.** If something is not clear because the speaker has referred to a person or an event that you are not familiar with, ask him or her to back up and explain. If you want the speaker to expand on a particular point, ask open-ended questions such as *"How do you feel about that?"* or *"Can you tell us some ways to improve?"*
4. **Feed back your understanding of the speaker's message.** Paraphrase, in your own words, your understanding of what the speaker has just said: for example, *"Do you mean . . . ?" "Am I right in assuming that we should . . . ?" "What I hear you saying is . . ."* or *"In other words, we. . . ."*

speaker's point of view and to consider how the speaker's perception of the situation may be different from your own. To improve your ability to critically view new information, be sure to listen for evidence that challenges as well as confirms your own point of view. This is especially important when there is no opportunity for feedback, such as when you are viewing "tabloid" television, listening to network TV news "sound bites," or reading Internet blogs. Analyze the source of the information and determine its validity and credibility. Ask yourself, "Why have I been given this information? Is it relevant, or am I just being used to advance the agenda of another person or group?" Critical listening skills will help you avoid perpetuating erroneous information simply because you heard it through gossip, saw it on TV, or read it on the Internet.

All of the communications filters identified in Figure 2.2 tend to distort your ability and willingness to listen, so activating your critical listening skills will take some effort. To help you in this skill development process, ask yourself:

- Does the speaker's reasoning make sense?
- What evidence is being offered to support the speaker's views?
- Do I know each point to be valid based on my own experience?
- Is each point based on a source that can be trusted?[18]

Empathic Listening

Another dimension to becoming a better listener involves empathy, which means understanding another person's feelings. Many workers today face serious personal problems and feel the need to talk about them with someone. They do not expect specific advice or guidance; they just want to spend some time with an empathic listener. Stephen Covey, the noted author and consultant, described **empathic listening** as listening with your ears, your eyes, and your heart.[19] If you want to practice empathic listening, adopt the following practices:

empathic listening Understanding another person's feelings; empathic listening involves your ears, your eyes, and your heart.

- *Avoid being judgmental.* Objectivity is the heart and soul of empathic listening. The person is communicating for emotional release and does not seek a specific response.
- *Acknowledge what is said.* You do not have to agree with what is being said, but you should let the person know you are able to understand his or her viewpoint.
- *Be patient.* If you are unable or unwilling to take the time to hear what the person has to say, say so immediately. Signs of impatience send a negative message to the person needing to talk.[20]

We live in a culture where empathic listening is quite rare. Interrupting has become all too common as people rush to fill every gap in the conversation. Nevertheless, empathic listening is greatly valued by those with personal or work-related problems—people want to spend time with a good listener.[21]

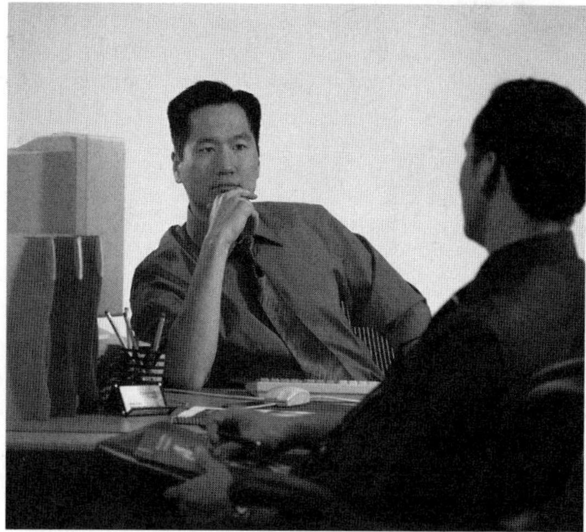

This supervisor listens carefully to an employee who needs assistance. He will ask questions and use his active listening skills to acquire the information needed to help the employee with a work-related problem. Active listening is a skill that can be learned.

Use Constructive Self-Disclosure

Self-disclosure is the process of letting another person know what you think, feel, or want. It is one of the important ways you let yourself be known by others. Self-disclosure can improve interpersonal communication, resolve conflict, and strengthen interpersonal relationships.

It is important to note the difference between self-disclosure and self-description. **Self-description** involves disclosure of nonthreatening information, such as your age, your favorite food, or where you went to school. This is information that others could acquire in some way other than by your telling them. Self-disclosure, by contrast, usually involves some degree of risk. When you practice self-disclosure, you reveal private, personal information that cannot be acquired from another source. Examples include your feelings about being a member of a minority group, job satisfaction, and new policies and procedures.

self-disclosure The act of revealing or exposing the self or aspects of the self.

self-description The disclosure of nonthreatening information.

The importance of self-disclosure, in contrast to self-description, is shown by the following situation. You work at a distribution center and are extremely conscious of safety. You take every precaution to avoid work-related accidents. But another employee has a much more casual attitude toward safety rules and often "forgets" to observe the proper procedures, endangering you and other workers. You can choose to disclose your feelings to this person or stay silent. Either way, your decision has consequences.

TOTAL PERSON INSIGHT

Albert J. Bernstein and **Sydney Craft Rozen**
Authors, ***Sacred Bull: The Inner Obstacles That Hold You Back at Work and How to Overcome Them***

"It's great when employees can read the subtle nuances of your behavior and figure out exactly what you require of them. But let's face it: Most people aren't mind readers. Even if they're smart, they may be oblivious to what's important to you—unless you spell it out for them."

Benefits Gained from Self-Disclosure

Before we discuss self-disclosure in more detail, let us examine four basic benefits you gain from openly sharing what you think, feel, or want.

1. *Increased accuracy in communication.* Self-disclosure often takes the guesswork out of the communication process. No one is a mind reader; if people conceal how they really feel, it is difficult for others to know how to respond to them appropriately. People who are frustrated by a heavy workload but mask their true feelings may never see the problem resolved. The person who is in a position to solve this problem may be oblivious to what's important to you—unless you spell it out.
2. *Reduction of stress.* Sidney Jourard, a noted psychologist who wrote extensively about self-disclosure, states that too much emphasis on privacy and concealment of feelings creates stress within an individual. Too many people keep their thoughts and feelings bottled up inside, which can result in considerable inner tension. When stress indicators like blood pressure, perspiration, and breathing increase, our immune function declines. The amount of stress that builds within us depends on what aspects of ourselves we choose to conceal. If you compulsively think about a painful human relations problem but conceal your thoughts and feelings, the consequence will likely be more stress in your life.[22]
3. *Increased self-awareness.* Chapter 1 stated that self-awareness is one of the major components of emotional intelligence at work. Daniel Goleman, author of *Working with Emotional Intelligence,* defines **self-awareness** as the ability to recognize and understand your moods, emotions, and drives, as well as their effect on others.[23] Self-awareness is the foundation on which self-development is built. To plan an effective change in yourself, you must be in touch with how you behave, the factors that influence your behavior, and how your behavior affects others. A young Asian associate at a financial services firm learned from her supervisor that she was perceived as not being assertive enough in her dealings with clients. As she reflected on this feedback and listened to views expressed by her female peers, the associate became aware of how her cultural background influenced her communication with clients. This feedback motivated her to modify her communication style.[24]

self-awareness Knowledge of oneself: one's thoughts, feelings, emotions, likes, and desires.

4. *Stronger relationships.* Another reward from self-disclosure is the strengthening of interpersonal relationships. When two people engage in an open, authentic dialogue, they often develop a high regard for each other's views. Often they discover they share common interests and concerns, and these serve as a foundation for a deeper relationship.

Guidelines for Appropriate Self-Disclosure

In the search for criteria to determine appropriate self-disclosure, many factors must be considered. How much information should be disclosed? How intimate should the information be? Under what conditions should the disclosures be made? The following guidelines will help you develop your self-disclosure skills.

1. *Use self-disclosure to repair damaged relationships.* Many relationships are unnecessarily strained. The strain often exists because people refuse to talk about real or imagined problems. Self-disclosure can be an excellent method of repairing a damaged relationship.

   If your actions have caused hurt feelings, anger, or deep-seated ill will, an apology may be in order. A sincere apology can have a tremendous amount of healing power. In addition, it may set the stage for improved communications in the future.

2. *Discuss disturbing situations as they happen.* Your reactions to a work-related problem or issue should be shared as soon after the incident as possible. It is often difficult to recapture a feeling once it has passed, and you may distort the incident if you let too much time go by. Your memory is not infallible. The person who caused the hurt feelings is also likely to forget details about the situation.
3. *Select the right time and place.* Remarks that otherwise might be offered and accepted in a positive way can be rendered ineffective not because of what we say but because of when and where we say it.[25] When possible, select a time when you feel the other person is not preoccupied and will be able to give you his or her full attention. Also, select a setting free of distractions.
4. *Avoid overwhelming others with your self-disclosure.* Although you should be open, do not go too far too fast. Many strong relationships are built slowly. The abrupt disclosure of highly emotional or intimate information may actually distance you from the other person. Your behavior may be considered threatening.

"I've had enough reports for one day. Bring me some gossip."

Test Prepper 2.3

Answers can be found on p. 237

True or False?

F 1. An important component of active listening is mentally preparing your response to a speaker as he/she is talking.

Multiple Choice

b 2. One of the best techniques to improve message clarity is to:
   a. send a message one time only, to avoid information overload.
   b. use parallel channels of communication.
   c. respond to messages quickly, without overthinking the response.
   d. send all messages as early in the morning as possible.

c 3. Which of the following skills is used by active listeners?
   a. Clarifying points by asking questions
   b. Using active verbs instead of passive verbs
   c. Accepting what is said by the speaker
   d. Listening for evidence that supports your point of view

c 4. At the end of their discussion of the productivity problems in Ron's department, Cole restates Ron's concerns: "In other words, Ron, we need to train your workers." Which aspect of active listening does Cole's statement exemplify?
   a. Giving the speaker full attention
   b. Developing a listening attitude
   c. Confirming understanding of the speaker's message by using feedback
   d. Clarifying by stating an opinion

d 5. When practicing empathic listening, a listener would do which one of the following?
   a. Ask, "Does the speaker's reasoning make sense?"
   b. Ask, "Is evidence being offered that supports the speaker's views?"
   c. Send an e-mail to confirm the conversation as a practice of parallel communication
   d. Acknowledge that he/she understands the speaker's point of view

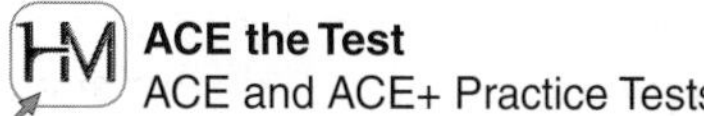

ACE the Test
ACE and ACE+ Practice Tests

COMMUNICATING VIA TECHNOLOGY

4 *Learn how to effectively communicate through technology.*

virtual offices Networks of workers who are connected by the latest technologies. These workers can "set up shop" wherever they are—at home, on an airplane, in a motel room—and communicate with coworkers via e-mail, cell phone, instant messaging, fax, or some other method.

telecommuting An arrangement that allows employees to work from their homes and enables people scattered all over the world to stay connected.

The traditional memos, letters, phone calls, and face-to-face conversations seem to be the exception rather than the rule in today's high-tech communications environment. Many organizations now maintain **virtual offices**, networks of workers connected by the latest technology. These workers can "set up shop" wherever they are—at home, on an airplane, in a motel room—and communicate with coworkers via e-mail, cell phone, instant messaging, fax, or some other method. **Telecommuting**, an arrangement that allows employees to work from their homes, enables people scattered all over the world to stay connected.

The advantages of using these technology-based communication alternatives are obvious. Time efficiency is unsurpassed because people can transmit simple or detailed information across all time zones, and receivers can retrieve the information at their convenience. Cost-effectiveness is unsurpassed because fiber-optic and satellite transmissions cost the consumer virtually pennies compared to traditional transworld phone calls.

In all the frantic speed with which information now flows, many people forget that communication still must be carefully created before it is transmitted. Voice mail can be frustrating and time-consuming if it is not handled properly, and poorly written e-mails can leave the impression that the sender is either poorly educated or careless.

Videoconferencing allows workers in different locations to have virtual meetings so team members and clients can visually connect.

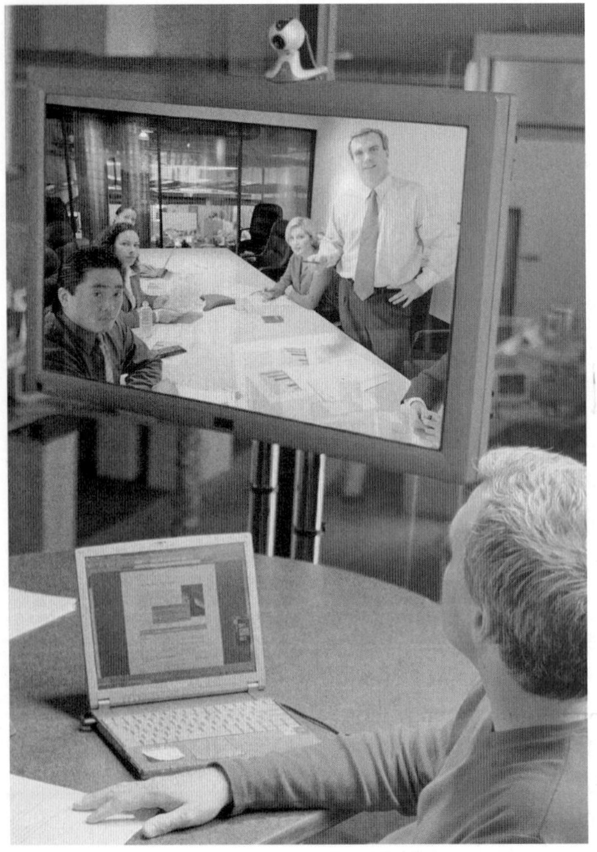

Voice Mail

Now that everyone is adjusting to the opportunities that immediate communication systems offer, nothing is more dismaying than playing phone tag (the exchange of several voice mails without successful transmission of the message). Whether you are on the sending or the receiving end, though, there are ways to avoid this counterproductive exercise in frustration.

When people call you and connect with your voice mail, be sure your recorded message includes your full name and when you will be retrieving your messages. If, for some reason, you will not be returning your calls for an extended time, edit your standard message to reflect this information so that your friends, customers, and colleagues will understand the delay and avoid repeated calls and duplicate messages. Forward your calls to another person's extension, if possible, or explain how the caller can reach a live person if the call is urgent. When you retrieve your messages, write down essential information, prioritize the messages in the order of importance, and return all of the calls as soon as possible.

When you are connected to another person's voice mail, state your full name, *a brief explanation of what information or action you need from that person* (the component most often neglected), your phone number, and the best time to reach you. All four components are necessary in order to avoid phone tag. Then, if the receiver reaches your voice mail when calling back, he or she can simply leave you a voice message with the information you wanted. The communication loop is complete.

E-mail

Technology has accelerated the pace of exchanging information today. People want answers and action now! Therefore, e-mail has become the standard format for most business and personal communication. In some cases, however, e-mail may be slower than a phone call or face-to-face meetings because you may have to wait days for a response to your message; plus, it takes time to compose an effective and accurate message.

E-mail takes careful planning and new writing skills. Those who read your e-mail will make judgments about your intelligence, competence, and attitude whether you want them to or not. Therefore, you need to carefully monitor not only what you write about but also how you word your messages. Here are some guidelines to follow:

Know Your Company's Policies

Most organizations monitor their employees' e-mail carefully. Keep in mind that even deleted messages live on indefinitely in the company's hard drives and may resurface. E-mail that might be sexually offensive could be considered sexual harassment and have serious ramifications.

HUMAN RELATIONS IN ACTION

E-mail Tips

- Do not send e-mail when you are angry or exhausted.
- When a face-to-face meeting is necessary, do not use e-mail as a substitute.
- When receiving large amounts of e-mail, selectively choose which ones you want to read by scanning the subject lines and deleting those that do not need a response.
- Make every attempt to create e-mail messages that are error free. Messages that contain errors may misrepresent your competence and give the wrong impression.
- Do not use e-mail to share rumors or innuendos or to say anything sensitive or critical that touches on someone's job competence.
- Avoid using unprofessional abbreviations such as BCNU for "Be seeing you," GG for "Got to go," or J/K for "Just kidding."
- Confine junk e-mail or personal e-mail to your friends and home computer and never transmit it through your company's computer system. Junk e-mail often contains attachments with viruses that could potentially shut down your entire organization.

Keep work-related messages professional and avoid sending personal e-mail messages on company time. A young analyst working in the Carlyle Group's Seoul office sent friends an e-mail in which he described his glamorous life that included a "harem of chickies," bankers catering to his "every whim," and other comments. Several people receiving the e-mail forwarded it to others in the financial community. Excerpts of it even appeared in the *New York Times*. The analyst was promptly fired.[26]

If you plan to join the millions of people who have created their own Web log, or blog, pay attention to your employer's policy. IBM has developed an eleven-point policy for employees who develop their own blog. Three of the IBM policy points are:

- Identify yourself and write in the first person. You must make it clear that you are speaking for yourself and not on behalf of IBM.
- Don't cite or reference clients, partners, or suppliers without their approval.
- Respect your audience. Don't use ethnic slurs, personal insults, or obscenities.[27]

Keep in mind that the information you include in your blog will be public for a long time.

Create an Appropriate E-mail Address

Carefully design your e-mail address to give the impression you want to convey. Addresses such as Crazylady@______.com or Buddyboy@______.com may be acceptable for personal e-mail but should never be used in a business setting. Your organization will generally have a specific format for your e-mail address that includes variations of your first and last names.

Although this may seem obvious, *always* make sure you are sending an e-mail to the correct address. This quick double-check will prevent delays and embarrassment for everyone involved if your message contains negative or potentially libelous comments about colleagues, or semiprivate information.

Use the *Subject:* Line

One of the best ways to set the stage for effective communications is to learn how to appropriately use the *Subject:* line available on all e-mail messages. It usually appears next to the sender's name on the receiver's screen. This brief introduction to your message will cue the receiver as to the probable content of your message. If your message is time-critical, add *Urgent* to the subject line, but be careful of overuse. When responding to another person's e-mail, be sure to forward the original subject line so that the receiver knows you are responding to his or her original request.

Watch Your Language

The biggest clue to your competence will be the words you use. The following are important things to remember when communicating:

- Be sure all words are spelled correctly and that there are no typographical errors. E-mails filled with typing errors convey an attitude of disrespect toward the reader.
- Be sure that you have selected the appropriate word—when choosing, for example, from there/their/they're; sight/site/cite; then/than; which/witch;

and so on. Do your verbs agree with their subjects? If your writing skills are limited, use software that includes grammar- and spelling-checkers.

- Keep your messages brief by summarizing your main points, indicate the action or response you are seeking, and be sure you provide all the details the receiver needs.
- Be very careful about the tone of your messages. Remove any potentially offending words and phrasing from your documents. Some people feel that they have to use stronger language to get a message across because the receiver cannot "hear" them. If you use solid capital letters in your e-mail, though, readers may think you are shouting at them.[28]
- The missing element in e-mail and other electronic communication is rapport, that bonding state that is easier to establish in person or by phone. Facial expressions, tone of voice, gestures—important social cues—are missing in e-mail.[29] Neither the sender nor the receiver can assume anything about the correspondent's frame of mind. Readers will not be able to tell if you are serious or being sarcastic, prying or simply curious, angry or merely frustrated. After creating your message, reread it as a stranger might. If words or phrases might be misconstrued, rewrite it so as to make clear exactly what you mean to say.

If your organization has been kind enough to provide you with Internet access and e-mail capabilities, respect the gift and use your account properly. In the information age, e-mail etiquette is just as important as other forms of business etiquette.[30]

TEST PREPPER 2.4

ANSWERS CAN BE FOUND ON P. 237

True or False?

___ 1. You should limit voice mail messages to 6 seconds or less, leaving only your name and phone number.

___ 2. Rapport is easier to establish via e-mail than over the telephone.

___ 3. In a virtual office, workers are connected to one another via the latest technology and do not have to be in the same physical location.

ACE the Test
ACE and ACE+ Practice Tests

Multiple Choice

___ 4. To use voice mail effectively, a worker should:
  a. keep messages a minimum of one week.
  b. always leave the outgoing greeting the same, lest callers become confused.
  c. jot down the essentials while listening and then delete the messages.
  d. use the system-default recorded greeting rather than recording in his/her own voice.

___ 5. Using capital letters throughout an e-mail message is the e-mail equivalent of:
  a. shouting.
  b. using profanity.
  c. asking for confidentiality.
  d. sexual harassment.

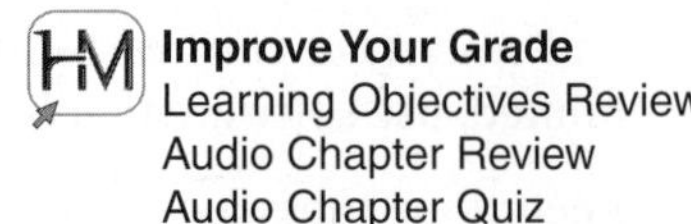

LEARNING OBJECTIVES REVIEW

1 *Understand the communication process.*

- Even with the major advances in technology-based communication, human involvement is necessary for successful communication in a work setting.
- Impersonal one-way communication methods can be used effectively to share basic facts, policies, and instructions.
- When feedback is necessary, interpersonal communication that involves a two-way exchange should be used.

2 *Identify and explain the filters that affect communication.*

- Messages are sent—and feedback is received—through a variety of filters that often distort the messages.
  - Semantics
  - Language and cultural barriers
  - Strong emotions
  - Negative attitudes
  - Role expectations
  - Gender roles
  - Nonverbal messages

3 *Identify ways to improve personal communication, including developing listening skills.*

- The sender and the receiver share equal responsibility for effective communication.
- Individuals can make their messages clearer by choosing words carefully, using repetition, timing the message correctly, and considering the receivers' preferences.
- Personal communication can also be improved by the use of active, critical, and empathic listening skills.
- Self-disclosure is the process of letting someone know what you think, feel, or want. Self-disclosure increases your accuracy in communication, reduces stress, increases self-awareness, and builds stronger relationships.

4 *Learn how to effectively communicate through technology.*

- Memos, letters, phone calls, and face-to-face conversations have been replaced, in many situations, by time-efficient and cost-effective, technology-based communication alternatives.
- Virtual offices, networks of workers connected by the latest technology, are now quite common.
- The increase in the use of e-mail, voice mail, teleconferencing, and other high-tech communication methods often creates human relations problems. Employees often forget that communication must still be carefully created before it is transmitted.

Career Corner

Q: I have just been "released" from the job I held for twelve years because my company was bought out by our competitor. I am highly skilled, competent, and dependable, but it's been a long time since I went on a job interview, and I'm scared to death. How should I communicate my strengths and commitment to a prospective employer? What happens if I blow it?

A: Fear is your greatest enemy, so be confident that many employers want to know that you are available. Remember that no one wants to hire a "victim," so do not refer to your "release" or your previous employer in a negative way. Memorize a positive statement that explains why you are looking for a new opportunity. It should focus on your strengths rather than on why you were released: for example, "My computer skills far exceeded the needs of my company's new owner." Be aware that your degree, references, wardrobe, and handshake get you in the door, but that interviews today often include probing questions that test your ability to react and respond quickly. Most interviewers expect applicants to ask their own series of questions, such as: How does this position fit into the organizational structure? Why is the position vacant? What are the opportunities for advancement? If you want the job at the conclusion of the interview, ask for it! Be sure to send a follow-up note to the interviewer that reemphasizes your strengths. If you feel you blew it, contact the interviewer by phone or letter to correct misleading or misinterpreted information. This type of persistence will show that you sincerely want the job. If you don't get the job, consider the interview a great practice session and enter the next one with renewed confidence!

Applying What You Have Learned

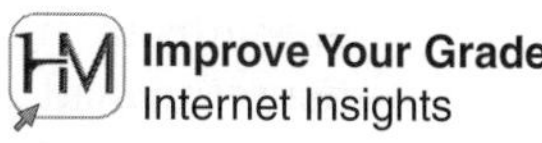

1. During the next week, study the listening habits of students in another class in which you are enrolled. Keep a journal of your observations by identifying the nonverbal behaviors you witness. Are they barriers to effective communication between the instructor and the student or do they enhance communication? How do you believe the students' nonverbal behaviors might affect the relationship between the instructor and the students?
2. Print out the most recent e-mails that you have sent or received and bring them to class. Analyze their effectiveness in terms of the e-mail tips in this chapter. Did the messages violate any of the tips? If so, which ones? How could these messages be improved?
3. Many times we take the conversation away from others and make it our own. This practice wastes time and is a major relationship killer. Here is how it works: At the beginning of the conversation, you tell the other person about a problem you are dealing with and, before you finish the story, the other person says, "I know what you mean," and then describes a personal experience that may or may not have anything to do with your problem. Once the other person takes over the conversation, a valuable exchange of ideas is probably lost. During the next week, monitor your conversations with friends, family members, and coworkers. How often did the other person attempt to take the conversation away from you? How often did you attempt to take over the conversation?[31]
4. To increase self-awareness in the area of communication complete the self-assessment form found on the website **college.hmco.com/pic/reeceSAS**.

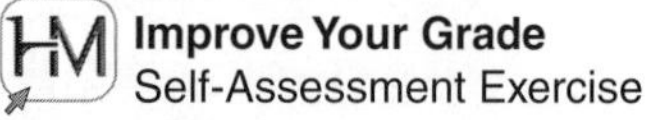

ROLE-PLAY EXERCISE

This role-play exercise is designed to improve your active listening skills. Carefully study Table 2.1, Active Listening Skills, and prepare to meet with another class member who wants to talk about his or her career plans. As this person talks, make every effort to apply the four active listening skills. Once the other person has finished speaking, discuss your career plans. When both of you have finished talking, discuss whether each felt the partner was really engaged in active listening. Did either of you find that the other person was distracted and not really paying attention? Be prepared to share your insights with your role-play partner, your instructor, and other class members.

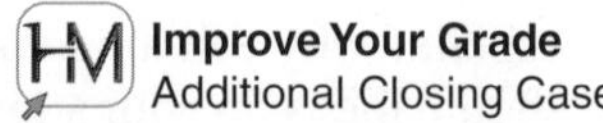

CASE 2.1

Fluid Communications

At the beginning of this chapter, you were introduced to the problems the administrators at Duke University Health System experienced when they discovered that for two months their surgeons had unknowingly used instruments that had been washed in a mixture of water and used hydraulic fluid instead of detergent and then sterilized with heat. Initially, no one noticed the mistake because the detergent containers had not been relabeled and the detergent normally used and the hydraulic fluid were the same color and were both odorless. Because surgical instruments are routinely treated with lubricants to prevent rusting, hospital administrators did not detect the problem despite complaints from medical staff that the surgical instruments seemed *unusually* slick and oily.

A few hours after the discovery, however, a crisis team had gathered to determine how to handle the potentially devastating situation. Within one week, letters went out to all 3,800 affected patients and their physicians apologizing for the mixup and telling them that it should pose little risk to their health. They were invited to call a hotline to report any changes in their health. A website was created to offer them information about the effects of hydraulic fluid on the body. The goal of the crisis team was to balance the urgency of getting the information out with the need for accuracy, especially in a world of business scandals where corporate attorneys prefer that top executives say nothing and public relations advisers want leaders to be frank.

Behind the scenes, Duke's Infection Control physicians began a vigilant surveillance program to monitor any spike in infections among the affected patients. The hotline calls were recorded, monitored, and analyzed. Scientists were brought in to conduct a chemical analysis of the used hydraulic fluid and to determine how it might harm humans. Surgery complications, new illnesses, and unusual complaints were analyzed and compared against normal rates for these problems. Despite these efforts, patients contacted attorneys and formed a support group claiming that Duke officials failed to take their concerns about ongoing health problems seriously.

In hindsight, hospital administrators admit they should have been more responsive to their patients' concerns. They discovered that sharing scientific results was not enough and that they needed to sympathize with their patients by considering not only their medical issues but also their concerns and anxieties. Dr. Michael Cuffe, Duke's vice president for medical affairs and patient-physician liaison, reported that administrators were doing all the right things internally, but they were not telling their patients what steps were being taken and did not provide the appropriate feedback to their concerns. Cuffe believes that patients who wanted to visit in person and talk about their concerns should have had that opportunity.[32]

Questions

1. Dr. Cuffe stated: "I see a heightened need to make sure the administration hears the concerns of patients. Not that they're deaf to it. But that's what needs to improve."[33] What steps could Duke administrators, or managers of any other organization, take to make sure the concerns of customers are heard?
2. How could the original problem have been intercepted before it became a health care crisis?
3. What filters were in place to block effective communication between the hospital administrators, medical staff, and affected patients?

Resources on the Web

Prepare for Class, Improve Your Grade, and ACE the Test. Student Achievement Series resources include:

- ACE and ACE+ Practice Tests
- Audio Chapter Quizzes
- Audio Chapter Reviews
- Learning Objective Reviews
- Career Snapshots
- Chapter Glossaries
- Chapter Outlines
- Crossword Puzzles
- Hangman Games
- Flashcards
- Audio Glossaries
- Internet Insights
- Self-Assessment Exercises
- Additional Closing Cases

To access these learning and study tools, go to **college.hmco.com/pic/reeceSAS**.

HM ManagementSPACE

3 Building High Self-Esteem

Self-efficacy and self-respect are central themes of the definition of self-esteem used in this chapter. For many people growth in both of these areas can be achieved through education.

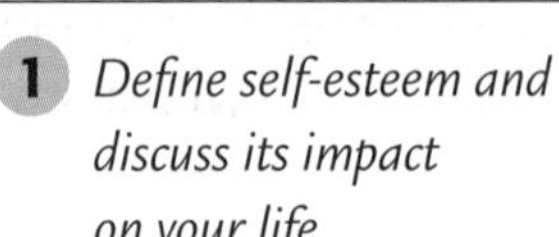

1 *Define self-esteem and discuss its impact on your life.*

2 *Understand how self-esteem is developed.*

3 *Identify the characteristics of people with low and high self-esteem.*

4 *Identify ways to raise your self-esteem.*

"Our level of self-esteem affects virtually everything we think, say, and do."

—Mary Ellen Donovan

Chapter Outline

Prepare for Class
Chapter Outline

5 *Understand the conditions organizations can create that will help workers raise their self-esteem.*

The Power of Self-Esteem

Shoshana Zuboff likes to reflect on some of the special students she taught at the Harvard Business School. Some students, she recalls, "threw themselves at learning as if their lives depended on it." One of those students, Edward, had a troubled past. His parents split up when he was a small boy, and he was on his own much of the time as his mother needed to work. Edward and his mother lived in a neighborhood where drugs and gangs were common. By the sixth grade, he was a drug dealer, and later he ended up in a penitentiary. Then he had the good fortune to meet a judge who offered him two years in a drug rehabilitation program in return for good behavior. After rehab, he got a job, enrolled in a community college, and made the dean's list several times.

A counselor encouraged Edward to set his sights high, so he applied and was accepted to an Ivy League school, where he studied business and economics. This success led to his acceptance into the Harvard Business School, where he met Professor Zuboff.

KEY TERMS

developmental psychology p. 56
external locus of control p. 59
guided imagery p. 65
inner critic p. 66
internal locus of control p. 60
mentor p. 63
self-concept p. 56
self-efficacy p. 54
self-esteem p. 54
self-respect p. 55
self-talk p. 66
talent p. 62
visualize p. 65

Prepare for Class
Chapter Glossary

Improve Your Grade
Flashcards
Hangman
Crossword Puzzle

Although Edward had accomplished a great deal since leaving the penitentiary, he felt a growing sense of shame over things he did not know. During one lecture, Professor Zuboff briefly mentioned the name of an author who had written about Auschwitz. After class, Edward asked, "What is Auschwitz?" Because of his disadvantaged childhood, he had missed out on many learning experiences that most students take for granted. To avoid giving away his deep-seated inner secret, he mastered many defense strategies to protect his image among his peers. Professor Zuboff noted, "He was haunted by the sense of not knowing what he didn't know or how to learn it."

With help from this caring professor and her husband, who agreed to serve as his mentor, Edward began a program of study designed to fill in the gaps in his education. His self-esteem improved greatly as his program of self-improvement unfolded. Today Edward runs a successful consulting firm that focuses on leadership and emotional intelligence.[1]

THE POWER OF SELF-ESTEEM

1 *Define self-esteem and discuss its impact on your life.*

The importance of self-esteem as a guiding force in our lives cannot be overstated. Tschirhart Sanford and Mary Ellen Donovan, the authors of *Women & Self-Esteem,* describe the power of self-esteem as follows:

> Our level of self-esteem affects virtually everything we think, say, and do. It affects how we see the world and our place in it. It affects how others in the world see and treat us. It affects the choices we make—choices about what we will do with our lives and with whom we will be involved. It affects our ability to both give and receive love. And, it affects our ability to take action to change things that need to be changed.[2]

Self-Esteem = Self-Efficacy + Self-Respect

Nathaniel Branden, author of *The Six Pillars of Self-Esteem* and *Self-Esteem at Work,* has spent the past three decades studying the psychology of self-esteem. He states that the ultimate source of **self-esteem** can only be internal: It is the relationship between a person's self-efficacy and self-respect. **Self-efficacy** is the belief that you can achieve what you set out to do.[3] When your self-efficacy is high, you believe you have the ability to act appropriately. When your self-efficacy is low, you worry that you might not be able to do the task, that it is beyond your abilities. Your perception of your self-efficacy can influence which tasks you take on and which ones you avoid. Albert Bandura, a professor at Stanford University and one of the foremost self-efficacy researchers, views this component of self-esteem as a resilient belief in your own abilities. According to Bandura, a major source of self-efficacy is the experience of mastery, in which success in one area builds your confidence to succeed in other areas.[4] For example, an administrative assistant who masters a sophisticated computerized accounting system is more likely to

self-esteem Belief in one's own abilities and of being capable of meeting life's challenges and being worthy of happiness.

self-efficacy The power to produce a positive attitude that affects one's self-esteem; the belief that one can achieve what one sets out to do.

HUMAN RELATIONS IN ACTION

The Power of Strong Self-Efficacy

Over the years many people we now know to be extremely intelligent and talented have had to develop a strong belief in themselves. If they had relied on others' opinions of their capabilities and potential, who knows where this world would be!

Walt Disney was fired by a newspaper editor for lack of ideas. He went bankrupt several times before he built Disneyland.

Thomas Edison's teacher said he was "too stupid to learn anything."

Fred Astaire recalls the 1933 memo from the MGM casting director that stated, "Can't act. Can't sing. Slightly bald. Can dance a little."

Vince Lombardi, successful football coach and motivational speaker and writer, recalls an expert's description of his talents: "He possesses minimal football knowledge and lacks motivation."

Albert Einstein did not speak until he was 4 years old and did not read until he was 7. His teacher described him as "mentally slow, unsociable, and adrift forever in foolish dreams."

tackle future complicated computer programs than is a person who feels computer illiterate and may not even try to figure out the new program, regardless of how well he or she *could* do it.

self-respect A component of self-esteem; what one thinks and feels about oneself.

Self-respect, the second component of self-esteem, is what you think and feel about yourself. Your judgment of your own value is a primary factor in achieving personal and career success. People who respect themselves tend to act in ways that confirm and reinforce this respect. People who lack self-respect may put up with verbal or physical abuse from others because they feel they are unworthy of praise and deserve the abuse. Nathaniel Branden believes that the healthier our self-esteem, the more inclined we are to treat others with respect, benevolence, goodwill, and fairness since we do not tend to perceive them as a threat, and since self-respect is the foundation of respect for others.[5]

Self-efficacy and self-respect are central themes of the definition of self-esteem adopted by the National Association for Self-Esteem. NASE defines self-esteem as "the experience of being capable of meeting life's challenges and being worthy of happiness."[6] It is having the conviction that you are able to make appropriate choices and decisions, and can be effective in the many roles you play in life, such as that of friend, daughter or son, husband or wife, employee or employer, leader, and so on. Your sense of competence is strengthened through accomplishing meaningful goals, overcoming adversities, and bouncing back from failure.

The NASE definition of self-esteem helps us make the distinction between authentic (healthy) self-esteem and false (unhealthy) self-esteem. Authentic self-esteem is not expressed by self-glorification at the expense of others or by the attempt to diminish others so as to elevate oneself. Arrogance, boastfulness, and overestimation of your abilities are more likely to reflect inadequate self-esteem rather than, as it might appear, too much self-esteem.

TEST PREPPER 3.1

ANSWERS CAN BE FOUND ON P. 237

True or False?

1. Arrogance, boastfulness, and overestimation of your abilities reflect false (unhealthy) self-esteem.
2. The ultimate source of self-esteem can only be external or achieved through praise from others.

Multiple Choice

3. T.J. has both high self-efficacy and high self-respect. Together, these indicate that T.J. also has:
   a. high self-esteem.
   b. low emotional intelligence.
   c. above-average intellectual capabilities.
   d. a supportive family.
4. People like Albert Einstein and Walt Disney succeeded because of their strong belief in themselves. In other words, like many other successful people, they had high:
   a. self-efficacy.
   b. regard for others.
   c. relationship-building skills.
   d. self-awareness.
5. People who lack self-respect are likely to:
   a. treat others with respect.
   b. treat others fairly.
   c. put up with verbal or physical abuse from others.
   d. stand up against abuse from others.

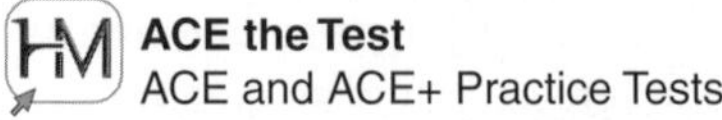

HOW SELF-ESTEEM DEVELOPS

Understand how self-esteem is developed.

self-concept The bundle of facts, opinions, beliefs, and perceptions about oneself that are present every moment of every day.

To understand the development of self-esteem, it is helpful to examine how you formed your self-concept. Your **self-concept** is the bundle of facts, opinions, beliefs, and perceptions about yourself that are present in your life every moment of every day.[7] The self-concept you have today reflects information you have received from others and life events that occurred throughout childhood, adolescence, and adulthood. You are *consciously* aware of some of the things you have been conditioned to believe about yourself. But many comments and events that have shaped your self-concept are processed at the *unconscious* level and continue to influence your judgments, feelings, and behaviors whether you are aware of them or not.[8]

Childhood

developmental psychology The study of the course and causes of developmental changes over a person's lifetime.

Researchers in the field of **developmental psychology** are concerned with the course and causes of developmental changes over a person's lifetime. They pay close attention to genetic and environmental factors (nature versus nurture).[9] Although space does not permit a detailed discussion here of cognitive, social, and emotional development during early childhood, we can state with conviction that developmental experiences during the first few years of life are extremely important. For example, too little attention from nurturing parents and too much television viewing can hinder healthy childhood development.[10]

Because childhood events are retained in your brain, poor performance in school, abusive or uncaring parents, or a serious childhood accident can be defining experiences in your life. Messages from siblings, teachers, and various authority figures can have a lasting impact on your self-concept. Consider the father who repeatedly says, "Real men don't cry," or places undue emphasis on successful performance during contact sports. These childhood experiences can form the foundation for your level of self-esteem that emerges later in life.

"Just remember, son, it doesn't matter whether you win or lose—unless you want Daddy's love."

Adolescence

The transition from childhood to adulthood can be a long and difficult period. At about age 11, children begin to describe themselves in terms of social relationships and personality traits. By the end of early adolescence, most youth are ready to develop a personal identity as a unique individual. Identity formation, the central task of adolescence, is usually more difficult for youth if their infancy and childhood resulted in feelings of shame, guilt, and inferiority.[11]

As adolescents attempt to resolve questions about self-worth, sexuality, and independence, they may "try out" alternative identities.[12] Teens often turn to movies, music videos, and magazines for guidance and attempt to emulate the unrealistic body images and fashions that their peers deem worthwhile. Adolescence can last well into the 20s as each person attempts to develop his or her own unique identity.

Parents and teachers can have a powerful effect on their teenagers' self-esteem. When they offer encouragement, support, enthusiasm, and commendation for achievements, they enable teens to learn how to take healthy risks, tolerate frustration, and feel proud of their accomplishments.

Adulthood

When you reach adulthood, you are greatly influenced by a time-reinforced self-concept that has been molded by people and events from all your past experiences. You have been bombarded over the years with positive and negative messages from your family, friends, teachers, supervisors, and the media. You may compare yourself to others, as was so common in adolescence, or you may focus on your own inner sense of self-worth. Emmett Miller, a noted authority on self-esteem, says that as adults we tend to define ourselves in terms of:[13]

1. *The things we possess.* Miller says this is the most primitive source of self-worth. If we define ourselves in terms of what we have, the result may be an effort to accumulate more and more material things to achieve a greater feeling of self-worth. The idea that we can compensate for self-doubt and insecurity with our checkbook is widely accepted in America.[14] People who define themselves in terms of what they have may have difficulty deciding "what is enough" and may spend their life in search of more material possessions.

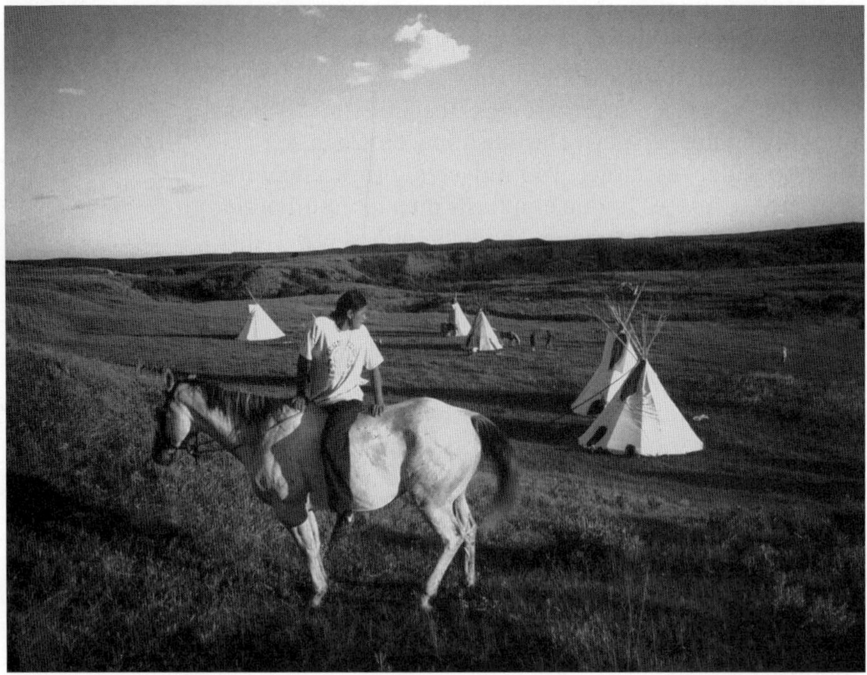

Most adolescents are attempting to resolve questions about self-worth, sexuality, and independence. David Rocky Mountain, a 13-year-old Lakota Native American, surveys a traditional campsite constructed by troubled teens from the Cheyenne River Sioux tribe in South Dakota. This "spiritual boot camp" provides youngsters with the opportunity to bond with their elders, who offer many valuable life lessons.

2. *What we do for a living.* Miller points out that too often our self-worth and identity depend on something as arbitrary as a job title. Amy Saltzman, author of *Downshifting,* a book on ways to reinvent (or redefine) success, says, "We have allowed our professional identities to define us and control us."[15] She points out that we have looked to outside forces such as the corporation, the university, or the media to provide us with a script for leading a satisfying, worthwhile life.
3. *Our internal value system and emotional makeup.* Miller says this is the healthiest way for people to identify themselves:

> If you don't give yourself credit for excellence in other areas of life, besides your job and material possessions, you've got nothing to keep your identity afloat in emotionally troubled waters. People who are in touch with their real identity weather the storm better because they have a more varied and richer sense of themselves, owing to the importance they attach to their personal lives and activities.[16]

As an adult, you will be constantly adjusting the level of your self-esteem as you cope with events at work and in your personal life. The loss of a job or being passed over for a promotion may trigger feelings of insecurity or depression. A messy divorce can leave you with feelings of self-doubt. An unexpected award may raise your spirits and make you feel better about yourself.

The Past Programs the Future

Phillip McGraw, better known as "Dr. Phil," has developed a one-sentence guide to understanding the importance of your self-concept: *The past reaches into the present, and programs the future, by your recollections and your internal rhetoric about*

TOTAL PERSON INSIGHT
Don Miguel Ruiz Author, ***The Four Agreements***

"How many times do we pay for one mistake? The answer is thousands of times. The human is the only animal on earth that pays a thousand times for the same mistake. The rest of the animals pay once for every mistake they make. But not us. We have a powerful memory. We make a mistake, we judge ourselves, we find ourselves guilty, and punish ourselves. . . . Every time we remember, we judge ourselves again, we are guilty again, and we punish ourselves again, and again, and again."

what you perceived to have happened in your life.[17] Past experiences and events, which McGraw describes as "defining moments," can influence your thinking for a lifetime and program your future. They get incorporated into your deepest understanding of who you are because they are often the focus of your internal dialogue—a process we call "self-talk." Later in this chapter, we will discuss how to avoid the influence of negative self-talk and build upon positive messages.

Self-Esteem Influences Your Behavior

3 *Identify the characteristics of people with low and high self-esteem.*

Your level of self-esteem can have a powerful impact on your behavior. Your sense of competence and resulting self-respect, the two components of self-esteem, stem from the belief that you are generally capable of producing the results in life that you want by making appropriate, constructive choices. This confidence makes you less vulnerable to the negative views of others, which then enables you to be more tolerant and respectful of others. People with healthy self-esteem tend to have a sense of personal worth that has been strengthened through various achievements and through accurate self-appraisal.[18]

Characteristics of People with Low Self-Esteem

1. *They tend to maintain an external locus of control.* People who maintain an **external locus of control** believe that their life is almost totally controlled by outside forces and that they bear little personal responsibility for what happens to them.[19] When something goes wrong, they have a tendency to blame something or someone other than themselves. Even when they succeed, they tend to attribute their success to luck rather than to their own expertise and hard work. They continually rely on other people to make them feel good about themselves, and therefore need an ever increasing dose of support from others to keep them going. When we rely too heavily on validation from external sources, we can lose control over our lives.[20]
2. *They are more likely to participate in self-destructive behaviors.* If you do not like yourself, there is no apparent reason to take care of yourself. Therefore, people with low self-esteem are more likely to drink too much, smoke too

external locus of control The belief that one's life is almost totally controlled by outside forces and that one bears little personal responsibility for what happens to oneself.

much, and eat too much. Some may develop an eating disorder such as bulimia or anorexia, often with devastating results.

3. *They tend to exhibit poor human relations skills.* Individuals with low self-esteem may have difficulty developing effective interpersonal skills. Workers with low self-esteem may reduce the efficiency and productivity of a group: They tend to exercise less initiative and hesitate to accept responsibility or make independent decisions and are less likely to speak up in a group and criticize the group's approach.

Characteristics of People with High Self-Esteem

internal locus of control The belief that one is able to shape one's life and take responsibility for oneself and one's actions.

1. *They tend to maintain an internal locus of control.* People who believe they are largely responsible for what happens to them maintain an **internal locus of control**. They make decisions for their own reasons based on their standards of what is right and wrong. They learn from their mistakes, but are not immobilized by them. They realize that problems are challenges, not obstacles. In his book *They All Laughed: From Lightbulbs to Lasers,* Ira Flatow examines the lives of successful, innovative people who had to overcome major obstacles to achieve their goals. He discovered that the common thread among these creative people was their ability to overcome disappointing events and press on toward their goals.
2. *They are able to feel all dimensions of emotion without letting those emotions affect their behavior in a negative way.* They realize emotions cannot be handled either by repressing them or by giving them free rein. Although you may not be able to stop feeling the emotions of anger, envy, and jealousy, you can control your thoughts and actions when you are under the influence of these strong emotions. Say to yourself, "I may not be able to control the way I feel right now, but I can control the way I behave."
3. *They are less likely to take things personally.* Don Miguel Ruiz, author of the best-selling book *The Four Agreements,* cautions us to avoid taking others' comments personally: "When you make it a strong habit not to take anything personally, you avoid many upsets in your life." He says that when you react strongly to gossip or strongly worded criticism ("You're so fat!"), you suffer for nothing. Ruiz notes that many of these messages come from people who are unable to respect you because they do not respect themselves.[21]
4. *They are able to accept other people as unique, talented individuals.* They learn to accept others for who they are and what they can do. Our multicultural work force makes this attitude especially important. Individuals who cannot tolerate other people who are "different" may find themselves out of a job. (See Chapter 7, "Valuing Work Force Diversity.") People with high self-esteem build mutual trust based on each individual's uniqueness.
5. *They have a productive personality.* They are optimistic in their approach to life and are capable of being creative, imaginative problem solvers. Because of this, they tend to be leaders and to be skillful in dealing with people. They have the ability to evaluate the dynamics of a relationship and adjust to the demands of the interaction. They do not resort to shifting the blame onto others if something goes wrong; instead, they help others accept the responsibility for their own actions. They are able to handle stress in a productive way by putting their problems and concerns into perspective and maintaining a balance of work and fun in their lives.[22]

TEST PREPPER 3.2, 3.3

ANSWERS CAN BE FOUND ON P. 237

True or False?

T 1. Researchers in developmental psychology pay close attention to nature versus nurture issues and how they impact developmental changes over the course of peoples' lifetimes.

F 2. Throughout adulthood it is best to stay focused on excellence achieved at work.

T 3. People with high self-esteem are able to feel and experience emotions and simultaneously control their behavior.

ACE the Test
ACE and ACE+ Practice Tests

Multiple Choice

c 4. The most primitive source of self-worth among adults is:
   a. occupation.
   b. internal value system.
   c. possessions.
   d. feedback from parents.

a 5. "Why do these things always happen to me? Others are always picking on me," says Teddy. It appears that Teddy is guided by:
   a. external locus of control.
   b. high expectations of others.
   c. healthy self-efficacy.
   d. internal locus of control.

HOW TO BUILD SELF-ESTEEM

4 *Identify ways to raise your self-esteem.*

"The level of our self-esteem is not set once and for all in childhood," says Nathaniel Branden. It can grow throughout our lives or it can deteriorate.[23] Healthy self-esteem comes from realizing what qualities and skills you have that you can rely on and then making a plan to build those qualities and skills that you want in the future. The person you will be tomorrow has yet to be created. Your new, higher level of self-esteem will not happen overnight. Such a change is the result of a slow, steady evolution that begins with the desire to overcome low self-esteem.

Search for the Source of Low Self-Esteem

Many people live with deep personal doubts about themselves but have difficulty determining the source of those feelings. They even have difficulty finding the right words to describe those negative feelings. People with low self-esteem are less likely to see themselves with great clarity. The self-image they possess is like a reflection in a warped funhouse mirror; the image magnifies their weaknesses and minimizes their strengths. To raise your self-esteem requires achieving a higher level of self-awareness and learning to accurately perceive your particular balance of strengths and weaknesses.[24]

- To start this process, take time to list and carefully examine the defining moments in your life. Pay special attention to those that were decidedly negative, and try to determine how these moments have shaped your current self-concept.
- Next, make a list of the labels that others have used to describe you.
- Study the list carefully, and try to determine which ones you have internalized and accepted. Have these labels had a positive or negative influence on your

concept of yourself? Phillip McGraw says, "If you are living to a label, you have molded for yourself a fictional self-concept with artificial boundaries."[25]

Identify and Accept Your Limitations

Become realistic about who you are and what you can and cannot do. Demanding perfection of yourself is unrealistic because no one is perfect. The past cannot be changed: Acknowledge your mistakes; learn from them; then move on.

Acting as an observer and detaching yourself from negative thoughts and actions can help you break the habit of rating yourself according to some scale of perfection and can enable you to substitute more positive and helpful thoughts. A good first step is learning to dislike a behavior you may indulge in, rather than condemning yourself. Criticizing yourself may make the behavior worse. If you condemn yourself for being weak, for example, how can you muster the strength to change?

Take Responsibility for Your Decisions

Psychologists have found that children who were encouraged to make their own decisions early in their lives have higher self-esteem than those who were kept dependent on their parents for a longer period of time. Making decisions helps you develop confidence in your own judgment and enables you to explore options. Take every opportunity you can to make decisions both in setting your goals and in devising ways to achieve them.

The attitude that you must be right all the time is a barrier to personal growth. With this attitude you will avoid doing things that might result in mistakes. Much unhappiness comes from the widespread and regrettable belief that it is important to avoid making mistakes at all costs.[26] Taking risks that reach beyond what you already know how to do can often be fun and extremely rewarding.

Engage in Strength Building

Over the past thirty years, the Gallup International Research and Education Center has researched the best way to maximize a person's potential. One of the most important findings can be summarized in a single sentence: Most organizations take their employees' strengths for granted and focus on minimizing their weaknesses. The research findings suggest that the best way to excel in a career is to maximize your strengths.[27]

The Gallup Organization research has been summarized in *Now, Discover Your Strengths* by Marcus Buckingham and Donald Clifton. The first step toward strength building is to discover your greatest talents. A **talent** is any naturally recurring pattern of thought, feeling, or behavior that can be productively applied. It is important to distinguish your natural talents from things you can learn. With practice, of

talent Any naturally recurring pattern of thought, feeling, or behavior that can be productively applied.

TOTAL PERSON INSIGHT

Fran Cox and Louis Cox Authors, ***A Conscious Life***

"There is little understanding in our culture that being an adult is an ongoing process of learning and self-correcting: Life is always changing, revealing what was previously unknown and unplanned for."

course, we can all get a little better at doing most things. However, to reach consistent, near perfect performances through practice alone is very difficult. Many successful salespeople have a talent for making new acquaintances and derive satisfaction from breaking the ice to make a connection with new people. They are intrigued with the unique qualities of each customer. They have a natural gift, enhanced through practice, for figuring out how to customize their sales presentation so it appeals to the unique needs of each customer. Without these talents, salespeople will struggle to achieve success.[28]

Strength building also requires the acquisition of knowledge and skill. As we prepare for a career, we must acquire certain factual knowledge. An accountant must know how to prepare a statement of cash flow. Nurses must know exactly how much Novocain is needed for a procedure. Skill, the application of knowledge, might be thought of as the "doing" part of strength building.[29]

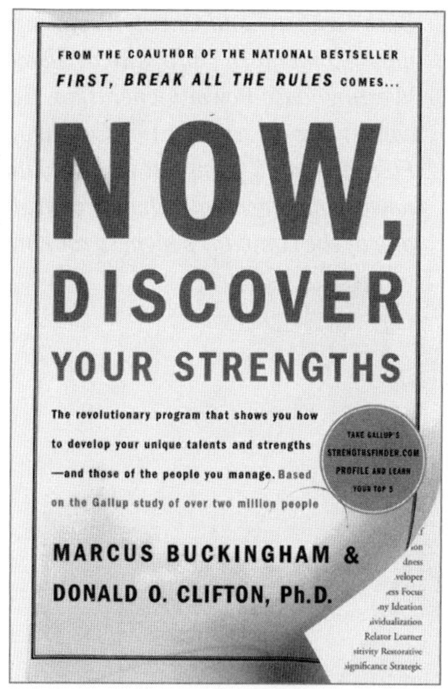

The authors of the best-selling book Now, Discover Your Strengths *encourage us to identify our dominant talents. Get involved in a wide range of activities and then pay close attention to how you feel about these experiences.*

Identifying Your Dominant Talents

Marcus Buckingham states that when we are not doing what we are truly good at, we are not living up to our greatest performance capabilities. He says that one effective way to identify your dominant talents is to step back and watch yourself as you try out different activities. Pay close attention to how you feel about these experiences. Take an elective course, volunteer to be chair of a committee, complete a summer internship, or accept a part-time job in an area that appeals to you. If you flourish in some activities but wither in others, analyze why this happened.

Buckingham's research indicates that the best managers spend 80 percent of their time trying to amplify their employees' strengths.[30] Chances are, however, you will not be working for a boss who encourages strength building. So, be prepared to assume responsibility for identifying your natural talents and building your strengths.

Seek the Support and Guidance of Mentors

Chip Bell, author of *Managers as Mentors: Building Partnerships for Learning,* defines a **mentor** as "someone who helps someone else learn something the learner would otherwise have learned less well, more slowly, or not at all."[31] In most organizations mentoring is carried out informally, but formal programs that systematically match mentors and protégés are common.

mentor A trusted friend or guide, tutor, or coach.

Improve Your Grade
Audio Glossary

Most people who have had a mentoring experience say it was an effective development tool. However, many surveys indicate that only a small percentage of employees say they have had a mentor. In today's fast-paced work environment, where most people have a heavy workload, you must be willing to take the initiative and build a mentor relationship. Warren Bennis, founding chairman of the Leadership Institute at the University of Southern California, states, "Being mentored isn't a passive game. It's nothing less than the ability to spot the handful of people who can make all the difference in your life."[32] Here are some tips to keep in mind.

1. *Search for a mentor who has the qualities of a good coach.* Mentors need to be accomplished in their own right, but success alone does not make someone a good mentor. Look for someone whom you would like to emulate, both in business savvy and in operating style. Be sure it is someone you trust enough to talk with about touchy issues.[33]

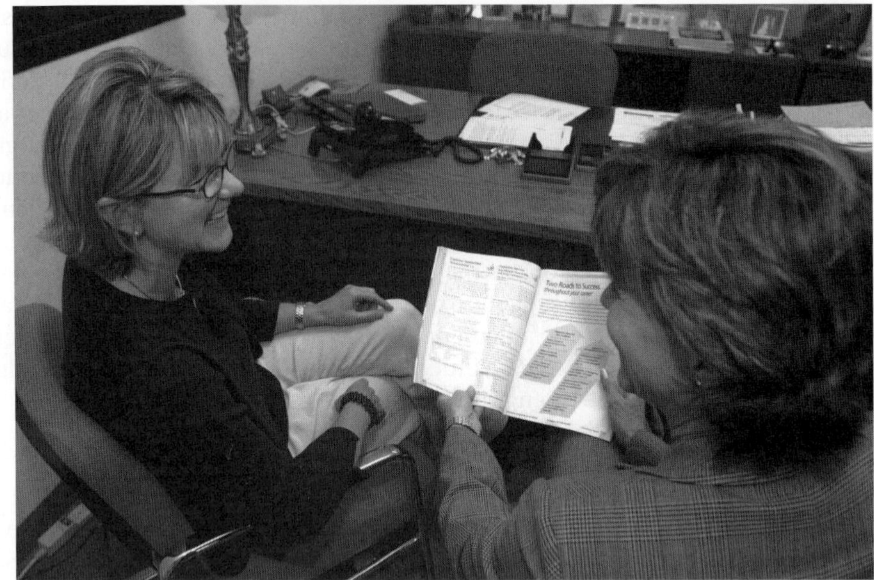

Beth Lay, left, and Christy Woodruff joined a mentoring program at Siemens Westinghouse Power Generation. Both women are veterans at this Orlando, Florida–based firm, but Lay is relatively new to management, while Woodruff is one of the company's highest-ranking women.

2. *Market yourself to a prospective mentor.* The best mentor for you may be someone who is very busy. Sell the benefits of a mentoring partnership. For example, point out that mentoring can be a mutually rewarding experience. Describe specific steps you will take to avoid wasting the time of a busy person. You might suggest that meetings be held during lunch or agree to on-line mentoring.[34]
3. *Use multiple mentors.* Some people feel the need for both internal and external mentors. An internal mentor, an experienced associate or supervisor, can provide guidance as you navigate the organizational bumps and potholes. An external mentor, someone who does not work for your company, can provide an objective, independent view of your skills and talents.[35] Many people benefit from short-term "learning partners" who will coach them on specific skills.

Although mentors are not mandatory for success, they certainly help. Indeed, there will always be days when you feel nothing you do is right. Your mentor can help repair damaged self-esteem and encourage you to go on. With the power of another person's positive expectations reinforcing your own native abilities, it is hard to fail.

Set Goals

Research points to a direct link between self-esteem and the achievement of personal and professional goals. People who set goals and successfully achieve them are able to maintain high self-esteem. Why? Because setting goals enables you to take ownership of the future. Once you realize that just about every behavior is controllable, the possibilities for improving your self-esteem are endless. Self-change may be difficult, but it's not impossible. Some people lack self-esteem because they haven't achieved enough goals and experienced the good feelings that come from success.[36]

The major principles that encompass goal setting are outlined in Table 3.1. Goal setting should be an integral part of your efforts to break old habits or form new ones. Before you attempt to set goals, engage in serious reflection. Make a list of the things you want to achieve, and then ask yourself this question: What goals are truly important to me? If you set goals that really excite you, desire will fuel your will to achieve them.[37]

Practice Guided Imagery

Guided imagery is one of the most creative and empowering methods for achieving your goals available today. It provides you with a way to harness the power of the mind and imagination to succeed at something. It can be used to help you relax, set goals (like losing weight), or prepare for a challenging opportunity such as interviewing for a new job. Some heart surgeons use guided imagery to calm their patients to help speed recovery. With a Walkman headphone, the patient hears carefully crafted, medically detailed messages that urge the person to relax and imagine themselves in a safe, comfortable place: "Feel the new strength flowing through you, through arteries that are wider and more open, more flexible with smoother surfaces than before."[38]

guided imagery A creative and empowering method that harnesses the power of the mind and the imagination to achieve goals through the use of visualization.

To **visualize** means to form a mental image of something. It refers to what you see in the mind's eye. Once you have formed a clear mental picture of what you want to accomplish, identify the steps needed to get there and then mentally rehearse them. The visualization process needs to be repeated over and over again. The following are some examples of visualization in real life:

visualize To form a mental image of something.

- Many athletes choreograph their performance in their imagination before competitions. Studies by the U.S. Olympic Training Center show that 94 percent of the coaches use mental rehearsal for training and competitions.[39]
- Artists rarely begin a work of art until they have an image of what they are going to create.

TABLE 3.1

Goal-Setting Principles

Goal setting gives you the power to take control of the present and the future. Goals can help you break old habits or form new ones. You will need an assortment of goals that address the different needs of your life. The following goal-setting principles should be helpful.

1. **Spend time reflecting on the things you want to change in your life.** Take time to clarify your motivation and purpose. Set goals that are specific, measurable, and realistic. Unrealistic goals increase fear, and fear increases the probability of failure.
2. **Develop a goal-setting plan that includes the steps necessary to achieve the goal.** Put the goal and the steps in writing. Change requires structure. Identify all activities and materials you will need to achieve your goal. Review your plan daily—repetition increases the probability of success.
3. **Modify your environment by changing the stimuli around you.** If your goal is to lose five pounds during a one-month period, make a weight chart so you can monitor your progress. You may need to give up desserts and avoid restaurants that serve huge portions. Gather new information on effective weight loss techniques, and seek advice from others. This may involve finding a mentor or joining a support group.
4. **Monitor your behavior, and reward your progress.** Focus on small successes, because each little success builds your reservoir of self-esteem. Reinforcement from yourself and/or others is necessary for change. If the passion for change begins to subside, remind yourself why you want to achieve your goal. Be patient—it takes time to change your lifestyle.

- Dancers physically and mentally rehearse their performances hundreds of times before ever stepping on stage. The same techniques can be used in the workplace.

Let's assume your team members have asked you to present a cost-saving plan to management. The entire team is counting on you. The visualization process should begin with identifying the steps you will take to get approval of the plan. What information will you present? What clothing will you wear? Will you use PowerPoint or some other visual presentation method? Will you use any printed documents? Once you have identified all important contingencies and strategies for success, visualize the actual presentation. See yourself walking into the room with your chin up, your shoulders straight, and your voice strong and confident. Picture yourself making appropriate eye contact with people in the room. The focus of your preparation should be on things within your control.

Use Positive Self-Talk

self-talk The internal dialogue that is carried on in the privacy of the mind; silently talking to oneself.

inner critic Negative thoughts about one's failures. A major step toward improving one's self-esteem is to understand how to respond to the negative influence of the inner critic.

Throughout most of your waking moments, you talk to yourself. **Self-talk** takes place in the privacy of your mind. It can be rational and productive, or it can be irrational and disruptive. When the focus of this internal conversation is on negative thoughts, you are usually less productive.[40] Some psychologists refer to these negative thoughts as your **inner critic**. The critic keeps a record of your failures but never reminds you of your strengths and accomplishments. A major step toward improving your self-esteem is to understand how to respond to the negative influence of your inner critic.[41]

When your inner critic talks to you, ask yourself, "Who is this voice that is reminding me of my past failures?" (see Figure 3.1). The chances are it is not your current boss or spouse, but someone in your past such as a teacher, coach, harsh parent, or sibling. Recognize that this critical voice is probably no longer relevant, and take the necessary steps to replace those negative messages with positive ones.[42] You can create effective, positive self-talk statements for each of your goals by using the following guidelines:

FIGURE 3.1

Self-Esteem Cycles

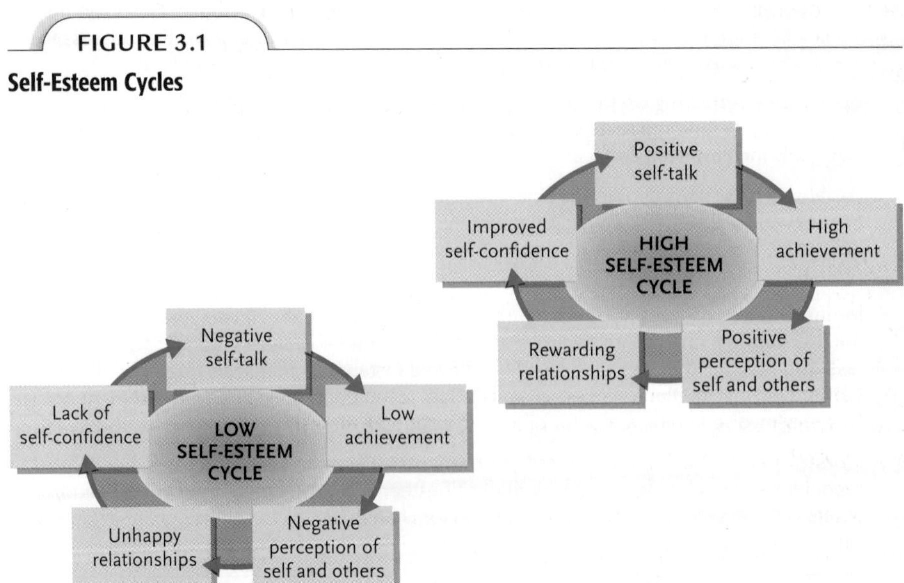

TABLE 3.2

Creating Semantically Correct Self-Talk

Wrong	Right
I can quit smoking.	I am in control of my habits.
I will lose twenty pounds.	I weigh a trim _____ pounds.
I won't worry anymore.	I am confident and optimistic.
Next time I won't be late.	I am prompt and efficient.
I will avoid negative self-talk.	I talk to myself, with all due respect.
I will not procrastinate.	I do it now.
I'm not going to let people walk all over me anymore.	I care enough to assert myself when necessary.

1. Be *specific* about the behavior you want to change. What do you want to do to increase your effectiveness? You should firmly believe that what you want is truly possible.
2. Begin each self-talk statement with a first-person pronoun, such as *I* or *my.* Use a present-tense verb, such as *am, have, feel, create, approve, do,* or *choose.* Don't say, "My ability to remember the names of other people will improve." Instead, focus on the present: "I *have* an excellent memory for the names of other people."
3. Describe the results you want to achieve. Be sure to phrase the statement as though you have already achieved what you want. Table 3.2 offers several general self-talk statements that might help you improve your self-esteem.[43]

This last step is critical. Because your brain is merely a computer filled with various data from all your past experiences, you need to use, literally, the correct words. When you think of the words *spider, tornado,* or *blue,* your brain develops an automatic understanding of each word and a response or image based on years of conditioning and training. If you are attempting to quit smoking, don't mention the word *smoke* in your self-talk because your brain will react to the word. "I will not smoke after dinner" conjures up an image in your subconscious mind, and your behavior follows accordingly. If your self-talk statements use the word *not,* you are probably sending the wrong message to your brain. Say instead, "I am in control of my habits" or "My lungs are clean."

Consider the following statement: "I will not eat chocolate for dessert." Now remove the word *not* from the statement, and the remaining words represent the message being sent to your brain. Does the remaining statement represent your goal? Be careful to semantically design your self-talk statements so that they take you in the direction you want to go; otherwise, they will take you straight toward what you don't want.

Keep in mind that positive self-talk that is truly effective consists of thoughts and messages that are realistic and truthful. It is rationally optimistic self-talk, not unfounded rah-rah hype. Positive internal dialogue should not be a litany of "feel good" mantras; it should be wholly consistent with your authentic self.[44]

TEST PREPPER 3.4

ANSWERS CAN BE FOUND ON P. 237

True or False?

___ 1. Acknowledging what you cannot do is a part of building self-esteem.

Multiple Choice

___ 2. The first step toward building healthy self-esteem as an adult is to:
   a. validate the inner critic.
   b. accept one's limitations.
   c. discover the source of one's low self-esteem.
   d. take responsibility for one's actions.

___ 3. Which of the following statements would be considered semantically correct self-talk?
   a. "I'm not going to let people walk all over me anymore."
   b. "I am confident and optimistic."
   c. "Next time I won't be late."
   d. "I will not smoke after dinner."

___ 4. Kenny's department supervisor, Darrell, has helped Kenny "learn the ropes" at his new job. Darrell's behavior exemplifies a(n):
   a. busybody.
   b. leader in control.
   c. mentor.
   d. active listener.

___ 5. Before her win in 2000 as the number-one kayaker in the United States, Kathy Ann Colin mentally rehearsed her performance. Colin successfully practiced:
   a. visualization.
   b. orientation.
   c. meditation.
   d. medication.

HM **ACE the Test**
ACE and ACE+ Practice Tests

ORGANIZATIONS CAN HELP

5 *Understand the conditions organizations can create that will help workers raise their self-esteem.*

HM **Improve Your Grade**
Career Snapshot

Even though each of us ultimately is responsible for raising or lowering our own self-esteem, we can make that task easier or more difficult for others. We can either support or damage the self-efficacy and self-respect of the people we work with, just as they have that option in their interactions with us. Organizations are beginning to include self-esteem modules in their employee- and management-training programs.

When employees do not feel good about themselves, the result will often be poor job performance. This view is shared by many human resource professionals. Many organizations realize that low self-esteem affects their workers' ability to learn new skills, to be effective team members, and to be productive. Research has identified five factors that can enhance the self-esteem of employees in any organization[45] (see Figure 3.2).

- *Workers need to feel valuable.* A major source of worker satisfaction is the feeling that one is valued as a unique person. Self-esteem grows when an organization makes an effort to accommodate individual differences, to recognize individual accomplishments, and to help employees build their strengths.
- *Workers need to feel competent.* Earlier in this chapter we noted that self-efficacy grows when people feel confident in their ability to perform job-related

tasks. One of the best ways organizations can build employee confidence is to involve employees in well-designed training programs.

- *Workers need to feel secure.* Employees are more likely to feel secure when they are well informed and know what is expected of them. Managers need to clarify their expectations and provide employees with frequent feedback regarding their performance.
- *Workers need to feel empowered.* Progressive organizations recognize that every employee has something to contribute to the organization and that limiting employees' contributions limits the organization's progress. When all employees are treated with respect and given the latitude for individual action within the defined limits of the organization, they are free to use their creativity and ingenuity to solve problems and make customers happy. This enables workers to develop a sense of personal responsibility and self-respect. To inhibit this freedom could induce resentful and eventually rebellious attitudes. Restrictions that suppress individuality can make people feel stunted and handicapped in the use of their personal skills, abilities, and resources.[46]
- *Workers need to feel connected.* People are likely to achieve high self-esteem when they feel their coworkers accept, appreciate, and respect them. Many companies are fostering these feelings by placing greater emphasis on mentoring and teamwork. Team-building efforts help promote acceptance and cooperation.

FIGURE 3.2

Factors That Enhance the Self-Esteem of Employees

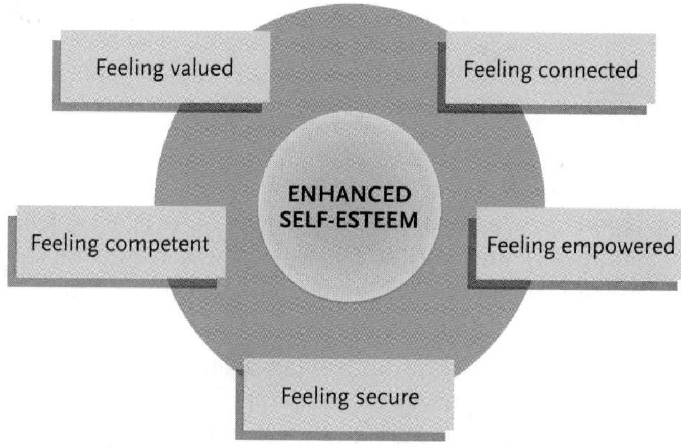

Test Prepper 3.5

Answers can be found on p. 237

True or False?

T 1. When employees have poor self-esteem, the result will often be poor performance.

F 2. Workers are more likely to achieve high self-esteem when they are prevented from comparing themselves with peers.

F 3. Employers are ultimately responsible for raising the self-esteem of their employees.

Multiple Choice

b 4. Will sends a handwritten note of thanks to new workers in his organization when they successfully complete their job training programs. Will is enhancing his workers' self-esteem by helping them to:

a. take ownership of their attitudes.
b. feel competent and valuable.
c. nurture their inner critics.
d. practice positive self-talk.

a 5. Which of the following organizational activities can help improve employees' feelings of competence?

a. Well-designed training programs
b. Accommodation of negative and positive attitudes
c. Restriction of employees' individual actions
d. Opposition to team-building efforts

ACE the Test
ACE and ACE+ Practice Tests

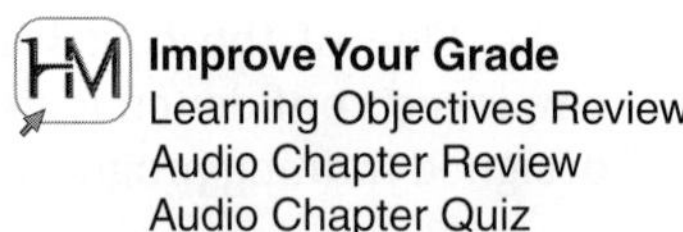

LEARNING OBJECTIVES REVIEW

1 *Define self-esteem and discuss its impact on your life.*

- Self-esteem is a combination of self-respect and self-efficacy.
- If you have high self-esteem, you are more likely to feel competent and worthy. If you have low self-esteem, you are more likely to feel incompetent, unworthy, and insecure.
- Self-esteem reflects your feelings of adequacy about the roles you play, your personality traits, your physical appearance, your skills, and your abilities.
- High self-esteem is the powerful foundation for a successful personal and professional life.

2 *Understand how self-esteem is developed.*

- A person starts acquiring and building self-esteem from birth. Developmental experiences in the first few years of life can significantly impact self-esteem. Siblings, teachers, and various authority figures can all have a lasting impact on a person's self concept.
- Adolescents often depend on social relationships to define their value and may compare themselves to media personalities.
- Adults often define themselves in terms of their possessions, jobs, or internal values.

3 *Identify the characteristics of people with low and high self-esteem.*

- People with high self-esteem tend to maintain an internal locus of control, manage their emotions, rarely take things personally, accept other people as unique and talented, and have productive personalities.
- People with low self-esteem tend to maintain an external locus of control, are likely to participate in self-destructive behaviors, and exhibit poor human relations skills. They often rely on the opinions of others to establish their inner self-worth.

4 *Identify ways to raise your self-esteem.*

- Search for the source of low self-esteem, accept your limitations, take responsibility for your decisions, engage in strength building and work with a mentor.
- Taking responsibility for your decisions and living with the consequences, positive or negative, can also help build self-esteem.
- Goal setting is an integral part of raising one's self-esteem.
- Guided imagery and positive self-talk can help overcome the inner critic that often interferes with personal and professional success.

5 *Understand the conditions organizations can create that will help workers raise their self-esteem.*

- Many organizations now realize that they need to help build employees' self-esteem and are doing so by making workers feel valuable, competent, and secure.
- Employers are empowering their employees to use their creativity and ingenuity to solve problems and make customers happy, which allows workers to develop a sense of personal responsibility.

CAREER CORNER

Q: The company I worked for recently merged with a giant corporation and I lost my job. Even though my previous employer has guaranteed that they will pay the expense of retraining me for a new career, I just can't seem to get motivated. I signed up for one class, but soon dropped it. I should have known I couldn't handle it. My former colleagues who are in the same situation are all much smarter than I am. I know that I'll never be as good as they are, so why should I even try? I'm not sure what there is in me that makes me avoid going back to school, but it is powerful. What can I do to gain more confidence?

A: It sounds like you are feeling down right now, and that is perfectly normal. Your world, as you knew it, has changed. Many people are going through the same thing in today's ever changing world of mergers, acquisitions, and company closings, so don't feel alone. Nevertheless, your self-esteem has been damaged and you need to take the necessary steps to repair and improve it. You need to stop comparing yourself to others, take a good look at your strengths, and build on them. Determine your skills, your values, and all those facets that make you unique. Though it may not be easy, it is not impossible to feel better about yourself. Trust your thoughts and intuitions. Do what makes you feel happy and fulfilled. Set realistic goals for yourself and take pride in your achievements, big and small. Replace negative self-talk with positive affirmations about your future. Exercise, eat right, and get plenty of sleep. Being exhausted and out of shape can leave you feeling more vulnerable, insecure, and anxious. Don't wait for someone else to take charge of your life and determine how you feel about yourself. Get acquainted with your potential and go for it!

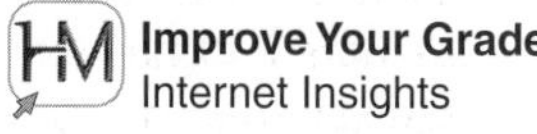

APPLYING WHAT YOU HAVE LEARNED

1. Review Table 3.1, Goal-Setting Principles. Work through each of the four principles in light of something you would like to change in your world. It could be a physical characteristic such as weight control or beginning an exercise regimen. It might be a component of your personality such as becoming more confident or assertive. Perhaps you would like to reexamine your career goals. Whatever your choice, write out your plan for change; then follow it through.
2. This chapter identified five characteristics of people with high self-esteem. Read each of the statements in the box below and rate yourself with this scale: **U** = Usually; **S** = Sometimes; **I** = Infrequently.
3. Draw a line down the center of a piece of paper and write **HIGH Self-Esteem** on top of the left column and **LOW Self-Esteem** on the top of the right column. In each column, record how your personal and professional interpersonal relationships might change if you maintained that level of self-esteem. Share your insights with your classmates.
4. To increase self-awareness in the area of self-esteem complete the self-assessment form found on the website **college.hmco.com/pic/reeceSAS**.

	U	S	I
I maintain an internal locus of control.	☑	❑	❑
I am able to feel all dimensions of emotions without letting these emotions affect my behavior in a negative way.	☑	❑	❑
I do not take things personally.	☑	❑	❑
I am able to accept other people as unique, talented individuals.	☑	❑	❑
I feel I have a productive personality.	☑	❑	❑

Improve Your Grade
Self-Assessment Exercise

ROLE-PLAY EXERCISE

Your have accepted a summer job with Bank of America. Throughout the summer you will replace tellers who are on vacation. In addition to earning money to pay next fall's college tution, you anticipate that this job will help you develop your customer service skills. To maximize the learning opportunities, and explore another area within the bank, you want to develop a mentor relationship with a senior vice president in the loan department. You have an appointment with Erin Brown, an experienced loan officer, tomorrow. In this role-play situation, you will meet with a class member who will assume the role of the loan officer, who is very busy and has scheduled the meeting to last no more than 15 minutes. During this short period of time you will need to explain why you need a mentor and market yourself to this prospective mentor. Prior to the role-play activity, review the information on mentoring in this chapter.

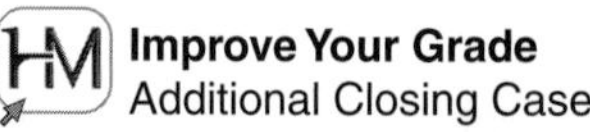

CASE 3.1

The Power of Mentoring

At the beginning of this chapter, you were introduced to Shoshana Zuboff and her husband, who served as mentors to Edward, the troubled youth who became a successful businessman with their support and guidance. Where would Edward be today if he had not met the Zuboffs? Tim Murphy, head football coach at Harvard University, explains the impact a mentor can have on young people. He sees his mentor role as that of a parent: You are not your mentees' buddy, so don't try to please them. Treat them with respect and expect the same in return. He found that some 18-, 19-, and 20-year-olds think they have all the answers, and it is not until they go through the bumps in life that they realize what their mentors told them was good advice after all.[47] Ronna Lichtenberg, author of *It's Not Business, It's Personal,* remembers when her mentor took her aside and said, "No, Ronna, you may not do that. . . . This is how we get things done."[48]

Betsy Bernard, president of AT&T, enjoys her role as a mentor to others within her organization. She listens to her mentees and determines the next opportunity for their development. She describes to them what she is dealing with on a daily basis to give mentees the opportunity to see things in a holistic way. Paul Muldoon, professor of creative writing at Princeton University and Pulitzer Prize winner for poetry, describes the responsibility of a mentor as extraordinary. He believes that mentors have to be enthusiastic and nurturing and states, "I want them to find a place where they can flourish." Dee Hock, founder and CEO emeritus of Visa International, compares the mentor/mentee relationship to "hitching a boat to an elegant cabin cruiser and being towed along in its wake."[49]

Many organizations today realize the value of developing formal and informal mentoring relationships among their employees. They know these relationships are critically important when it is time to pass knowledge along to the next generation of workers. Larry Aloz, author of *Effective Teaching and Mentoring,* declares, "I think what people are finding is that in times of change and turmoil, we reach out for stability and guidance. Mentors give us a sense of continuity. They have been there before. They have advice for us. They have experience to pass on."[50] Mack Tilling, CEO of Instill Corporation, says, "Being able to talk about your work with an experienced executive can help anyone—even a CEO—make better decisions. Mentors help you see things in a way that you might not have thought about."[51]

Questions

1. Mentoring programs help bring new employees up to speed with what is going on in the organization and often help employees advance in the organization. What elements of a mentoring program contribute to building an employee's self-esteem?
2. A well-developed mentoring program can make a major contribution to the success of an organization, yet many companies do not have such programs. What are some reasons why some organizations do not support mentoring programs?
3. Would you prefer the formal approach to mentoring programs within organizations, or would you prefer the informal approach? Explain your reasoning.

Resources on the Web

Prepare for Class, Improve Your Grade, and ACE the Test. Student Achievement Series resources include:

- ACE and ACE+ Practice Tests
- Audio Chapter Quizzes
- Audio Chapter Reviews
- Learning Objective Reviews
- Career Snapshots
- Chapter Glossaries
- Chapter Outlines
- Crossword Puzzles
- Hangman Games
- Flashcards
- Audio Glossaries
- Internet Insights
- Self-Assessment Exercises
- Additional Closing Cases

To access these learning and study tools, go to **college.hmco.com/pic/reeceSAS**.

HM ManagementSPACE

4 Personal Values Influence Ethical Choices

Top executives at WorldCom helped engineer the largest accounting fraud in corporate history. The victims of corporate crime include both investors and the employees who lose their jobs. As this protester notes, the outcome is often "Jobs lost, hopes crushed."

1. *Explain the personal benefits of developing a strong sense of character.*
2. *Understand how personal values are formed.*
3. *Understand values conflicts and how to resolve them.*
4. *Learn how to make the right ethical decisions based on your personal value system.*

"Your behavior is a reflection of what you truly believe. Values are personal beliefs and preferences that influence your behavior."

—Hyrum Smith

Chapter Outline

Prepare for Class
Chapter Outline

5 *Understand the danger of corporate crime and the steps being taken to eliminate it.*

Valuing Your Decisions

Scott Sullivan, former chief financial officer at WorldCom, was looking forward to living in his new 30,000-square-foot estate located in Boca Raton, Florida. The house has ten bedrooms, twelve bathrooms, and seven hand-carved stone fireplaces. It features an eighteen-seat movie theater and a two-bedroom boathouse overlooking a private lake. Instead of moving into this luxury house, Mr. Sullivan will be spending the next five years in a federal prison. He was found guilty of participating in the $11 billion accounting fraud at WorldCom (since renamed MCI). Sullivan and his boss, former CEO Bernie Ebbers, were at the center of the largest accounting fraud in corporate history.[1]

During the past few years we have seen a large number of corporate scandals involving publicly traded companies. Managers employed by Enron, Adelphia Communications, Tyco International, Rite Aid, ImClone, and other well-known companies have been found guilty of various white-collar crimes. Later in this

KEY TERMS

character *p. 76*
codes of ethics *p. 88*
core values *p. 78*
ethics *p. 84*
integrity *p. 76*
internal values conflict *p. 82*
modeling *p. 81*
values *p. 77*
values conflict *p. 82*
values drift *p. 81*
whistleblower *p. 89*

Prepare for Class
Chapter Glossary

Improve Your Grade
Flashcards
Hangman
Crossword Puzzle

chapter, we will examine some of the factors that motivate corporate leaders to engage in fraud and other crimes.[2]

Of course, it would not be fair to focus our attention on unethical behavior at the top of the organization and ignore the misdeeds of employees in the lower ranks. One third of all employees steal from their employers, and employee theft is the fastest-growing crime in the United States.[3]

The new generation of workers are occupationally and educationally ambitious. They are coming of age at a time when our culture is placing a great deal of emphasis on self-gratification, the crossing of many moral boundaries, and the breaking of many social taboos. This chapter will help you understand how to make the right ethical decisions based on a values system that embraces honor and integrity. It will help you understand how your values are formed, how to clarify which values are important to you, and how to resolve human relations problems that result when your personal values conflict with others' values.

CHARACTER, INTEGRITY, AND MORAL DEVELOPMENT

1 *Explain the personal benefits of developing a strong sense of character.*

character Personal standards of behavior, including honesty, integrity, and moral strength; the main ingredient that is sought in leaders.

Former U.S. senator Al Simpson said, "If you have character, that's all that matters; and if you don't have character, that's all that matters, too."[4] **Character** is composed of personal standards of behavior, including honesty, integrity, and moral strength. It is the main ingredient we seek in our leaders and the quality that earns us respect in the workplace. In *The Corrosion of Character,* author Richard Sennett says that we have seen a decline of character that can be traced to conditions that have grown out of our fast-paced, high-stress, information-driven economy.[5] He notes that many people are no longer connected to their past, to their neighbors, and to themselves.

integrity The basic ingredient of character that is exhibited when congruence is achieved between what one knows, what one says, and what one does.

Integrity is the basic ingredient of character that is exhibited when you achieve congruence between what you know, what you say, and what you do.[6] When your behavior is in tune with your professed standards and values—when you practice what you believe in—you have integrity. When you say one thing but do something else, you *lack* integrity.

How important is it to be viewed as a person with integrity and a strong sense of character in the eyes of your friends, family members, fellow workers, and leaders? When you look closely at the factors that contribute to warm friendships,

TOTAL PERSON INSIGHT
Roy Chitwood President, **Max Sacks International**

"A person's true character can be judged by how he treats those who can do nothing for him."

strong marriages, successful careers, and successful organizations, you quickly come to the conclusion that character and integrity are critical.

You are not born with these qualities, so what can a person do to build his or her character? One approach, recommended by author Stephen Covey, is to keep your commitments. "As we make and keep commitments, even small commitments, we begin to establish an inner integrity that gives us the awareness of self-control and courage and strength to accept more of the responsibility for our own lives."[7] Covey says that when we make and keep promises to ourselves and others, we are developing an important habit. We cannot expect to maintain our integrity if we consistently fail to keep our commitments.

How Personal Values Are Formed

2 *Understand how personal values are formed.*

Hyrum Smith, author of *The 10 Natural Laws of Successful Time and Life Management,* says that certain natural laws govern personal productivity and fulfillment. One of these laws focuses on personal beliefs: Your behavior is a reflection of what you truly believe.[8] **Values** are the personal beliefs and preferences that influence your behavior. They are deep-seated in your personality. To discover what really motivates you, carefully examine what it is you value.

values The personal beliefs and preferences that influence one's behavior.

Table 4.1 details the values clarification process. These five steps can help you determine whether or not you truly value something. Many times you are not consciously aware of what is really driving your behavior because values exist at

TABLE 4.1

A Five-Part Valuing Process to Clarify and Develop Values

- **Thinking:** We live in a confusing world where making choices about how to live our lives can be difficult. Of major importance is developing critical thinking skills that help distinguish fact from opinion and supported from unsupported arguments. Learn to think for yourself. Question what you are told. Engage in higher-level thinking that involves analysis, synthesis, and evaluation.
- **Feeling:** This dimension of the valuing process involves being open to your "gut level" feelings. If it doesn't "feel right," it probably isn't. Examine your distressful feelings such as anger, fear, or emotional hurt. Discover what you prize and cherish in life.
- **Communicating:** Values are clarified through an ongoing process of interaction with others. Be an active listener and hear what others are really saying. Be constantly alert to communication filters such as emotions, body language, and positive and negative attitudes. Learn to send clear messages regarding your own beliefs.
- **Choosing:** Your values must be freely selected with no outside pressure. In some situations, telling right from wrong is difficult. Therefore, you need to be well informed about alternatives and the consequences of various courses of action. Each choice you make reflects some aspect of your values system.
- **Acting:** Act repeatedly and consistently on your beliefs. One way to test whether something is of value to you is to ask yourself, "Do I find that this value is persistent throughout all aspects of my life?"

Source: Howard Kirschenbaum, *Advanced Values Clarification* (La Jolla, Calif.: University Associates, 1977).

different levels of awareness.[9] Unless you clarify your values, life events are likely to unfold in a haphazard manner. Once you are aware of your value priorities, you are in a better position to plan and initiate life-changing activities.

Identifying Your Core Values

core values Values that a person consistently ranks higher than other values and that give a definite picture of the kind of person he or she would want to be.

Hyrum Smith says that everything starts with your **core values**, those values that you consistently rank higher than others. When you are able to identify your core values, you have a definite picture of the kind of person you want to be and the kind of life you want to have. Anne Mulcahy, an executive at Xerox Corporation and a mother of two sons, says she and her husband make decisions at home and work based on their core values: "Our kids are absolutely the center of our lives—and we never mess with that."[10] Maura FitzGerald, CFO of FitzGerald Communications, Inc., a public relations firm, asks all her employees to adhere to the "FitzGerald Family Values" before accepting a job with her company. All her workers carry with them a wallet-size card listing the organization's basic operating principles, one of which is "Never compromise our integrity—this is our hallmark."[11]

We often need to reexamine our core values when searching for a job. Joanne Ciulla, author of *The Working Life,* says taking a job today is a matter of choosing among four core values: high salary, security, meaningful work, and lots of time off.[12] Needless to say, most jobs would require putting at least one of these values on the back burner.

Focus on Your Life's Purpose

Jack Canfield, Brian Tracy, and other authorities on the development of human potential emphasize how important it is to define your purpose in life. Canfield says, "Without purpose as the compass to guide you, your goals and action plans may not ultimately fulfill you." To get from where you are today to where you want to be, you have to know two things: where are you today and where you want to get to.[13] Once you have identified your core values, defining your purpose in life will be much easier.

Influences That Shape Your Values

As you engage in the values clarification process, it helps to reflect on those things that have influenced your values, such as people and events of your generation, your family, religious groups, your education, the media, and people you admire.

People and Events

Table 4.2 provides a summary of some of the key events and people that have shaped the values of four generations: the Matures, the Baby Boomers, Generation X, and Generation Y, sometimes called Millennials. Although workers of different ages want basically the same things—the opportunity for personal growth, respect, and a fair reward for work done well—they can have very different ideas about what these mean.

- An older baby boomer might believe that respect is due when someone spends many years on the job.
- To a Generation Xer, respect is expected when someone displays competence.

TABLE 4.2

People and Events Have Influenced the Formation of Values for Four Groups of Americans: Matures, Baby Boomers, Generation X, and Generation Y (sometimes called Millennials)
This means that today's work force represents the broadest range of ages and values in American history.

Matures (born 1928–1945)	Baby Boomers (born 1946–1964)	Generation X (born 1965–1976)	Generation Y (born 1977–1994)
Eisenhower	Television	AIDS	Corporate downsizing
MacArthur	The Cold War	The Wellness movement	Ethics scandals
The A-bomb	The space race	Watergate	Digital technology
Dr. Spock	The Civil Rights Act	Glasnost	24/7 economy
John Wayne	The pill	The Oklahoma City bombing	Jeff Bezos
The Great Depression	The drug culture	MTV	9/11 terrorist attacks
World War II	Gloria Steinem	The World Wide Web	Iraq War
The New Deal	The Vietnam War	Information economy	Income gap
	JFK and MLK assassinations	Work/Life balance concerns	Globalization

- Someone born during the early years of the baby-boom generation might be satisfied with feedback during annual or semiannual performance reviews.
- Generation Xers, as a group, have a need to see results almost daily and receive frequent feedback on their performance.

Analyzing the traits of any large population can lead to unfair and unrealistic stereotyping. But generational differences shaped by sociological, political, and economic conditions can be traced to differences in values.[14]

Your Family

Katherine Paterson, author of books for children, says being a parent these days is like riding a bicycle on a bumpy road—learning to keep your balance while zooming full speed ahead, veering around as many potholes as possible.[15] Parents must assume many roles, none more important than moral teacher. In many families in contemporary society, one parent must assume full responsibility for shaping children's values. Some single parents—those overwhelmed with responsibility for career, family, and rebuilding their own personal lives—may lack the stability necessary for the formation of the six pillars of character. And in two-parent families, both parents may work outside the home and at the end of the day may lack the time or energy to intentionally direct the development of their children's values. The same may be true for families experiencing financial pressures or the strains associated with caring for elderly parents.

Religious Groups

Many people learn their value priorities through religious training. This may be achieved through the accepted teachings of a church, through religious literature such as the Koran and the Bible, or through individuals in churches or synagogues who are positive role models. Some of the most powerful spiritual leaders do not have formal ties to a particular religion. John Templeton is one example. He is a successful investor and one of the greatest philanthropists of the modern age. Templeton says the only real wealth in our lives is spiritual wealth. Over the years, he has given over $800 million to fund forgiveness, conflict-resolution, and character-building projects.[16]

Religious groups that want to define, instill, and perpetuate values may find an eager audience. Stephen Covey and other social observers say that many people are determinedly seeking spiritual and moral anchors in their lives and in their work. People who live in uncertain times seem to attach more importance to spirituality.[17] Healthy spirituality is discussed in Chapter 9.

Education

Many parents, concerned that their children are not learning enough about moral values and ethical behavior, want character education added to the curriculum. In support of these views, Thomas Lickona, professor of education at the State University of New York, says children have very little sense of right and wrong, so schools must help out. Educators are concerned about the constant barrage of messages children are getting about behavior in corporate America. Twenty grade schools, middle schools, and high schools in New York and Chicago are currently testing an ethics curriculum created by Junior Achievement, whose mission is to teach youngsters about the free-enterprise system.[18]

Several nonprofit organizations have responded to the call for more character education in our public schools, colleges, and universities.

- The Josephson Institute of Ethics (www.josephsoninstitute.org) has formed the Character Counts Coalition, an alliance of organizations that addresses the issue of character development in educational institutions and organizations throughout the country. This coalition has developed a variety of grassroots training activities involving what it refers to as the "six pillars of character": trustworthiness, respect, responsibility, fairness, caring, and citizenship.[19]
- The Character Education Partnership (www.character.org) is attempting to rally business leaders to champion character education within their companies and encourage character training within the schools located in their communities.
- The Institute for Global Ethics, or IGE (www.globalethics.org), is dedicated to promoting ethical action in a global context.
- The Center for Corporate Ethics, or CCE (www.ethics-center.com), is a division of the IGE. The CCE has developed tools, techniques, and training programs aimed at reducing the likelihood and risks of ethical lapses.

The Media

Some social critics say that if you are searching for signs of civilization gone rotten, you can simply tune in to the loud and often amoral voices of mass entertainment on television, radio, and the Internet. They point out that viewers too often see people abusing and degrading other people without any significant consequences.

Mainstream television, seen by a large number of young viewers, continues to feature a great deal of violence and antisocial behavior.

Is there a connection between violence in the media and violence in real life? The American Academy of Pediatrics and the American Psychiatric Association report that repeated exposure to violent imagery desensitizes children and increases the risk of violent behavior.[20] Research has also found a connection between heavy television viewing and depressed children. More research is needed to help us fully understand the extent of the influence of the media on our culture's values.

"I swear I wasn't looking at smut—I was just stealing music."

People You Admire

In addition to being influenced by the media, you have probably also done some **modeling**—you have shaped your behavior to resemble that of people you admire and embraced the qualities those people demonstrate. The heroes and heroines you discover in childhood and adolescence help you form a "dominant value direction."[21] The influence of modeling is no less important in our adult life. Most employees look to their leaders for moral guidance. Unfortunately, there is a shortage of leaders who have a positive impact on ethical decision making. A recent survey found that less than half of employees in large organizations think their senior leadership is highly ethical.[22] In addition to role models at work, you may be influenced by religious leaders, sports figures, educators, and others whom you admire.

modeling Shaping behavior to resemble that of people one admires and embracing the qualities those people demonstrate.

Avoiding Values Drift

Once you have examined the various influences on your values and have clarified what is important to you now that you are an adult (see Table 4.1), you also need to be aware of **values drift**, the slow erosion of your core values over time—those tiny changes that can steer you off course. When you observe lying, abuse, theft, or other forms of misconduct at work or feel pressure to make ethical compromises, carefully and intentionally reflect on the values you hold dear and choose the appropriate ethical behavior that maintains your character and integrity. Monitor your commitment to your values and make adjustments when necessary to get your life back on track. In his book *Conversations with God,* Neal Donald Walsch discusses the process of building a strong foundation for your daily decisions as they lead you toward your life's goals. He suggests: "Do not dismantle the house, but look at each brick, and replace those which appear broken, which no longer support the structure."[23] This careful examination of each of your values in light of each day's decisions will help keep you on track throughout your life.

values drift The slow erosion of core values over time.

TEST PREPPER 4.1, 4.2

ANSWERS CAN BE FOUND ON P. 237

True or False?

___ 1. Making and keeping promises to ourselves and to others is an important step in developing and maintaining character and integrity.

___ 2. Major events, such as the Cold War for the baby boomers, can influence people's values.

Multiple Choice

___ 3. John and Gail teach their children to behave according to a strict moral code, yet they lie about their ages and underreport their income to the IRS. John and Gail's behavior can best be described as lacking in:
   a. character.
   b. integrity.
   c. religious convictions.
   d. self-worth.

___ 4. The popular WWJD (What Would Jesus Do?) wristbands demonstrate that for many of today's youth, Jesus Christ is a relevant:
   a. role model.
   b. object of scorn.
   c. butt of a joke.
   d. father figure.

___ 5. When you experience misconduct or feel pressure to make ethical compromises at work, you need to be vigilant to prevent:
   a. modeling.
   b. values drift.
   c. peer favoritism.
   d. religious pressure.

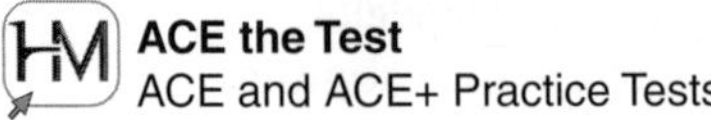

VALUES CONFLICTS

3 *Understand values conflicts and how to resolve them.*

values conflict The clash between the personal values of different people.

One of the major causes of conflict within an organization is the clash between the personal values of different people. There is no doubt about it; people are different. They have different family backgrounds, religious experiences, educations, role models, and media exposure. These differences can pop out anywhere and anytime people get together. Many observers suggest that organizations look for **values conflicts** when addressing such problems as declining quality, absenteeism, and poor customer service. The trouble may lie not so much in work schedules or production routines as in the mutual distrust and misunderstanding brought about by clashes in workers' and managers' value preferences. The late Peter Drucker, author of *The Practice of Management,* said: "Organizations are no longer built on force but on trust. The existence of trust between people does not mean that they like one another. It means that they understand one another. Taking responsibility for relationships is therefore an absolute necessity. It is a duty."[24]

Internal Values Conflicts

internal values conflict A conflict in which a person is forced to choose between two or more strongly held values.

A person who is forced to choose between two or more strongly held values is experiencing an **internal values conflict**. Soon after the World Trade Center was attacked by terrorists, many people began to reexamine their values. Some decided to spend more time with family and friends, thinking that although overtime might be an opportunity to make more income, it was also an obstacle to maintaining a commitment to their family. Some workers also decided that their "work and spend" lifestyle no longer made sense. Before the terrorist attacks, a 28-year-old market research manager described herself as "very driven" and motivated to acquire things. Following September 11, she said, "Maybe I don't need all this stuff."[25]

A recent study of Generation Xers by Catalyst, a group that seeks to advance women in business, found that members of this group are seeking a well-rounded life. They are not frenetic job hoppers as some social commentators maintain, but traditionalists at heart. They value company loyalty and are inclined to stay with their current company. Earning a great deal of money is not nearly as important to these Xers as having the opportunity to share companionship with family and friends. They are able to prioritize their values and make their decisions accordingly.[26]

How you resolve internal values conflicts depends on your willingness to rank your core values in the order of their importance to you. Prioritizing your values will help you make decisions when life gets complicated and you have to make difficult choices. If one of your values is to be an outstanding parent and another is to maintain a healthy body, you should anticipate an internal values conflict when a busy schedule requires a choice between attending your daughter's soccer game and your weekly workout at the fitness center. However, when you rank which value is most important, the decision will be much easier.

Values Conflicts with Others

As we have noted, four distinct generations have come together in the workplace. Employees from each generation bring with them different experiences and expectations. Values conflicts are more likely in this environment. These conflicts require effective human relations skills.

How will you handle a tense situation where it is obvious your values conflict with those of a colleague? You may discover your supervisor is a racist and you strongly support the civil rights of all people. One option is to become indignant and take steps to reduce contact with your supervisor. The problem with being indignant is that it burns your bridges with someone who can influence your growth and development within the organization. The opposite extreme would be

HUMAN RELATIONS IN ACTION

The Fall of Arthur Andersen

When Barbara Toffler was a consultant for Arthur Andersen, she and some of her colleagues were under considerable pressure to sell their consulting services at inflated prices. Ironically, Toffler was at the time head of the Ethics and Responsible Business Practices Group at Arthur Andersen. In her book *Final Accounting—Ambition, Greed, and the Fall of Arthur Andersen,* she recalls a difficult luncheon meeting with a former client. At one point he said, "You were selling us stuff you didn't think we needed." Then he spoke the words that were most painful: "Barbara, this is not the you I used to know." The company that once stood for trust and accountability ended ninety years of service under a cloud of scandal and shame.

to do nothing. But when we ignore unethical or immoral behavior, we compromise our integrity, and the problem is likely to continue and grow.[27] With a little reflection, you may be able to find a response somewhere between these two extremes. If your supervisor tells a joke that is demeaning to members of a minority group, consider meeting with her and explaining how uncomfortable these comments make you feel. When we confront others' lapses in character, we are strengthening our own integrity.

PERSONAL VALUES AND ETHICAL CHOICES

4 *Learn how to make the right ethical decisions based on your personal value system.*

ethics Principles that define behavior that is right, good, and proper and that draw the line between right and wrong.

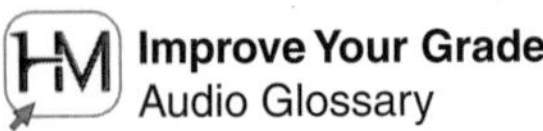

Ethics refers to principles that define behavior as right, good, and proper. Your ethics, or the code of ethics of your organization, does not always dictate a single moral course of action, but it does provide a means of evaluating and deciding among several options.[28] Ethics determines where you draw the line between right and wrong.

As competition in the global marketplace increases, moral and ethical issues can become cloudy. Although most organizations have adopted the point of view that "good ethics is good business," exceptions do exist. Some organizations encourage, or at least condone, unethical behaviors. Surveys show that many workers feel pressure to violate their ethical standards in order to meet business objectives.[29] Thus, you must develop your own personal code of ethics.

Every job you hold will present you with new ethical and moral dilemmas. And many of the ethical issues you encounter will be very difficult. Instead of selecting from two clear-cut options—one right, one wrong—you often face multiple options.[30]

How to Make the Right Ethical Choices

According to the Association of Certified Fraud Examiners, unethical acts by workers cost U.S. businesses more than $600 billion a year.[31] The following guidelines may help you avoid being part of this growing statistic.

Learn to Distinguish Between Right and Wrong

Although selecting the right path can be difficult, a great deal of help is available through books, magazine articles, and a multitude of on-line resources. Support may be as close as your employer's code of ethics, guidelines published by your professional organization, or advice provided by an experienced and trusted colleague at work. In some cases, you can determine the right path by *restraining* yourself from choosing the *wrong* path. For example:

- Just because you have the power to do something does not mean it is the proper thing to do.
- Just because you have the right to do something does not mean it is right to do.
- Just because you want to do something does not mean you should do it.
- Choose to do more than the law requires and less than the law allows.[32]

Companies that focus on their employees' values, like allowing dogs in the workplace, is an example of the idea that if employees feel valued they will be more committed to the organization.

Don't Let Your Life Be Driven by the Desire for Immediate Gratification

Progress and prosperity have almost identical meanings to many people. They equate progress with the acquisition of material things. One explanation is that young business leaders entering the corporate world are under a great deal of pressure to show the trappings of success—a large house or an expensive car, for example.

Some people get trapped in a vicious cycle: They work more so that they can buy more consumer goods; then, as they buy more, they must work more. They fail to realize that the road to happiness is not paved with Rolex watches, Brooks Brothers suits, and a Lexus. Chapter 5 offers support for finding satisfaction through nonfinancial resources that make the biggest contribution to a fulfilling life.

Make Certain Your Values Are in Harmony with Those of Your Employer

You may find it easier to make the right ethical choices if your values are compatible with those of your employer. Many organizations have adopted a set of beliefs, customs, values, and practices that attract a certain type of employee (see Figure 4.1). Harmony between personal and organizational values usually leads to success

TOTAL PERSON INSIGHT

Dan Rice and Craig Dreilinger
Management Consultants;
Authors, ***Rights and Wrongs of Ethics Training***

"Nothing is more powerful for employees than seeing their managers behave according to their expressed values and standards; nothing is more devastating to the development of an ethical environment than a manager who violates the organization's ethical standards."

FIGURE 4.1

Biogen's Values

Source: Watson Wyatt Data Services, "Watson Wyatt's Human Capital Index," *Workforce,* August 2002 [cited 17 November 2005]. Available from www.workforce.com/archive/article/23/27/06; INTERNET.

Biogen's Values

Biogen's success is based on its people. Everyone is considered a leader. The core of leadership is integrity and courage—characteristics they seek in every Biogen employee. The shared values listed below represent how they aspire to lead and work together. Part of the biotech company's performance-appraisal process includes evaluating whether employees lived up to these company values.

- Hire only the highest quality talent.
- Communicate and then obtain alignment to our strategy and goals.
- Tell the truth.
- Face the facts, admit mistakes, accept criticism, learn from it, and improve.
- Build teams.
- Forcefully resist adding layers, procedures, and bureaucracy.
- Assume your position responsibilities are a starting point, not a limitation.
- Weigh the risks carefully but do not hesitate to innovate or to encourage and reward innovation and initiative.
- See change as an opportunity, not a threat.
- Serve and defend with equal energy our customers', our employees', and our shareholders' interests.

for the individual as well as the organization. Enlightened companies realize that committed employees give them their competitive edge and are taking values seriously. They realize that reconciling corporate and employee values helps to cement the ethical environment within the organization. Before you select an organization in which to build your career, determine what the organization stands for and then compare those values to your own priorities.[33]

BMS Software in Houston, Texas, provides a work environment where you can find sustenance for the whole self—mind, body, and spirit. Employees can pump iron in the gym, enjoy a gourmet meal, or participate in massage therapy. The self-contained community offers an array of services (banking, dry cleaning, hair salon, etc.), and there is a large kitchen with free fruit, popcorn, soda, and coffee on each floor of the company's two glass towers. You live comfortably at BMS, but you also work long hours. Many employees work 10- to 12-hour days.[34] Some people would feel comfortable working for this company, but others would be unhappy about the long hours.

TEST PREPPER 4.3, 4.4

ANSWERS CAN BE FOUND ON P. 237

True or False?

___ 1. According to Peter Drucker, the existence of trust between individuals means that the individuals like one another.

___ 2. Values conflicts with others are more likely to occur in work environments that include members of different generations.

___ 3. It is typically easier to make the correct ethical choices in the workplace if your personal values are in line with the values of your employer.

HM **ACE the Test**
ACE and ACE+ Practice Tests

Multiple Choice

___ 4. Recent job seekers are more likely to ask an employer:
   a. about salary and benefits.
   b. if they have an organizational SWAT team.
   c. about the company's formal code of ethics.
   d. if they will have to be drug tested.

___ 5. Which of the following statements correctly describes the stance of many successful organizations regarding ethics?
   a. Good ethics stifles profits.
   b. Good ethics is good business.
   c. Bad ethics is good business.
   d. Good ethics constitutes staying just within the law.

Corporate Values and Ethical Choices

 5 *Understand the danger of corporate crime and the steps being taken to eliminate it.*

Improve Your Grade
Career Snapshot

When organizations consistently make ethical decisions that are in the best interest of their stakeholders—employees, customers, stockholders, and the community—they are considered good corporate citizens because they are socially responsible.

- The list "The 100 Best Corporate Citizens" published by *Business Ethics* magazine reminds us that a company can be socially responsible and still achieve excellent earnings.
- In her *BusinessWeek* article "A Conscience Doesn't Have to Make You Poor," Susan Scherreik interviewed stockholders who invest only in companies that are good corporate citizens. One stated, "I see the damage that many companies do to people's health and the environment by polluting or creating dangerous products. Investing in them makes no sense because these companies won't flourish in the long run."[35]

Corporate Crime

Many organizations have gotten into serious trouble by ignoring ethical principles. In recent years, the media have carried headlines concerning organizations involved in corporate crime.

- A top Air Force acquisition official admitted that she steered billions of dollars' worth of contracts to Boeing Company out of gratitude for Boeing's hiring of her daughter. The procurement scandal cost Boeing billions in lost defense contracts.[36]
- Bernard Ebbers was found guilty of masterminding a record $11 billion accounting fraud that toppled WorldCom. Investors, former employees, and others experienced large financial losses.[37]
- A unit of Exide Technologies, the maker of automotive batteries, agreed to plead guilty to fraud and pay criminal fines of $27.5 million. Exide admitted to supplying inferior batteries to Sears, Roebuck & Company, trying to cover up the defects, and spending $80,000 to bribe a Sears battery buyer.[38]

Those items represent only a small fraction of the corporate crime that took place in recent years. Many offenders are not caught or brought to trial. But, on the positive side, recent surveys indicate that a large majority of America's major corporations are actively trying to build ethics into their organizations.

- At Simmons Bedding Company, the commitment to conducting business with integrity can be traced to 1870, the year the company was founded. Every Simmons employee is guided by a four-part code of ethics: be fair, respect the individual, act from integrity, and foster growth and development.[39]
- At Harley-Davidson the soul of the "Hog" can be traced to values that emphasize strong working relationships. The company's idea of a healthy working relationship is embedded in five formal values that constitute a code of

behavior for everyone:[40] tell the truth; be fair; keep your promises; respect the individual; and encourage intellectual curiosity.

- Honesty tops the list of employee expectations at Swanson Russell Associates, a marketing communications firm in Lincoln, Nebraska. The mandate is carefully reviewed during new-employee orientation and it's posted in every employee's work area.[41]

Many say they have difficulty determining the right course of action in difficult "gray-area" situations. And even when the right ethical course of action is clear, competitive pressures sometimes lead well-intentioned managers astray.[42] Tom Chappell, author of *The Soul of a Business,* explains why organizations often have difficulty doing what is morally right and socially responsible: "It's harder to manage for ethical pursuits than it is to simply manage for profits."[43]

How to Prevent Corporate Crime

Establish and Support a Strong Code of Ethics

codes of ethics Written statements of what an organization expects in the way of ethical behavior and of what behaviors are acceptable or improper in the workplace. The focus is on core organization values.

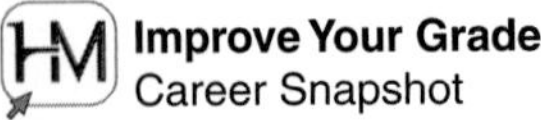

We have recently seen an increase in ethical initiatives that make ethics a part of core organizational values. **Codes of ethics**, written statements of what an organization expects in the way of ethical behavior, can give employees a clear indication of what behaviors are acceptable or improper.[44] An ethics code can be a powerful force in building a culture of honesty, but only if it is enforced without exception. The list of corporate values at Enron Corporation included respect, integrity, communication, and excellence. As events have shown, these values did not prevent unethical conduct at the highest levels of the company. Empty values statements create cynical and dispirited employees and undermine managerial credibility.[45]

Hire with Care

Thomas Melohn, president of North American Tool & Die, Inc., located in San Leandro, California, says the key to operating a successful company is to first identify a guiding set of values and then "make sure you find people who have those values and can work together."[46] He says the hiring process should be given a very high priority. Melohn never hires any employee without checking references and conducting a lengthy job interview.

Some companies use integrity tests (also called honesty or character tests) to screen out dishonest people. Two standardized tests designed to measure honesty are the Reid Report (www.reidlondonhouse.com) and the newer Career Ethic Inventory (www.careerethic.com). These tests are helpful, but they are not a substitute for rigorous interviewing and reference checks. Resumés that include exaggerations or outright fabrications tell you a lot about the integrity of the applicants.[47]

Provide Ethics Training

Many ethical issues are complex and cannot be considered in black-and-white moral terms. It is for this and other reasons that ethics training has become quite common. In some cases, the training involves little more than a careful study of the company ethics code and its implications for day-to-day decision making. In other cases, employees participate in in-depth discussions of ethical decisions.

Can colleges and universities teach ethics? In the wake of numerous corporate scandals, business schools have been criticized for producing graduates who are

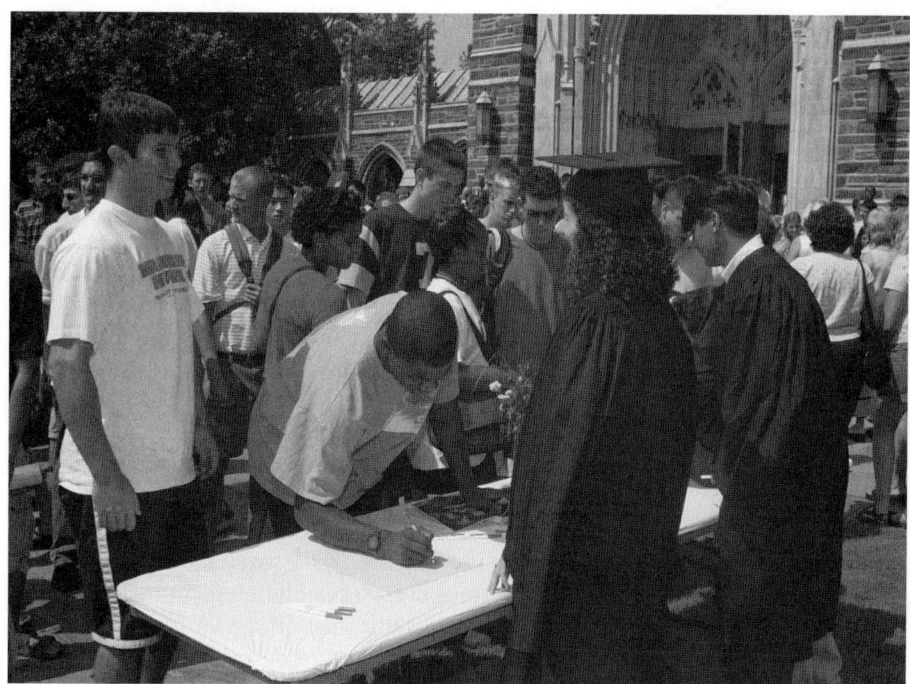

Business schools are trying a host of new methods to teach MBAs lasting lessons in ethical behavior. Duke University is encouraging students to think about the importance of ethical decision making by requiring them to sign an ethics pledge.

obsessed with making money regardless of the ethical consequences. In response to this criticism, business schools are trying a host of new methods, including required ethics courses and honor codes. At Ohio University, the Fisher College of Business created a new honor code that students are required to sign. The code states: "Honesty and integrity are the foundation from which I will measure my actions."[48]

Develop Support for Whistleblowing

When you discover that your employer or a colleague is behaving illegally or unethically, you have three choices. You can keep quiet and keep working. You can decide you can't be party to the situation and leave. Or you can report the situation in the hope of putting a stop to it. When you reveal wrongdoing within an organization to the public or to those in positions of authority, you are a **whistleblower**.

whistleblower A person who reveals wrongdoing within an organization to the public or to those in positions of authority.

- FBI attorney Coleen Rowley wrote a memo to FBI director Robert Mueller claiming that the department ignored the pleas of the Minneapolis field office to investigate Zacarias Moussaoui, who was subsequently indicted as a September 11 coconspirator.
- Cynthia Cooper informed WorldCom's board of directors that illegal accounting procedures covered up $3.8 billion in corporate losses.
- Enron vice president Sherron Watkins wrote a letter to Enron chairman Kenneth Lay alerting him to the illegal accounting procedures that misled stockholders about Enron's financial picture.

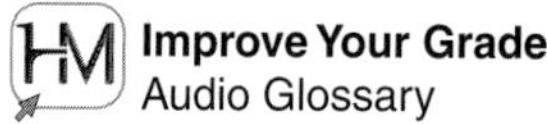

All three of these women tried to keep their concerns "in-house" by speaking the truth to executives in a position of power, not to the public. As details exploded in the media, these women were plunged into the public eye. *Time* magazine

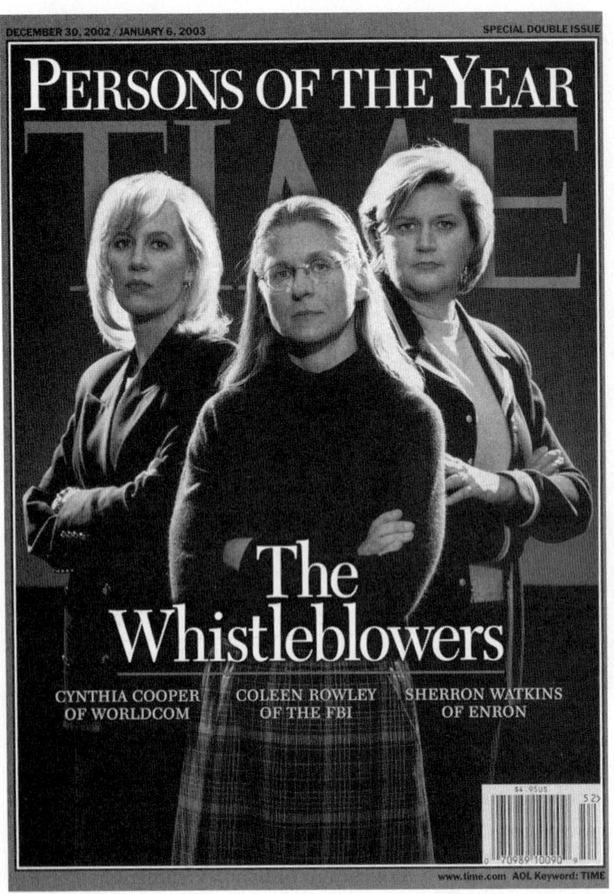

Cynthia Cooper, Coleen Rowley, and Sherron Watkins, whistleblowers at three prominent organizations, were selected as Time *magazine's "Persons of the Year." They helped give corporate and government misconduct national attention.*

proclaimed them "Persons of the Year for 2002" and made them national celebrities, but their personal and professional lives were permanently altered, as their jobs, their health, and their privacy were threatened.[49]

Because of these women—and a multitude of other whistleblowers—organizations now have a legal responsibility to support whistleblowing. Executives who attempt to retaliate can be held criminally liable. The Occupational Safety and Health Administration (OSHA) fields the complaints of individuals who make a disclosure—to a supervisor, law enforcement agency, or congressional investigator—that could have a "material impact" on the value of the company's shares. If the company attempts to retaliate, the whistleblower has ninety days to report the incident to the Department of Labor, which can order the organization to rehire the whistleblower without going to court.[50]

Your fellow colleagues may resent the disruption your revelations cause in their lives. They may be impressed with your integrity, but not everyone will be on your side in your struggle to do what is right and ethical. Your efforts may result in months or even years of emotional and financial turmoil. A survey conducted by the National Whistleblower Center in Washington, D.C., showed that half of the whistleblowers were fired because of their actions. Most reported being unable to acquire new jobs because prospective employers perceived them as troublemakers. Others faced demotions or were placed in jobs with little impact or importance.[51]

Each individual must make his or her own decision as to whether the disturbing unethical offense is worth the personal cost. Table 4.3 lists four questions potential whistleblowers should ask themselves before taking action.

Values and Ethics in International Business

If the situation is complex on the domestic scene, values and ethical issues become even more complicated at the international level. American business firms are under great pressure to avoid doing business with overseas contractors that permit human rights violations such as child labor, low wages, and long hours in their factories. The 1977 Foreign Corrupt Practices Act prohibits U.S. companies from using bribes or kickbacks to influence foreign officials, and many industrial nations have signed a multinational treaty outlawing corporate bribery. But monitoring illegal activities throughout the world is a difficult task. Doing business in the global marketplace continues to be an ethical minefield with illegal demands for bribes, kickbacks, or special fees standing in the way of successful transactions. American businesses acknowledge that it is difficult to compete with organizations from other countries that are not bound by U.S. laws. However, according to the International Business Ethics Institute (www.business-ethics.org), there has been significant progress in the last few years, thanks to both national imperatives and polite but firm pressure from the American business community.

TABLE 4.3

Whistleblower Checklist

Experts say that people who are thinking about blowing the whistle on their company should ask themselves four important questions before doing so.

1. **Is this the only way?**
   Do not blow the whistle unless you have tried to correct the problem by reporting up the normal chain of command and gotten no results. Make sure your allegations are not minor complaints.
2. **Do I have the goods?**
   Gather documentary evidence that proves your case, and keep it in a safe place. Keep good notes, perhaps even a daily diary. Make sure you are seeing fraud, not merely incompetence or sloppiness.
3. **Why am I doing this?**
   Examine your motives. Do not act out of frustration or because you feel underappreciated or mistreated. Do not embellish your case, and do not violate any confidentiality agreements you may have.
4. **Am I ready?**
   Think through the impact on your family. Be prepared for unemployment and the possibility of being blacklisted in your profession. Last but not least, consult a lawyer.

Source: Paula Dwyer and Dan Carney, with Amy Borrus and Lorraine Woellert in Washington and Christopher Palmeri in Los Angeles, "Year of the Whistleblower," *BusinessWeek,* December 16, 2002, pp. 107–108.

- Kevin Tan, the Shanghai director of the marketing research firm Frank, Small & Associates, believes U.S. companies have been a very positive role model for the rest of the business world. Even though it is understood by many in the global business community that violations do occur, the question is often one of degree.
- Paul Jensen, a consultant working for U.S., European, and Japanese interests in China, suggests: "What every internal manager has to do is find what he's personally comfortable with. That's a combination of the company's standards and his personal standards."[52]

TEST PREPPER 4.5

ANSWERS CAN BE FOUND ON P. 237

True or False?

___ 1. In order to effectively compete with companies from other nations, U.S. companies are allowed under the Foreign Corrupt Practices Act to use bribes or kickbacks to influence foreign officials.

___ 2. When Sherron Watkins of Enron wrote a letter to chairman Kenneth Lay alerting him to illegal accounting procedures, she was acting as a whistleblower.

___ 3. Organizations may have difficulty doing what is morally correct because it is easier to manage for profits than to manage for ethical pursuits.

___ 4. A code of ethics is a strong force for building an ethical workplace, even if the code is enforced only sporadically.

ACE the Test
ACE and ACE+ Practice Tests

Improve Your Grade
Learning Objectives Review
Audio Chapter Review
Audio Chapter Quiz

LEARNING OBJECTIVES REVIEW

1 *Explain the personal benefits of developing a strong sense of character.*

- A strong sense of character grows out of your personal standards of behavior.
- When you consistently behave in accordance with your values, you maintain your integrity.

2 *Understand how personal values are formed.*

- Your values are the personal importance you give to an object or idea.
- People's values serve as the foundation for their attitudes, preferences, opinions, and behaviors.
- Your core values are largely formed early in life and are influenced by people and events in your life, your family, religious groups, your education, the media, and people you admire.

3 *Understand values conflicts and how to resolve them.*

- Internal values conflicts arise when you must choose between strongly held personal values.
- Values conflicts with others, often based on age, racial, religious, gender, or ethnic differences, require skilled intervention before they can be resolved.

4 *Learn how to make the right ethical decisions based on your personal value system.*

- Once you have clarified your personal values, your ethical decisions will be easier.
- You must learn to distinguish right from wrong, avoid the pursuit of immediate gratification, and choose an employer whose values you share.
- Shared values unify employees in an organization by providing guidelines for behavior and decisions.

5 *Understand the danger of corporate crime and the steps being taken to eliminate it.*

- Corporate values and ethics on both the domestic and the international levels are receiving increasing attention because of the devastating effect and expense of corporate crime.
- Many organizations are developing ethics codes to help guide employees' behavior, hiring only those individuals who share their corporate values, offering ethics training opportunities to all employees, and supporting whistleblowing.
- Values and ethics become even more complex at the international level. As a result, the individuals involved will need to consciously examine their values and ethical standards to deal effectively with differing values structures around the world.

CAREER CORNER

Q: I will soon graduate from college and would like to begin my career with an organization that shares my values. I have carefully examined what is most important to me and believe I know the type of organizational culture in which I can thrive. But how do I discover the "real" values of an organization when my interviews are permeated with buzzwords such as *family-friendly* and *teamwork-oriented*? How can I determine whether they truly mean what they seem to say?

A: Getting beyond the standard questions about your hours, pay, and job title is important if you want to build a satisfying and successful career within an organization. But direct questions about an organization's values often result in well-rehearsed answers from the interviewer. Try using *critical incident* questions such as "How did your organization handle the September 11 crisis?" or "Tell me about the heroes in your organization." Ask whether they have a formal code of ethics and how ethical misconduct is disciplined. And don't depend solely on the interviewer's answers. Seek out an honest current or former employee who will tell you the unvarnished truth about the organization. Listen carefully to the language used during your interviews. Do you hear a lot of talk about "love," "caring," and "intuition," or do you hear statements like "We had to send in the SWAT team," "They beat their brains out," and "We really nailed them!" If possible, sit in on a team meeting with your potential coworkers. Be forthright about work/life values, and make them a standard part of your interview process. A perfect match between your values and your potential employer's values is hard to find, so be patient. You may need to compromise.

APPLYING WHAT YOU HAVE LEARNED

1. Guilt and loss of self-respect can result when you say or do things that conflict with what you believe. One way to feel better about yourself is to "clean up" your integrity. Make a list of what you are doing that you think is wrong. Once the list is complete, look it over and determine if you can stop these behaviors. Consider making amends for things you have done in the past that you feel guilty about.[53]
2. In groups of four, discuss how you would react if your manager asked you to participate in some sort of corporate crime. For example, the manager could ask you to help launder money from the company, give a customer misleading information, or cover up a budget inaccuracy and keep this information from reaching upper management. You might want to role-play the situation with your group. Follow up with class discussion.
3. One of the great challenges in life is the clarification of our values. The five-part valuing process described in Table 4.1 can be very helpful as you attempt to identify your core values. Select one personal or professional value from the following list, and clarify this value by applying the five-step process.
   a. Respect the rights and privileges of people who may be in the minority because of race, gender, ethnicity, age, physical or mental abilities, or sexual orientation.
   b. Conserve the assets of my employer.
   c. Utilize leisure time to add balance to my life.
   d. Maintain a healthy lifestyle.
   e. Balance the demands of my work and personal life.
4. To increase self-awareness in the area of personal values complete the self-assessment form found on the website **college.hmco.com/pic/reeceSAS**.

Improve Your Grade
Self-Assessment Exercise

ROLE-PLAY EXERCISE

You are currently employed by a pharmaceutical wholesaler that sells prescription drugs to hospitals in a three-county area. Each morning you help other employees fill orders that arrive via computer or the telephone. Once the orders are completed and loaded into delivery vans, you spend the rest of the day delivering products to hospitals. Although others help fill the orders, you are responsible for the accuracy of each order and for timely delivery. Corey Houston, a fellow employee, performs the same duties, but delivers items to hospitals in a different territory. Over the past two months you have noticed that Corey sometimes makes poor ethical choices. For example, the company's reimbursement for lunch is a maximum of $8. Corey packs each day's lunch and never eats at a restaurant. At the end of each week, however, Corey's reimbursement form claims the maximum amount for each meal. Once Corey bragged about earning an extra $40 each week for meals that were not purchased. Corey owns a small landscaping business on the side and sometimes uses the company van to transport items to customers. Recently you drove by a Home Depot store and noticed Corey loading bags of mulch into the company van. At one point you thought about talking with the supervisor about these ethical lapses, but decided to talk with Corey first. Another class member will assume the role of Corey Houston. Try to convince Corey that some of these on-the-job activities are unethical.

CASE 4.1

Employee Theft

The media often focus on corporate crime and the executives involved. However, as we mentioned in the opening vignette of this chapter, the fastest-growing crime in the United States is employee theft. Recent surveys indicate that companies lose over $50 billion annually as employees steal time, money, and supplies from their employers. Employee theft comes in a variety of forms.

- Employees who pilfer pens, scissors, tape, and other office supplies may begin to refer jokingly to the supply room as the "gift shop."
- Padding an expense account with an extra meal or exaggerated tips to servers and baggage handlers may provide enough extra income to pay for the extended child care necessary while an employee is on a business trip.
- A salesperson who is a single parent may tell the boss that a customer needs additional time so returning to the office will be delayed, when in reality the employee's child has a dental appointment.
- An employee's aging father "dies" each time the employee changes employers, thus gaining the employee the paid time off for bereavement leave.
- The person in charge of arrangements for various luncheons within an organization routinely over-orders and takes the "extra" food home.

Theft of this nature is often rationalized as a perk of the job. Some employees may feel that they are underpaid and that they are entitled to these little extras. This larcenous sense of entitlement may come from disgruntled employees who feel they are not appreciated, so they take matters into their own hands. It is true that there are a lot of bad examples at the top of many organizations, and it may be easy to blame top executives for fostering a culture of dishonesty, but does that justify the lack of character and integrity of lower-level employees?[54]

Questions

1. Research indicates that employee misconduct tends to increase in companies where mergers, acquisitions, and restructurings are under way. Why do you think this happens?
2. If your boss is so demanding that you have to lie to protect family time, will you do it? For example, if you have to miss a staff meeting or refuse a business trip to fulfill the needs of your family, will you fabricate work-related or health reasons? Are there any alternatives to lying? Explain.
3. If you were the employer, how would you handle each of the instances above?

RESOURCES ON THE WEB

Prepare for Class, Improve Your Grade, and ACE the Test. Student Achievement Series resources include:

- ACE and ACE+ Practice Tests
- Audio Chapter Quizzes
- Audio Chapter Reviews
- Learning Objective Reviews
- Career Snapshots
- Chapter Glossaries
- Chapter Outlines
- Crossword Puzzles
- Hangman Games
- Flashcards
- Audio Glossaries
- Internet Insights
- Self-Assessment Exercises
- Additional Closing Cases

To access these learning and study tools, go to **college.hmco.com/pic/reeceSAS**.

HM ManagementSPACE

5 Attitudes Can Shape Your Life

Fish tossing demonstrations at Seattle's famous Pike Place Fish Market attract a large audience every day. This business is known for its playful company culture that creates a high energy, fun atmosphere.

1. *Understand the impact of employee attitudes on the success of individuals as well as organizations.*
2. *List and explain the ways people acquire attitudes.*
3. *Describe attitudes that employers value.*
4. *Learn how to change your attitudes and the attitudes held by others.*

"The last of the human freedoms is to choose one's attitude in any given set of circumstances."

—Viktor Frankl, Auschwitz survivor and author

Chapter Outline

- **Attitudes Are Learned**
  - Root Causes of Negative Attitudes
  - The Powerful Influence of Attitudes
  - The Age of Information Mandates Attitude Changes
- **How Attitudes Are Formed**
  - Socialization
  - Peer and Reference Groups
  - Rewards and Punishment
  - Role Model Identification
  - Cultural Influences
- **Attitudes Valued by Employers**
  - Basic Interpersonal Skills
  - Self-Motivation
  - Openness to Change
  - Team Spirit
  - Health Consciousness
  - Appreciation of Coworker Diversity
  - Honesty
- **How to Change Attitudes**
  - Changing Your Own Attitude
  - Helping Others Change Their Attitudes
- **Organizations' Efforts Toward Improving Employees' Attitudes**

HM **Prepare for Class**
Chapter Outline

5 *Understand what adjustments organizations are making to develop positive employee attitudes.*

The Fish Movement

Workers at Seattle's famous Pike Place Fish Market have a cold, wet job. Fish guts, blood, and scales produce a strong stench during their 12-hour shifts. However, when you visit the fish market, you will find that the workers are not downtrodden about their environment.[1] They laugh and joke as they toss fish to each other and over the heads of those who are standing at the counter waiting to pay for their purchases. Some customers even participate in the fish-tossing antics and make spectacular "catches" themselves. Pike Place employees' attitudes, expressed through their energetic clowning, seem contagious.

Not all organizations encourage this type of atmosphere at work. In companies where managers are very controlling, *play* is a four-letter word that means activities that disrupt efforts to be efficient. That's one of the reasons John Christensen, CEO of ChartHouse Learning, coauthored the training books *Fish!*, *Fish! Tales*, and *Fish! Sticks* and created video and management training programs based on the workplace atmosphere at Pike Place. He wanted to provide an opportunity for managers to learn how to instill a positive, productive atmosphere at work. He knew that a playful corporate culture can be created but cannot be mandated. Customers can tell the difference between employees who truly enjoy their jobs and those who are following a company mandate to have a positive attitude. Even Pike Place's owner, John Yokoyama, admits that he was once a grouchy and difficult boss. Then he "got some training" and realized that change was possible.[2] Yokoyama and millions of others have discovered that joyful, lighthearted attitudes occur naturally when people enjoy what they are doing.

Those who embrace what has become known as the "Fish Movement" believe in two basic ideas. First, they believe that a positive attitude is a good thing. Second, they believe that in most situations one can learn to adapt and accept one's current circumstances even if at first they seem undesirable.[3] It's all a matter of attitude.

KEY TERMS

Prepare for Class
Chapter Glossary

Improve Your Grade
Flashcards
Hangman
Crossword Puzzle

ATTITUDES ARE LEARNED

1 *Understand the impact of employee attitudes on the success of individuals as well as organizations.*

attitudes Thoughts that are accepted as true and that lead one to think, feel, or act positively or negatively toward a person, idea, or event.

Attitudes are merely thoughts that you have accepted as true and that lead you to think, feel, or act positively or negatively toward a person, idea, or event. They represent an *emotional readiness* to behave in a particular manner.[4] You are not born with these thoughts; you learn them. Therefore, it is reasonable to conclude that you can learn new attitudes and/or change old ones.

Your values, those beliefs and preferences you feel are important, serve as a foundation for your attitudes. For example, if you believe your religion is important, you may form negative attitudes toward those people and activities that restrict your religious privileges and positive attitudes toward those who support your convictions. Your attitudes, in turn, serve as a motivation for your behavior (see Figure 5.1). So, when someone attempts to interfere with your right to practice your religion, you might become angry and retaliate. But you also have the freedom to choose another response. Perhaps another value comes into play—peace—and it seems more important than "defending" yourself. So, instead of retaliating, you decide to just ignore the interference. The most amazing things can happen once you realize that you can choose which attitude you will act upon.

Root Causes of Negative Attitudes

Some people are positive thinkers and see daily obstacles as opportunities rather than roadblocks. Others tend to dwell on things that can go wrong. Generally speaking, positive attitudes generate positive results and negative attitudes generate negative results. If attitudes are a choice (we can choose our thoughts), why would anyone *choose* to think negatively? There are several factors that exist individually or blend together to produce negative attitudes. We will briefly describe some common root causes of negative attitudes.[5]

FIGURE 5.1

The Relationship Among Values, Attitudes, and Behaviors

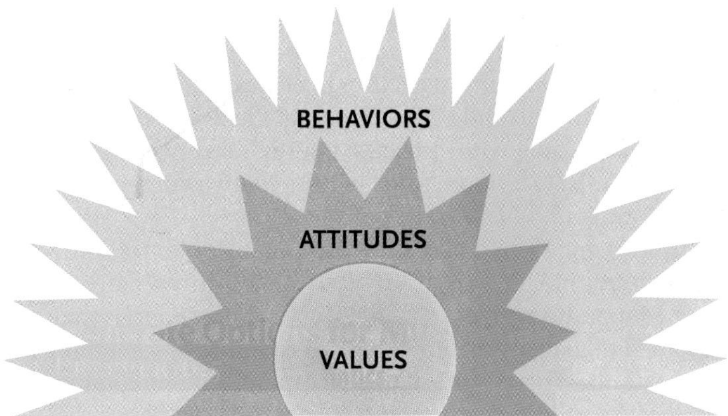

Low Self-Esteem

In Chapter 3 we describe people with low self-esteem as those who lack a sense of personal worth and tend to embrace negative thoughts about the future. This negative outlook influences their ability to get along with others.

Unresolved Conflict

Unresolved conflict can be very costly in terms of lost productivity at work, broken marriages, and lost friendships. Chapter 8 is devoted to conflict resolution strategies.

Work That Is Not Satisfying

Many workers rebel against the monotony of repetitious job functions or working for a boss who fails to recognize work well done. Employers need to develop job designs that provide a sense of achievement, challenge, variety, and personal growth.

Fear or Uncertainty

Negative attitudes can sometimes be traced to feelings of fear or uncertainty. This can happen when someone takes a sliver of fact, rumor, or observation and expands it into something dramatically negative.

TOTAL PERSON INSIGHT

Price Pritchett Chairman, **EPS Solutions**

"The biggest career challenges these days are *perceptual . . . psychological.* Not technical. Not even skills-based. The major adjustments we need to make are mental. For example, how we frame things at work. The way we process events in our head. Our attitudes and outlook about how our jobs and organizations now have to operate."

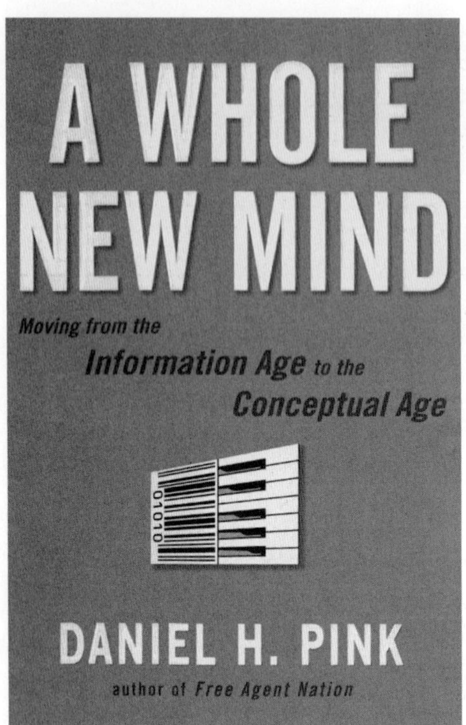

Daniel H. Pink, author of A Whole New Mind, *predicts that one of the major players in the new conceptual age will be the empathizer. These workers have the ability to imagine themselves in someone else's position and understand what that person is feeling.*

empathizer A person who can imagine himself or herself in someone else's position and understand what that person is feeling.

The Powerful Influence of Attitudes

One of the most significant differences between high and low achievers is choice of attitude. People who go through life with a positive attitude are more likely to achieve their personal and professional goals. People who filter their daily experiences through a negative attitude find it difficult to achieve contentment or satisfaction in any aspect of their lives. Jack Welch, the former chairman and CEO of General Electric, believes that an organization needs people with "positive energy" and needs to get rid of those people who inject the work force with "negative energy"—even if they are high performers.[6]

Attitudes represent a powerful force in any organization. An attitude of trust, for example, can pave the way for improved communication and greater cooperation between an employee and a supervisor. But when trust is absent, a manager's sincere attempts to improve something may be met with resistance. These same actions by management, filtered through attitudes of trust and hope, may result in improved worker morale.

The Age of Information Mandates Attitude Changes

During the early stages of the information age, many of the best jobs were filled by people who were proficient at reasoning, logical thinking, and analysis. But as the information age unfolded and the global economy heated up, organizations discovered that it often takes more than quick and accurate information communicated through advanced technology to retain their clients and customers. In many cases, two competing firms, such as banks, may offer customers the same products at the same prices and use the same information technology. The competitive advantage is achieved through superior customer service provided by well-trained employees with effective interpersonal skills.

Daniel Pink, author of *A Whole New Mind,* says we are moving from the information age to the conceptual age. He predicts that one of the major players in the conceptual age will be the **empathizer**. Empathizers have the ability to imagine themselves in someone else's position and understand what that person is feeling. They are able to understand the subtleties of human interaction.[7] For example, several medical schools have come to the conclusion that empathy is a key element of compassionate medical care. Medical school students at Harvard, Columbia, and Dartmouth are learning that an important part of health care diagnosis is contained in the patient's story. They are trained how to identify the subtle details of a patient's condition through caring, compassionate attitudes.[8]

Technology, in its many forms, will continue to make a major contribution to the workplace. However, we must seek a better balance between "high tech" and "high touch." Leadership, for example, is about empathy. It is about having the ability to relate to and to connect with people. Pink states: "Empathy builds self-awareness, bonds parent to child, allows us to work together, and provides the scaffolding for our morality."[9]

Test Prepper 5.1

Answers can be found on p. 237

True or False?

____ 1. In the age of information, an organization's competitive advantage is often gained through superior advanced technology, diminishing the need for customer service.

Multiple Choice

____ 2. An attitude is a(n):
   a. foundation for a person's values.
   b. relatively simple, one-dimensional emotion about a person or object.
   c. unchangeable way of thinking and behaving.
   d. collection of thoughts accepted as true, leading one to think, feel, and behave either positively or negatively.

____ 3. Employers are usually concerned about employees' job satisfaction because:
   a. the more they know about job satisfaction, the more they can manipulate workers into better performance.
   b. current laws governing human resource policies require that managers implement a plan to link behavior with attitude for each employee.
   c. employees' attitudes are an accurate reflection of the behaviors that underlie them.
   d. they realize the importance of the link between job satisfaction (attitude) and behavior (job performance).

____ 4. Leslie and Taylor are equally intelligent, skilled, and attractive. Leslie views ordinary problems as opportunities to learn instead of insurmountable roadblocks to success. Taylor is easily discouraged by routine obstacles. The main difference between Leslie and Taylor is that:
   a. concerning everyday difficulties, Taylor is more realistic than Leslie is.
   b. Leslie has more friends among coworkers than Taylor has.
   c. Taylor's self-esteem is higher than Leslie's is.
   d. Leslie has a positive attitude toward problem solving and Taylor does not.

____ 5. Which one of the following is not likely to cause a negative attitude?
   a. High self-esteem
   b. Fear of uncertainty
   c. Unsatisfying work
   d. Unresolved conflicts

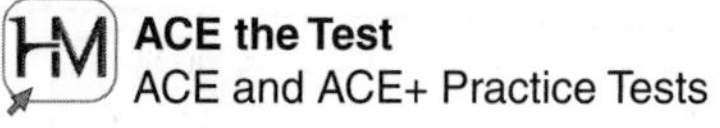

How Attitudes Are Formed

2 *List and explain the ways people acquire attitudes.*

Throughout life you are constantly making decisions and judgments that help form your attitudes. These attitude-shaping decisions are often based on behaviors your childhood authority figures told you were right or wrong, behaviors for which you were rewarded or punished. The role models you select and the various environmental and organizational cultures you embrace also shape your attitudes.

Socialization

The process through which people are integrated into a society by exposure to the actions and opinions of others is called **socialization**.[10] As a child, you interacted with your parents, family, teachers, and friends. Children often feel that statements

socialization The process through which people are integrated into a society by exposure to the actions and opinions of others.

Dale Carnegie, an innovator in self-responsibility and self-improvement, believed that one's attitude could be shaped simply by the way they look at a situation.

made by these authority figures are the "proper" things to believe. For example, if a parent declares, "People who live in big, expensive houses either are born rich or are crooked," the child may hold this attitude for many years. In some cases, the influence is quite subtle. Children who observe their parents recycling, using public transportation instead of a car to get to work, and turning off the lights to save electricity may develop a strong concern for protection of the environment.

Peer and Reference Groups

As children reach adolescence and begin to break away psychologically from their parents, the **peer group** (people their own age) can have a powerful influence on attitude formation. In fact, peer-group influence can sometimes be stronger than the influence of parents, teachers, and other adult figures. With the passing of years, reference groups replace peer groups as sources of attitude formation in young adults. A **reference group** consists of several people who share a common interest and tend to influence one another's attitudes and behaviors. The reference group may act as a point of comparison and a source of information for the individual member. In the business community, a chapter of the American Society for Training and Development or of Sales & Marketing Executives International may provide a reference group for its members.

peer group A group of people of similar age that can have a powerful influence on attitude formation.

reference group Several people who share a common interest and tend to influence one another's attitudes and behaviors.

Rewards and Punishment

Attitude formation is often related to rewards and punishment. People in authority generally encourage certain attitudes and discourage others. Naturally, individuals tend to develop attitudes that minimize punishments and maximize rewards. A child who is praised for sharing toys with playmates is more likely to develop positive attitudes toward caring about other people's needs. Likewise, a child who receives a weekly allowance in exchange for performing basic housekeeping tasks learns an attitude of responsibility.

As an adult, you will discover that your employers will continue to attempt to shape your attitudes through rewards and punishment at work. Many organizations are rewarding employees who take steps to stay healthy, avoid accidents, increase sales, or reduce expenses.

Role Model Identification

Most young people would like to have more influence, status, and popularity. These goals are often achieved through identification with an authority figure or a role model. A **role model** is that person you most admire or are likely to emulate. As you might expect, role models can exert considerable influence—for better or for worse—on developing attitudes.

role model A person who is admired and likely to be emulated.

In most organizations, supervisory and management personnel have the greatest impact on employee attitudes. The new dental hygienist and the recently hired auto mechanic want help adjusting to their jobs. They watch their supervisors' attitudes toward safety, cost control, accuracy, grooming, and customer relations and tend to emulate the behavior of these role models. Employees pay more attention to what their supervisors *do* than to what they *say*.

Cultural Influences

Our attitudes are influenced by the culture that surrounds us. **Culture** is the sum total of knowledge, beliefs, values, objects, and ethnic customs that we use to adapt to our environment. It includes tangible items, such as food, clothing, and furniture, as well as intangible concepts, such as education and laws.[11]

culture The sum total of knowledge, beliefs, values, objects, and ethnic customs that people use to adapt to their environment.

Today's organizations are striving to create corporate cultures that attract and keep productive workers in these volatile times. When employees feel comfortable in their work environment, they tend to stay.

- When it comes to providing a strong, "fun," corporate culture, Icarian Inc., a provider of on-line software that helps companies hire and manage their work forces, is a prime example of going the extra mile. Balloons and roller-hockey gear are everywhere, and pet dogs frolic in the hallways. Employees work hard, and at break time they play hard with chess, Ping-Pong, and other games in the lunchroom. Employees are encouraged to work at home, and community volunteerism is rewarded with time off to participate. After-hours events include wine tasting and barbecues. Happy workers, CEO Doug Merritt believes, are bound to be productive.[12]
- Executives at MBNA, the highly successful credit card company, understand that satisfied employees are more likely to provide excellent customer service. Every day the 23,000 MBNA employees are given a gentle reminder that the customer comes first. The words THINK OF YOURSELF AS A CUSTOMER are printed over every doorway of every office. Each year this Delaware-based company makes *Fortune* magazine's list of the 100 best companies to work for.[13]
- The U.S. Marines have developed an eleven-week basic training program that has a dramatic impact on those who complete it. Recruits emerge as self-disciplined Marines who are physically fit, courteous to their elders, and drug free. Many have had to overcome deep differences of class and race and have learned to live and work as a team. They live in an organizational culture where a hint of racism can end a career and the use of illegal drugs is minimized by a zero-tolerance policy.[14]

HUMAN RELATIONS IN ACTION

Attitudes Shape Starbucks Policies

The person who created an American institution—Starbucks—is a modern-day Horatio Alger. Howard Schultz grew up on some of Brooklyn's meaner streets and lived in a cramped apartment in a public housing project. Throughout his youth, he experienced things that shaped the attitudes he would later bring to Starbucks. He recalls coming home one day to find his father lying on the couch with a broken ankle. His father couldn't work, so he lost his job. Because the family had no medical benefits, its tight finances became even tighter. Recalling that early life experience, Schultz said, "I will never forget that episode; I never want that to happen to our employees." That is why thousands of part-time Starbucks workers have full medical benefits.

TEST PREPPER 5.2

ANSWERS CAN BE FOUND ON P. 237

True or False?

___ 1. When children learn to value a quality family life over material possessions through observing the actions of their parents, they are experiencing the process of socialization.

___ 2. As adolescents pass into adulthood, peer groups tend to replace reference groups as a primary source of attitude influence.

___ 3. Punishments and rewards ultimately have little influence on the formation of attitudes.

Multiple Choice

___ 4. During adolescence, which source of influence on attitude formation is often the strongest?
  a. Parents
  b. Peer group
  c. Teachers
  d. Celebrities

___ 5. An important point that employers should remember concerning role models in the workplace is that:
  a. workers' role models are more likely to be coworkers at their level, not supervisors or upper management personnel.
  b. their influence on new workers is negligible.
  c. their influence may be either positive or negative.
  d. employees pay more attention to what their supervisors say than to what they do.

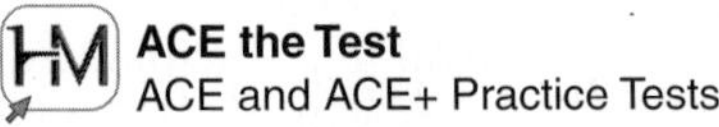

ATTITUDES VALUED BY EMPLOYERS

Describe attitudes that employers value.

Many organizations have discovered the link between workers' attitudes and profitability. This discovery has led to major changes in the hiring process. Employers today are less likely to assume that applicants' technical abilities are the best indicators of their future performance. They have discovered that the lack of technical skills is not the primary reason why most new hires fail to meet expectations. It is their lack of interpersonal skills that counts.[15]

Whether you are looking for your first career position, anticipating a career change, or being retrained for new opportunities, you may find the following discussion helpful concerning what attitudes employers want in their employees.

Basic Interpersonal Skills

In this information-based, high-tech, speeded-up economy, we are witnessing an increase in workplace incivility. Rude behavior in the form of high-decibel cellphone conversations, use of profanity, or failure to display simple courtesies such as saying "thank you" can damage workplace relationships. As we note in Chapter 6, incivility is the ultimate career killer.

Self-Motivation

People who are self-motivated are inclined to set their own goals and monitor their own progress toward those goals. Their attitude is "I am responsible for this job."

They do not need a supervisor hovering around them making sure they are on task and accomplishing what they are supposed to be doing. Many find ways to administer their own rewards after they achieve their goals. Employers often retain and promote those employees who take the initiative to make their own decisions, find better ways of doing their jobs, read professional publications to learn new things, and monitor the media for advances in technology.

"I'M BACK, MR. WILSON. I THOUGHT I'D GIVE YOU ANOTHER CHANCE TO BE *NICE*."

Dennis the Menace

Openness to Change

In the age of information, the biggest challenge for many workers is adjusting to the rapidly accelerating rate of change. Some resistance to change is normal merely because it may alter your daily routine. However, you will get into trouble if you choose the following three attitudes:[16]

1. *Stubbornness.* Some workers refuse to be influenced by someone else's point of view. They also find fault with every new change.
2. *Arrogance.* Employees who reject advice or who give the impression that they do not want retraining or other forms of assistance send the wrong message to their employer.
3. *Inflexibility.* Displaying a closed mind to new ideas and practices can only undermine your career advancement opportunities.

Team Spirit

In sports, the person who is a "team player" receives a great deal of praise and recognition. A team player is someone who is willing to step out of the spotlight, give up a little personal glory, and help the team achieve a victory. Team players are no less important in organizations. Employers are increasingly organizing employees into teams (health teams, sales teams, product development teams) that build products, solve problems, and make decisions.

Health Consciousness

The ever growing cost of health care is one of the most serious problems facing companies today. Many organizations are promoting wellness programs for all employees as a way to keep costs in line. These programs include tips on healthy eating, physical-fitness exercises, and stress management practices, as well as other forms of assistance that contribute to a healthy lifestyle. Employees who actively participate in these programs frequently take fewer sick days, file fewer medical claims, and bring a higher level of energy to work. Some companies even give cash awards to employees who lose weight, quit smoking, or lower their cholesterol levels.

Appreciation of Coworker Diversity

To value diversity in the work setting means to make full use of the ideas, talents, experiences, and perspectives of all employees at all levels within the organization. People who differ from each other often add richness to the organization. An old adage states: If we both think alike, one of us is not necessary.

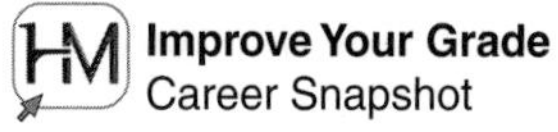
Improve Your Grade
Career Snapshot

Development and utilization of a talented, diverse work force can be a key to success in a period of fierce global competition. Women and people of color make up a large majority of the new multicultural, global work force. Many people, however, carry prejudiced attitudes against those who differ from them. They tend to "prejudge" others' value based on the color of their skin, gender, age, religious preference, lifestyle, political affiliation, or economic status. Although deeply held prejudices that often result in inappropriate workplace behaviors are difficult to change, employers are demanding these changes. Chapter 7 contains specific guidance on how to develop positive attitudes toward joining a diverse work force.

Honesty

Honesty and truthfulness are qualities all employers are searching for in their employees. This is because relationships depend on trust. An honest employee's attitude is "I owe my coworkers the truth." If you cannot be honest with your employer, customers, fellow workers, and friends, they cannot trust you, and strong relationships will be impossible.

Test Prepper 5.3

Answers can be found on p. 237

True or False?

___ 1. Lack of technical skills is the primary reason most new hires fail to meet employer expectations.

Multiple Choice

___ 2. Tamika works with Sue, Hakeem, and John to produce quality control software. She shares credit and blame with her team in their successes and failures. In the age of information, Tamika's attitude reflects the importance of:
   a. loyalty to one's company.
   b. privacy in the workplace.
   c. being a team player.
   d. workplace diversity.

___ 3. Cary's supervisor says, "I never need to check on Cary to make sure he's on task. He sets his own goals and monitors his progress toward them." Cary's supervisor believes that Cary is:
   a. self-conscious.
   b. self-motivated.
   c. self-aware.
   d. self-actualized.

___ 4. Employees who are concerned about their own wellness:
   a. are a drain on profitability because of their constant use of health-related assistance programs.
   b. reduce their employers' costs in the long run.
   c. abuse sick leave more often than others do because they usually are hypochondriacs.
   d. exhibit less energy at work because they wear themselves out pursuing physical fitness on their own time.

___ 5. Avon, a leader in the cosmetics industry, has a very diverse work force. Which of the following is most likely to be true of Avon?
   a. Its benefits costs are higher than average.
   b. Its talent level is lower than average.
   c. It cannot demand that employees overcome prejudices that they may harbor against their coworkers.
   d. It has an advantage in global competition over companies with less diverse work forces.

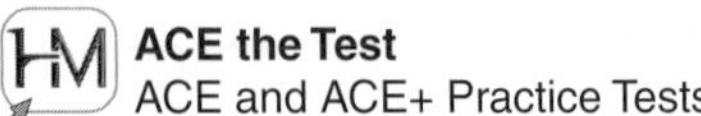

How to Change Attitudes

4 *Learn how to change your attitudes and the attitudes held by others.*

If you are having difficulty working with other team members, if you feel you were overlooked for a promotion you should have had, or if you go home from work depressed and a little angry at the world, you can almost always be sure you need an attitude adjustment. Unfortunately, people do not easily adopt new attitudes or discard old ones. It is difficult to break the attachment to emotionally laden beliefs. Yet attitudes *can* be changed. There may be times when you absolutely hate a job, but you can still develop a positive attitude toward it as a steppingstone to another job you actually do want. There will be times as well when you will need to help colleagues change their attitudes so that you can work with them more effectively. And, of course, when events, such as a layoff, are beyond your control, you can accept this fact and move on. It is often said that life is 10 percent what happens to you and 90 percent how you react to it. Knowing how to change attitudes in yourself and others can be essential to effective interpersonal relations—and your success—in life.

Changing Your Own Attitude

You are constantly placed in new situations with people from different backgrounds and cultures. Each time you go to a new school, take a new job, get a promotion, or move to a different neighborhood, you may need to alter your attitudes to cope effectively with the change. The following attitudes will help you achieve positive results in today's world.

Choose Happiness

In his best-selling book *The Art of Happiness,* the Dalai Lama presents happiness as the foundation of all other attitudes. He suggests that the pursuit of happiness is the purpose of our existence. Survey after survey has shown that unhappy people tend to be self-focused, socially withdrawn, and even antagonistic. Happy people, in contrast, are generally found to be more sociable, flexible, and creative and are able to tolerate life's daily frustrations more easily than unhappy people.[17]

HUMAN RELATIONS IN ACTION

Who Moved My Cheese?

Several years ago, Spencer Johnson wrote *Who Moved My Cheese?* In this small book, which has been on the bestseller list for more than seven years, Johnson introduces the reader to a fable on how to cope positively with change. He recognizes that change is a basic fact of life, so learning to cope with it is an important life strategy. Johnson's most important message is that instead of seeing change as the end of something, you need to learn to see it as a beginning. Breaking through your fear of change is a very important attitude shift in our fluid, ever changing working world.

TOTAL PERSON INSIGHT

His Holiness the Dalai Lama and **Howard C. Cutler**
Coauthors, ***The Art of Happiness***

"We don't need more money, we don't need greater success or fame, we don't need the perfect body or even the perfect mate—right now, at this very moment, we have a mind, which is all the basic equipment we need to achieve complete happiness."

Michael Crom, executive vice president of Dale Carnegie Training, believes that happiness is the state of mind that permits us to live life enthusiastically. He views enthusiasm as an energy builder and as the key to overcoming adversity and achieving goals.[18] But how can you become happy and enthusiastic when the world around you is filled with family, career, and financial crises on a daily basis? Most psychologists, in general, agree that happiness or unhappiness at any given moment has very little to do with the conditions around us, but rather with how we perceive our situation, how satisfied we are with what we have.[19] For example, if you are constantly comparing yourself to people who seem smarter, more attractive, or wealthier, you are likely to develop feelings of envy and frustration. By the same token, you can achieve a higher level of happiness by reflecting on the good things you have received in life.[20]

Embrace Optimism

Optimistic thoughts give rise to positive attitudes and effective interpersonal relationships. When you are an optimist, your coworkers, managers, and—perhaps most important—your customers feel your energy and vitality and tend to mirror your behavior.

It does not take long to identify people with an optimistic outlook. Optimists are more likely to bounce back after a demotion, layoff, or some other disappointment. According to Martin Seligman, professor of psychology at the University of Pennsylvania and author of *Learned Optimism,* optimists are more likely to view problems as merely temporary setbacks on their road to achieving their goals. They focus on their potential success rather than on their failures.[21]

Pessimists, in contrast, tend to believe bad events will last a long time, will undermine everything they do, and are their own fault. A pessimistic pattern of thinking can have unfortunate consequences. Pessimists give up more easily when faced with a challenge, are less likely to take personal control of their life, and are more likely to take personal blame for their misfortune.[22] Often pessimism leads to **cynicism**, which is a mistrusting attitude regarding the motives of people. When you are cynical, you are constantly on guard against the "misbehavior" of others.[23] If you begin to think that everyone is screwing up, acting inconsiderately, or otherwise behaving inappropriately, cynicism has taken control of your thought process, and it is time to change.

cynicism A mistrusting attitude regarding the motives of people.

If you feel the need to become a more optimistic person, you can spend more time visualizing yourself succeeding, a process that is discussed in Chapter 3. Monitor your self-talk, and discover whether or not you are focusing on the negative aspects of the problems and disappointments in your life or are looking at them as learning experiences that will eventually lead you toward your personal and professional goals. Try to avoid having too much contact with pessimists, and refuse to be drawn into a group of negative thinkers who see only problems, not solutions. Attitudes can be contagious.

Think for Yourself

One of the major deterrents to controlling your own attitude is the power of "group think," which surfaces when everyone shares the same opinion. Individuals can lose their desire and ability to think for themselves as they strive to be accepted by team members, committee members, or coworkers in the same department. You are less likely to be drawn into group think if you understand that there are two overlapping relationships among coworkers. *Personal relationships* develop as you bond with your coworkers. When you share common interests and feel comfortable talking with someone, the bonds of friendship may grow very strong. You form small, intense groups. But there still exists the larger group—the organization. Within this setting, *professional relationships* exist for just one purpose: to get the job done.[24] Having two kinds of relationships with the same people can be confusing.

Let's assume you are a member of a project team working on a software application. The deadline for completion is rapidly approaching, yet the team still needs to conduct one more reliability test. At a team meeting, one person suggests that the final test is not needed because the new product has passed all previous tests, and it's time to turn the product over to marketing. Another member of the team, a close friend of yours, enthusiastically supports this recommendation. You have serious concerns about taking this shortcut but hesitate to take a position that conflicts with that of your friend. What should you do? In a professional relationship, your commitment to the organization takes precedence—unless, of course, it is asking you to do something morally wrong.[25]

Keep an Open Mind

We often make decisions and then refuse to consider any other point of view that might lead us to question our beliefs. Many times our attitudes persist even in the presence of overwhelming evidence to the contrary. If you have been raised in a family or community that supports racist views, it may seem foreign to you when your colleagues at work openly accept and enjoy healthy relationships with people whose ethnicity is different from your own. Exposing yourself to new information and experiences beyond what you have been socialized to believe can be a valuable growth experience.

In his book *The 100 Absolutely Unbreakable Laws of Business Success,* Brian Tracy suggests reflecting on the "Law of Flexibility." He said, "You are only as free in life as the number of well-developed options you have available to you." The more thoroughly you open your mind to the options available to you, the more freedom you have.[26] This flexibility to see beyond what you thought was true and examine others' perspectives could be one of the most powerful tools you have to inspire the rest of your life.

Helping Others Change Their Attitudes

As the Serenity Prayer (Figure 5.2) expresses, you have a choice whether to accept circumstances or try to change them. Sometimes we *can* do more than just change our attitude—perhaps we can change a condition over which we have no absolute

FIGURE 5.2

Serenity Prayer

Source: "Serenity Prayer" by Dr. Reinhold Niebuhr.

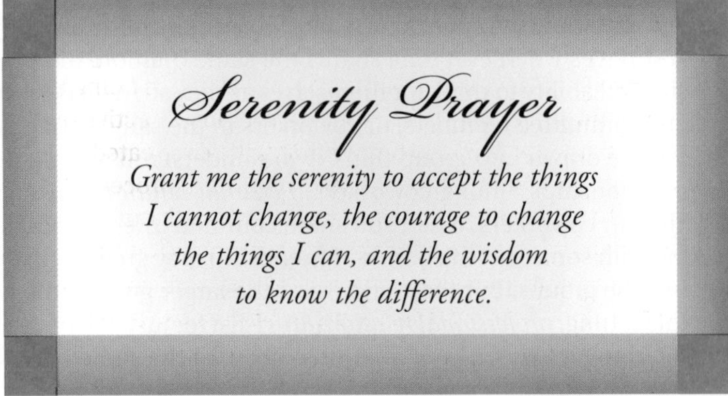
Serenity Prayer
Grant me the serenity to accept the things
I cannot change, the courage to change
the things I can, and the wisdom
to know the difference.

control but which we might be able to influence. For example, at some point you may want to help another person change his or her attitude about something. If you try to beg, plead, intimidate, or even threaten him or her into thinking differently, you probably will get nowhere. This process is similar to attempting to push a piece of yarn across the top of a table. When you *push* the yarn in the direction you want it to go, it gets all bent out of shape. However, when you gently *pull* the yarn with your fingertips, it follows you wherever you want it to go. Two powerful techniques can help you pull people in the direction you want them to go:

1. Change the *conditions* that precede the behavior.
2. Change the *consequences* that follow the behavior.

Change the Conditions

If you want people to change their attitudes, identify the behaviors that represent the poor attitudes and alter the conditions that *precede* the behavior. Consider the following situation.

A new employee in a retail store is having a problem adjusting to her job. The manager needed her on the sales floor as soon as possible, so he rushed through her job training procedures without taking time to answer her questions. Now she finds there are many customers' questions she cannot answer, and she has trouble operating the computerized cash register. She wants to quit, and her negative attitudes are affecting her job performance and the way she handles her customers.

The manager could easily have prevented this employee's negative attitudes by answering all her questions *before* she was placed on the sales floor. Perhaps he could have asked an experienced salesperson to stay with her as she helped her first few customers. Above all, he could have displayed a caring, supportive attitude toward her.

Change the Consequences

Another way to help other people change their attitudes is to alter what happens *after* they exhibit the behavior you are attempting to change. A simple rule applies:

When an experience is followed by positive consequences, the person is likely to repeat the behavior. When an experience is followed by negative consequences, the person will likely stop the behavior. For example, if you are a supervisor, and several of your employees are consistently late for work, you might provide some form of negative consequence each time they are tardy, such as a verbal reprimand or reduced pay. Keep in mind, however, that we tend to focus attention on the people who exhibit disruptive attitudes and to ignore the employees exhibiting the attitudes we want to encourage. Saying "Thank you for being here on time. I really appreciate your commitment" can be an extremely effective reward for those who arrive at work on time. Behaviors rewarded will be repeated.

An attitude is nothing more than a personal thought process. We cannot control the thinking that takes place in someone else's mind, but we can sometimes influence it. And sometimes we can't do that either, so we have to set certain rules of behavior. Some organizations have come to the conclusion that behavior that offends or threatens others must stop. It may be impossible to stop someone from thinking prejudicial thoughts, but you can establish a zero-tolerance policy regarding acts that demean or threaten others.[27]

Test Prepper 5.4

Answers can be found on p. 237

Multiple Choice

___ 1. "Develop an attitude of gratitude," writes Sarah Ban Breathnach, best-selling author of self-improvement books. This statement shows that one can choose happiness by:
   a. reflecting on the good things one has received in life.
   b. being more sociable.
   c. becoming more self-focused to understand better what one needs to be happy.
   d. comparing oneself to others who seem smarter and more attractive.

___ 2. Martin mistrusts his coworkers, always assuming that they are out to get him personally. Martin has an attitude of:
   a. pessimism.
   b. learned optimism.
   c. cynicism.
   d. temperamental optimism.

___ 3. Georgia strongly desires to fit in among her department peers and therefore tends to support the perceptions of her department members. Georgia is exhibiting signs of:
   a. cynicism.
   b. group think.
   c. optimism.
   d. independent thought.

___ 4. François observes his employees' behavior on the job and thanks them personally when they show evidence of their commitment to the company's goals. François is trying to influence his employees' attitudes by:
   a. changing the conditions that precede their behavior.
   b. maintaining an authoritarian leadership style.
   c. focusing on the consequences of their behavior.
   d. providing negative reinforcement.

___ 5. Changing a negative attitude is:
   a. impossible because attitudes are enduring.
   b. easy but not significant.
   c. challenging but critical to continued growth and success.
   d. difficult, and rarely results in long-lasting benefits.

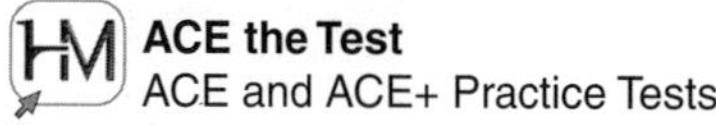

Organizations' Efforts Toward Improving Employees' Attitudes

5 *Understand what adjustments organizations are making to develop positive employee attitudes.*

Most companies realize that an employee's attitude and performance cannot be separated. When employees have negative attitudes about their work, their job performance and productivity suffer. When Thomas Kuwatsch, vice president of the German information technology company Nutzwerk, discovered that employees' whining was cutting into productivity and costing the company an average of $17,600 a year, he formed the "two moans and you're out" policy. A clause in employees' contracts requires them to be in a good mood to keep their jobs. Everyone can complain, but employees must present a solution or better idea to overcome the problem they are complaining about.[28]

When employees have positive attitudes, job performance and productivity are likely to improve. One CEO of a software company has stated, "The way you get superior performance is to get people's passionate loyalty and belief. That means being flexible and giving your people what they need to do a great job."[29]

People who are asked what they most want from their job typically cite mutual respect among coworkers, interesting work, recognition for work well done, the chance to develop skills, and so forth. Of course, workers expect the pay to be competitive, but they want so much more. As author and management consultant Peter Drucker says, "To make a living is not enough. Work also has to make a life."[30] Organizations are finding creative ways to influence worker attitudes. The following companies made *Fortune* magazine's list of the 100 best companies to work for.[31]

At Mango's Tropical Café in Miami, Florida, dance classes help employees embrace the look and feel of the company's culture, which emphasizes fun and multicultural celebration. These classes also build friendships, trust, and teamwork.

- Plante & Moran is an accounting firm with a human touch and a sense of humor. The company describes itself as "relatively jerk-free." Full-time employees get at least four weeks of paid vacation.
- Baptist Health Care is a hospital that the competition tries to imitate. Top management maintains close contact with all employees, and employee-led initiatives have resulted in low turnover among registered nurses. Periodic open-forum meetings give employees a chance to voice concerns or make suggestions.
- Adobe Systems, a successful Silicon Valley firm, strives to generate camaraderie among its employees. It schedules frequent all-hands meetings, job rotations, and Friday night parties. Perks include a fitness center with trainer, seasonal farmers' market, and basketball court.

What do these organizations have in common? Each has given thought to the attitudes that are important for a healthy work environment and has taken steps to shape these attitudes. Many organizations are attempting to improve employee attitudes and productivity by enhancing the quality of their employees' work life.

TEST PREPPER 5.5

ANSWERS CAN BE FOUND ON P. 237

True or False?

F 1. Although employees with positive attitudes are more pleasant to work with, they rarely perform better than those with negative attitudes.

ACE the Test
ACE and ACE+ Practice Tests

Multiple Choice

C 2. Many contemporary workplaces are attempting to improve their employees' attitudes by:

a. terminating employees who criticize the company.
b. reducing the pay of employees with negative attitudes.
c. enhancing the quality of employees' work lives.
d. sending employees to psychotherapy.

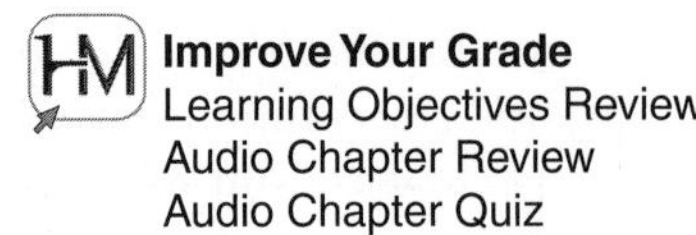

LEARNING OBJECTIVES REVIEW

1 *Understand the impact of employee attitudes on the success of individuals as well as organizations.*

- Attitudes are merely thoughts that you have accepted as true and that lead you to think, feel, or act positively or negatively toward a person, idea, or event.
- Negative attitudes are caused by low self-esteem, unresolved conflicts, work that is not satisfying, and fear of uncertainty.
- Employees' attitudes and performance cannot be separated. When employees display a positive attitude toward their work and coworkers, teamwork and productivity improve. When employees display a caring attitude toward their customers, the business is likely to enjoy a high degree of customer loyalty and repeat business.
- Because of the ready availability of advanced technology, competitive advantage is now frequently gained through superior customer service skills and employees with strong interpersonal abilities.

2 *List and explain the ways people acquire attitudes.*

- Children acquire attitudes through socialization.
- Adolescents rely heavily on their peer groups (people of their own age) in the development of attitudes.
- For adults, the primary influence of peer groups is reference groups (several people who share a common interest).
- Role models (people you most admire or are likely to emulate) can exert considerable influence—for better or for worse—on developing attitudes.
- Our attitudes are influenced by the culture (the knowledge, beliefs, values, objects, and ethnic customs) that surrounds us.
- However, attitudes are not set in stone. You always have the power to choose your attitude toward any situation.

3 *Describe attitudes that employers value.*

- Employers hire and attempt to retain employees who have basic interpersonal skills, are self-motivated, accept change, are team players, are concerned about their health, value coworker diversity, and are honest.

4 *Learn how to change your attitudes and the attitudes held by others.*

- You can decide to change your attitudes by choosing to be happy, becoming an optimist, thinking for yourself without undue pressure from others, and keeping an open mind.
- You can help others change their attitudes by altering the conditions that lead to negative behaviors, such as by providing effective training so that the employee's job performance and personal satisfaction improve.
- You can also alter the consequences following people's behavior by providing positive consequences if you want them to have a positive attitude toward their behavior and repeat it, and negative consequences to deter them from participating in that behavior again.

5 *Understand what adjustments organizations are making to develop positive employee attitudes.*

- Employers realize that money alone will not make employees happy.
- Organizations are taking steps to improve employee attitudes by enhancing the quality of their work life.

Career Corner

Q: Two years ago I left a job I loved when the executives of an exciting new company offered me a position that seemed to have tremendous potential. I gave my two weeks' notice and jumped to the new employer. I worked day and night to help the new company be successful and enhance my climb to the top of it. Last week I was informed that it is declaring bankruptcy next month. I am choosing how I react to this devastating news and am trying not to panic, but I need advice on how to approach my former employer about returning to my old position. I still see some of my former colleagues socially, and they believe that there might be an opportunity to return to my old job. What can I do to enhance my chances at reentry?

A: You are not alone! Many workers grab new job opportunities when they believe the grass might be greener on the other side, only to discover they were better off in the first location. You were smart when you offered two weeks' notice before leaving your position. This considerate attitude toward your colleagues and customers will speak well for you during your reentry attempt. Determine what new skills you learned with the new organization and how those skills might be transferred to your former employer. Did you learn to effectively handle multiple priorities simultaneously, work faster, or take more risks? Point out why this new knowledge makes you even more valuable to your former employer. Who knows, they may reinstate you in a higher position than before!

Keep in mind that returning to your previous employer may not be your only choice. You could choose to look at this forced change as an opportunity to explore options you never considered before. Are there other employers in your field that might consider your experience an asset? Are your skills transferable to another career path? Keep an open mind as you examine your future.

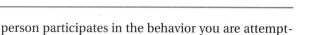

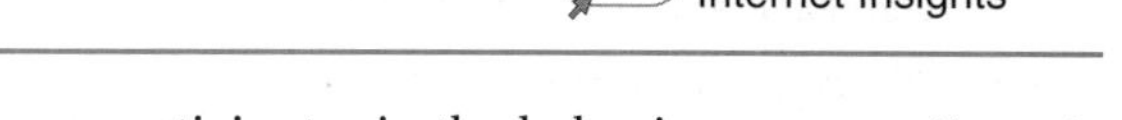

Applying What You Have Learned

1. Describe your attitudes concerning

   a. a teamwork environment
   b. health and wellness
   c. life and work
   d. learning new skills

   How do these attitudes affect you on a daily basis? Do you feel you have a positive attitude in most situations? Can you think of someone you have frequent contact with who displays negative attitudes toward these items? Do you find ways to avoid spending time with this person?
2. Identify an attitude held by a friend, coworker, or spouse that you would like to see changed. Do any conditions that precede this person's behavior fall under your control? If so, how could you change those conditions so the person might change his or her attitude? What positive consequences might you offer when the person behaves the way you want? What negative consequences might you impose when the person participates in the behavior you are attempting to stop?
3. For a period of one week, keep a diary or log of positive and negative events. Positive events might include the successful completion of a project, a compliment from a coworker, or just finding time for some leisure activities. Negative events might include forgetting an appointment, criticism from your boss, or simply looking in the mirror and seeing something you don't like. An unpleasant news story might also qualify as a negative event. At the end of one week, review your entries and determine what type of pattern exists. Also, reflect on the impact of these events. Did you quickly bounce back from the negative events, or did you dwell on them all week? Did the positive events enhance your optimism? Review the root causes of negative attitudes, and try to determine if any of these factors influence your reaction to negative or positive events.
4. To increase self-awareness in the area of attitudes complete the self-assessment form found on the website **college.hmco.com/pic/reeceSAShumrel**.

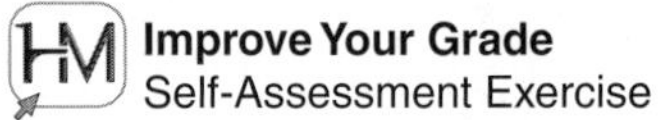

ROLE-PLAY EXERCISE

In this role-play excercise you will be attempting to change the attitudes of a friend who is a chronic underachiever. He has a great deal of potential, but he does things at work that result in self-sabotage. For example, he tends to procrastinate and often misses deadlines. When he does complete a project, his approach is to get by with the least amount of effort. When things don't go well at work, he tends to blame others. You will meet with another member of your class who will assume the role of your friend. Prior to the meeting, think about things you might say or do that would help your friend develop the attitudes that employers value today.

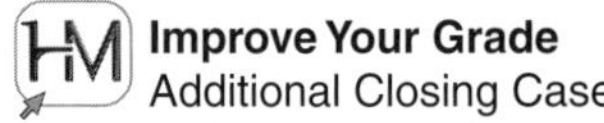

CASE 5.1

Life Is Good at the Pike Place Fish Market

The popular books *Fish!*, *Fish! Tales*, and *Fish! Sticks*, mentioned at the beginning of this chapter, present a business philosophy that focuses on building employees' commitment to their employers and organizations. This philosophy is applicable to almost every organization because it is based on the idea that most people like working in happy places, so they are more likely to stay on the job and do a better job. While some people might argue that these "feel-good" attitudes are "soft skills" and do not affect the bottom line, a spokesperson for a very large organization said that the savings they experienced as a result of implementing the *Fish!* philosophy was in the millions of dollars because of employee retention.

The philosophy emphasizes four ways that companies can help employees and workers can help themselves.

- *Play.* A sense of playfulness makes a huge difference between those who perceive their jobs as no fun and those who have fun doing their jobs. When employees are having as much fun as they can at whatever they are doing, they generate a spirit of innovation and creativity.
- *Be there.* Don't daydream about what you could be doing and things you do not have. Make the most of where you are. Listen in depth to customers' and colleagues' concerns or ideas. When you really focus

on a conversation and postpone other activities such as answering phone calls or processing paperwork, you avoid communicating indifference to the other person.

- *Make someone's day.* Delight customers instead of grudgingly doing the bare minimum. Do favors for others, even those who make you uncomfortable, and your job will become much more rewarding.
- *Choose your attitude.* People often add unnecessary stress to their lives because they stay upset with certain aspects of their job that they cannot control, rather than focusing on how they can make things better.

First Essex Bank chairman and CEO Leonard Wilson admits that "*Fish!* isn't going to make horrible, inexperienced employees into good employees. . . . But most workers can give an extra 10 to 40 percent. . . . *Fish!* is a way to get at an employee's 'pool of discretionary effort.'"[32]

Questions

1. Which of the four *Fish!* principles do you believe can have the most dramatic effect on employees' productivity? Explain your answer.
2. What would you say to someone who sincerely believed that the *Fish!* principles were ridiculous and frivolous?
3. Would you like to work for a *Fish!* organization? Why or why not?
4. Identify workers and/or organizations that you believe have caught on to the powerful impact of this "attitude adjustment" program. How can you tell? What effect has it had on the individuals' and/or the organizations' success?

RESOURCES ON THE WEB

Prepare for Class, Improve Your Grade, and ACE the Test. Student Achievement Series resources include:

- ACE and ACE+ Practice Tests
- Audio Chapter Quizzes
- Audio Chapter Reviews
- Learning Objective Reviews
- Career Snapshots
- Chapter Glossaries
- Chapter Outlines
- Crossword Puzzles
- Hangman Games
- Flashcards
- Audio Glossaries
- Internet Insights
- Self-Assessment Exercises
- Additional Closing Cases

To access these learning and study tools, go to **college.hmco.com/pic/reeceSAS**.

HM ManagementSPACE

6 Developing a Professional Presence

Apple computers have a lot in common with Lexus automobiles, BMW motorcycles, Starbucks Coffee, and Craftsman tools. Each is a *brand* that receives the highest quality ratings and consistently lives up to expectations.

1. *Explain the importance of professional presence and discuss the factors that contribute to a favorable first impression.*
2. *Define* image *and describe the factors that form the image you project to others.*
3. *List and discuss factors that influence your choice of clothing for work.*
4. *Explain how your facial expression, entrance and carriage, voice, and handshake impact your work image.*

"Developing a strong personal brand involves all the little ways in which you express your feelings about yourself and present yourself to others."

—David McNally & Karl D. Speak

Chapter Outline

HM **Prepare for Class**
Chapter Outline

Brand Yourself

5 *Understand how manners contribute to improved interpersonal relations in the workplace.*

What do Apple computers and BMW motorcycles have in common? Each is a consumer product with a cult following. These brands have become a form of self-expression for those who own them. They have achieved brand personality through unique design and performance attributes. The Macintosh brand seems to communicate youthful, independent, and creative qualities. BMW motorcycles have a loyal following of riders who feel these bikes are superior in quality, performance, and design. A brand is more than the product. The best brands build an emotional connection with the consumer.[1]

Why introduce the concept of brands in a book devoted to human relations? Because branding can play a crucial role in your career success. The authors of *Be Your Own Brand: A Breakthrough Formula for Standing Out from the Crowd* say branding can have a significant impact on your relationships, career, and life.[2] Developing a strong personal brand involves all the little

KEY TERMS

Prepare for Class
Chapter Glossary

Improve Your Grade
Flashcards
Hangman
Crossword Puzzle

ways in which you express your feelings about yourself and present yourself to others.

Dave Olsen, chief coffee guru with Starbucks, was once asked to describe the most important factor contributing to the company's success. Was it the coffee? The employees working behind the counter? The design of the stores? Olsen thought about the question for a while and then said, "Everything matters." When it comes to developing your own personal brand, everything matters.[3]

PROFESSIONAL PRESENCE—AN INTRODUCTION

1 *Explain the importance of professional presence and discuss the factors that contribute to a favorable first impression.*

There are many personal and professional benefits to be gained from a study of the concepts in this chapter. You will acquire new insights regarding ways to communicate positive impressions during job interviews, business contacts, and social contacts made away from work. You will also learn how to shape an image that will help you achieve your fullest potential in the career of your choice. Image is a major component of brand development.

This is not a chapter about ways to make positive impressions with superficial behavior and quick-fix techniques. We do not discuss the "power look" or the "power lunch." The material in this chapter will not help you become a more entertaining conversationalist or win new customers by pretending to be interested in their hobbies or families. Stephen Covey, author of *The Seven Habits of Highly Effective People*, says that the ability to build effective, long-term relationships is based on character strength, not quick-fix techniques. He notes that outward attitude and behavior changes do very little good in the long run *unless* they are based on solid principles governing human effectiveness. These principles include service (making a contribution), integrity and honesty (which serve as a foundation of trust), human dignity (every person has worth), and fairness.[4]

Professional Presence—A Definition

professional presence A dynamic blend of poise, self-confidence, control, and style that enables a person to command respect in any situation.

We are indebted to Susan Bixler, author of *Professional Presence*, for giving us a better understanding of what it means to possess professional presence. **Professional presence** is a dynamic blend of poise, self-confidence, control, and style that empowers us to be able to command respect in any situation.[5] Once acquired, it permits us to project a confidence that others can quickly perceive the first time they meet us. Obviously, to *project* this confidence, you need to *feel* confident.

Bixler points out that, in many cases, the credentials we present during a job interview or when we are being considered for a promotion are not very different from those of other persons being considered. It is our professional presence that permits us to rise above the crowd. Debra Benton, a career consultant, says, "Any boss with a choice of two people with equal qualifications will choose the one with style as well as substance."[6]

Professional Presence at the Job Interview

Professional business attire is recommended for interviews and client meetings to convey a clean, well-groomed, and organized image.

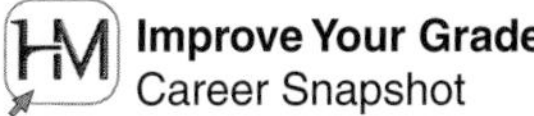

Professional presence has special meaning when you are preparing for a job interview. In most cases you are competing against several other applicants, so you can't afford to make a mistake. A common mistake among job applicants is failure to acquire background information on the employer. Without this information, it's difficult to prepare questions to ask during the interview, and decisions about what to wear will be more difficult.

Keep in mind that regardless of the dress code of the organization, it's always appropriate to dress conservatively. If you arrive for an interview wearing torn jeans and a T-shirt, the person conducting the interview may think you are not serious about the job. The expectation of most employers is that the job applicant will be well groomed and dressed appropriately.

One of the most important objectives of a job interview is to communicate the image that you are someone who is conscientious, so be prepared. If possible, visit the place of business before your interview. Observe the people already working there; then dress one step up in terms of professional appearance. What's most important is that you show that you care enough to make a good impression.

The Importance of Making a Good First Impression

As organizations experience increased competition for clients, patients, or customers, they are giving new attention to the old adage "First impressions are lasting ones." Research indicates that initial impressions do indeed tend to linger. Therefore, a positive first impression can be thought of as the first step in building a long-term relationship.

Of course, it is not just first contacts with clients, patients, customers, and others that are important. Positive impressions should be the objective of every contact. Many organizations have learned that in the age of information, high tech without high touch is not a winning formula.

The Primacy Effect

The development of professional presence begins with a full appreciation of the power of first impressions. The tendency to form and retain impressions quickly at the time of an initial meeting illustrates what social psychologists call a **primacy effect** in the way people perceive one another. The general principle is that initial information tends to carry more weight than information received later. First impressions establish the mental framework within which a person is viewed, and information acquired later is often ignored or reinterpreted to coincide with this framework.[7]

primacy effect The tendency to form and retain impressions quickly at the time of an initial meeting.

Ann Demarais and Valerie White, founders of First Impressions, Inc. (www.firstimpressionsconsulting.com), note that in a first impression others see only a very small sample of you, a tiny percentage of your life. But to them, that small sample represents 100 percent of what they know of you. And they will weigh initial information much more heavily than later information.[8]

TOTAL PERSON INSIGHT

Susan Bixler and **Nancy Nix-Rice**
Authors, ***The New Professional Image***

"Books are judged by their covers, houses are appraised by their curb appeal, and people are initially evaluated on how they choose to dress and behave. In a perfect world this is not fair, moral, or just. What's inside should count a great deal more. And eventually it usually does, but not right away. In the meantime, a lot of opportunities can be lost."

The First Few Seconds

Malcolm Gladwell (www.gladwell.com), a best-selling author, learned a great deal about the power of first impressions a few years ago when he let his close-cropped hair grow wild. His life changed immediately. He got far more speeding tickets and was routinely pulled out of airport security lines for special attention. People he met knew nothing about him except that he had shaggy hair, but they were ready to think the worst.[9]

Gladwell was inspired to try to understand what happens beneath the surface of rapidly made decisions. His findings later appeared in *Blink: The Power of Thinking Without Thinking.* He says most of us would like to think our decision making is the result of rational deliberation, but in reality most decisions are made subconsciously in a split second.[10]

Most people assess another person very quickly and then settle on a general perception of that individual. It is very difficult for us to reverse that first impression. Paula rushed into a restaurant for a quick lunch—she had to get back to her office for a 1:30 p.m. appointment. At the entrance of the main dining area was a sign reading "Please Wait to Be Seated." A few feet away, the hostess was discussing a popular movie with one of the waitresses. The hostess made eye contact with Paula but continued to visit with the waitress. In this situation, Paula immediately formed a negative impression of the hostess, even though no words were exchanged. She quickly left the restaurant. Unfortunately, the hostess may not have been fully aware of the negative impression she communicated to the customer.

Assumptions Versus Facts

assumptions Ideas that are taken for granted or believed to be true.

The impression you form of another person during the initial contact is made up of both assumptions and facts. Most people tend to rely more heavily on **assumptions** during the initial meeting. If a job applicant sits slumped in the chair, head bowed and shoulders slack, you might assume the person is not very interested in the position. If the postal clerk fails to make eye contact during the transaction and does not express appreciation for your purchase, you may assume this person treats everyone with indifference. Needless to say, the impression you form of another person during the initial contact can be misleading. The briefer the encounter with a new acquaintance, the greater the chance that misinformation will enter into your perception of the other person. The authors of a popular book on first impressions state that "depending on assumptions is a one-way ticket to big surprises and perhaps disappointments."[11]

Where Is Your Emotional Focus?

Making a good first impression means making the person you meet feel positive about you. When you make contact with someone, it is not uncommon to focus on yourself. You talk to someone at a party or a meeting, and you think about how you feel—whether you are comfortable, bored, nervous, intimidated, and so on. But do you think about the impression you are making on the other person? Do you think about how the other person is feeling during the initial contact? The authors of *First Impressions—What You Don't Know About How Others See You* say that focusing on how the other person feels is the secret to making a positive first impression.[12]

Cultural Influence

Cultural influences, often formed during the early years of our life, lead us to have impressions of some people even before we meet them. People often develop stereotypes of entire groups. Although differences between cultures are often subtle, they can lead to uncomfortable situations. We need to realize that the Korean shopkeeper is being polite, not hostile, when he puts change on the counter and not in your hand. Some Asian students do not speak up in class out of respect for the teacher, not boredom.[13]

cultural influences Impressions and ideas usually formed in the early years of life that can lead people to form ideas about other people and things even before they are encountered.

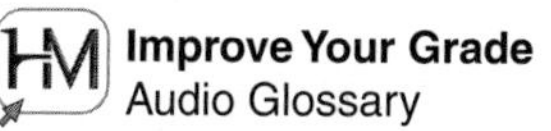

Many American companies are attempting to create a new kind of workplace where cultural and ethnic differences are treated as assets, not annoyances. Recently, Walt Disney, known for its squeaky-clean dress and grooming standards, announced it was loosening grooming rules for workers at its theme parks. Under the new policy, male workers can wear braids provided they are above the collar and neatly tied close to the scalp in straight rows. Female workers at Disney have been able to braid their hair for years.[14]

Norine Dresser, author of *Multiculture Manners—New Rules of Etiquette for a Changing Society*, notes that it is becoming more difficult for organizations to develop policies that do not offend one ethnic group or another. She argues that it is the collective duty of the mainstream to learn the customs and practices of established minority groups as well as the ways of the latest arrivals from other countries.[15]

HUMAN RELATIONS IN ACTION

Snap Judgments and Future Relationships

A group of 164 incoming first-year college students were paired by sex and asked to talk for three, six, or ten minutes. The students were then asked to rate how much they liked the other person, assess how much the two had in common, and make predictions about their future relationship with that person. After nine weeks, the university researchers conducted a follow-up survey and found that the best predictor of the relationships that had developed was how positively the subjects had rated their partners after the first, quick meeting.

TEST PREPPER 6.1

ANSWERS CAN BE FOUND ON P. 237

Multiple Choice

___ 1. One of the most important ways to establish a positive professional presence from the very first impression is to:
   a. avoid eye contact, lest one be thought too aggressive.
   b. be the first to speak.
   c. wear appropriate attire for the people one will contact and the places one will visit.
   d. relax your posture, slumping forward to enhance two-way communication.

___ 2. Garry is interviewing for a position at corporate headquarters this morning. How long does he have to create a good impression?
   a. A few seconds
   b. About 5 minutes
   c. Around an hour
   d. 2 hours at most

ACE the Test
ACE and ACE+ Practice Tests

___ 3. Self-confidence, style, poise, and control are all integral to:
   a. attractive appearance.
   b. professional presence.
   c. animal magnetism.
   d. self-efficacy.

___ 4. "You never get a second chance to make a good first impression." This statement encapsulates the:
   a. recency effect.
   b. surface effect.
   c. control effect.
   d. primacy effect.

___ 5. Yasuo, an exchange student from Japan, never speaks in class. His professor assumes that Yasuo is bored. In fact, Yasuo's culture indicates that he is being quiet because:
   a. he is hostile toward the professor.
   b. he holds the professor in contempt.
   c. he respects the professor.
   d. he lacks language skills.

THE IMAGE YOU PROJECT

2 *Define* image *and describe the factors that form the image you project to others*

image A term used to describe how other people feel about you. It can reveal your inherent qualities, your competence, and your attitude.

Image is a term used to describe how other people feel about you. In every business or social setting, your behaviors and appearance communicate a mental picture that others observe and remember. This picture determines how they react to you.

Think of image as a tool that can reveal your inherent qualities, your competence, your attitude, and your leadership potential. If you wish to communicate your professional capabilities and create your own brand, begin by scrutinizing your attitudes; only then can you invest the time and energy needed to refine and enhance your personal image.

In many respects, the image you project is very much like a picture puzzle, as illustrated in Figure 6.1. It is formed by a variety of factors, including manners, self-confidence, voice quality, versatility, integrity (see Chapter 4), entrance and carriage, facial expression, surface language, competence, positive attitude, and handshake. Each of these image-shaping components is under your control, though some are harder to develop than others. As you reflect on the image you want to project, remember that a strong personal brand is built from the inside out.

FIGURE 6.1

Major Factors That Form Your Image

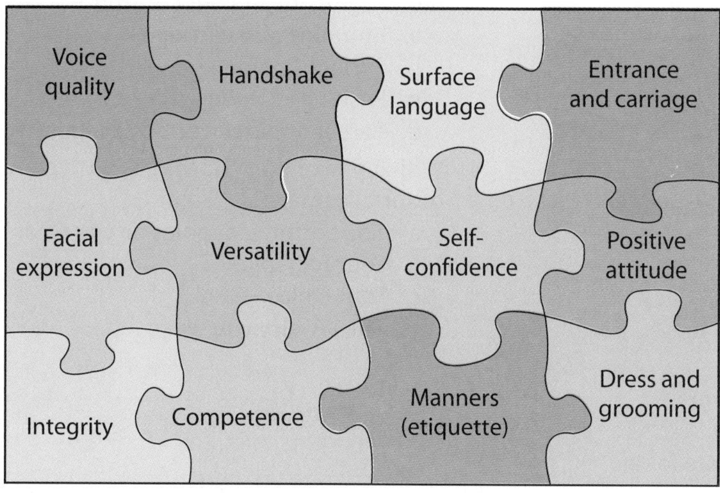

Surface Language

As noted earlier, we base opinions about other people on both facts and assumptions. Unfortunately, assumptions often carry a great deal of weight. Many of the assumptions we develop regarding other people are based on **surface language**, a pattern of immediate impressions conveyed by what we *see*—in other words, by appearance. The clothing you wear, your hairstyle, the fragrances you use, and the jewelry you display all combine to make a statement about you to others.

surface language A pattern of immediate impressions conveyed by what one sees.

According to many writers familiar with image formation, clothing is particularly important. Although a more relaxed dress code has evolved in some employment areas, people judge your appearance long before they judge your talents. It would be a mistake not to take your career wardrobe seriously. Bixler suggests that those making career wardrobe decisions should keep in mind that three things haven't changed:[16]

1. *If you want the job, you have to look the part.* Establish personal dress and grooming standards appropriate for the organization where you wish to work. Before you apply for a job, try to find out what the workers there are wearing. If in doubt, dress conservatively. Casual dress can convey indifference.
2. *If you want the promotion, you have to look promotable.* A good rule to follow is to dress for the job you want, not the job you have. If you are currently a bank teller and want to become a branch manager, identify the successful branch managers and emulate their manner of dress.
3. *If you want respect, you have to dress as well as or better than your industry standards.* One would expect to find conservative dress standards in banking, insurance, accounting, and law, and more casual dress standards in advertising, sports entertainment, and agriculture. Spend time researching the dress and grooming standards in the industry in which you hope to find a job.

TEST PREPPER 6.2

ANSWERS CAN BE FOUND ON P. 237

Multiple Choice

a 1. Which of the following is *not* an important component of a person's image?
   a. Natural hair color
   b. Positive attitude
   c. Voice quality
   d. Surface language

d 2. Ellen wants to be promoted from associate professor to head of the Sociology Department at her college. Ellen should:
   a. conform closely to the clothing norms for all associate professors of sociology.
   b. dress like the college president.
   c. let her inner qualities and hard work speak for her.
   d. project the appearance appropriate for a department head *before* she seeks the promotion.

d 3. Which one of these image-shaping components is outside of your control?
   a. Entrance and carriage
   b. Surface language
   c. Positive attitude
   d. Career apparel worn by a fellow worker

c 4. Which one of the following is *not* a component of surface image?
   a. The perfume or cologne you wear
   b. Your hairstyle
   c. Your college GPA
   d. The jewelry you wear

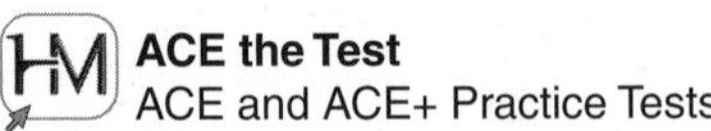

SELECTING YOUR CAREER APPAREL

3 *List and discuss factors that influence your choice of clothing for work.*

Millions of American workers wear a uniform especially designed for a particular job. The judges on the U.S. Supreme Court and the technicians at the local Midas Muffler and Brake shop have one thing in common—both groups wear a special uniform to work. Companies that have initiated extensive career apparel programs rely on uniforms to project an image of consistent quality, good service, and uniqueness.

Enterprise Rent-A-Car, the nation's largest recruiter of college students, requires its 52,000 workers to follow conservative dress and grooming policies. Men, for example, follow twenty-six rules that include no beards (unless medically necessary) and dress shirts with coordinated ties. Female employees follow thirty dress code guidelines, including one for skirt length (skirts must not be shorter than two inches above the knee) and one for mandatory stockings. Why does Enterprise choreograph how its employees look? The company maintains that its personal appearance and grooming standards give it a marketing advantage.[17]

The uniforms worn by United Parcel Service employees, airport screeners, and the employees at your local restaurant might be classified as special-design **career apparel**. In addition to special-design uniforms, there is another type of career apparel, somewhat less predictable, worn by large numbers of people in the labor force. Here are two examples:

career apparel A uniform especially designed for a particular job or clothing prescribed by dress code guidelines.

- A male bank loan officer would be appropriately dressed in a tailored gray or blue suit, white shirt, and tie. This same person dressed in a colorful blazer, sport shirt, and plaid slacks would be seen as too casual in most bank settings.

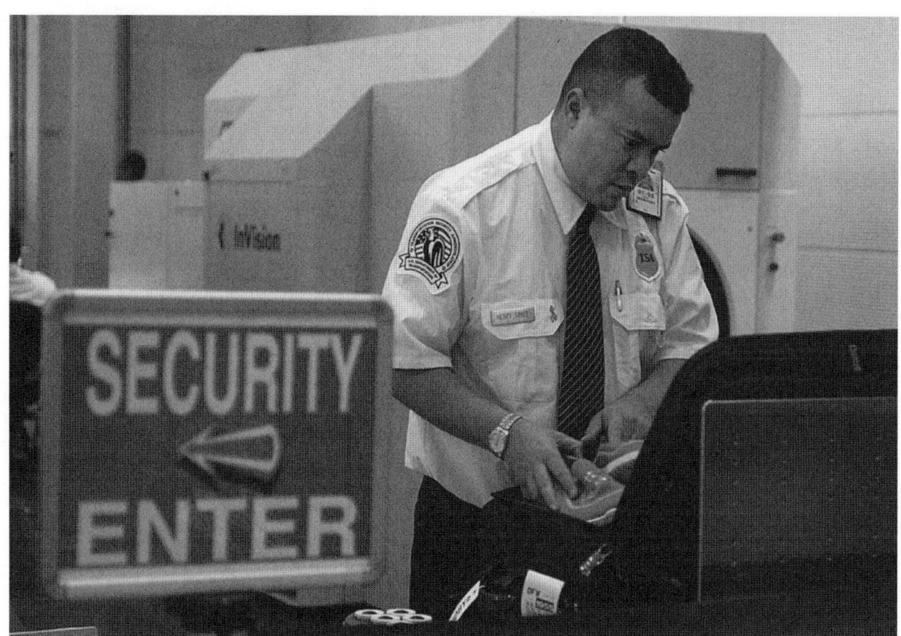

Many American workers wear a uniform that is especially designed for a particular job. This airport security officer wears a uniform that communicates authority. It complements the serious nature of his work.

- A technician employed by an auto dealership that sells new cars would be appropriately dressed in matching gray, tan, or blue shirt and pants. The technician would be inappropriately dressed in jeans and a T-shirt.

Many organizations seek advice about career apparel from image consultants who have received certification from the Association of Image Consultants International (www.aici.org) or Global Protocol, Inc. (www.globalprotocol.com). The demand for etiquette and protocol consultants has increased in recent years.[18]

Wardrobe Engineering

The term **wardrobe engineering** was first used by John Molloy, author of *Dress for Success,* to describe how clothing and accessories can be used to create a certain image. This concept was later refined by several other noted image consultants in hundreds of books and articles on dress and grooming. Although these authors are not in complete agreement on every aspect of dress, they do agree on the four basic points presented in Table 6.1. Use this information as a guide. Although you should consider the dress and grooming standards of others in your field, don't give in to blind conformity. As noted by one consultant, "Effective packaging is an individual matter based on the person's circumstances, age, weight, height, coloring, and objectives."[19]

wardrobe engineering The activity and decision making regarding how clothing and accessories can be used to create a certain image.

The Business Casual Look

The term **business casual** is used to describe the movement toward dress standards that emphasize greater comfort and individuality. Business casual is clothing that allows you to feel comfortable at work but looks neat and professional. It usually means slacks, khaki pants, collared long-sleeved shirts and blouses, and shoes with socks or hosiery. It usually does not include jeans, T-shirts, shorts, sneakers, or sandals.[20]

business casual A dress standard that emphasizes greater comfort and individuality.

HM **Improve Your Grade**
Audio Glossary

TABLE 6.1

Factors Influencing Your Choice of Clothing for Work

Dress codes are undergoing changes, and this complicates the selection of clothing for work. Use the four factors described here for guidance.

1. *Products and services offered.* In some cases the organization's products and services more or less dictate a certain type of dress. For example, a receptionist employed by a well-established law firm is likely to wear clothing that is conservative, modest, and in good taste. These same dress standards would apply to a pharmaceutical sales representative who calls on medical doctors.
2. *Type of person served*. Research indicates that first impressions created by dress and grooming are greatly influenced by unconscious expectations. Throughout life we become acquainted with real estate salespeople, nurses, police officers, and others employed in a wide range of occupations. We form mental images of the apparel common to each of these occupations. When we encounter someone whose appearance does not conform to our past experiences, we often feel uncomfortable.
3. *Desired image projected by the organization.* Some companies establish dress codes that help shape the image they project to the public. Walt Disney Company, for example, maintains a strict dress and grooming code for all its theme-park employees. They are considered "cast members" and must adhere to dress and grooming standards that complement the image projected by Disney theme parks.
4. *Geographic region*. Dress in the South and Southwest tends to be more casual than dress in the Northeast. Climate is another factor that influences the clothing people wear at work.

Some companies are relaxing dress codes and allowing workers to dress casually. Although no precise definition of business casual exists, the following casual dress guidelines are typical.

1. *Wear dressier business clothing when meeting with customers or clients.* You should avoid creating inconsistencies between your message and your appearance. Workers at ProVox Technologies Corporation, based in Roanoke, Virginia, keep company-designed ProVox shirts and khakis in the office for client visits.[21]
2. *Respect the boundary between work and leisure clothing.* Victoria's Secret once sold body-hugging spandex tube tops as workplace wear. Anne Fisher of *Fortune* magazine's "Ask Annie" career advice column says, "As a rule, people should avoid wearing anything that shows so much skin that it distracts other people from their work." How about body piercing, tattoos, orange hair (or other colors not found in nature), three-day stubble, no socks, micro-mini skirts, or rubber flip-flops? In some cases, you will be guided by company policy. At Ford Motor Company, "nonoffensive" tattoos are permitted and body piecing is acceptable if it does not pose safety risks. Subway Restaurants permit "discrete" tattoos, but body piercing is limited to one piercing per ear.[22] Of course, some dress code violations fall into the "unwritten" category. If you wear a nose ring to work, you may be sending the wrong message to the person responsible for your next promotion.
3. *Wear clothing that is clean and neat and that fits well.* Casual dress codes tend to emphasize the importance of this guideline.

Do not let "dress-down" influences rob you of common sense. You don't get a second chance to make a good first impression, so select your casual clothing with care. If you have to ask yourself, "Is this clothing acceptable?" you probably shouldn't wear it to work.

TEST PREPPER 6.3

ANSWERS CAN BE FOUND ON P. 237

True or False?

T 1. As a general rule, people should avoid wearing anything that shows too much skin to work, as it distracts others in the workplace.

F 2. High-end flip-flops and sneakers are now widely accepted as typical business casual wear.

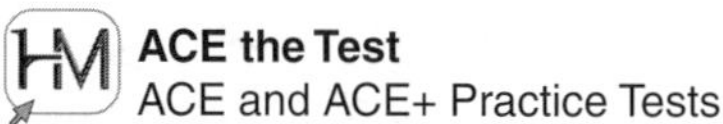

Multiple Choice

b 3. Sara is making an effort to "package" herself so that she will stand out from other job applicants. This process is called:
   a. career development.
   b. wardrobe engineering.
   c. primacy effect awareness.
   d. branding.

b 4. Which of the following items is often a component of business casual attire?
   a. Short-sleeved T-shirt
   b. Khaki slacks
   c. French-cuffed dress shirt
   d. Pantyhose

FACTORS THAT MAKE AN IMPACT

4 *Explain how your facial expression, entrance and carriage, voice, and handshake impact your work image.*

Your Facial Expression

After your overall appearance, your face is the most visible part of you. Facial expressions are the cues most people rely on in initial interactions. They provide the clues by which others read your mood and personality.

Studies conducted in nonverbal communication show that facial expressions strongly influence people's reactions to each other. The expression on your face can quickly trigger a positive or negative reaction from those you meet. How you rate in the "good-looks" department is not nearly as important as your ability to communicate positive impressions with a pleasant smile and eye contact.

If you want to identify the inner feelings of another person, watch the individual's facial expressions closely. A frown may tell you "something is wrong." A pleasant smile generally communicates "things are OK." Everyone has encountered a "look of surprise" or a "look that could kill." These facial expressions usually reflect inner emotions more accurately than words. The smile is the most recognizable signal in the world. People everywhere tend to trust a smiling face.[23]

Your Entrance and Carriage

The way you enter someone's office or a business meeting can influence the image you project, says Susan Bixler. She notes that "your entrance and the way you carry yourself will set the stage for everything that comes afterward."[24] A nervous or apologetic entrance may ruin your chances of getting a job, closing a sale, or getting the raise you have earned. If you feel apprehensive, try not to let it show in your body language. Hold your head up, avoid slumping forward, and try to project self-assurance. To get off to the right start and make a favorable impression, follow these words of advice from Bixler: "The person who has confidence in himself or herself indicates this by a strong stride, a friendly smile, good posture, and a genuine sense of energy. This is a very effective way to set the stage for a productive meeting. When you ask for respect visually, you get it."[25] Bixler says the key to making a successful entrance is simply believing—and projecting—that you have a reason to be there and have something important to present or discuss.

Your Voice Quality and Speech Habits

The tone of your voice, the rate of speed at which you speak (tempo), the volume of your speech, your ability to pronounce words clearly (diction), and your speech habits contribute greatly to the image you project. Consider these real-world examples:

- Regina Tell, court reporter at a liability trial involving Merck & Company's painkiller Vioxx, said the rapid speech patterns of the attorneys was "killing her." She reported that they spoke at a rate of over 300 words a minute, or more than 100 words a minute faster than average people speak.[26]
- Kristy Pinand, a youthful-looking 23-year-old, routinely used "teen speak" when talking to colleagues and clients. Words such as *cool* and *like* were frequently part of her speech pattern. With feedback from her supervisor, she was able to correct the problem.[27]
- A senior project manager at a major financial-services company was surprised when his boss blamed his thick Brooklyn accent for his stalled advancement in the company. Despite his MBA, the project manager was speaking too fast and skipping many consonants. His frequent use of *deeze* and *doze* created the impression that he was poorly educated and inarticulate.[28]

A conscious effort to improve your voice begins with awareness. A tape or video recording of your conversations will help you identify problem areas. If you hear a voice that is too monotone, too nasal, too high-pitched, too weak, too insincere, or too loud, you can target the problem for improvement. With practice and the use of a tape recorder, you can change your voice quality and speech habits.

If you routinely receive requests to repeat yourself, the problem may be your accent, or something as simple as your breathing. You may not be breathing correctly, leaving your words soft and inaudible. If you are looking for professional help, consider working with a voice coach or a speech pathologist. You may also want to join Toastmasters International, a professional organization dedicated to effective personal and public communication.

Your Handshake

When two people first meet, a handshake is usually the only physical contact between them. A handshake is a friendly and professional way to greet someone or to take leave, regardless of gender. The handshake can communicate warmth, genuine concern for the other person, and strength. It can also communicate aloofness, indifference, and weakness. The message you send the other party through your handshake depends on a combination of the following factors:

1. *Degree of firmness.* Generally speaking, a firm (but not viselike) grip communicates a caring attitude, whereas a weak grip communicates indifference.
2. *Degree of dryness of hands.* A moist, clammy palm is unpleasant to feel and can communicate the impression that you are nervous. People who have this problem often remove the moisture with a clean handkerchief.
3. *Duration of grip.* There are no specific guidelines for the ideal duration of a grip. Nevertheless, by extending the handshake just a little, you can often communicate a greater degree of interest in and concern for the other person.
4. *Depth of interlock.* A full, deep grip is more likely to convey friendship to the other person. Position your hand to make complete contact with the other person's hand. Once you have connected, close your thumb over the back of the other person's hand and give a slight squeeze.[29]
5. *Eye contact during handshake.* Visual communication can increase the positive impact of your handshake. Maintaining eye contact throughout the handshaking process is important when two people greet each other.[30]

Most individuals have shaken hands with hundreds of people but have little idea whether they are creating positive or negative impressions. It is a good idea to obtain this information from those coworkers or friends who are willing to provide you with candid feedback. Like all other human relations skills, the handshake can be improved with practice.

Test Prepper 6.4

Answers can be found on p. 237

True or False?

____ 1. As an indication of respect to others, it is important to lower your head upon first meeting business associates.

____ 2. Improving your voice and speech habits begins with an awareness of what you say and how you say it.

Multiple Choice

____ 3. Alan pays particular attention to his facial expression in business settings because he realizes that it is the second most noticeable part of himself, ranking after:

a. voice quality.
b. self-confidence.
c. overall appearance.
d. a handshake.

____ 4. Which of the following items sends a poor message to the recipient of a handshake?

a. A firm (not vicelike) grip
b. Extending the grip of the handshake just a little
c. Making complete contact with the other person's hand
d. Avoiding eye contact during the handshake

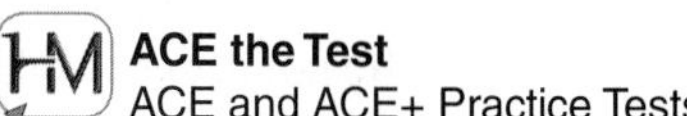

ETIQUETTE FOR A CHANGING WORLD

5 *Understand how manners contribute to improved interpersonal relations in the workplace.*

Why are so many etiquette guides crowding bookstore shelves? And why are many organizations hiring consultants to conduct classes on etiquette guidelines? Well, one reason is that we need advice on how to avoid annoying other people and what to do if they annoy us. In today's fast-paced, often tense, work environment, we have to work a little harder to maintain a climate of fairness, kindness, and mutual respect.[31]

etiquette A set of guidelines or traditions based on kindness, efficiency, and logic.

Etiquette (sometimes called *manners* or *protocol*) is a set of traditions based on kindness, efficiency, and logic.[32] Letitia Baldrige, author and etiquette consultant, says, "It's consideration and kindness and thinking about somebody other than oneself."[33] Sometimes we need new etiquette guidelines to deal with our changing world. Today smoking at work is usually prohibited or restricted to a certain area. Meetings often begin with the announcement "Please silence your cell phones and beepers." And the nearly universal use of e-mail has spawned hundreds of articles on e-mail etiquette (see Chapter 2). A diverse work force has created many new challenges in the area of protocol.

Although it is not possible to do a complete review of the rules of etiquette, we will discuss those that are particularly important in an organizational setting.

Dining Etiquette

Job interviews and business meetings are frequently conducted at breakfast, lunch, or dinner, so be aware of your table manners. To illustrate decisions you might need to make during a business meal, let's eavesdrop on Tom Reed, a job candidate having a meal with several employees of the company he wants to work for. After introductions, the bread is passed to Tom. He places a roll on the small bread-and-butter plate to the right of his dinner plate. Soon, he picks up the roll, takes a bite, and returns it to the plate. Midway through the meal, Tom rises from his chair, places his napkin on the table, and says, "Excuse me; I need to make a potty run." So far, Tom has made four etiquette blunders: The bread-and-butter plate he used belongs to the person seated on his right; his own is to the left of his dinner plate. When eating a roll, he should break off one piece at a time and butter the piece as he is ready to eat it. The napkin should have been placed on his chair, indicating his plan to return. (When departing for good, leave it to the left of your plate.) And finally, the words *potty run* are too casual for a business meal. A simple statement such as, "Please excuse me; I'll be back in just a moment," would be adequate.

There are some additional table manners to keep in mind. Do not begin eating until the people around you have their plates. If you have not been served, however, encourage others to go ahead. To prevent awkward moments during the meal, avoid ordering food that is not easily controlled, such as ribs, spaghetti, chicken with bones, or lobster.

Meeting Etiquette

Business meetings should start and end on time, so recognize the importance of punctuality. Anne Marie Sabath, owner of a firm that provides etiquette training for business employees, says,"We teach people that if you're early, you're on time, and if you're on time, in reality, you're late." Showing up late for any meeting will be viewed as rudeness by coworkers, your boss, and your clients. Do not feel obligated to comment on each item on the agenda. Yes, sometimes silence is golden. In most cases, you should not bring up a topic unless it is related to an agenda item. If you are in charge of the meeting, end it by summarizing key points, reviewing the decisions made, and recapping the responsibilities assigned to individuals during the meeting. Always start and end the meeting on a positive note.[34]

Cell Phone Etiquette

New technologies often bring new annoyances, and the cell phone is no exception. *Cell phone contempt* surfaces in offices, restaurants, houses of worship, and many other places. Cell phone etiquette is based on a few simple guidelines. First, it's not acceptable to use your cell phone at business meetings, in elevators, or at restaurants. If you receive a call at a restaurant, take the call outside the dining area. When making or receiving a call, talk in a normal speaking voice. Too often cell phone users talk louder than normal because they feel the need to compensate for the size of small phones. Try to confine your calls to private areas; it's rude to inflict your conversation on people near you.[35] Finally, if a coworker or friend insists on "staying connected" at all times and you find this behavior annoying, confront the person. However, choose your words carefully. If a coworker takes a call at a meeting, for example, you might say, "When you answer your cell phone it makes the group feel unimportant and as if we don't have your full attention."[36]

Conversational Etiquette

When you establish new relationships, avoid calling people by their first name too soon. Never assume that work-related associates prefer to be addressed informally

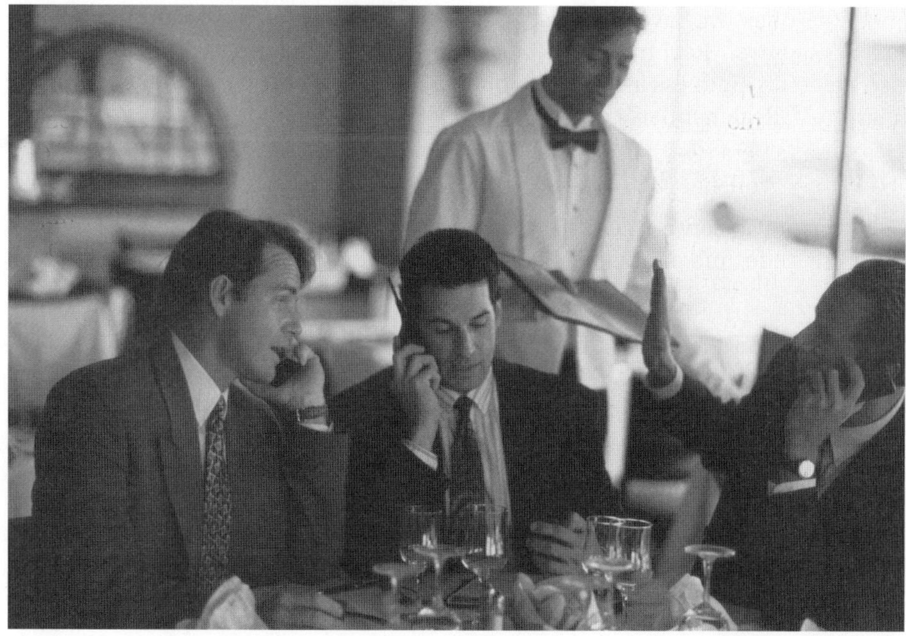

How would you like to be seated next to three people who are talking on their cell phones?If you receive a call at a restaurant, take the call outside the dining area. It's rude to inflict your conversation on people seated near you.

by their first names. Use titles of respect—Ms., Mr., Professor, or Dr.—until the relationship is established. Too much familiarity will irritate some people. When the other person says, "Call me Ruth" or "Call me John," it is alright to begin using the person's first name.

A conversation that includes obscene language can create problems in the workplace. Although the rules about what constitutes profanity have changed over the years, inappropriate use of foul language in front of a customer, a client, or, in many cases, a coworker is a breach of etiquette. An obscenity implies lack of respect for your audience. Also, certain language taboos carry moral and spiritual significance in most cultures. Obscene language is often cited by persons who file sexual harassment charges.[37]

Networking Etiquette

Networking—making contact with people at meetings, social events, or other venues—is an effective job-search method. Networking is also important to salespeople searching for prospects and to professionals (accountants, lawyers, consultants, etc.) who need to build a client base.

When you meet people at an event, tell them your name and what you do. Avoid talking negatively about any aspect of your current job or your life. In some cases you will need to make a date to call or meet with the new contact later. After the event, study your contacts and follow up.

Send a *written* thank-you note if someone has been helpful to you or generous with his or her time. You might also consider sending a newspaper or magazine article as an "information brief," since one goal of networking is information exchange.[38]

We have given you a brief introduction to several areas of etiquette. This information will be extremely helpful as you develop a strong personal brand. Remember that good etiquette is based on consideration for the other person. If you genuinely respect other people, you will have an easier time developing your personal approach to business manners. You will probably also agree with most of the etiquette "rules" we have been discussing. Nancy Austin, coauthor of *A Passion for Excellence*, says, "Real manners—a keen interest in and a regard for somebody else, a certain kindness and at-ease quality that add real value—can't be faked or finessed."[39] Real manners come from the heart.

Incivility—The Ultimate Career Killer

Civility in our society is under siege. In recent years we have witnessed an increase in coarse, rude, and obnoxious behavior. Unfortunately, some of the most outra-

TOTAL PERSON INSIGHT

Judith Martin Author

"In a society as ridden as ours with expensive status symbols, where every purchase is considered a social statement, there is no easier or cheaper way to distinguish oneself than by the practice of gentle manners."

geous behavior by athletes, coaches, politicians, and business leaders has been rewarded with wealth and influence.

As noted in Chapter 1, civility is the sum of the many sacrifices we are called upon to make for the sake of living together. At work, it may involve refilling the copier paper tray after using the machine or making a new pot of coffee after you take the last cup. It may mean turning down your radio so workers nearby are not disturbed or sending a thank-you note to someone who has helped you complete a difficult project. Small gestures, such as saying "Please" and "Thank you" or opening doors for others, make ourselves and others more content. Learning to discipline your passions so as to avoid obnoxious behavior will demonstrate also your maturity and self-control.

TEST PREPPER 6.5

ANSWERS CAN BE FOUND ON P. 237

True or False?

F 1. Meeting etiquette requires that you display interest by commenting on each meeting agenda item.

F 2. It is perfectly acceptable to use your cell phone in an elevator or a restaurant.

Multiple Choice

C 3. Conversational etiquette dictates that:
   a. work-related associates prefer to be addressed informally by their first name.
   b. professionals such as medical doctors should never be addressed by their first name.
   c. we should use titles of respect—Ms., Miss, Mr., Professor, or Dr.—until the relationship is established.
   d. informality is the key to developing rapport.

b 4. Workplace etiquette is more important now than ever because of:
   a. gender differences.
   b. greater diversity in the workplace.
   c. health and wellness concerns.
   d. increased substitution of virtual contact for face-to-face encounters.

a 5. Which one of the following actions displays poor dining etiquette?
   a. Placing your napkin on the table when excusing yourself to go to the restroom
   b. Using the bread-and-butter plate to the left of your dinner plate
   c. Waiting to eat until everyone has been served
   d. Breaking off a piece of a roll and buttering the piece before eating it

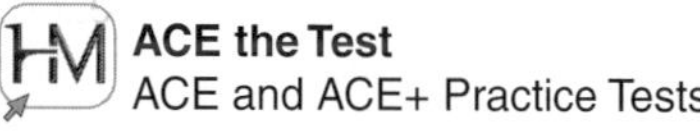

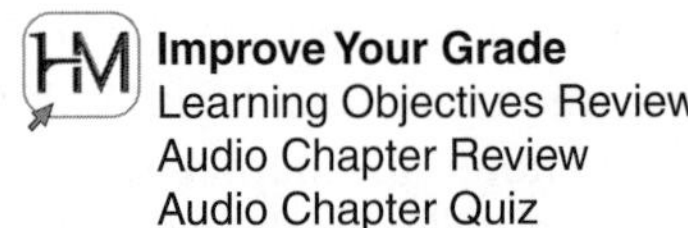

LEARNING OBJECTIVES REVIEW

1 *Explain the importance of professional presence and discuss the factors that contribute to a favorable first impression.*

- Professional presence is a dynamic blend of poise, self-confidence, control, and style. Once acquired, it permits you to be perceived as self-assured and competent.
- People tend to form impressions of others quickly at the time they first meet them (primacy effect), and these first impressions tend to be preserved.
- The impression you form of another person during the initial contact is made up of assumptions and facts. Assumptions are often based on perceptions of surface language—the pattern of immediate impressions conveyed by appearance.

2 *Define* image *and describe the factors that form the image you project to others.*

- *Image* is a term used to describe how other people feel about you. In every business or social setting, your behaviors and appearance communicate a picture that others observe and remember.
- Image is formed by a variety of factors:
  - manners
  - self-confidence
  - voice quality
  - versatility
  - integrity
  - entrance and carriage
  - facial expression
  - surface language
  - competence
  - positive attitude
  - handshake

3 *List and discuss factors that influence your choice of clothing for work.*

- Image consultants contend that discrimination on the basis of appearance is a fact of life. Clothing is an important part of the image you communicate to others.
- Four factors tend to influence your choice of clothing for work:
  - (1) the products or services offered by the organization
  - (2) the type of person served
  - (3) the desired image projected by the organization
  - (4) the region where you work.

4 *Explain how your facial expression, entrance and carriage, voice, and handshake impact your work image.*

- Beyond your clothing choices, many physical factors can influence your workplace image.
  - Facial expressions strongly influence people's reactions to each other.
  - People with confidence, a strong stride, a friendly smile, and great energy carry themselves well.
  - Tone of voice, tempo, volume, diction, and habits all contribute to your image. Any of these can make an unfavorable impression if not delivered correctly.
  - A handshake can communicate warmth, concern, and strength if done correctly, and aloofness, indifference, and weakness when it is not.

5 *Understand how manners contribute to improved interpersonal relations in the workplace.*

- Manners, sometimes called etiquette or protocol, are traditions based on kindness, efficiency, and logic.
- Dining, meeting, cell phone, conversational, and networking etiquette are all important in the workplace.

CAREER CORNER

Q: In the near future I will begin my job search, and I want to work for a company that will respect my individuality. Some companies are enforcing strict dress and grooming codes and other policies that, in my opinion, infringe on the rights of their employees. How far can an employer go in dictating my lifestyle?

A: This is a good question, but one for which there is no easy answer. For example, most people feel they have a right to wear the fragrance of their choice, but many fragrances contain allergy-producing ingredients. In some employment settings, you will find "non-fragrance" zones. Secondhand smoke is another major issue in the workplace because most research indicates that it can be harmful to the health of workers. Rules regarding body piercings, hair length, and the type of clothing that can be worn to work have also caused controversy. There is no doubt that many companies are trying to find a balance between their interests and the rights of workers. Enterprise Rent-A-Car has placed restrictions on the length of an employee's hair and established over twenty-five dress code guidelines for its employees. The company believes employee appearance is crucial to its success. The best advice I can give you is to become familiar with the employer's expectations *before* you accept a job. The company has a responsibility to explain its personnel policies to prospective employees, but sometimes this information is not covered until after a person is hired.

APPLYING WHAT YOU HAVE LEARNED

HM **Improve Your Grade**
Internet Insights

1. Many people complain that interrupting has become a major annoyance. You begin speaking and someone finishes your sentence. Marilyn Vos Savant, author of the "Ask Marilyn" column, recommends a technique that can stop interrupters. When someone interrupts you, stop speaking abruptly and say "What?" This will highlight the interruption, and the person who interrupts you will be forced to repeat himself or herself too, which is an unpleasant experience. Repeat this method, if necessary, until the offender lets you complete your sentences. Marilyn Vos Savant says you should save this method for *chronic* interrupters.[40]
2. You have assumed the duties of sales manager at a new Lexus automobile dealership that is scheduled to open in three weeks. You will hire and train all salespeople. What types of career apparel would you recommend to members of your sales team? What grooming standards would you recommend?
3. The first step toward improving your voice is to hear yourself as others do. Listen to several recordings of your voice on a dictation machine, tape recorder, or VCR, and then complete the following rating in the box below. Place a checkmark in the appropriate space for each quality.

Quality	Major Strength	Strength	Weakness	Major Weakness
Projects confidence	______	______	______	______
Projects enthusiasm	______	______	______	______
Speaking rate is not too fast or too slow	______	______	______	______
Projects optimism	______	______	______	______
Voice is not too loud or too soft	______	______	______	______
Projects sincerity	______	______	______	______

Improve Your Grade
Self-Assessment Exercise

ROLE-PLAY EXERCISE

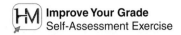

After spending eight years working for a well-established kitchen design firm, you established your own company. Whitehall Design Kitchens is the area's premier kitchen design studio. You have partnered with the industry's finest artisans and suppliers and can offer exotic veneers, gourmet appliances, unique hand carvings, and modern cabinetry to people who want their kitchen to be an extension of their image and lifestyle. You cater to an upscale clientele who appreciate quality, beauty, and fine craftsmanship. At the present time you employ five design consultants. The newest member of your design team, Dera Corian, is a talented designer who recently completed the Certified Kitchen Design (CKD) professional designation. She has excellent design skills, but often she does not project the upscale image of Whitehall Design Kitchens. Although she is well paid, Dera likes to shop at discount clothing stores, always searching for a great bargain. Very often her clothing and accessories communicate a "thrift store" image that clashes with the upscale image of Whitehall Design Kitchens. You have decided to meet with Dera and try to encourage her to adopt a wardrobe that is more appropriate for the clientele she serves. You will meet with another class member who will assume the role of Dera Corian.

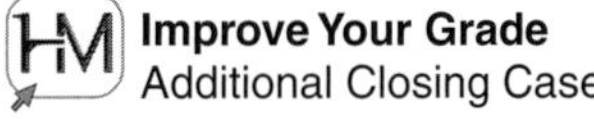

CASE 6.1

Do You Want to Be Your Own Brand?

About twenty years ago Toyota Motor Company decided to develop a line of luxury automobiles that would compete with Mercedes-Benz, BMW, Cadillac, and Lincoln. After several years of research and development, the Lexus brand was born. Today, Lexus cars are recognized by automobile writers and consumers as the best mass-produced luxury cars. They stand for quality.

Branding, a concept that has been used in the field of marketing for over fifty years, has recently surfaced as a personal development strategy. Using the principles of successful brand development, many people are positioning themselves to stand for something—to say something important about themselves that will affect how others perceive them. The authors of *Be Your Own Brand* note that the concept of brand in business has a well-defined meaning: "A brand is a perception or emotion, maintained by a buyer or a prospective buyer, describing the experience related to doing business with an organization or consuming its products or services."[41] In a personal context, you can think of it this way: "Your brand is a perception or emotion, maintained by somebody other than you, that describes the total experience of having a relationship with you."[42]

The key to understanding the concept of personal and business branding is understanding the nature and needs of a relationship. L. L. Bean has become a major force in outdoor and casual clothing by implementing business practices that build customer loyalty and repeat business. In addition to selling quality products, this company works hard to build a trusting relationship with its customers.

Personal brand development begins with self-management practices that help you create and strengthen relationships with other people. Early in his career, Jerry Seinfeld decided he would never use profanity in his comedy routines. This personal decision forced him to use more creativity, and he became a stronger comedian. Jeff Bezos, founder of Amazon.com, recalls an early life experience that changed the way he viewed relationships. He made a comment to his grandmother that hurt her feelings. Later his grandfather met with him privately and said, "You'll learn one day that it's much harder to be kind than clever."[43] This insight has helped Bezos in his professional life.

To develop a distinctive brand that will help you in your interactions with others may require making some changes in your life. To become distinctive, you must stand for something. What you stand for relates to your values. Thus a strong personal brand is generally built from the inside out. But to some extent you can also decide what type of image you want these values to project. This may require changes in your manners, dress, voice quality, facial expression, posture, or behaviors that reflect your integrity.

Questions

1. Given this brief introduction to brand development, would you consider taking steps to develop a distinctive personal brand? Explain your answer.
2. Experts in personal brand development say that employees should align their values with their employer's values. Do you agree with this recommendation?
3. Association of Image Consultants International says its members help clients achieve authenticity, credibility, and self-confidence. Would you consider hiring a personal consultant to help you grow in these areas? Explain.
4. If you decide to develop a personal brand, what changes will you make in your life?

RESOURCES ON THE WEB

Prepare for Class, Improve Your Grade, and ACE the Test. Student Achievement Series resources include:

- ACE and ACE+ Practice Tests
- Audio Chapter Quizzes
- Audio Chapter Reviews
- Learning Objective Reviews
- Career Snapshots
- Chapter Glossaries
- Chapter Outlines
- Crossword Puzzles
- Hangman Games
- Flashcards
- Audio Glossaries
- Internet Insights
- Self-Assessment Exercises
- Additional Closing Cases

To access these learning and study tools, go to **college.hmco.com/pic/reeceSAS**.

HM ManagementSPACE

7 Valuing Work Force Diversity

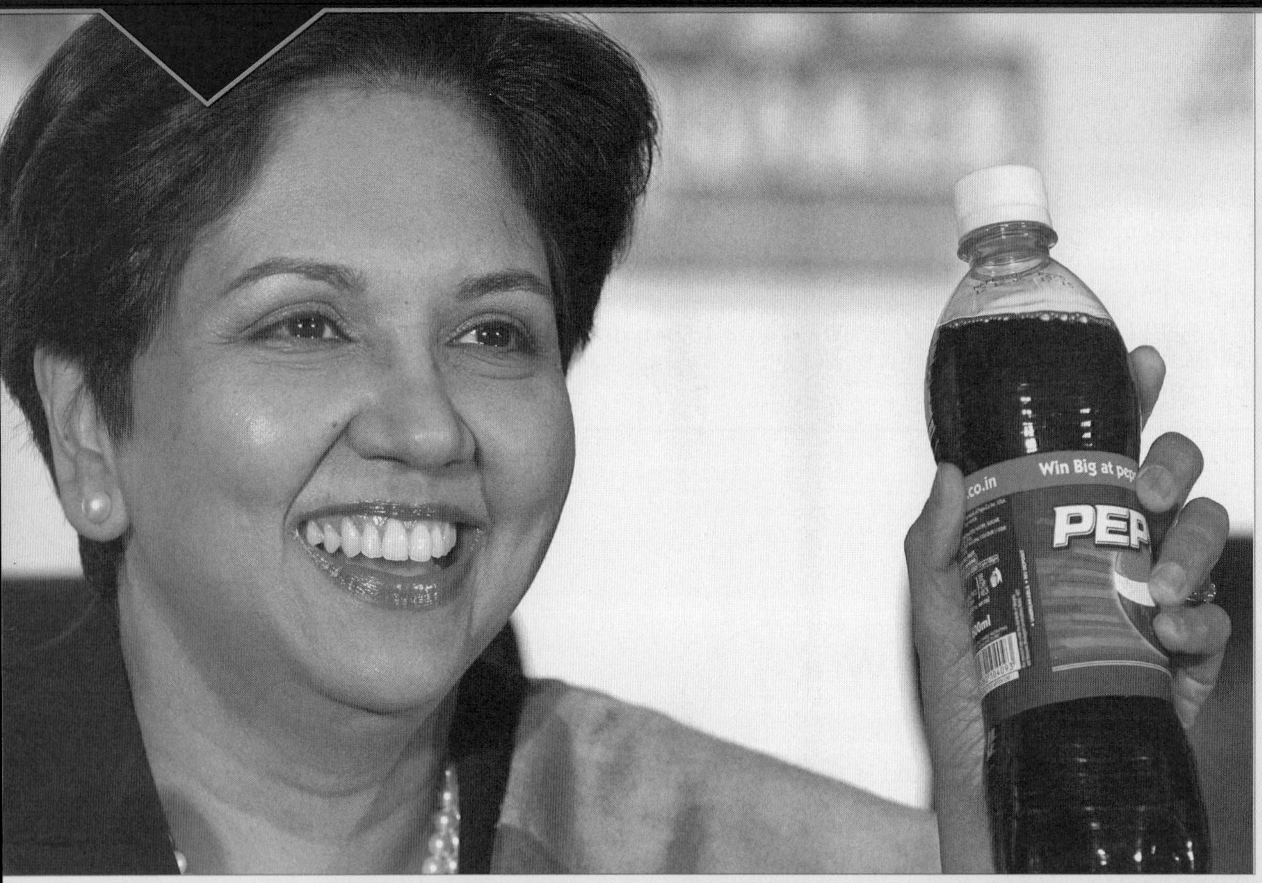

PepsiCo Incorporated used to have a reputation as a mostly white male fraternity, but things have changed. Indra K. Noogi, Chief Executive Officer of PepsiCo, is a strong leader in the area of corporate diversity. Several of PepsiCo's top officers are minorities.

1 *Define the primary and secondary dimensions of diversity.*

2 *Explain how prejudiced attitudes are formed.*

3 *Develop an awareness of the various forms of discrimination in the workplace.*

4 *Understand why organizations are striving to develop organizational cultures that value diversity.*

"No matter who you are, you're going to have to work with people who are different from you."

—J. T. "Ted" Childs, Jr.

Chapter Outline

Prepare for Class
Chapter Outline

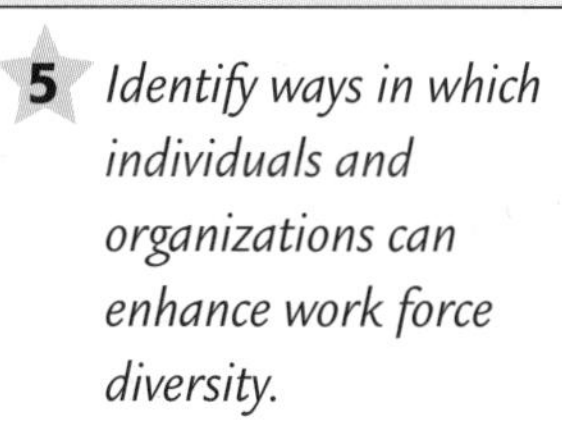

5 *Identify ways in which individuals and organizations can enhance work force diversity.*

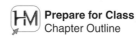

6 *Explain the current status of affirmative action programs.*

A Mixed Bag

A growing number of companies realize that they need a work force that reflects the changing demographics of their customers. Diversity is not simply a matter of doing the right thing; it is a business imperative. PepsiCo Incorporated used to have a reputation as a mostly white-male fraternity, but things have changed. People of color now hold 17 percent of the management jobs at midlevel and above, and women hold nearly 30 percent. Indra K. Noogi, CEO of PepsiCo, is leading the diversity initiative.

KEY TERMS

Prepare for Class
Chapter Glossary

Improve Your Grade
Flashcards
Hangman
Crossword Puzzle

She believes that diversity promotes innovation and better decision making. New products inspired by employees include a wasabi-flavored snack aimed at Asian Americans, guacamole-flavored Doritos chips aimed at Hispanics, and Mountain Dew Code Red, which appeals to African Americans.[1]

Harley-Davidson, the Milwaukee-based motorcycle maker, concluded many years ago that its sales would falter unless it expanded beyond its traditional white male customers. To attract people of color and women, the company needed employees who reflected the customer base they wanted to attract. Over the past decade, Harley-Davidson has worked hard to attract both women and minority managers.[2]

WORK FORCE DIVERSITY

1 *Define the primary and secondary dimensions of diversity.*

America has always served as host to a kaleidoscope of the world's cultures, and the diversity movement is likely to continue. Growing minority and immigrant populations will contribute to increased racial and ethnic diversity. The American work force is becoming more racially and ethnically diverse, increasingly female, and increasingly older.[3] Foreign-born population trends are presented in Figure 7.1.

In the past, most U.S. organizations attempted to assimilate everyone into one "American" way of doing things. Labor unions were formed so that everyone would be treated the same. The women's rights movement began when women wanted to be treated just like men in the workplace. The emphasis now, however, is on **valuing diversity**, which means appreciating everyone's uniqueness, respecting dif-

valuing diversity A business imperative that recognizes the importance of a work force that reflects the demographics of customers.

FIGURE 7.1

Foreign-Born Population Trend

Source: Reprinted from the April 24, 2000, issue of *BusinessWeek* by special permission, copyright © 2000 by The McGraw-Hill Companies, Inc.

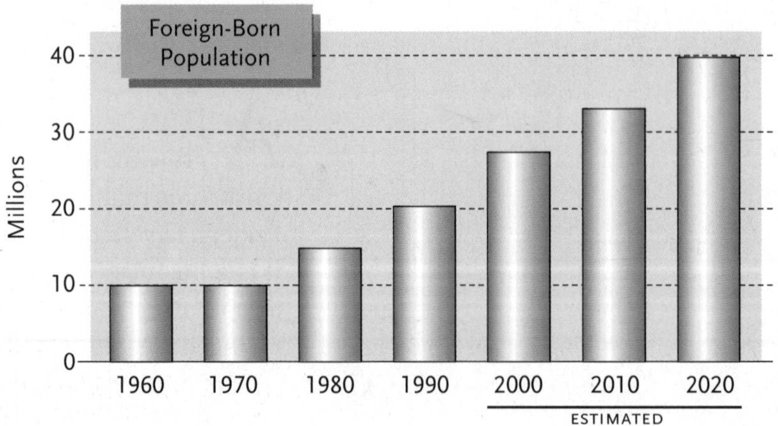

FIGURE 7.2

Primary and Secondary Dimensions of Diversity

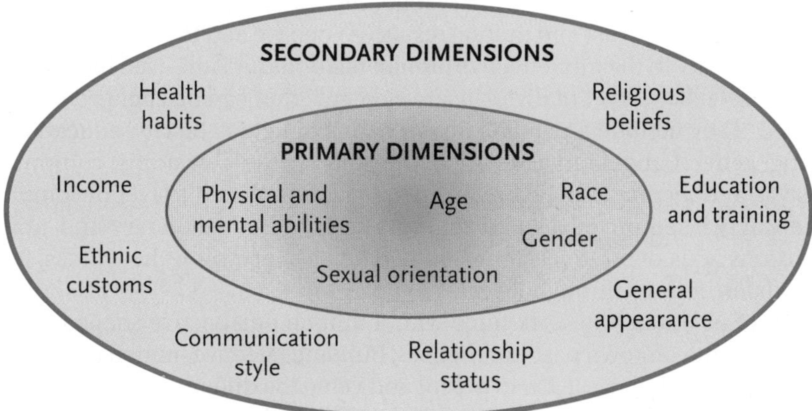

ferences, and encouraging every worker to make his or her full contribution to the organization. Organizations that foster the full participation of all workers will enjoy the sharpest competitive edge in the expanding global marketplace.

Dimensions of Diversity

There are primary and secondary dimensions of diversity. The **primary dimensions** are core characteristics of each individual: age, race, gender, physical and mental abilities, and sexual orientation (see Figure 7.2). Together they form an individual's self-image and the filters through which each person views the rest of the world. These inborn elements are interdependent; no one dimension stands alone. Each exerts an important influence throughout life. Marilyn Loden and Judy Rosener

primary dimensions Inherited characteristics, such as physical and mental abilities, age, race, gender, and sexual orientation.

Eastman Kodak Company has worked hard to increase minority representation at all levels. The company realizes that fostering diversity in their workplace in an important business practice.

describe individual primary dimensions in their book *Workforce America!* They say, "Like the interlocking segments of a sphere, they represent the core of our individual identities."[4]

The greater the number of primary differences between people, the more difficult it is to establish trust and mutual respect. When we add the secondary dimensions of diversity to the mix, effective human relations become even more difficult. The **secondary dimensions** of diversity are elements that can be changed or at least modified. They include a person's health habits, religious beliefs, education and training, general appearance, relationship status, ethnic customs, communication style, and income (see Figure 7.2). These factors all add a layer of complexity to the way we see ourselves and others. The blend of secondary and primary dimensions adds depth to each person and helps shape his or her values, priorities, and perceptions throughout life.[5]

secondary dimensions Characteristics that are not inherited, such as health habits, religious beliefs, income, ethnic customs, communication style, relationship status, general appearance, education, and training.

Each of us enters the work force with a unique perspective shaped by these dimensions and our own past experiences. Building effective human relationships is possible only when we learn to accept and value the differences in others. Without this acceptance, both primary and secondary dimensions of diversity can become roadblocks to further cooperation and understanding.

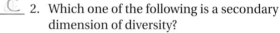

TEST PREPPER 7.1

ANSWERS CAN BE FOUND ON P. 237

Multiple Choice

___ 1. Concerning diversity, current trends in U.S. organizations include:
   a. valuing diversity by appreciating individual uniqueness and differences.
   b. continuing past strategies of assimilating people with differences.
   c. ignoring civil rights laws.
   d. excluding people whose race, gender, or culture differs significantly from that of the organizations' managers.

___ 2. Which one of the following is a secondary dimension of diversity?
   a. Age
   b. Race
   c. General appearance
   d. Gender

___ 3. Which one of the following is a primary dimension of diversity?
   a. Mental abilities
   b. Religious beliefs
   c. Education
   d. Relationship status

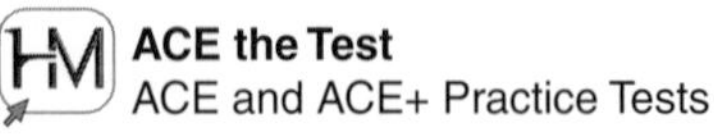

ACE the Test
ACE and ACE+ Practice Tests

PREJUDICED ATTITUDES

2 *Explain how prejudiced attitudes are formed.*

prejudice A premature judgment or opinion that is formed without examination of the facts.

stereotypes Perceptions, beliefs, and expectations about members of some group.

Improve Your Grade
Audio Glossary

Prejudice is a premature judgment or opinion that is formed without examination of the facts. Throughout life we often prejudge people in light of their primary and secondary dimensions. Rather than treat others as unique individuals, prejudiced people tend to think in terms of **stereotypes**—perceptions, beliefs, and expectations about members of some group. In most cases, a stereotype involves the false assumption that all members of a group share the same characteristics.

TOTAL PERSON INSIGHT

J. T. "Ted" Childs, Jr. Vice President, **IBM Global Workforce Diversity**

"No matter who you are, you're going to have to work with people who are different from you. You're going to have to sell to people who are different from you, and buy from people who are different from you, and manage people who are different from you."

The most common and powerful stereotypes focus on observable personal attributes such as age, gender, and ethnicity.[6]

Prejudiced attitudes and the resulting stereotypes are more likely to change when we take time to learn more about specific members of a particular group. For example, twenty years ago, women were often viewed as indecisive, passive, and too emotional to succeed in leadership positions. As the work force became increasingly female, men and women began working together and learning that leadership ability might *not* be gender-related. Now that women occupy a greater proportion of management and executive positions, stereotypes formed by prejudiced attitudes are contradicted by facts.

How Prejudicial Attitudes Are Formed and Retained

Three major factors contribute to the development of prejudice: childhood experiences, ethnocentrism, and economic conditions.

Childhood Experiences

Today's views toward others are filtered through the experiences and feelings of childhood. Children watch how their family members, friends, teachers, and other authority figures respond to different racial, ethnic, and religious groups. As a result, they form attitudes that may last a lifetime, unless new information replaces the old perceptions. Prejudicial attitudes are not unalterable. Whatever prejudice is learned during childhood can be unlearned later in life.[7] The Declaration of Tolerance (see Figure 7.3) provides helpful suggestions on ways to avoid developing prejudicial attitudes.

Ethnocentrism

The tendency to regard our own culture or nation as better or more "correct" than others is called **ethnocentrism**. The word is derived from *ethnic,* meaning a group united by similar customs, characteristics, race, or other common factors, and *center.* **Ethnicity** refers to the condition of being culturally rather than physically distinctive.[8] When ethnocentrism is present, the standards and values of our own culture are being used as a yardstick to measure the worth of other cultures.

ethnocentrism The tendency to regard one's own culture or nation as better or more "correct" than others.

ethnicity The condition of being culturally rather than physically distinctive.

Improve Your Grade
Audio Glossary

In their book *Valuing Diversity,* Lewis Brown Griggs and Lente-Louise Louw compare ethnocentrism in an organization to icebergs floating in an ocean. We can see the tips of icebergs above the water level, just as we can see our diverse coworkers' skin color, gender, mannerisms, and job-related talents and hear the words they use and their accents. These are basically "surface" aspects of a person that others can easily learn through observation. However, just as the enormous breadth of an iceberg's base lies beneath the water's surface, so does the childhood

FIGURE 7.3

Declaration of Tolerance

Source: Adapted from "101 Tools For Tolerance: Simple Ideas for Promoting Equity and Celebrating Diversity." Copyright © 2000, Southern Poverty Law Center, Montgomery, Alabama. *101 Tools for Tolerance* is available free from the SPLC. For more information, visit *www.splcenter.org* or send a fax to (334) 264-7310. Reprinted by permission of Southern Poverty Law Center.

Declaration of Tolerance

Tolerance is a personal decision that comes from a belief that every person is a treasure. I believe that America's diversity is its strength. I also recognize that ignorance, insensitivity, and bigotry can turn that diversity into a source of prejudice and discrimination.

To help keep diversity a well-spring of strength and make this country a better place for all, I pledge to have respect for people whose abilities, beliefs, cultures, race, sexual identity, or other characteristics are different from my own.

To fulfill this pledge, I will . . .

- examine my own biases and work to overcome them,
- set a positive example for my family and friends,
- work for tolerance in my own community, and
- speak out against hate and injustice.

____

Signature

Please sign and mail a copy to:
National Campaign for Tolerance,
400 Washington Avenue
Montgomery, AL 36104.

conditioning of people from different cultures. As icebergs increase in number and drift too close together, they are likely to clash at their base even though there is no visible contact at the water's surface.[9] As organizations increase the diversity of their work force, the potential for clashes resulting from deep-seated cultural conditioning and prejudiced attitudes also increases.

Economic Factors

When the economy goes through a recession or depression, and housing, jobs, and other necessities become scarce, people's prejudices against other groups often increase. If enough prejudice is built up against a particular group, members of that group may be barred from competing for jobs. The recent backlash against immigrants can be traced, in part, to a fear that the new arrivals will take jobs that would otherwise be available to American workers. Prejudice based on economic factors has its roots in people's basic survival needs, and, as a result, it is very hard to eliminate.

Rising income and wealth inequality in America is viewed by many as a serious barrier to racial harmony. Ronald Walters, University of Maryland political scien-

TOTAL PERSON INSIGHT

Sherlyn Chew Creator, **The Purple Bamboo Orchestra**

"To bring Chinese music to an African American church, it means that when we leave Chinatown we are promoting our culture. If we stay in Chinatown, we're only preserving it. If you're going to promote cultural understanding, it has to be to all people of all walks of life."

tist, says, "You can only have meaningful racial reconciliation when people of roughly equal socioeconomic status can reach across the divide of race."[10] The gap in well-being between whites and nonwhites barely changed throughout the booming 1990s and remains huge. The racial divide in wealth (value of all assets) and income shows no sign of narrowing.[11]

TEST PREPPER 7.2

ANSWERS CAN BE FOUND ON P. 237

True or False?

T 1. In most cases stereotypes involve the false assumption that all members of a group share the same characteristics.

F 2. The most powerful stereotypes focus on characteristics such as education and mental ability.

F 3. People's prejudices toward one another tend to increase during times of economic prosperity.

T 4. Clashes related to ethnocentrism are more likely to arise in a workplace with increased diversity.

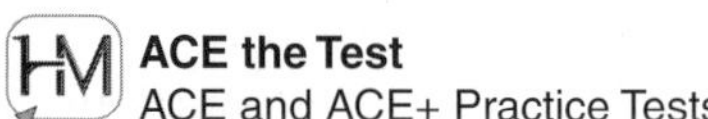

ACE the Test
ACE and ACE+ Practice Tests

Multiple Choice

b 5. Throughout the 1990s, the difference between U.S. whites and nonwhites in terms of economic well-being:

a. narrowed considerably because of the gains of nonwhites in a booming economy.
b. stayed about the same, with whites significantly better off than nonwhites.
c. became the largest in the nation's history.
d. stayed about the same, although the difference was much smaller than during the 1980s because of strict enforcement of employment discrimination laws.

THE MANY FORMS OF DISCRIMINATION

3 *Develop an awareness of the various forms of discrimination in the workplace.*

Discrimination is behavior based on prejudiced attitudes. If, as an employer, you believe that overweight people tend to be lazy, that is a prejudiced attitude. If you refuse to hire someone simply because that person is overweight, you are engaging in discrimination.

discrimination Behavior based on prejudiced attitudes, such as refusing to hire someone simply because that person is overweight.

Individuals or groups that are discriminated against are denied equal treatment and opportunities afforded to the dominant group. They may be denied

Improve Your Grade
Audio Glossary

employment, promotion, training, or other job-related privileges on the basis of race, lifestyle, gender, or other characteristics that have little or nothing to do with their qualifications for a job.

Gender

Discrimination based on gender has been, and continues to be, the focus of much attention. The traditional roles women have held in society have undergone tremendous changes in the past few decades. Women enter the work force not only to supplement family income but also to pursue careers in previously all-male professions. Men have also been examining the roles assigned them by society and are discovering new options for themselves. Most companies have recognized that discrimination based on gender is a reality and are taking steps to deal with the problem.

Age

Oscar winner Paul Newman climbs into a race car every chance he gets, even though he is in his 80s. He was proud to be codriver of one of the cars that competed in the 2005 Rolex 24-hour endurance race held at Daytona International Speedway.[12] The people who make up today's work force are working longer and living longer. Meaningful employment is a source of well-being for many of these workers. Yet, many workers over 50 face discrimination based on age.

There is the widespread perception that older workers are unable or unwilling to adapt to accelerating change.[13] This stereotypical notion exists in spite of studies indicating that workers 55 and over are productive, cost-effective employees who can be trained in new technologies as easily as younger people. Because of prejudice, workers over 50 take nearly twice as long to find a new job as do younger people.[14] Many must accept positions that pay considerably less than their previous job.

According to recent reports from the Equal Employment Opportunity Commission (EEOC), age discrimination is on the rise. As companies search for ways to cut costs, they often find creative ways to get rid of older workers (see Table 7.1) and replace them with younger workers who earn less. The rise in age discrimina-

TABLE 7.1

Age-Related Discriminatory Practices

Many organizations have fostered cultures of age bias. This bias is expressed in a variety of age-related discriminatory practices:

- Cutting off older workers from job-related training and career development opportunities
- Excluding older workers from important activities
- Favoring younger job applicants over older, better-qualified candidates
- Forcing older workers out of the work force with negative performance evaluations
- Pressuring older workers to accept financial incentives and retire early

Source: Sheldon Steinhauser, "Age Bias: Is Your Corporate Culture in Need of an Overhaul?" *HRMagazine*, July 1998.

tion complaints is also due to our aging work force. By 2015, workers 55 and older will make up nearly 20 percent of the work force.[15]

Some companies have discovered that employees in their 50s and 60s have valuable knowledge and experience and are taking steps to retain these older workers. They realize the value of senior staff members passing along "institutional memory," giving the new generation of employees the advantage of learning from the past so that they can effectively direct the future of the organization. Often those who are nearing retirement serve as mentors who can offer guidance and advice unclouded by personal ambition.[16] Many progressive companies are taking steps to retain older workers. These retention tools include phased retirement, portable jobs for people who want to live in warmer climates in the winter, and part-time projects for retirees.[17]

- At Home Depot, older employees serve as a powerful draw to young shoppers needing help with home improvement projects.
- West Pac Banking Corporation, a large financial-services company, recently recruited 950 workers over age 45 as financial planners. Older clients prefer advisers with experience.

Race

Few areas are more sensitive and engender more passion than issues surrounding race. **Race** denotes a category of people who are perceived as distinctive on the basis of certain biologically inherited traits such as skin color or hair texture.[18] Because people cannot change these inherited traits, they can easily become victims of discrimination.

race A category of people who are perceived as distinctive on the basis of certain biologically inherited traits such as skin color or hair texture.

Throughout American history we have seen attempts to place people in racial categories and judge them as racial symbols rather than as unique individuals. During World War II, many Japanese Americans of Japanese ancestry were confined in concentration camps because they were considered a security threat, merely because of their racial heritage. Until the mid-1960s, some African Americans were not allowed to drink from public water fountains, to sit anywhere but in the rear of public transportation, or to attend public schools established for white children only. Because of the war on terrorism, today's "racial" targets often include immigrants from Pakistan, Iraq, and other Middle Eastern countries, as well as their American-born children.

The Myth of Race

Critics of racial categories view them as social inventions that intensify and reinforce racist beliefs and actions. They believe that one way to break down racial barriers and promote a race-free consciousness is to get rid of traditional racial categories (see Table 7.2). A growing number of geneticists and social scientists reject the view that "racial" differences have an objective or scientific foundation.[19] The American Anthropological Association (AAA) has taken the official position that "race" has no scientific justification in human biology. The AAA position is that "there is as much genetic variability between two people from the same 'racial group' as there is between two people from any two different 'racial' groups."[20]

It is important to keep in mind that some race categories include people who vary greatly in terms of ethnicity. The Asian label includes a wide range of groups, such as Vietnamese, Filipinos, Chinese, and Koreans, with distinct histories and languages. The label *African American* does not take into consideration the enormous linguistic, physical, and cultural diversity of the peoples of Africa.[21]

Since interracial relationships are now much more common than they were before, millions of Americans are of mixed races that do not fit the usual general categories. Golf champion Tiger Woods (his father is African American and his mother is from Thailand) is proud of his multiracial background. He joins a growing number of Americans who believe that identities can evolve, that people needn't be locked into the identities bestowed on them at birth. As a result, respondents to U.S. census forms are now provided the opportunity to check one or more boxes from sixty-three racial options.[22]

Race as Social Identity

Although races are not scientifically defensible, they are "real" socially, politically, and psychologically. Race and racism affect our own self-perception and how we are treated by others. Groups that are working to build ethnic pride, such as Native

TABLE 7.2

Traditional Nonwhite Race Categories

African American	Persons who descended from peoples of African origin. The term *Black* is often used to describe persons of African ancestry.
Hispanic	This is the broadest term used to encompass Spanish-speaking peoples in both American hemispheres. The widely used term *Latino* is generally restricted to persons of Latin American descent.
Asian	The term *Asian* is preferred over *Oriental* for persons of East, Southeast, and South Asian ancestry, such as Chinese, Koreans, Japanese, Indonesians, and Filipinos.
Native American	This term refers to peoples indigenous to America. However, the term *Indian* is sometimes used as a term of pride and respect by Native Americans.

Source: American Heritage Dictionary, 4th ed. (Boston: Houghton Mifflin, 2000), pp. 105, 189–190, 832, 1171.

Americans, oppose efforts to get rid of the traditional racial categories, which they consider part of a positive identity. Many feel that this system of racial categories is necessary to create minority-voting districts and to administer an array of federal laws and programs designed to ensure that minorities get equal housing, education, health care, and employment opportunities.[23] That is why the federal government has assured the public that the agencies responsible for enforcement of nondiscriminatory housing laws, employment laws, and so forth will break down the many census report categories in ways that allow them to enforce the current laws.

Joshua Hochschild had to leave his assistant professorship at Wheaton College after he converted to Catholicism. Wheaton College is an evangelical Protestant college based in Wheaton, Illinois.

Religion

Discrimination based on a person's religious preference has been an issue throughout history. Christianity is the most commonly practiced religion in the United Sates, and Judaism is the second.[24] During the 1930s, however, many Christian Americans considered Jews a separate "race" and treated them accordingly. Religion has always had the power to fracture and divide people of faith. Members of various denominations often lack tolerance for beliefs that differ from their own.

Wheaton College, an evangelical Protestant college in Illinois, was very pleased to have Assistant Professor Joshua Hochschild teach students about medieval Roman Catholic thinkers. But when the popular teacher converted to Catholicism, the college fired him. Associate Professor Susan Anderson of Appalachian State University was a faculty candidate at Baylor University several years ago. Baylor is the largest Baptist university in the world. The president asked her how she would integrate the Bible into her accounting classes. He also asked her why she was a member of the Methodist faith. Although the department faculty voted to extend her a job offer, the decision was vetoed by Baylor's administration. Religious colleges are increasingly "hiring for mission," even at the cost of eliminating more academically qualified candidates.[25]

Today the headlines document the pervasive discrimination of Muslims in the workplace. They are often ridiculed for their daily prayer routine. Misunderstandings seem to occur frequently over relatively minor issues such as Muslim women's right to wear head scarves and Muslim men's right to maintain facial hair. With more than 5 million Muslims in America, Islam is expected to soon surpass Judaism and become the second most practiced religion in the United States. The EEOC has reported an increase in discrimination complaints brought by Muslims, Arabs, Middle Easterners, South Asians, and Sikhs. Even those who are American born but are perceived to be members of these groups because of physical features can become victims of this type of discrimination.

Disability

The Americans with Disabilities Act (ADA) sets forth requirements for businesses with fifteen or more employees. It bans discrimination against workers and customers with disabilities and requires employers to make "reasonable accommodations" so that the disabled can access and work in the workplace. It covers a wide range of disabilities, including mental impairments, AIDS, alcoholism, visual impairments, and physical impairments that require use of a wheelchair (visit www.adata.org). Although legal protection is in place, the employment rate for people with disabilities ages 21 to 64 is only 38 percent.[26]

Disabled people who want to work face several problems.

- Many of the jobs performed by people with disabilities are being outsourced abroad. Doug Schalk lost his position as a call-center customer representative at Vanguard Car Rental USA Incorporated when it transferred his job to India.
- Many of the low-paying service-sector jobs often filled by those with disabilities do not provide adequate health benefits to meet the needs of disabled workers.[27]
- Some employers are simply unwilling to hire people who are blind or use a wheelchair and to accommodate their needs with ramps, power doors, Braille signage, and voice-activated technology. They fail to see that these adjustments might serve as a gateway to valuable, hard-working employees, a new customer base, and an economic opportunity.

The good news is that several companies are setting a good example with major programs to accommodate both employees and customers with disabilities (see Table 7.3). In addition, many corporate diversity training programs include sessions on disability awareness and employment.

TABLE 7.3

Enabling Those with Disabilities

Company	Type of Assistance
Crestar Bank	Provides voice-activated technology for disabled customer service representatives. Makes special services available to customers with disabilities.
Honeywell	Participates in Able to Work program, a consortium of 22 companies that find ways to employ disabled persons. Uses its high-tech innovations to assist employees with disabilities.
Johnson & Johnson	Has established a comprehensive disability management program that tailors work assignments to employees returning to work after an injury.
Caterpillar	Serves as a model of high-tech accessibility for the disabled; sponsors Special Olympics.
America OnLine	Has agreed to work with the National Federation of the Blind to ensure that AOL content is largely accessible to the blind.

Sources: John Williams, "The List—Enabling Those with Disabilities," *BusinessWeek,* March 6, 2000, p. 8; "The New Work Force," *BusinessWeek,* March 20, 2000, pp. 64–74; and Douglas M. Towns, "What Internet Companies Must Know About the Americans with Disabilities Act." [cited on 23 February 2006]. Available from www.gigalaw .com; INTERNET.

Sexual Orientation

Discrimination based on a person's sexual orientation is motivated by *homophobia,* an aversion to homosexuals. Not long ago, gays and lesbians went to great lengths to keep their sexuality a secret. But today many gays and lesbians are "coming out of the closet" to demand their rights as members of society. Indeed, many young people entering the work force who are used to the relative tolerance of college campuses refuse to hide their orientation once they are in the workplace.

Gay rights activists are working hard to create awareness that discrimination based on sexual orientation is no less serious than discrimination based on age, gender, race, or disability. Activists are also working to rid the workplace of antigay behaviors such as offensive jokes, derogatory names, or remarks about gays. An atmosphere in which gays and lesbians are comfortable about being themselves is usually more productive than an atmosphere in which they waste their time and energy maintaining alternate, and false, personalities.

In recent years we have witnessed several workplace trends favorable to gay and lesbian employees.

- More than 80 percent of *Fortune* 500 companies include sexual orientation in their antidiscrimination policies, and some companies have established lesbian and gay employee associations that provide a point of contact for previously invisible employees.
- A majority of the nation's top 500 companies now extend medical benefits to same-sex partners. Some major companies such as American Express and J. P. Morgan & Company are targeting recruiting efforts at gay and lesbian college students.[28]

What kind of people take blind kids mountain climbing?
The same ones who take paraplegics sailing and amputees horseback riding.
THE NATIONAL SPORTS CENTER FOR THE DISABLED
To participate, volunteer, or help financially, visit www.nscd.org

The National Sports Center for the Disabled's mission is to positively impact the lives of people with any physical or mental challenge. Today, the NSCD is one of the largest outdoor therapeutic recreational agencies in the world. Thousands of lessons are provided each year.

Many state and local governments have passed laws that help protect gays and lesbians from discrimination and violence. Policies aimed at preventing verbal and physical harassment of homosexual students have been adopted by many public schools and colleges. In some cases, these initiatives have generated considerable controversy. Some religious and conservative groups have actively opposed these violence-prevention efforts, believing that they promote homosexuality.[29]

Subtle Forms of Discrimination

A person who feels he or she has been the victim of discrimination based on gender, age, race, abilities, or sexual orientation can take legal action by filing a complaint with his or her state's office of the Equal Employment Opportunity

HUMAN RELATIONS IN ACTION

Meeting Someone with a Disability

Here are a few suggestions for making a good impression. If the person . . .

. . . **is in a wheelchair.** Sit down, if possible. Try to chat eye to eye. Don't touch the wheelchair. It is considered within the boundaries of an individual's personal space.

. . . **has a speech impediment.** Be patient, actively listen, and resist the urge to finish his or her sentences.

. . . **is accompanied by a guide dog.** Never pet or play with a guide dog; you will distract the animal from its job.

. . . **has a hearing loss.** People who are deaf depend on facial expressions and gestures for communication cues. Speak clearly and slowly. Speak directly to the person, not to an interpreter or assistant if one is present.

Commission. However, while state and federal laws protect individuals from discrimination based on these issues, they do not specifically protect workers from the more subtle forms of discrimination. For example, those who graduated from an Ivy League college may treat coworkers who graduated from state-funded colleges as inferior. Overweight employees might experience degrading remarks from coworkers. Those who speak with a distinct regional accent may hear snickers behind their back at work. People who do not value differences often equate a difference with a deficiency.

HUMAN RELATIONS IN ACTION

Tools for Tolerance: Workplace

- Hold a "diversity potluck" lunch. Invite coworkers to bring foods that reflect their cultural heritage.
- Suggest ways to overcome any barriers that might prevent people of color and women from succeeding.
- Value the input of every employee. Reward managers who do.
- Push for equitable leave policies. Provide paid maternity and paternity leave.
- Start a mentoring program that pairs employees of different ages, such as seniors with entry-level workers.
- Vary your lunch partners. Seek out coworkers of different backgrounds, from different departments, and at different levels in the company.

In its valuing diversity training program, Kaiser Permanente identifies twenty concrete examples of human differences that might cause discrimination among its workers. The list includes the standard diversity issues, but it also identifies characteristics such as education, politics, personal history, and socioeconomic status.[30] Since there are no laws regarding these issues, employees need to understand the negative impact of these subtle forms of discrimination and take responsibility for creating an atmosphere where they are not tolerated.

What Can You Do?

What should you do if you discover you are the target of some form of subtle, unprotected discrimination because you are different from others at work? If you want to stay in the organization, you will need to determine whether the "difference" is something you can change—your weight, the way you dress, your manner of speaking. If the difference is something you cannot or choose not to change, you may need to address the situation directly. Review the assertiveness guidelines in Chapter 8. Your assertiveness may help change other people's attitudes and in turn alter their discriminatory behaviors.

TEST PREPPER 7.3

ANSWERS CAN BE FOUND ON P. 237

True or False?

T 1. Islam is expected to soon surpass Judaism and become the second most practiced religion in the United States.

F 2. Because of the legal protection in place by the ADA, almost 75 percent of Americans with disabilities are employed.

Multiple Choice

C 3. Jim is a 46-year-old man who has worked full-time as an accountant for over twenty years. Despite years of superior work performance, he lost his job in his company's recent downsizing. "We can replace Jim with a 30-year-old and save $25,000 per year in salary and benefit costs," says the company's comptroller. Which of the following is the most likely reason that Jim lost his job?

a. Gender discrimination
b. Subtle discrimination
c. Age discrimination
d. Name discrimination

b 4. Employers who expect gay and lesbian employees to keep their private lives under wraps at work:

a. are breaking federal laws.
b. cause those employees to be more isolated and less productive.
c. are trying only to protect the majority of heterosexual workers, who would rather not work with gays or lesbians.
d. engage in a legal form of age discrimination since homosexual employees are likely to be younger than heterosexual employees.

d 5. Critics arguing for the elimination of traditional racial categories use all the following arguments to support their position except:

a. racial categories are social inventions that intensify and reinforce racist beliefs and actions.
b. there is no objective or scientific foundation for racial differences.
c. racial categories do not take into account the wide variance of people within a racial category.
d. racial districts are necessary to create minority-voting districts for fair representation.

HM **ACE the Test**
ACE and ACE+ Practice Tests

THE ECONOMICS OF VALUING DIVERSITY

4 *Understand why organizations are striving to develop organizational cultures that value diversity.*

The new millennium has brought a strong shift away from the traditional pattern of treating everyone the same and toward valuing diversity in a work setting. This means that a company intends to make full use of the ideas, talents, experiences, and perspectives of all employees at all levels of the organization. Joe Watson, a recruiter of minorities, believes that if you want to satisfy clients and customers from diverse backgrounds, you need a diverse mix of employees who are more likely to understand them. People from various cultural and ethnic backgrounds can offer different perspectives and stimulate creativity. "This type of inclusion," says Watson, "isn't about joining hands and singing 'Kumbaya.' This is about improving corporate performance."[31]

A study conducted by the Society for Human Resource Management revealed that diversity initiatives within organizations can affect an organization's bottom line by reducing costs associated with turnover, absenteeism, and low productivity. In addition, efforts to value workers' and customers' diversity reduce complaints and litigation and improve the organization's public image.[32] Organizations that pursue diversity and make it part of their culture usually outperform companies that are less committed to diversity.

The price tag for *not* helping employees learn to respect and value each other is enormous. Many highly skilled and talented employees will leave an organization that does not value diversity. A comment, gesture, or joke delivered without malice but received as an insult will create tension among workers and customers alike. Valuable time will be wasted clarifying miscommunication and misunderstandings. Recognizing the value of diversity and managing it as an asset can help eliminate these negative effects.

TOTAL PERSON INSIGHT

Lewis Brown Griggs and **Lente-Louise Louw**
Authors, ***Valuing Diversity: New Tools for a New Reality***

"More and more, organizations can remain competitive only if they can recognize and obtain the best talent; value the diverse perspectives that come with talent born of different cultures, races, and genders; nurture and train that talent; and create an atmosphere that values its workforce."

MANAGING DIVERSITY

5 *Identify ways in which individuals and organizations can enhance work force diversity.*

managing diversity The process of creating an organizational culture in which the primary and secondary dimensions of diversity are respected.

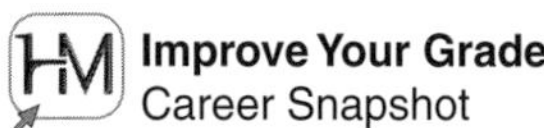

Managing diversity is the process of creating an organizational culture in which the primary and secondary dimensions of diversity are respected. This process can be a challenge now that the work force is composed of so many different nationalities. Managers at some Marriott Hotels work with employees from thirty different countries. The employees who are part of the Toyota Formula 1 race team represent twenty-seven nationalities. Even some small retail stores have become a kind of United Nations. The Kroger supermarket in Durham, North Carolina, has employees from ten countries. The issue is further complicated when an organization's diverse work force is in global satellite offices separated by thousands of miles. Microsoft's research unit, for example, is staffed by 700 multinational scientists and engineers working in six laboratories on three continents.[33]

What Individuals Can Do

People tend to hang on to their prejudices and stereotypes. If certain white people believe people of color are inferior, they are likely to notice any incident in which a person of color makes a mistake. But when a person of color exhibits competence and sound decision-making abilities, these same white people may not notice, or they may attribute the positive results to other circumstances. You cannot totally eliminate prejudices that have been deeply held and developed over a long time. But you can take steps to change those attitudes and behaviors that may have a negative impact on your employer's efforts to enhance diversity.

1. *Learn to look critically and honestly at the particular myths and preconceived ideas you have been conditioned to believe about others.* Contact among people of different races, cultures, and lifestyles can break down prejudice when people join together for a common task. The more contact there is among culturally diverse individuals, the more likely it will be that stereotypes based on myths and inaccurate generalizations will not survive.
2. *Develop a sensitivity to differences.* Do not allow gender-based, racist, or antigay jokes or comments in your presence. If English is not a person's native language, be aware that this person might interpret your messages differently from what you intended. When in doubt as to the appropriate behavior, ask questions. "I would like to open the door for you because you are in a wheelchair, but I'm not sure whether that would offend you. What would you like me to do?"
3. *Develop your own diversity awareness program.* The starting point might be creation of a "diversity profile" of your friends, coworkers, and acquaintances. How much diversity do these individuals have in terms of race? Ethnicity? Religion? Assess the cultural diversity reflected in the music you listen to and the books you read. Visit an ethnic restaurant and try to learn about more than the food. Study Islam, Buddhism, and other faiths that may be different from your own.[34]

What Organizations Can Do

A well-planned and well-executed diversity program can promote understanding and defuse tensions between employees who differ in age, race, gender, religious beliefs, and other characteristics. Programs that are poorly developed and poorly executed often backfire, especially in organizations where bias and distrust have festered for years. A comprehensive diversity program has three pillars:[35] organizational commitment, employment practices, and training and development (see Figure 7.4).

Organizational Commitment

Catalyst, a research and advisory group, conducted a survey of 106 global companies to determine why these companies use diversity strategies as part of their overall business plan. Nearly 90 percent said their diversity program was designed to help them gain a competitive advantage.[36] When the objective of the diversity initiative is to achieve a stronger competitive position, the commitment is usually quite strong.

Companies that see diversity programs as a quick-fix *event*—a one-day workshop that promotes the advantages of a diverse work force—often create greater, not less, divisiveness among workers. Companies that see diversity programs as a *process* know that the key to a successful diversity program is long-term commitment.

FIGURE 7.4

Three Pillars of Diversity

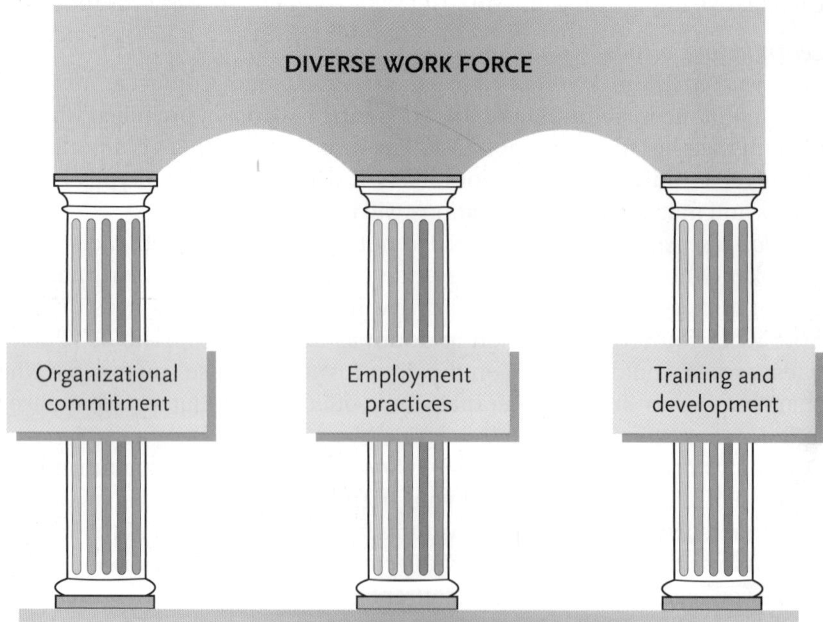

- At Consolidated Edison, responsibility for diversity extends to the entire management team. Each of the 2,100 officers and managers is reviewed and compensated in part for his or her success in hiring, promoting, and retaining minorities. PepsiCo, the soft drink maker, links bonuses to diversity performance. Both of these companies made "America's 50 Best Companies for Minorities" list published by *Fortune*.[37]
- Coca-Cola Company has been a strong backer of civil rights, but it has not always been a model for diversity in corporate America. Former black employees sued the company, alleging vast discrepancies in pay, promotions, and performance evaluations. Reporting on the lawsuit, *BusinessWeek* said, "The cola giant needs a cultural overhaul. Just as Texaco needed to scrub its 'oil rig' culture clean of racism, Coke needs to scrap the insular environment that ex-employees say is dominated by good ol' boys. . . ." After paying $192.5 million to settle a race discrimination class-action lawsuit in 2000, the company took steps to strengthen its diversity program. In 2002, Coca-Cola made the *Fortune* list of best companies for minorities.[38]

Employment Practices

To achieve work force diversity, organizations need to design a plan that actively recruits men and women of different ethnicities, family situations, disabilities, and sexual orientations. Diversity should not be limited to race and gender. One approach is to make a special effort to plug into networks that are often ignored by corporate recruiters. Many communities have established groups such as the Center for Independent Living for those with limited abilities, the Family Service League for displaced homemakers and single parents, and Parents, Families, and Friends of Lesbians and Gays. All of these groups can help identify employees.

Organizations must also foster a climate for retention. Newly hired people who are different from the majority must often contend with an atmosphere of tension, instability, and distrust and may soon lose the desire to do their best work. Subtle biases often alienate these employees and create unnecessary stress. An organization that makes every effort to make *all* employees comfortable will reduce this stress and thus benefit from low turnover and high individual and team performance levels.

Training and Development

To develop a culture that values and enhances diversity, organizations need training programs that give managers and employees the tools they need to work more effectively with one another regardless of their backgrounds. These programs can also reduce an organization's liability for discrimination.

Lockheed Martin Corporation launched an educational awareness program called "Diversity Dialogue: Building an Inclusive Workplace." Managers receive training on how to lead diversity discussions. This effort recognizes that employees need to talk about diversity just as they might spend time talking about how to improve quality. Managers are also introduced to Lockheed's new Diversity Maturity Model, which measures the company's progress in creating an inclusive environment.[39]

Done well, diversity training programs can promote harmony, reduce conflict, and help give the organization a competitive advantage. Training programs that are poorly designed and delivered by incompetent trainers, however, can end up alienating and offending employees. Participants should learn specific behaviors that will not be condoned and the basic rules of civil behavior. We may not be able to stop people from bringing their prejudices to work, but they can learn to act as though they have none.

TEST PREPPER 7.4, 7.5

ANSWERS CAN BE FOUND ON P. 237

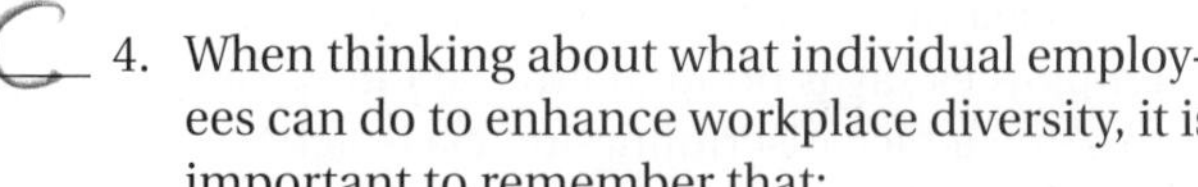

True or False?

T 1. The more contact there is among culturally diverse individuals, the less likely that stereotypes based on myths and inaccurate generalizations will survive.

Multiple Choice

C 2. The effects of failing to value diversity in the workplace include:
  a. lower employee turnover because of a more homogeneous work force.
  b. fewer complaints of discrimination.
  c. increased labor costs because of higher absenteeism and employee turnover.
  d. savings on labor costs.

a 3. A powerful way to reduce intolerance in the workplace is to:
  a. reward managers who value and enhance diversity.
  b. reduce the number of ethnic food options in the company cafeteria.
  c. provide ways for employees of the same racial or ethnic backgrounds to socialize together informally at work.
  d. eliminate parental leave benefits.

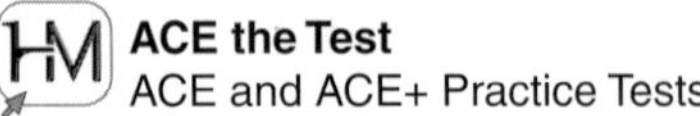

C 4. When thinking about what individual employees can do to enhance workplace diversity, it is important to remember that:
  a. men are more likely to be prejudiced than are women.
  b. examining one's social conditioning only reinforces one's prejudices.
  c. one cannot completely eliminate prejudices that have been held over a long period of time.
  d. being sensitive to differences between individuals indicates lingering prejudice.

d 5. The three pillars of diversity are:
  a. age, gender, and race.
  b. race, employment practices, and promotion.
  c. age, training and development, and organizational commitment.
  d. employment practices, training and development, and organizational commitment.

b 6. Most diversity programs that fail do so because:
  a. they lack support from the state and federal government.
  b. they are not comprehensive and do not have the full support of top management.
  c. they do not meet federal guidelines.
  d. they focus too much attention on race.

AFFIRMATIVE ACTION: YESTERDAY AND TODAY

6 *Explain the current status of affirmative action programs.*

The Civil Rights Act of 1964 marked the beginning of antidiscrimination employment legislation. In an attempt to make up for past discrimination in the workplace, most organizations are required to take affirmative (positive) action to include women and racial minorities in the work force (see Table 7.4). Various laws have been passed to expand the list of *protected* individuals beyond women and racial minorities. The updated list includes those who share the following characteristics:

- Sex/gender (women, including those who are pregnant)
- Racial or ethnic origin (not limited to those of color)
- Religion (special beliefs and practices: e.g., attire, holidays)
- Age (individuals over 40)
- Individuals with disabilities (physical or mental)
- Sexual orientation (some state and city laws, not federal laws)
- Military experience (Vietnam-era veterans)
- Marital status (same-gender couples; some state laws, not federal laws)

Affirmative action plans (AAPs) are the formal documents that employers compile annually for submission to various enforcement agencies, including the EEOC. The documents clarify the organizations' efforts to actively seek out, employ, and develop the talents of individuals from the various protected classes. The affirmative action programs that fulfill the AAPs of many organizations include the following:[40]

affirmative action plans The documents that clarify an organization's efforts to actively seek out, employ, and develop the talents of individuals from protected classes.

1. Active recruitment of women and minorities
2. Elimination of prejudicial questions on employment application forms
3. Establishment of specific goals and timetables for minority hiring
4. Validation of employment testing procedures

Affirmative action allowed a tremendous influx of diverse individuals through the front door of thousands of schools and organizations. Many were able to work their way into advanced, top-level positions. At the same time, however, affirmative action reinforced the historical view that the members of protected groups are not qualified for various positions and therefore need assistance just to get a job.

The Affirmative Action Debate

Many people say it is time to rethink affirmative action or even eliminate it. Recent political and legal interpretations of affirmative action have stimulated a nationwide debate over the merits of any program that grants preferential treatment to

TABLE 7.4

Organizations Subject to Affirmative Action Rules and Regulations

- All private employers of 15 or more people who are employed 20 or more weeks per year
- All educational institutions, public and private
- State and local governments
- Public and private employment agencies
- Labor unions with 15 or more members
- Joint labor/management committees for apprenticeships and training

Source: From *Human Resource Management* with West Group Product Booklet, 10th edition, by Mathis/Jackson, © 2003. Reprinted with permission of South-Western, a division of Thomson Learning: www.thomsonrights.com, fax 800-730-2215.

specific groups. The following are common arguments voiced by those who want to end preferential policies:[41]

- *Preferences are discriminatory.* They tend to discriminate against those who are not members of the "right" race or gender, such as white men. Preferential policies often give a leg up to those who have suffered no harm, while holding back those who have done no wrong.
- *Preferences do not make sense, given changing demographics.* The population eligible for affirmative action continues to grow several times faster than the "unprotected" population. Hugh Davis Graham, author of *Collision Course,* believes the future of affirmative action programs is threatened because of the explosive growth in the number of people immigrating to the United States. Recent immigrants are eligible for affirmative action programs originally designed to empower minorities.[42]

Those who say affirmative action causes companies to hire and promote less qualified people fail to realize that the hiring process usually goes beyond the abilities, knowledge, and skills of the job candidate and includes additional merit-based factors, such as education and experience. When these factors are included in the hiring process, recipients of affirmative action are less likely to feel stigmatized. The way people react to a preferential selection procedure will often depend on how well it is structured and implemented.[43]

The concept of affirmative action and the means for implementing it will continue to be challenged in the courts for years to come. A recent Supreme Court ruling (*Grutter v. Bollinger*) states that an employer can legally give preferential treatment to applicants based on their race when the intent is to create a diverse workplace environment. However, if the hiring process resembles a quota system, which involves reserving a specific number of positions for protected class members, it will likely be considered illegal.

TEST PREPPER 7.6

ANSWERS CAN BE FOUND ON P. 237

True or False?

F 1. Affirmative action programs have completely failed to get an influx of diverse individuals into the workplace and higher education system.

T 2. In most cases an employer can legally give preference to applicants based on their race if the intention is to create a diverse workplace.

F 3. It is completely legal to have a hiring process that involves reserving a certain number of positions for protected class members.

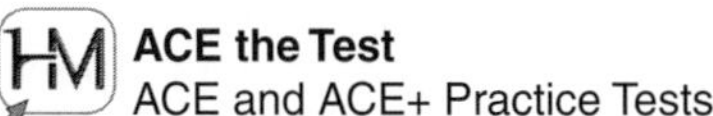

Multiple Choice

C 4. Affirmative action programs in organizations are an outgrowth of which of the following?
   a. The Americans with Disabilities Act of 1991
   b. The companies' organizational commitment to team building
   c. The Civil Rights Act of 1964
   d. The companies' training and development agendas

b 5. One of the strongest arguments advanced by opponents of affirmative action is that:
   a. members of minority groups are often inferior workers.
   b. preferences are discriminatory.
   c. preferences help only white males.
   d. preemployment testing eliminates discrimination.

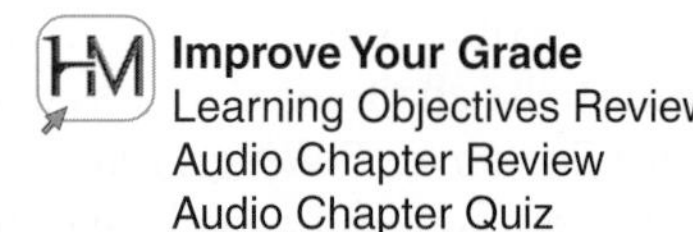

LEARNING OBJECTIVES REVIEW

1 *Define the primary and secondary dimensions of diversity.*

- Primary dimensions of diversity are core aspects of each individual; they include gender, age, race, physical and mental abilities, and sexual orientation.
- Secondary dimensions are aspects that can be altered, including health habits, religious beliefs, ethnic customs, communication style, relationship status, income, general appearance, and education and training.

2 *Explain how prejudiced attitudes are formed.*

- Prejudice is an attitude based partly on observation of others' differences and partly on ignorance, fear, and cultural conditioning.
- Prejudiced people tend to see others as stereotypes rather than as individuals.
- Prejudicial attitudes are formed through the effects of childhood experiences, ethnocentrism, and economic factors.

3 *Develop an awareness of the various forms of discrimination in the workplace.*

- Discrimination is behavior based on prejudicial attitudes.
- Groups protected by law from discrimination in the workplace include people who share characteristics such as gender, age, race, abilities, religion, and sexual orientation.
- More subtle discrimination can arise when individuals have different appearances or educational backgrounds. These subtle forms of discrimination may not be illegal, but they are disruptive to a productive work force.

4 *Understand why organizations are striving to develop organizational cultures that value diversity.*

- A well-planned and well-executed diversity program can promote understanding and diffuse tensions.
- To remain competitive, organizations must value the contributions of all of their diverse workers and make full use of their ideas and talents.

5 *Identify ways in which individuals and organizations can enhance work force diversity.*

- Individuals can enhance diversity by letting go of their stereotypes and learning to critically and honestly evaluate their prejudiced attitudes as they work and socialize with people who are different.
- Organizations must commit to valuing individual differences and implementing effective employment practices that respect and enhance diversity. Their diversity training programs should be an ongoing process rather than a one-time event. They need to seek out, employ, and develop employees from diverse backgrounds.

6 *Explain the current status of affirmative action programs.*

- Affirmative action guidelines have helped bring fairness in hiring and promotion to many organizations.
- Some people believe these guidelines are discriminatory because they allow preferential treatment for the people they were designed to protect. These preferences may no longer make sense, critics say, given the changing demographics of today's work force.

Career Corner

Q: I am a call-center technician for a global computer manufacturer whose headquarters is in Simi Valley, California. My office is in New Delhi. We take calls from customers all over the world who are asking for help solving their computer problems. Although we have been trained to use simple semantics as we try to assess callers' situations and offer them advice accordingly, some customers get irritated and verbally abusive when they realize English is my second language. My supervisor says that handling customers' discriminatory behaviors is part of my job. I am the sole supporter of my family and must keep this job, as it is one of the best opportunities in New Delhi. Should I expect my employer to protect me from this verbal abuse, or is there a better way to handle these callers?

A: Your employers have a vested interest in keeping their customers *and* employees happy. Discriminatory behavior in any form can have a major effect on their competitive advantage in the global marketplace. Rest assured; they want to solve this problem. Talk with them and ask for training that will help you handle callers who may be making judgments about your competence before you are allowed to exhibit your knowledge and expertise.

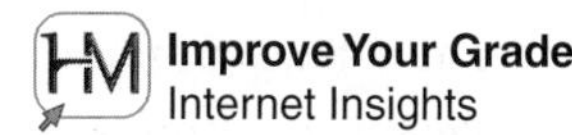

Applying What You Have Learned

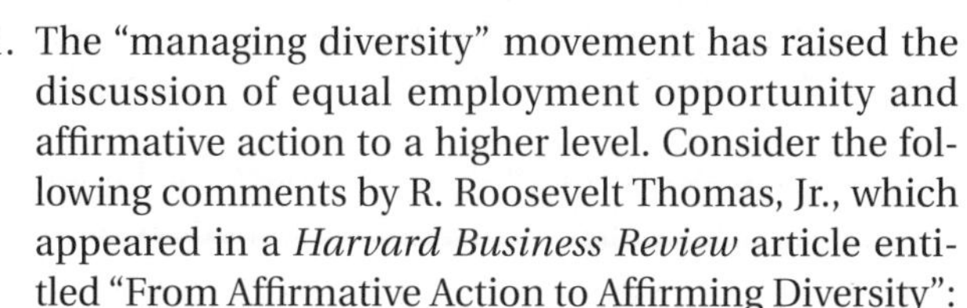

1. The "managing diversity" movement has raised the discussion of equal employment opportunity and affirmative action to a higher level. Consider the following comments by R. Roosevelt Thomas, Jr., which appeared in a *Harvard Business Review* article entitled "From Affirmative Action to Affirming Diversity":

    > Managers usually see affirmative action and equal employment opportunity as centering on minorities and women, with very little to offer white males. The diversity I'm talking about includes race, gender, creed, and ethnicity but also age, background, education, function, and personality differences. The objective is not to assimilate minorities and women into a dominant white male culture but to create a dominant heterogeneous culture.[44]

    What does "dominant heterogeneous culture" mean to you? Consider your former or current workplace. How would the atmosphere at work be different if Roosevelt got his wish? Be specific.
2. For one week, keep a diary that records every instance in which you see actions or hear comments that reflect outmoded, negative stereotypes. For instance, watch a movie, and observe whether the villains are all of a particular race or ethnic group. As you read textbooks from other courses you are taking, notice whether the pictures and examples reflect any stereotypes. Listen to your friends' conversations, and notice any time they make unfair judgments about others based on stereotypes. Finally, reflect on your own attitudes and perceptions. Do you engage in stereotyping?

    Share your experiences with class members, and discuss what steps you can take to help rid the environment of negative stereotyping.
3. Meet with someone who is a member of a racial or ethnic group different from your own, and attempt to build a relationship by discussing the things that are important to each of you. As you get to know this person, become aware of his or her beliefs and attitudes. Try not to be diverted by accent, grammar, or personal appearance; rather, really listen to the person's thoughts and ideas. Search for things you and your new acquaintance have in common, and do not dwell on your differences.

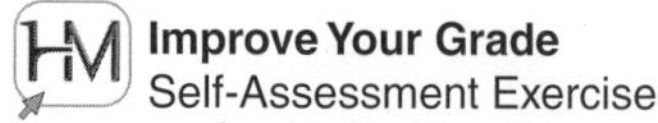

ROLE-PLAY EXERCISE

You are currently supervising six skilled tool and die makers. Until recently the work group was working as a productive team and was free of any serious interpersonal relationship problems. Then the work climate began to change. One day Kira Purcell, the most experienced employee, hung a small poster in the work area. The poster featured a biblical quotation that spoke to the evils of homesexual relationships. The headline at the top of the poster read "The Homosexual Plague." One day, during lunch break, the poster disappeared. Someone in the group apparently removed it. Purcell complained that removal of the poster was no different from stealing tools from her work area. Purcell was upset and the next day replaced the poster with one that featured another biblical quotation with the headline "moral perversity." You explained the problem to the owner of the company, and he suggested that you meet with Purcell and request that no more posters be displayed in the work area. You will meet with another class member who will assume the role of Kira Purcell. Try to convince your role-play partner that these posters are inappropriate in a work setting.

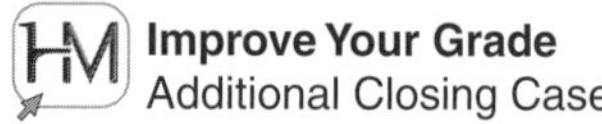

CASE 7.1

The Baggage of Bigotry

Bigots are people who are strongly partial to their own group, religion, race, lifestyle, and so on and intolerant of those who differ from them. Bigotry, prejudiced attitudes expressed through intolerant behaviors, has long been a part of American history, as witnessed by slavery, anti-gay hate crimes, anti-Semitism, and terrorist stereotyping. Bigoted ideas do not arise spontaneously; they are learned. If they are learned, they can be changed.

The "No Place for Hate" campaign in the Houston, Texas, schools was designed to help young people respect diversity. The hope is that if children learn this lesson early enough, they will reject bigotry for life and thereby rid the world of this historical baggage. Jordan's Queen Rania attended an English school in her native Kuwait that had children from Europe, Africa, the Far East, and the United States. She acknowledges that her interactions with the children from various cultures helped her realize that those things that make everyone similar far outweigh those things that make them different. At the end of the day, everyone wants the same thing out of life.

Research shows that prejudiced attitudes are fluid and that when we become conscious of our bigotry, we can take active and successful steps to combat it. In experiments, researchers have discovered that as people become consciously aware of their prejudices, they feel guilty and try harder to rid themselves of them. Once you become aware of your bigoted tendencies, feel guilty about them, and have the desire to overcome them, the cure is meaningful contact with and knowledge about different cultures.

Today it is easy to obtain information about different countries and cultures through the Internet, TV news, and journalists' reports from various regions of the world. As neighborhoods are integrated with various cultures from around the world, people learn to live with and respect their neighbors' traditions. Biases change when members of racially mixed groups cooperate to accomplish shared goals.[45]

Questions

1. Do any of your family members exhibit bigotry? If so, where do you believe those attitudes originated? Do you share the same beliefs? Why or why not?
2. Do bigots come in only one color? Explain your reasoning.
3. Is racial profiling a form of bigotry? Explain your reasoning.
4. What would the workplace be like if we could end bigotry? What would the world be like? Where do we start this process?

RESOURCES ON THE WEB

Prepare for Class, Improve Your Grade, and ACE the Test. Student Achievement Series resources include:

ACE and ACE+ Practice Tests	Chapter Glossaries	Audio Glossaries
Audio Chapter Quizzes	Chapter Outlines	Internet Insights
Audio Chapter Reviews	Crossword Puzzles	Self-Assessment Exercises
Learning Objective Reviews	Hangman Games	Additional Closing Cases
Career Snapshots	Flashcards	

To access these learning and study tools, go to **college.hmco.com/pic/reeceSAS**.

HM ManagementSPACE

8 Resolving Conflict and Achieving Emotional Balance

Joe Louis Arena in Detroit, home of the Detroit Red Wings, is shown empty. The National Hockey League became the first professional sports league in North America to cancel an entire season. There were no winners in this conflict.

1. *List and describe some of the major causes of conflict in the work setting.*
2. *Utilize assertiveness skills in conflict situations.*
3. *Understand when and how to implement effective negotiation skills.*
4. *Identify key elements of the conflict resolution process.*
5. *Describe how emotions influence our thinking and behavior.*

"In reality, conflicts can serve as opportunities for personal growth . . ."

—Dudley Weeks

Chapter Outline

- A New View of Conflict
  - Finding Root Causes of Conflict
- Resolving Conflict Assertively
  - How to Become More Assertive
- Learn to Negotiate Effectively
  - Think Win/Win
  - Beware of Defensive Behaviors
  - Know That Negotiating Styles Vary
- Conflict Resolution Process
  - Step One: Decide Whether You Have a Misunderstanding or a True Disagreement
  - Step Two: Define the Problem and Collect the Facts
  - Step Three: Clarify Perceptions
  - Step Four: Generate Options for Mutual Gain
  - Step Five: Implement Options with Integrity
- Emotional Balance—An Introduction
  - Achieving Emotional Balance—A Daily Challenge
  - Emotional Intelligence
  - Emotional Expression
  - The Emotional Factor at Work
- Factors That Influence Our Emotions
  - Temperament
  - Unconscious Influences
  - Cultural Conditioning
- Coping with Your Anger and the Anger of Others
  - Managing Your Anger
  - Effective Ways to Express Your Anger
  - How to Handle Other People's Anger
- Strategies for Achieving Emotional Control
  - Identifying Your Emotional Patterns
  - Fine-Tuning Your Emotional Style

Prepare for Class
Chapter Outline

6 *Describe the major factors that influence our emotional development.*

7 *Learn how to deal with your anger and the anger of others.*

8 *Describe strategies for achieving emotional control.*

An Icy Conflict

If you are a die-hard hockey fan, you will probably always remember the 2004–2005 season. The season was canceled because the National Hockey League and the NHL Players Association could not settle an ongoing labor dispute, and for the first time since 1919, the Stanley Cup was not awarded.

The NHL became the first professional sports league in North America to cancel an entire season because of a labor conflict. The conflict over economic issues began when the owners of the NHL's 30 professional teams locked out the 700 members of

KEY TERMS

anger *p. 189*
aggressive behavior *p. 174*
assertive behavior *p. 174*
conflict *p. 170*
conflict resolution process *p. 181*
emotion *p. 185*
emotional intelligence *p. 186*
lose/lose approach *p. 178*
nonassertive behavior *p. 174*
temperament *p. 188*
unconscious mind *p. 188*
win/lose approach *p. 177*
win/win approach *p. 178*

Prepare for Class
Chapter Glossary

Improve Your Grade
Flashcards
Hangman
Crossword Puzzle

the players' union when their collective-bargaining agreement expired. Negotiations spanned a ten-month period before an agreement could be reached. During that time teams lost an estimated $2 billion in revenue from tickets, media, sponsorships, and concessions, while players lost approximately $1 billion in salaries. Team office personnel and stadium attendants were laid off, and Canadian government agencies that owned the stadiums lost rental income. The Canadian government estimated that the country's gross domestic product was reduced by 170 million Canadian dollars as a result of the cancelled season.[1]

The lost NHL season and the lost revenue associated with the conflict are a reminder of how difficult and expensive it can be when conflicts cannot be effectively resolved. While disputes within most organizations are not of this magnitude, companies pay a high price for conflict. Often productivity drops, work relationships suffer, and energy is wasted as workers become increasingly angry, stressed, and defensive.[2] It is estimated that managers spend about 20 percent of their time resolving disputes among staff members.[3] This chapter offers workers and managers alike specific guidelines for effectively and productively resolving a variety of conflicts.

A NEW VIEW OF CONFLICT

1 *List and describe some of the major causes of conflict in the work setting.*

conflict A clash between incompatible people, ideas, or interests.

Improve Your Grade
Audio Glossary

Most standard dictionaries define **conflict** as a clash between incompatible people, ideas, or interests. These conflicts are almost always perceived as negative experiences in our society. But when we view conflict as a negative experience, we may be hurting our chances of dealing with it effectively. In reality, conflicts can serve as opportunities for personal growth if we develop and use positive, constructive conflict resolution skills.[4]

Much of our growth and social progress comes from the opportunities we have to discover creative solutions to conflicts that surface in our lives. Dudley Weeks, professor of conflict resolution at American University, says conflict can provide additional ways of thinking about the *source* of conflict and open up possibilities for improving a relationship.[5] When people work together to resolve conflicts, their solutions are often far more creative than they would be if only one person addressed the problem. Creative conflict resolution can shake people out of their mental ruts and give them a new point of view.

Too much agreement is not always healthy in an organization. Employees who are anxious to be viewed as "team players" may not voice concerns even when they have doubts about a decision being made. Four years before the first flight of space shuttle *Challenger,* some NASA engineers discovered problems with the O-ring seals, but these concerns were disregarded. Howard Schwartz, in his book *Narcissistic Process and Corporate Decay,* described the *Challenger* disaster as a tragic example of the "exportation of conflict."[6] Meaningful conflict can be the key to producing healthy, successful organizations because conflict is necessary for effective problem solving and for effective interpersonal relationships.[7] As Mark

Twain once said, "It were not best that we should all think alike; it is difference of opinion that makes horse races."[8] The problem isn't with disagreements, but with how they are resolved.

Finding the Root Causes of Conflict

If left unattended, weeds can take over a garden and choke all the healthy plants. When inexperienced gardeners cut weeds off at the surface instead of digging down to find the roots, the weeds tend to come back twice as strong. Conflicts among people at work often follow the same pattern. Unless the root of the conflict is addressed, the conflict is likely to recur. If the root cause appears to stimulate *constructive* conflict, it can be allowed to continue. However, as soon as the symptoms of *destructive* conflict become apparent, steps need to be taken to correct the problem that is triggering it.[9] This segment of the chapter discusses the most common causes of conflicts in the workplace.

Organizational Change

Organizational change is one of the seven root causes of conflict. In most organizations there is tension between opposing forces for stability (maintain the status quo) and change. If management wants to shift more health care costs onto

HUMAN RELATIONS IN ACTION

Needed: Serious Negotiations

As the automobile industry struggles with escalating labor costs and imminent bankruptcies, stockholders and managers realize that adjustments must be made. Lower labor costs offshore represent a viable cost-cutting opportunity for management, but are cause for conflict among unionized laborers in the United States. Delphi CEO Robert "Steve" Miller has a four-point plan to help his organization emerge from bankruptcy that might become the standard for other struggling manufacturers.

- **Change employee expectations.** Workers in China and Mexico work for approximately $7,000 a year. It is going to be very difficult for those with manual-labor jobs in the United States to maintain their current lifestyle if they want to compete with their offshore counterparts.
- **Rewrite the social contract.** Reduce the current unionized workers' benefits from $65 an hour to $20. If the union leaders don't agree, ask the U.S. Bankruptcy Court to void the current labor contract entirely.
- **Don't worry about a strike.** There is nothing to be gained. A strike would only accelerate the bankruptcy process and increase the number of plants that would have to be closed.
- **Get the government to help with health care.** Lobby legislators to create policies that take the burden of health care costs off employers and put it onto taxpayers.

workers, tension may surface. With too much stability, the organization may lose its competitive position in the marketplace. With too much change, the mission blurs and employee anxiety develops.[10]

Ineffective Communication

A major source of personal conflict is the misunderstanding that results from ineffective communication. In Chapter 2 we discussed the various filters that messages must pass through before effective communication can occur. In the work setting, where many different people work closely together, communication breakdowns are inevitable.

Often it is necessary to determine if the conflict is due to a misunderstanding or a true disagreement. If the cause is a *misunderstanding*, you may need to explain your position again or provide more details or examples to help the other person understand. If a *disagreement* exists, one or both parties have to be persuaded to change their position on the issue. Those involved in the conflict can attempt to explain their position over and over again, but until someone changes, the root problem will persist.[11] This issue is discussed in greater detail later in this chapter.

Value and Culture Clashes

In Chapter 4 you read that differences in values can cause conflicts between generations, among men and women, and among people with different value priorities. Today's diverse work force reflects a kaleidoscope of cultures, each with its own unique qualities. The individual bearers of these different cultural traditions could easily come into conflict with one another. The issues may be as simple as one person's desire to dress in ethnic fashion and a supervisor's insistence on strict adherence to the company dress code, or as complex as work ethics.

Work Policies and Practices

Interpersonal conflicts can develop when an organization has unreasonable or confusing rules, regulations, and performance standards. The conflicts often surface when managers fail to tune in to employees' perceptions that various policies are unfair. Managers need to address the source of conflict rather than suppress it. Conflict also surfaces when some workers refuse to comply with the rules and neglect their fair share of the workload.

Adversarial Management

Under adversarial management, supervisors may view their employees and even other managers with suspicion and distrust and treat them as "the enemy." Employees usually lack respect for adversarial managers, resenting their authoritarian style and resisting their suggestions for change. This atmosphere makes cooperation and teamwork difficult.

Competition for Scarce Resources

It would be difficult to find an organization, public or private, that is not involved in downsizing or cost cutting. The result is often destructive competition for scarce resources such as updated computerized equipment, administrative support personnel, travel dollars, salary increases, or annual bonuses. When budgets and cost-cutting efforts are not clearly explained, workers may suspect coworkers or supervisors of devious tactics.

HUMAN RELATIONS IN ACTION

Fire the Client?

Lisa Zwick knew that her client, the CEO of an Internet start-up company, was a problem. He was irritable and extremely hard to work with. When he called her California home at 5:00 A.M. one Monday morning from his New York City hotel room and asked her to order a limousine for him, she refused and took the issue to her boss. With his support, Lisa fired the client, telling him, "This isn't working out for several reasons; but most of all, you're a jerk!" Many firms are concluding that firing cantankerous clients can be a good business decision. One company fired a client who was bringing in $1 million a year, or 20 percent of the company's revenue, for making nasty, digging comments about employees. The owner of the company believed that if the irritating client was going to drive her employees crazy, the relationship wasn't worth it. Her respected employees replaced the lost business and have since doubled revenue to $10 million.

Personality Clashes

There is no doubt about it: Some people just don't like each other. They may have differing communication styles, temperaments, or attitudes. They may not be able to identify exactly what it is they dislike about the other person, but the bottom line is that conflicts will arise when these people have to work together. Even people who get along well with each other in the beginning stages of a work relationship may begin to clash after working together for many years.

Test Prepper 8.1

Answers can be found on p. 237

True or False?

____ 1. Conflict resolution is typically more creative when an individual works alone to create a resolution.

____ 2. Unless the root cause of conflict is addressed, conflict is likely to reoccur.

Multiple Choice

____ 3. Which of the following is true about conflict in organizations?

a. The existence of conflict is a symptom of poor management.
b. The outcome of disagreement is less productivity and creativity in an organization.
c. Too much agreement within an organization may be unhealthy.
d. Experts agree that growth and social progress are inhibited by conflict.

____ 4. Today's increase in workplace diversity exacerbates which source of conflict?

a. Culture clashes
b. Adversarial management
c. Work policies and practices
d. Noncompliance

____ 5. Corporation XYZ is merging with Corporation ABC. If there is conflict in the newly formed organization, the root cause will likely be:

a. organizational change.
b. ineffective communication.
c. adversarial management.
d. personality clashes.

ACE the Test
ACE and ACE+ Practice Tests

RESOLVING CONFLICT ASSERTIVELY

2 *Utilize assertiveness skills in conflict situations.*

Conflict is often uncomfortable whether it is in a personal or professional setting. People sometimes get hurt and become defensive because they feel they are under attack personally. Because we have to work or live with certain people every day, it is best to avoid harming these ongoing relationships. But many people don't know how to participate in and manage conflict in a positive way. Many professionals advise going directly to the offending person and calmly discussing his or her irritating behavior, rather than complaining to others.[12] Figure 8.1, "Dealing with People You Can't Stand," offers specific strategies you might use. By taking those steps to change *your* behavior, you might facilitate a powerful change in theirs. Keep in mind that some people are unaware of the impact of their behavior, and if you draw their attention to it, they may change it.

Whereas these strategies may be comfortable for some people, such a direct approach may be very uncomfortable for many others. People who attempt to avoid conflict by simply ignoring things that bother them are exhibiting **nonassertive behavior**. Nonassertive people often give in to the demands of others, and their passive approach makes them less likely to make their needs known. If you fail to take a firm position when such action is appropriate, customers, coworkers, and supervisors may take advantage of you, and management may question your abilities.

nonassertive behavior The attempt to avoid conflict by simply ignoring it.

Assertive behavior, on the other hand, provides you the opportunity to stand up for your rights and express your thoughts and feelings in a direct, appropriate way that does not violate the rights of others. It is a matter of getting the other person to understand your viewpoint.[13] People who exhibit appropriate assertive behavior skills are able to handle their conflicts with greater ease and assurance while maintaining good interpersonal relations.

assertive behavior Standing up for one's rights and expressing one's thoughts and feelings in a direct, appropriate way.

Some people do not understand the distinction between being aggressive and being assertive. **Aggressive behavior** involves expressing your thoughts and feelings and defending your rights in a way that *violates* the rights of others. Aggressive people may interrupt, talk fast, ignore others, and use sarcasm or other forms of verbal abuse to maintain control.

aggressive behavior Expressing one's thoughts and feelings and defending one's rights in a way that violates the rights of others.

Table 8.1 may give you a clearer understanding of how nonassertive, assertive, and aggressive individuals respond when confronted with conflict situations.

How to Become More Assertive

Entire books have been written that describe how to improve your assertiveness skills. Several years ago the American Management Association (www.amanet.org) began offering skill development seminars that focus on assertiveness training, including Assertiveness Training for the New or Prospective Manager and Assertiveness Training for Women in Business.[14] Enrollees have the opportunity to achieve greater credibility by learning how to handle tough situations with composure and confidence. Whether you choose to read the books or participate in assertiveness training, know that you can communicate your wants, dislikes, and feelings in a clear, direct manner without threatening or attacking others. Here are three practical guidelines that will help you develop your assertiveness skills.

FIGURE 8.1

Dealing with People You Can't Stand

Source: Adapted from Rick Brinkman and Rick Kirschner, *Dealing with People You Can't Stand* (New York: McGraw-Hill, 1994); Don Wallace and Scott McMurray, "How to Disagree (without being disagreeable)," *Fast Company*, November 1995, p. 146; Kris Maher, "The Jungle," *Wall Street Journal*, April 15, 2003, p. B8; Jared Sandberg, "Sabotage 101: The Sinister Art of Back-Stabbing," *Wall Street Journal*, February 11, 2004, p. B1.

THE BULLY	Bullies find ways to manipulate or control others. They are pushy, ruthless, loud, and forceful and tend to intimidate you with in-your-face arguments. They assume that the end justifies the means. **Strategy:** Keep your cool. Immediately respond calmly and professionally to let the bully know you are not a target: "When you're ready to speak to me with respect, I'll be ready to discuss this matter." Walk away from a ranting bully. Ask the bully to fully explain what he or she is trying to say or do, and then paraphrase your understanding of the bully's real intentions.
THE BACKSTABBER	They present themselves as your friend but do everything in their power to sabotage your relationships with your supervisors, coworkers, and clients. They use tactics such as withholding information from you and then suggesting to others that you are incompetent, witless, and worthy of demotion. **Strategy:** Once you've discovered your saboteur, tell key people that the person is, in fact, not a friend, which takes power from the backstabber and reveals the smear campaign.
THE WHINER	They wallow in their woe, whine incessantly about the injustices that surround them, and carry the weight of the world on their shoulders. **Strategy:** Listen and write down their main points. Interrupt and get specifics so you can identify and focus on possible solutions. If they remain in "it's hopeless" mode, walk away saying, "Let me know when you want to talk about a solution."
THE JERK	They tend to be self-centered, arrogant, manipulative, and goal-oriented. They trust no one and refuse to collaborate with others. They may take pot-shots at you during meetings, but avoid one-on-one confrontations. They lack empathy, but can be great sweet-talkers to the boss. **Strategy:** They do not respond to normal pleas to change their behavior, so just back off. Do not take their bait, limit your contact with them, avoid conflict when possible, and always be on guard.
THE KNOW-IT-ALL	They will tell you what they know, but they won't bother listening to your "clearly inferior" ideas. Often they really don't know much, but they don't let that get in the way. They exaggerate, brag, and mislead. **Strategy:** Acknowledge their expertise, but be prepared with your facts. Use "I" statements, such as "From what I've read and experienced . . ."
THE NEBBISH	When faced with a crucial decision, they keep putting it off until it's too late and the decision makes itself, or they say yes to everything but follow through on nothing. **Strategy:** Help them feel comfortable and safe in their rare decisions to move forward, and stay in touch until the decision is implemented. Arrange deadlines and describe the consequences that will result when they complete the tasks and what will happen if they don't.
THE EXPLODERS	They throw tantrums that can escalate quickly. When they blow their tops, they are unable to stop. When the smoke clears and the dust settles, the cycle begins again. **Strategy:** When an explosion begins, assertively repeat the individual's name to get his or her attention, or repeat a neutral comment such as "Stop!" Calmly address what they said in their first few sentences, which usually reveals the real problem. Give them time to regain self-control. Suggest they take time out to cool down, and then listen to their problems in private.

TABLE 8.1

Behaviors Exhibited by Assertive, Aggressive, and Nonassertive Persons

	Assertive Person	Aggressive Person	Nonassertive Person
In conflict situations	Communicates directly	Dominates	Avoids the conflict
In decision-making situations	Chooses for self	Chooses for self and others	Allows others to choose
In situations expressing feelings	Is open, direct, honest, while allowing others to express their feelings	Expresses feelings in a threatening manner; puts down, inhibits others	Holds true feelings inside
In group meeting situations	Uses direct, clear "I" statements: "I believe that . . ."	Uses clear but demeaning "you" statements: "You should have known better . . ."	Uses indirect, unclear statements: "Would you mind if . . . ?"

In the beginning, take small steps.

Being assertive may be difficult at first, so start with something that is easy. You might decline the invitation to keep the minutes at the weekly staff meeting if you feel others should assume this duty from time to time. If you are tired of eating lunch at Joe's Diner (the choice of a coworker), suggest a restaurant that you would prefer. If someone insists on keeping the temperature at a cool 67 degrees and you are tired of being cold all the time, approach the person and voice your opinion. Asking that your desires be considered is not necessarily a bad thing.

Use communication skills that enhance assertiveness.

A confident tone of voice, eye contact, firm gestures, and good posture create nonverbal messages that say, "I'm serious about this request." Using "I" messages can be especially helpful in cases where you want to assert yourself in a nonthreatening manner. If you approach the person who wants the thermostat set at 67 degrees and say, "You need to be more considerate of others," the person is likely to become defensive. However, if you say, "I feel uncomfortable when the temperature is so cool," you will start the conversation on a more positive note.

Be soft on people and hard on the problem.

The goal of conflict resolution is to solve the problem but avoid doing harm to the relationship. Of course, relationships tend to become entangled with the problem, so there is a tendency to treat the people and the problem as one. Your coworker Terry is turning in projects late every week, and you are feeling a great deal of frustration each time it happens. You must communicate to Terry that each missed deadline creates serious problems for you. Practice using tact, diplomacy, and patience as you keep the discussion focused on the problem, not on Terry's personality traits.

TEST PREPPER 8.2

ANSWERS CAN BE FOUND ON P. 237

True or False?

___ 1. It is sometimes necessary to use aggressive behavior to resolve conflict.

Multiple Choice

___ 2. During her conference with Dan, Sandy listens carefully to Dan's complaints about anything and everything; identifies and writes down specific problems; and finally tells Dan that they will talk again when Dan is ready to discuss solutions. Judging by her handling of Dan, Sandy believes that Dan is a:

a. whiner.
b. know-it-all.
c. jerk.
d. backstabber.

ACE the Test
ACE and ACE+ Practice Tests

___ 3. Which of the following is true for developing assertiveness skills?

a. Be hard on people and hard on the problem.
b. Be hard on the problem and soft on people.
c. Focus on achieving a win/lose outcome.
d. Begin communications with "you" statements rather than "I" statements.

___ 4. In a group meeting an assertive person is likely to say which of the following statements?

a. "I believe we should use the XYZ company."
b. "You are wrong. We should not use the ABC company."
c. "Would you mind if we went with the XYZ company."
d. "You should have known better than to hire the MLN company."

LEARN TO NEGOTIATE EFFECTIVELY

3 *Understand when and how to implement effective negotiation skills.*

In the past, the responsibility for negotiating an effective resolution to conflicts was often given to supervisors, department heads, team leaders, shop stewards, mediators, and other individuals with established authority and responsibility. Today, many companies have organized workers into teams and are empowering those workers to solve their own problems whenever possible. This means that every employee needs to learn how to effectively negotiate satisfactory resolutions to conflicts. Danny Ertel, author and consultant in the area of negotiations, says, "Every company today exists in a complex web of relationships, and the shape of that web is formed, one thread at a time, through negotiations,"[15] Team assignments, compensation, promotions, and work assignments are just a few of the areas where you can apply negotiation skills.

Think Win/Win

There are basically three ways to approach negotiations: win/lose, lose/lose, and win/win. When you use the **win/lose approach**, you are attempting to reach your goals at the expense of the other party's. For example, a manager can say, "Do as I say or find a job somewhere else!" The manager wins; the employee loses. Although this approach may end the conflict on a short-term basis, it doesn't usually address

win/lose approach The attempt to reach one's goals at the expense of the other party.

Soon after celebrating their 15th wedding anniversary Elaine and Michael Honig decided to get a divorce. As joint owners of the successful Honig Vineyard, the divorce could have created serious problems. However, they decided to remain friends as well as business partners after the divorce.

the underlying cause of the problem. It may simply sow the seeds of another conflict because the "losers" feel frustrated. (This strategy may be effective in those rare instances when it is more important to get the job done than it is to maintain good human relations among the work force.)

When the **lose/lose approach** is used to settle a dispute, each side must give in to the other. If the sacrifices are too great, both parties may feel that too much has been given. This strategy can be applied when there is little time to find a solution through effective negotiation techniques, or when negotiations are at a standstill and no progress is being made. Union-management disputes, for example, often fall into the lose/lose trap when neither side is willing to yield. In these cases an arbitrator, a neutral third party, may be called in to impose solutions on the disputing parties.

In general, the win/lose and lose/lose approaches to negotiating create a "we versus they" attitude among the people involved in the conflict, rather than a "we versus the problem" approach. "We versus they" (or "my way versus your way") means that participants focus on whose solution is superior, instead of working together to find a solution that is acceptable to all. Each person tends to see the issue from his or her viewpoint only and does not approach the negotiations in terms of reaching the goal.

The basic purpose of the **win/win approach** to negotiating is to fix the problem—not the blame! Don't think hurt; think help. Negotiating a win/win solution to a conflict is not a debate where you are attempting to prove the other side wrong; instead, you are engaging in a dialogue where each side attempts to get the other side to understand its concerns and both sides then work toward a mutually satisfying solution. Your negotiations will go better when you shift your emphasis from a tactical approach of how to counter the other person's every comment to discovering a creative solution that simple haggling obscures.[16]

Perhaps the most vital skill in effective negotiations is listening. When you concentrate on learning common interests, not differences, the nature of the negotiations changes from a battle to win to a discussion of how to meet the objectives of everyone involved in the dispute (see Figure 8.2).

lose/lose approach A tactic used to settle a dispute whereby each side must give in to the other.

win/win approach The use of a creative solution or dialogue so that each party understands the concerns of the other party and both sides work toward a mutually satisfying solution.

Improve Your Grade
Audio Glossary

Beware of Defensive Behaviors

Effective negotiations are often slowed or sidetracked completely by defensive behaviors that surface when people are in conflict with each other. When one person in a conflict situation becomes defensive, others may mirror this behavior. In a short time, progress is slowed because people stop listening and begin thinking about how they can defend themselves against the other person's comments.

We often become defensive when we feel our needs are being ignored. Kurt Salzinger, Executive Director for Science at the American Psychological Association, reminds us that conflicts are often caused by unfulfilled needs for things such as dignity, security, identity, recognition, or justice. He says, "Conflict is often exacerbated as much by the process of the relationship as it is by the issues."[17] Determining the other person's needs requires careful listening and respect for views

FIGURE 8.2

Negotiation Tips From Best-Sellers

Source: Rob Walker, "Take It or Leave It: The Only Guide to Negotiating You Will Ever Need," *Inc.,* August 2003, p. 81.

Rob Walker reviewed several of the best-selling books on negotiation, including *Getting to Yes, You Can Negotiate Anything, The Negotiation Tool Kit,* and *The Power of Nice.* He discovered a few basic negotiating tips that recur in these popular advice books:

- Stay rationally focused on the issue being negotiated.
- Exhaustive preparation is more important than aggressive argument.
- Think through your alternatives.
- The more options you feel you have, the better a negotiating position you'll be in.
- Spend less time talking and more time listening and asking good questions. Sometimes silence is your best response.
- Let the other side make the first offer. If you're underestimating yourself, you might make a needlessly weak opening move.

that differ from your own. If you feel you are trapped in a win/lose negotiation and can hear yourself or the other person becoming defensive, do everything in your power to refocus the discussion toward fixing the problem rather than defending your position.

Know That Negotiating Styles Vary

Depending on personality, assertiveness skills, and past experiences in dealing with conflict in the workplace, individuals naturally develop their own negotiating styles. But negotiating is a skill, and people can learn how and when to adapt their style to deal effectively with conflict situations.

Robert Maddux suggests that there are five different behavioral styles that can be used during a conflict situation. These styles are based on the combination of two factors: assertiveness and cooperation (see Figure 8.3). He takes the position that different styles may be appropriate in different situations.

Avoidance Style (Uncooperative/Nonassertive)

This style is appropriate when the conflict is too minor or too great to resolve. Any attempt to resolve the conflict might result in damaging a relationship or simply wasting time and energy.

Accommodating Style (Cooperative/Nonassertive)

This style is appropriate when resolving the conflict is not worth risking damage to the relationship or general disharmony. Individuals who use this approach relinquish their own concerns to satisfy the concerns of someone else.

FIGURE 8.3

Behavioral Styles for Conflict Situations

Source: Adapted from Robert B. Maddux's *Team Building: An Exercise in Leadership,* Crisp Publications, Inc., Menlo, Calif., 1986, p. 53. Reprinted by permission of the publisher.

High degree of assertiveness
X
Win/Lose Style
Confrontational, aggressive. Must win at any cost.
X
Problem-Solving Style
Needs of both parties are legitimate and important. High respect for mutual support. Assertive and cooperative.
Low degree of cooperation
X
High degree of cooperation
COMPROMISING STYLE
Important that all parties achieve basic goals and maintain good relationships. Aggressive but cooperative.
Avoidance Style
Nonconfrontational. Ignores or passes over issues. Denies issues are a problem.
X
Accommodating Style
Agreeable, nonassertive. Cooperative even at the expense of personal goals.
X
Low degree of assertiveness

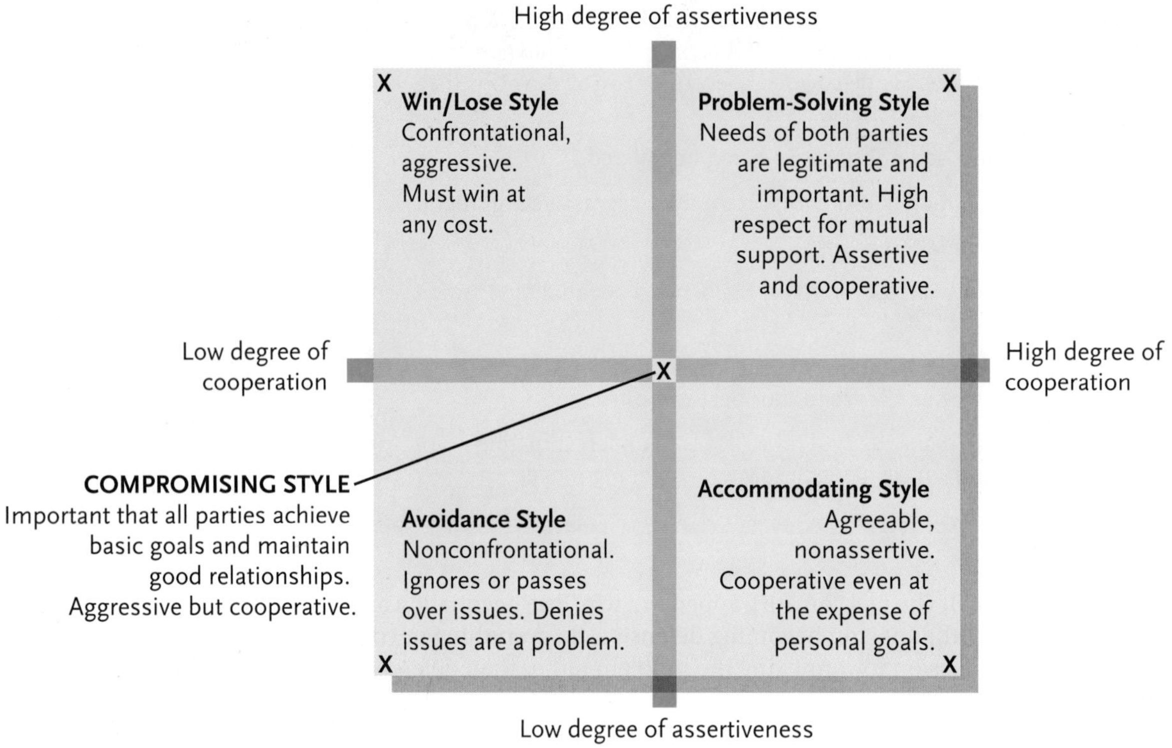

Win/Lose Style (Uncooperative/Aggressive)

This style may be appropriate when the conflict involves "survival of the fittest," when you must prove your superior position, or when your opinion is the most ethically or professionally correct.

Problem-Solving Style (Assertive/Cooperative)

This style is appropriate when all parties openly discuss the issues and a mutually beneficial solution can be found without anyone making a major concession. Problem solvers attempt to uncover underlying issues that may be at the root of the problem and then focus the discussion toward achieving the most desirable outcome.

Compromising Style (Moderately Aggressive/Moderately Cooperative)

This style is appropriate when no one person or idea is perfect, when there is more than one good way to do something, or when you must give to get what you want. Compromise attempts to find mutually acceptable solutions to the conflict that partially satisfy both sides. Never use this style when unethical activities are the cause of the conflict.

© King Features Syndicate

TEST PREPPER 8.3

ANSWERS CAN BE FOUND ON P. 237

True or False?

T 1. Negotiating is a skill, and people can learn how and when to adapt their style for effective conflict resolution.

Multiple Choice

b 2. When it comes to negotiating, the most crucial skill is:
   a. speaking articulately.
   b. listening well.
   c. standing one's ground.
   d. aggressively seeking victory.

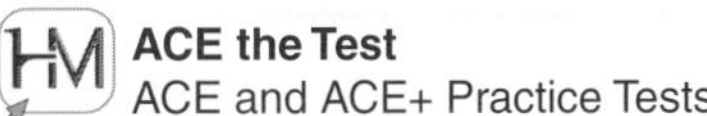
ACE the Test
ACE and ACE+ Practice Tests

d 3. Clare is known as a "My-Way-or-the-Highway" type of supervisor. Clare's approach to conflict is typically:
   a. win/win.
   b. compromise.
   c. optimize.
   d. win/lose.

b 4. When resolving the conflict is not worth potentially damaging the interpersonal relationship, this conflict resolution style is appropriate.
   a. Avoidance
   b. Accommodation
   c. Compromise
   d. Win/lose

CONFLICT RESOLUTION PROCESS

4 *Identify key elements of the conflict resolution process.*

The **conflict resolution process** consists of five steps that can be used at work and in your personal life. To apply the five steps requires understanding and acceptance of everything we have discussed up to this point in the chapter: application of assertiveness skills, understanding how to deal with various types of difficult people, support for the win/win approach to conflict resolution, and learning how to negotiate.

conflict resolution process A process that includes understanding and acceptance, the application of assertiveness skills, knowledge of how to deal with various types of difficult people, support for the win/win approach to conflict resolution, and negotiation.

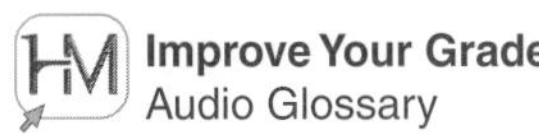
Improve Your Grade
Audio Glossary

Step One: Decide Whether You Have a Misunderstanding or a True Disagreement

David Stiebel, author of *When Talking Makes Things Worse!*, says a misunderstanding is a failure to accurately understand the other person's point. A disagreement, in contrast, is a failure to agree that would persist despite the most accurate understanding. In a true disagreement, people want more than your explanation and further details; they want to change your mind.[18] When we fail to realize the distinction between these two possibilities, a great deal of time and energy may be wasted. Consider the following conflict situation.

As Sarah entered the driveway of her home, she could hardly wait to share the news with her husband Paul. Late that afternoon she had met with her boss and learned she was the number one candidate for a newly created administrative position. Sarah entered the house and immediately told Paul about the promotion opportunity. In a matter of seconds, it became apparent that he was not happy about the promotion. He said, "We don't need the extra money, and you do not need the headaches that come with an administrative position." Expecting a positive response, Sarah was very disappointed. In the heat of anger, Sarah and Paul both said things they would later regret.

If Sarah and Paul had asked each other a few questions, this conflict might have been avoided. Prior to arriving home, Sarah had already weighed the pros and cons of the new position and decided it was not a good career move; however, she wanted her husband's input before making the final decision. This conflict was not a true disagreement, in which one person tries to change the other person's mind; it was a misunderstanding that was the result of incomplete information. If Sarah and Paul had fully understood each other's position, it would have become clear that a true disagreement did not exist.

Step Two: Define the Problem and Collect the Facts

The saying "A problem well defined is a problem half solved" is not far from the truth. It is surprising how difficult this step can be. Everyone involved needs to focus on the real cause of the conflict, not on what has happened as a result of it. At this stage, it is helpful to have everyone write a one- or two-sentence definition of the problem. When everyone is allowed to define the problem, the real cause of the conflict will often surface.

As you begin collecting information about the conflict, it may be necessary to separate facts from opinions or perceptions. Ask questions that focus on who is involved in the conflict, what happened, when, where, and why. What policies and procedures were involved?

Conflict resolution in the age of information offers us new challenges. As we are faced with information overload, we may be tempted to use the information we already have rather than search for the new information needed to guide a decision.[19]

Step Three: Clarify Perceptions

Your perception is your interpretation of the facts surrounding the situations you encounter. Perceptions can have a tremendous influence on your behavior. In a conflict situation, it is therefore very important that you clarify all parties' perceptions of the problem. You can do this by attempting to see the situation as others see it. Take the case of Laura, a sales representative who was repeatedly passed over for a promotion even though her sales numbers were among the best in the department.

Over a period of time Laura became convinced that she was the victim of gender discrimination. She filed charges with the Equal Employment Opportunity Commission (EEOC), and a hearing was scheduled. When Laura's boss was given a chance to explain his actions, he described Laura as someone who was very dedicated to her family. He said, "It's my view that she would be unhappy in a sales management position because she would have to work longer hours and travel more." He did not see his actions as being discriminatory. Laura explained that she valued the time she spent with her husband and children but achieving a management position was an important career goal. Laura's and her boss's perceptions of the same situation were totally different.

Step Four: Generate Options for Mutual Gain

Once the basic problem has been defined, the facts surrounding it have been brought out, and everyone is operating with the same perceptions, everyone involved in the conflict should focus on generating options that will fix the problem. Some people,

Snapping at Each Other?
If there's one thing every company doing business on a global scale wants to avoid, it's the delay, cost and uncertainty of litigation in a foreign court.
That's why more and more companies entering into cross-border agreements are turning to the International Centre for Dispute Resolution™, a division of the American Arbitration Association, for assistance in drafting conflict resolution clauses.
So when conflicts arise, parties can turn to our experienced case managers and expert neutrals, utilizing our internationally recognized rules and procedures, to resolve the issues in a timely, fair and non-litigious manner.
For more information on international dispute resolution services that take the bite out of even the most complex cross-border dispute, call 1-800-311-3799 or visit us from anywhere around the globe at www.adr.org.
ICDR
International Centre for Dispute Resolution

The International Centre for Dispute Resolution (ICDR) offers conflict resolution assistance to organizations that are doing business on a global scale. Cross-border disputes can sometimes be very complicated.

however, do not consider generating options to be part of the conflict resolution process. Rather than broadening the options for mutual gain, some individuals want to quickly build support for a single solution. The authors of the best-selling book *Getting to Yes* say, "In a dispute, people usually believe that they know the right answer—their view should prevail. They become trapped in their own point of view."[20]

Step Five: Implement Options with Integrity

The final step in the conflict resolution process involves finalizing an agreement that offers win/win benefits to those in conflict. Sometimes, as the conflict resolution process comes to a conclusion, one or more parties in the conflict may be tempted to win an advantage that weakens the relationship. This might involve hiding information or using pressure tactics that violate the win/win spirit and weaken the relationship. Even the best conflict solutions can fail unless all conflict partners serve as "caretakers" of the agreement and the relationship.[21]

Establish timetables for implementing the solutions, and provide a plan to evaluate their effectiveness. On a regular basis, make a point to discuss with others how things are going to be sure that old conflict patterns do not resurface. Conflict resolution agreements must be realistic and effective enough to survive as the challenges of the future confront them. Avoid the temptation to implement quick-fix solutions that may prove to be unsatisfactory in a few weeks.[22]

TEST PREPPER 8.4

ANSWERS CAN BE FOUND ON P. 237

True or False?

___ 1. A misunderstanding and a disagreement are basically the same thing.

Multiple Choice

___ 2. When you attempt to see the situation as others see it, you are performing which step of conflict resolution?
   a. Step four: Generate options for mutual gain
   b. Step five: Implement options with integrity
   c. Step three: Clarify perceptions
   d. Step two: Define the problem and collect the facts

___ 3. In a dispute, if people believe they know the correct answer and they become trapped in their point of view, they are failing which step of conflict resolution?
   a. Step four: Generate options for mutual gain
   b. Step five: Implement options with integrity
   c. Step three: Clarify perceptions
   d. Step two: Define the problem and collect the facts

___ 4. When Cheryl finalizes an agreement with her employees for a new project, develops timelines for implementation, and generates methods for evaluating success, she is performing what step of conflict resolution?
   a. Step four: Generate options for mutual gain
   b. Step five: Implement options with integrity
   c. Step three: Clarify perceptions
   d. Step two: Define the problem and collect the facts

HM **ACE the Test**
ACE and ACE+ Practice Tests

EMOTIONAL BALANCE—AN INTRODUCTION

5 *Describe how emotions influence our thinking and behavior.*

An **emotion** is a strong, temporary feeling that is positive or negative. Emotional experiences tend to alter the thought processes by directing attention toward some things and away from others. Emotions energize our thoughts and behaviors.[23]

emotion A strong, temporary feeling (such as anger or fear) that is positive or negative.

Throughout each day our feelings are activated by a variety of events (see Figure 8.4). You might feel a sense of joy after learning that a coworker has just given birth to a new baby. You might feel overpowering grief after learning that your supervisor was killed in an auto accident. Angry feelings may surface when you discover that someone borrowed a tool without your permission. Once your feelings have been activated, your mind interprets the event. In some cases, the feelings trigger irrational thinking: "No one who works here can be trusted!" In other cases, you may engage in a rational thinking process: "Perhaps the person who borrowed the tool needed it to help a customer with an emergency repair." The important point to remember is that we can choose how we behave. We can gain control over our emotions.

Achieving Emotional Balance—A Daily Challenge

The need to discover ways to achieve emotional balance has never been greater. To be successful in these complex times, we need to be able to think and feel simultaneously. People make choices dictated primarily by either their heads (reason) or their hearts (feelings). The thinking function helps us see issues logically; the feeling function helps us be caring and human.[24] Many organizations are spawning fear, confusion, anger, and sadness because the leaders lack emotional balance.

The basic emotions that drive us—such as fear, love, grief, greed, joy, and anger—have scarcely changed over the years. However, we are now seeing enormous differences in the expression of emotions. Today, people are much more likely to engage in aggressive driving, misbehave at public events, or become abusive when they are unhappy with service. In the workplace many people experience emotional pain because of disagreeable bosses.

FIGURE 8.4

Behavior Is Influenced by Activating Events

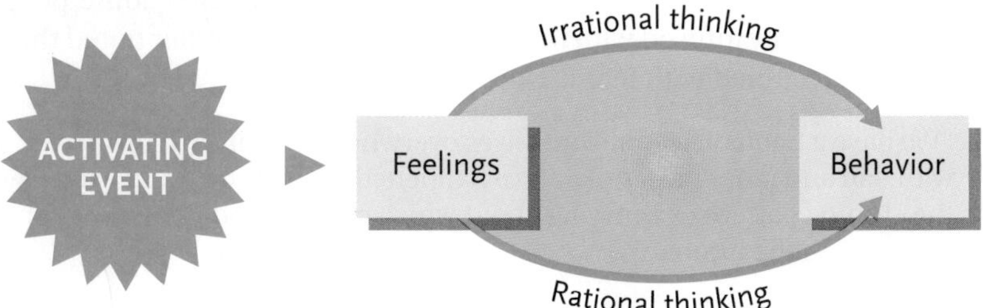

Emotional Intelligence

emotional intelligence The ability to recognize our own feelings and those of others; to manage emotions well in ourselves and in our relationships.

Daniel Goleman, author of several popular books on emotional intelligence, challenges the traditional view of the relationship between IQ and success. He says there are widespread exceptions to the rule that IQ predicts success: "At best, IQ contributes about 20 percent to the factors that determine life success, which leaves 80 percent to other forces.[25] **Emotional intelligence** can be described as the ability to monitor and control one's emotions and behavior at work and in social settings. Whereas standard intelligence (IQ) deals with thinking and reasoning, emotional intelligence (EQ) deals more broadly with building social relationships and controlling one's emotions. Several studies indicate that EQ can be increased through a combination of awareness and training. [26] The focus of Goleman's research is the human characteristics that make up what he describes as *emotional competence*. The emotional competence framework is made up of two dimensions.[27]

Personal Competence

This term refers to the competencies that determine how we manage ourselves. Recognizing one's emotions and their effects, keeping disruptive emotions and impulses in check, and maintaining standards of honesty and integrity represent a few of the competencies in this category.

Social Competence

This refers to the competencies that determine how we handle relationships. Sensing others' feelings and perspectives, listening openly and sending convincing messages, and negotiating and resolving disagreements represent some of the competencies in this category.

Although IQ tends to be stable throughout life, emotional competence is learnable and tends to increase throughout our life span. The emotional competencies that really matter for work can be learned.

Emotional Expression

We sometimes suffer from a lack of emotional balance because we learn to inhibit the expression of certain emotions and to overemphasize the expression of others. Some families, for example, discourage the expression of love and affection. Some people are taught from an early age to avoid expressing anger. Others learn that a public display of grief (crying, for example) is a sign of weakness. If as a child you were strongly encouraged to avoid the expression of anger, fear, love, or some other emotion, you may repress or block these feelings as an adult.[28]

Emotional imbalance also develops if we become fixated on a single emotion. The high incidence of violent crime in America has motivated some people to become almost totally infused with the emotion of fear. One writer noted that people who are preoccupied with fear may be intensifying the problem:

> "We have a habit of keeping ourselves overwhelmed, through the news media, with bad and scary things that have happened all over the world each day; and the chronic pattern of worrying about which of these bad things might happen to us in the future."[29]

To focus on one emotion to the exclusion of others creates a serious imbalance within us.

The Emotional Factor at Work

Emotions play a critical role in the success of every organization, yet many people in key decision-making positions—leaders with outstanding technical skills—fail to understand the important role emotions play in a work setting. In part, the problem can be traced to leadership training that emphasizes that "doing business" is a purely rational or logical process. Some leaders learn to value only those things that can be arranged, analyzed, and defined. One consultant put the problem into proper perspective when he said, "We are still trying to do business as if it requires only a meeting of the minds instead of a meeting of the hearts."[30]

Tim Sanders, former chief solutions officer at Yahoo!, says, "How we are perceived as human beings is becoming increasingly important in the new economy." He notes that compassion is an important key to long-term personal success. This is the human ability to reach out with warmth through eye contact, physical touch, or words. It is a quality machines can never possess.[31]

At Umpqua Bank, every element of the culture is focused on great customer service. Here we see a customer and his friend relaxing at an Umpqua branch bank in Portland, Oregon.

Relationship Strategy

Emotional undercurrents are present in almost every area of every organization. Most banks, hospitals, retail firms, hotels, and restaurants realize that they need a relationship strategy—a plan for establishing, building, and maintaining quality relationships with customers. Cosco Systems, for example, measures itself by the quality of its relationships with customers. Salespeople achieve their bonuses based in large part on customer satisfaction instead of on gross sales or profit.[32]

Frontline employees, those persons responsible for delivering quality service and building relationships, engage in "emotional labor," and those who have frequent contact with the public often find the work very stressful.[33] *Emotional labor*, which taxes the mind, is often more difficult to handle than physical labor, which strains the body. For this reason, frontline employees need the support of leaders who are both caring and competent.

Test Prepper 8.5

Answers can be found on p. 237

True or False?

____ 1. The basic emotions that drive people have changed little over the years. However, people today are more likely to exhibit road rage and abusive reactions to poor service.

____ 2. Most studies indicate that EQ (emotional intelligence) cannot be changed through training and remains mostly constant throughout life.

ACE the Test
ACE and ACE+ Practice Tests

Multiple Choice

____ 3. Feelings that influence thought and behavior are called:

a. emotions. c. negativity.
b. reinforcers. d. positivity.

____ 4. According to author Daniel Goleman, approximately what percentage of a person's life success is attributable to the intelligence quotient, or IQ?

a. 80 percent c. 40 percent
b. 50 percent d. 20 percent

FACTORS THAT INFLUENCE OUR EMOTIONS

6 *Describe the major factors that influence our emotional development.*

The starting point in achieving greater emotional control is to determine the source of emotional difficulties. Why do we sometimes display indifference when the expression of compassion would be more appropriate? Why is it so easy to put down a friend or coworker and so hard to recognize that person's accomplishments? Why do we sometimes worry about events that will never happen? To answer these and other questions, it is necessary to study the factors that influence our emotional development.

Temperament

temperament A person's individual style of expressing needs and emotions; it is biological and genetically based.

Temperament refers to a person's individual style of expressing needs and emotions; it is biological and genetically based. It reflects heredity's contribution to the beginning of an individual's personality.[34] Researchers have found that certain temperamental characteristics are apparent in children at birth and remain somewhat stable over time. For example, the traits associated with extroversion and introversion can be observed when a baby is born. Of course, many events take place between infancy and adulthood to alter or shape a person's temperament. Personality at every age reflects the interplay of temperament and of environmental influences, such as parenting.[35]

Unconscious Influences

unconscious mind The part of the mind of which we are unaware. A vast storehouse of forgotten memories, desires, ideas, and frustrations.

The **unconscious mind** is a vast storehouse of forgotten memories, desires, ideas, and frustrations, according to William Menninger, founder of the famed Menninger Foundation.[36] He noted that the unconscious mind can have a great influence on behavior. It contains memories of past experiences as well as memories of feelings associated with past experiences. The unconscious is active, continuously influencing conscious decision-making processes.

Although people cannot remember many of the important events of the early years of their lives, these incidents do influence their behavior as adults. Joan Borysenko offers this example:

> Inside me there is a seven-year-old who is still hurting from her humiliation at summer camp. Her anguish is reawakened every time I find myself in the presence of an authority figure who acts in a controlling manner. At those moments, my intellect is prone to desert me, and I am liable to break down and cry with the same desolation and helplessness I felt when I was seven.[37]

This example reminds us that childhood wounds can cause us to experience emotions out of proportion to a current situation. Also, we often relive the experience in a context very different from the one we experienced as a child. A worker who is strongly reprimanded by an angry supervisor may experience the same feelings that surfaced when he was scolded by his mother for breaking an expensive vase.

Cultural Conditioning

A professor at Dartmouth College said, "Culture is what we see and hear so often that we call it reality. Out of culture comes behavior."[38] Culture helps shape just about every aspect of our behavior and our mental processes. Culture is frequently associated with a particular country; but actually, most countries are multicultural. African Americans, Hispanic Americans, Asian Americans, and American Indians represent a few of the subcultures within the United States.[39]

Coping with Your Anger and the Anger of Others

7 *Learn how to deal with your anger and the anger of others.*

Anger may be defined as the thoughts, feelings, physical reactions, and actions that result from unacceptable behavior by others. Anger is almost always a response to perceived injustice, and may dissolve with a deeper understanding of the cause. Anger in the workplace is clearly on the rise. In a survey conducted by Marlin Company, a national workplace communication company, 52 percent of respondents said their colleagues need help managing anger. The authors of *Anger Kills* say that about 20 percent of the general population has levels of hostility high enough to be dangerous to their health.[40]

anger A strong feeling of displeasure, usually of antagonism.

Managing Your Anger

Learning to deal with their own anger and the anger of other people is one of the most sophisticated and mature skills people are ever required to learn. Intense anger takes control of people and distorts their perceptions, which is why angry people often make poor decisions.[41]

Dr. Art Ulene, author of *Really Fit Really Fast,* says the first step in anger management is to monitor your anger. How often do you get angry each day? What are the causes of irritation in your life? How upsetting is each episode of anger? How well do you manage each episode? Ulene suggests using a diary or journal to record this information. This self-monitoring activity will help you determine the impact of anger in your life. Record not only the source of the irritation but the feelings that surfaced when you became angry. Also record the behaviors you displayed when angry. Ulene says that people who monitor their behavior carefully see positive results: "Without even trying, their behavior begins to change in ways that are usually desirable."[42]

What makes you angry? The anger journal will help you identify your most common anger triggers. You may find that irritations and annoyances such as traffic delays, interruptions,

Did you hear me? Anger control has been a challenge for Bobby Knight. Here we see the Texas Tech coach yelling at an official during a game against Baylor University.

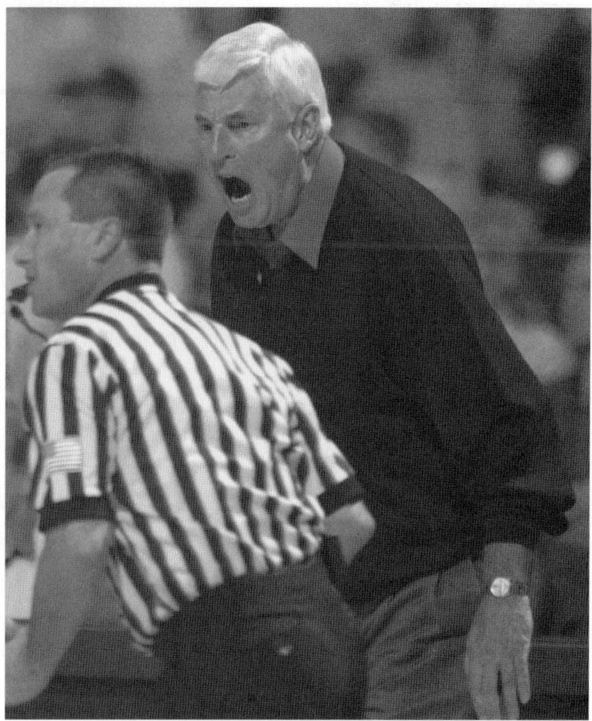

or loud noise are very irritating. You may discover that your anger is frequently connected to disappointment in someone or to some annoying event.

Intense anger often takes the form of rage. In addition to road rage, air rage, and customer rage, we are witnessing more incidents of "workplace rage." Workplace rage can take the form of yelling, verbal abuse, and physical violence. It is more likely to occur when workers are stressed by long hours, unrealistic deadlines, cramped quarters, excessive e-mail, lack of recognition, bullying incidents, or some combination of these factors.

Effective Ways to Express Your Anger

Buddha said, "You will not be punished for your anger, you will be punished by your anger." Buddhist teachings tell us that patience is the best antidote to aggression.[43] Intense anger that is suppressed will linger and become a disruptive force in your life unless you can find a positive way to get rid of it. Expressing feelings of anger can be therapeutic, but many people are unsure about the best way to self-disclose this emotion. To express anger in ways that will improve the chances that the other person will receive and respond to your message, consider these suggestions:

1. *Avoid reacting in a manner that could be seen as emotionally unstable.* If others see you as reacting irrationally, you will lose your ability to influence them.[44] Failure to maintain your emotional control can damage your image.
2. *Do not make accusations or attempt to fix blame.* It would be acceptable to begin the conversation by saying, "I felt humiliated at the staff meeting this morning." It would not be appropriate to say, "Your comments at the morning staff meeting were mean-spirited and made me feel humiliated." The latter statement invites a defensive response.[45]
3. *Express your feelings in a timely manner.* The intensity of anger can actually increase with time. Also, important information needed by you or the person who provoked your anger may be forgotten or distorted with the passing of time.
4. *Be specific as you describe the factors that triggered your anger, and be clear about the resolution you are seeking.* The direct approach, in most cases, works best.

In some cases the person who triggers your anger may be someone you cannot confront without placing your job in jeopardy. For example, one of your best customers may constantly complain about the service he receives. You know he receives outstanding service, and you feel anger building inside you each time he complains. But any display of anger may result in loss of his business. In this situation you rely on your rational thinking power and say to yourself, "This part of my work is very distasteful, but I can stay calm each time he complains."

TOTAL PERSON INSIGHT

Pema Chödrön Author and Buddhist Teacher

"We can suppress anger or act it out, either way making things worse for ourselves and others. Or we can practice patience: wait, experience the anger and investigate its nature."

How to Handle Other People's Anger

Dealing with other people's anger may be the most difficult human relations challenge we face. The following skills can be learned and applied to any situation where anger threatens to damage a relationship.

1. *Recognize and accept the other person's anger.* The simple recognition of the intense feelings of someone who is angry does a lot to defuse the situation.[46] In a calm voice you might say, "I can see that you are very angry," or "It's obvious that you are angry."
2. *Encourage the angry person to vent his or her feelings.* By asking questions and listening carefully to the response, you can encourage the person to discuss the cause of the anger openly. Try using an open-ended question to encourage self-disclosure: "What have I done to upset you?" or "Can you tell me why you are so angry?"
3. *Do not respond to an angry person with your own anger.* To express your own anger or become defensive will only create another barrier to emotional healing. When you respond to the angry person, keep your voice tone soft. Keep in mind the old biblical injunction, "A soft answer turns away wrath."[47]
4. *Give the angry person feedback.* After venting feelings and discussing specific details, the angry person will expect a response. Briefly paraphrase what seems to be the major concern of the angry person, and express a desire to find ways to solve the problem. If you are at fault, accept the blame for your actions and express a sincere apology.

Test Prepper 8.6, 8.7

Answers can be found on p. 237

True or False?

____ 1. The unconscious mind is active, continuously influencing conscious decision-making processes.

____ 2. Anger in the workplace is clearly in decline.

____ 3. If you are trying to express your anger, you should try to do so in a timely manner, as feelings of anger can intensify with time.

Multiple Choice

____ 4. In the United States, intense media focus on violence and crime causes many people to experience:
   a. emotional imbalance because of exaggerated belligerent reactions.
   b. emotional imbalance because of exaggerated fearful reactions.
   c. greater emotional balance because of additional information about the world.
   d. greater emotional balance as they realize that they are not victims.

____ 5. ____is the thoughts, feelings, actions, and physical reactions that result from unacceptable behavior by others.
   a. Temperament
   b. Cultural conditioning
   c. Emotion
   d. Anger

____ 6. Susan is starting an anger management process. Her first step will be to:
   a. monitor her anger by recording episodes of anger in a journal.
   b. suppress her anger.
   c. identify who is to blame for her anger.
   d. display the anger, no matter what the circumstances are.

ACE the Test
ACE and ACE+ Practice Tests

STRATEGIES FOR ACHIEVING EMOTIONAL CONTROL

8 *Describe strategies for achieving emotional control.*

Each day we wake up with a certain amount of mental, emotional, and physical energy that we can spend throughout the day. If we allow our "difficult" emotions to deplete our energy, we have no energy to change our life or to give to others.[48] The good news is that we can learn to discipline the mind and banish afflicting thoughts that create needless frustration and waste energy. In this, the final part of the chapter, we share with you some practical suggestions for achieving greater control of the emotions that affect your life.

Identifying Your Emotional Patterns

We could often predict or anticipate our response to various emotions if we would take the time to study our emotional patterns—to take a running inventory of circumstances that touch off jealousy, fear, anger, or some other emotion. Journal entries can help you discover emotional patterns. Record not only your conscious feelings, such as anxiety or guilt, but feelings in your body, such as a knot in your stomach or muscle tension.

If you don't feel comfortable with journal writing, consider setting aside some quiet time to reflect on your emotional patterns. A period of quiet reflection will help you focus your thoughts and impressions. Becoming a skilled observer of your own emotions is one of the best ways to achieve greater emotional control.

In addition to journal writing and quiet reflection, there is one more way to discover emotional patterns. At the end of the day, construct a chart of your emotional landscape. Make a chart (see Table 8.2) of the range of emotions you experienced and expressed during the day.[49] Your first entry might be "I woke up at 6:00 A.M. and immediately felt ______." The final entry might be "I left the office at 5:30 P.M. with a feeling of ______." What emotions surfaced throughout your workday? Resentment? Creative joy? Anxiety? Boredom? Contentment? Anger? Reflect on the completed chart and try to determine which patterns need to be changed. For example, you might discover that driving in heavy traffic is a major energy drain. Repeat this process over a period of several days in order to identify your unique emotional patterns.

TOTAL PERSON INSIGHT

Gerard Egan Author, ***You and Me***

"It's unfortunate that we're never really taught how to show emotion in ways that help our relationships. Instead, we're usually told what we should not do. However, too little emotion can make our lives seem empty and boring, while too much emotion, poorly expressed, fills our interpersonal lives with conflict and grief. Within reason, some kind of balance in the expression of emotion seems to be called for."

TABLE 8.2

Charting Your Emotional Landscape

Time	Circumstance	Emotion
6:00 A.M.	Alarm goes off. Mind is flooded by thoughts of all the things that must be done during the day.	Anxiety
7:10 A.M.	Depart for work. Heavy traffic interferes with plan to arrive at work early.	Anger and helplessness
8:00 A.M.	Thirty-minute staff meeting scheduled by the boss lasts fifty minutes. No agenda is provided. Entire meeting seems a waste of time.	Anger and frustration
9:35 A.M.	Finally start work on creative project.	Contentment
10:15 A.M.	Progress on project interrupted when coworker enters office, sits down, and starts sharing gossip about another coworker.	Anger and resentment
11:20 A.M.	Progress is made on creative project.	Contentment
1:45 P.M.	Creative project is complete and ready for review.	Joy and contentment
2:50 P.M.	Give project to boss for review. She says she will not be able to provide any feedback until morning. This delay will cause scheduling problems.	Frustration
4:00 P.M.	Attend health insurance update seminar sponsored by human resources department. No major changes are discussed.	Boredom
5:40 P.M.	Give up on a search for a missing document, turn off computer, and walk to parking lot.	Relief and fatigue

Fine-Tuning Your Emotional Style

Once you have completed the process of self-examination and have identified some emotional patterns you want to change, it is time to consider ways to fine-tune your emotional style. Bringing about discipline within your mind can help you live a fuller, more satisfying life. Here are four things you can begin doing today.

- *Take responsibility for your emotions.* How you view your emotional difficulties will have a major influence on how you deal with them. If your frustration is triggered by thoughts such as "I can never make my boss happy" or "Things always go wrong in my life," you may never achieve a comfortable emotional state. By shifting the blame to other people and events, you cannot achieve emotional control.
- *Put your problems into proper perspective.* Why do some people seem to be at peace with themselves most of the time while others seem to be in a perpetual state of anxiety? People who engage in unproductive obsessing are unable or unwilling to look at problems realistically and practically, and they view each disappointment as a major catastrophe. To avoid needless misery, anxiety, and emotional upsets, use an "emotional thermometer" with a scale of 0 to 100. Zero means that everything is going well, and 100 denotes something life-threatening or truly catastrophic. Whenever you feel upset, ask yourself to come up with a logical number on the emotional thermometer. If a problem

surfaces that is merely troublesome but not terrible, and you give it 60 points, you are no doubt overreacting. This mental exercise will help you avoid mislabeling a problem and feeling upset as a result.[50]

- *Take steps to move beyond negative emotions such as envy, anger, jealousy, or hatred.* Some people are upset about things that happened many years ago. Some even nurse grudges against people who have been dead for years. The sad thing is that the negative feelings remain long after we can achieve any positive learning from them.[51] Studies of divorce, for example, indicate that anger and bitterness can linger a long time. Distress seems to peak one year after the divorce, and many people report that it takes at least two years to move past the anger.[52] When negative emotions dominate one's life, whatever the reason, therapy or counseling may provide relief. Learning to release unwanted patterns of behavior is very important.

- *Give your feelings some exercise.* Several prominent authors in the field of human relations have emphasized the importance of giving our feelings some exercise. Leo Buscaglia, author of *Loving Each Other,* says, "Exercise feelings. Feelings have meaning only as they are expressed in action."[53] Sam Keen, author of *Fire in the Belly,* said, "Make a habit of identifying your feelings and expressing them in some appropriate way."[54] If you have offended someone, how about sending that person a note expressing regret? If someone you work with has given extra effort, why not praise that person's work? Make a decision to cultivate positive mental states like kindness and compassion. A sincere feeling of empathy, for example, will deepen your connection to others.

Every day of our personal and work life we face some difficult decisions. One option is to take only actions that feel good at the moment. In some cases, this means ignoring the feelings of customers, patients, coworkers, and supervisors. Another option is to behave in a manner that is acceptable to the people around you. If you choose this option, you will have to make some sacrifices. You may have to be warm and generous when the feelings inside you say, "Be cold and selfish." You may have to avoid an argument when your feelings are insisting, "I'm right and the other person is wrong!" To achieve a positive emotional state often requires restructuring our ways of feeling, thinking, and behaving.

TEST PREPPER 8.8

ANSWERS CAN BE FOUND ON P. 237

True or False?

____ 1. Making a decision to cultivate positive mental states such as empathy and compassion can help to change emotional patterns.

____ 2. If you shift blame from yourself to other people for negative situations in your life, you can start to gain emotional control.

____ 3. Negative and difficult emotions can create frustration and waste personal energy.

Multiple Choice

____ 4. One of the best ways to achieve emotional control is to:

a. vent emotions immediately when you feel them so they never become too great.
b. become a skilled observer of your own emotions through journaling or reflection.
c. attempt to ignore your emotions so they do not gain too much importance.
d. stay away from people who cause you to lose emotional control.

____ 5. Sally has identified some emotional patterns she would like to change. What would you recommend Sally do next?

a. Find out who is to blame for her negative emotional patterns
b. Try to hang on to emotions such as envy or anger in order to stay motivated
c. Try to ignore these emotional patterns so that they go away
d. Put her problems into perspective

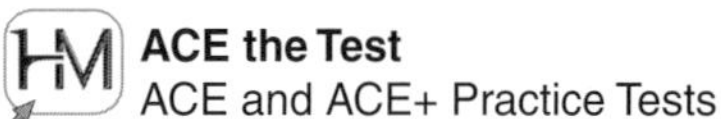

Improve Your Grade
Learning Objectives Review
Audio Chapter Review
Audio Chapter Quiz

LEARNING OBJECTIVES REVIEW

1 *List and describe some of the major causes of conflict in the work setting.*

- Conflicts among people at work happen every day and can arise because of:
  - changes within the organization
  - poor communication
  - values and culture clashes
  - confusing work policies and practices
  - competition for scarce resources
  - adversarial management
- While unresolved conflicts can have a negative effect on an organization's productivity, a difference of opinion sometimes has a positive effect by forcing team members toward creative and innovative solutions to problems.

2 *Utilize assertiveness skills in conflict situations.*

- Assertiveness skills are necessary when you want to maintain your rights during a conflict with someone else but want to avoid being overly aggressive and interfering with others' rights.
- Begin building assertiveness skills by tackling relatively minor issues first until you gain the confidence to take on those who try to take away your power. Use "I" statements rather than "you" statements so that the other person does not become defensive. Focus on fixing the problem rather than attacking the other person.

LEARNING OBJECTIVES REVIEW (CONTINUED)

3 *Understand when and how to implement effective negotiation skills.*

- You can vastly improve your human relations skills when dealing with difficult people by learning when and how to intentionally implement Robert Maddux's five negotiating styles.
- These styles include the avoidance style (uncooperative/nonassertive), accommodating style (cooperative/nonassertive), win/lose style (uncooperative/aggressive), problem-solving style (assertive/cooperative), and compromising style (moderately aggressive/moderately cooperative).

4 *Identify key elements of the conflict resolution process.*

- Step one: Decide whether you have a misunderstanding or a true disagreement.
- Step two: Define the problem and collect the facts.
- Step three: Clarify perceptions.
- Step four: Generate options for mutual gain.
- Step five: Implement options with integrity.

5 *Describe how emotions influence our thinking and behavior.*

- An emotion can be thought of as a feeling that influences our thinking and behavior.
- Feelings are activated by a variety of events. Angry feelings may surface when another employee borrows something without your permission. Feelings of grief will very likely follow the loss of a close friend.

6 *Describe the major factors that influence our emotional development.*

- Our emotional development is influenced by:
  - temperament (the biological shaper of personality)
  - our unconscious mind
  - cultural conditioning
- Throughout the long process of emotional development, we learn different ways to express our emotions.

7 *Learn how to deal with your anger and the anger of others.*

- Appropriate expressions of anger:
  - contribute to improved interpersonal relations
  - help us reduce anxiety
  - give us an outlet for unhealthy stress
- We must also learn how to handle other people's anger.

8 *Describe strategies for achieving emotional control.*

- Emotional control is an important dimension of emotional style.
- The starting point in developing emotional control is to identify your current emotional patterns. One way to do this is to record your anger experiences in a diary or journal.
- Additional ways to identify emotional patterns include setting aside time for quiet reflection and developing a chart of your emotional landscape.

Career Corner

Q: The old adage "Fool me once, shame on you. Fool me twice, shame on me!" has become a reality in my career search. Last year I accepted a position with an ad agency where the owners did not disclose they were married to each other until after I was on the job. I quit after nine months when I discovered they expected me to lie to clients about the size of the agency. I accepted my next job with an event-production company, even though the hiring supervisor made disparaging remarks about the person who had previously held my position. It is now obvious that this supervisor acts condescendingly toward everyone, including me. I should have recognized the clues that indicated I was heading into these bad-boss environments. How can I avoid falling into another bad situation now that I am once again looking for a job?

A: Many applicants ignore warning signs about their prospective supervisors, yet the type of person you will be working with is one of the most important factors you should consider when job hunting. Prepare a list of ideal traits you would want in your next supervisor and a second list of what bothers you most about your current one, and then quiz present and past employees about your prospective boss while keeping your itemized lists in mind. Ask them and your interviewer direct questions such as "Who was your employee of the year and why was that employee selected?" "Give me an example of how an employee's unethical conduct is handled." "During a recent crisis within the organization, who was the 'hero' and why?" "What is your employee retention rate?" If your stomach aches throughout an interview, talk about your feelings with a friend so that you can separate bad-boss anxiety from normal interview jitters. Don't let financial pressure dictate whether you take any job. Good luck!

Applying What You Have Learned

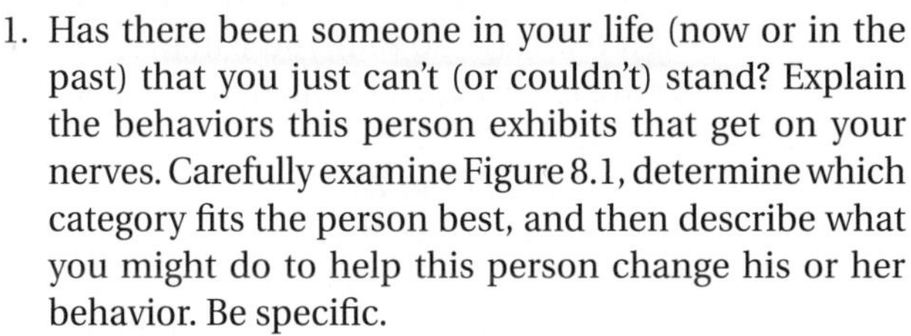

1. Has there been someone in your life (now or in the past) that you just can't (or couldn't) stand? Explain the behaviors this person exhibits that get on your nerves. Carefully examine Figure 8.1, determine which category fits the person best, and then describe what you might do to help this person change his or her behavior. Be specific.
2. To develop your assertiveness skills, find a partner who will join you for a practice session. The partner should assume the role of a friend, family member, or coworker who is doing something that causes you a great deal of frustration. (The problem can be real or imaginary.) Communicate your dislikes and feelings in a clear, direct manner without threatening or attacking. Then ask your partner to critique your assertiveness skills. Participate in several of these practice sessions until you feel confident that you have improved your assertiveness skills.
3. To learn more about the way you handle anger, record your anger responses in a journal for a period of five days. When anger surfaces, record as many details as possible. What triggered your anger? How intense was the anger? How long did your angry feelings last? Did you express them to anyone? At the end of the five days, study your entries and try to determine whether any patterns exist. If you find this activity helpful, consider keeping a journal for a longer period of time.
4. To learn more about how emotions influence your thinking and behavior, complete each of the following sentences. Once you have completed them all, reflect on your written responses. Can you identify any changes you would like to make in your emotional style?

   a. "When someone makes me angry, I usually . . ."
   b. "The most common worry in my life is . . ."
   c. "When I feel compassion for someone, my response is to . . ."
   d. "My response to feelings of grief is . . ."
   e. "When I am jealous of someone, my response is to . . ."

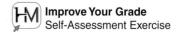

Improve Your Grade
Self-Assessment Exercise

ROLE-PLAY EXERCISE

Assume the role of a business manager for a large hospital. About three weeks ago you received some incomplete medical records from Ashley Carver, the physician in charge of the emergency room. With a red pen, you marked the areas that were incomplete and sent the forms back to the doctor. You attached a terse note that requested the forms be returned within twenty-four hours. Three days passed without a reply, and your anger increased each day. Finally, you sent the doctor an e-mail that basically accused Dr. Carver of incompetence in the area of medical record keeping. The doctor phoned you immediately and said the entire emergency room staff had been extremely busy and did not have a moment to spare. You replied that timely and accurate record keeping is the responsibility of every physician employed by the hospital. Unfortunately, your tone of voice and your selection of words were totally inappropriate. Basically, you treated Dr. Carver like a child who had misbehaved, and the doctor hung up on you. You immediately felt like a fool and regretted your behavior. The next day, the completed forms were returned to you. You have decided to meet with Dr. Carver. Your goal is to repair the damaged relationship and set the stage for effective communications in the future. Prior to meeting with another class member who will assume the role of Dr. Carver, review the information on resolving conflicts.

CASE 8.1

Couples Combat

According to a study conducted by the University of Denver, marital distress costs companies $6.8 billion in lost productivity. At any given time, one in every six employees has some sort of personal problem, including conflict with a significant other, that directly affects his or her productivity. These employees are three times more likely to think about quitting their job.

In an attempt to intercept this productivity hemorrhage, many organizations are taking a proactive approach to help their employees solve their marital conflicts before they happen. Managers are being taught how to help employees maintain healthy marriages and other personal relationships outside work by maintaining adequate staffing levels to avoid excessive overtime, discouraging workaholism, offering travel benefits for partners of employees who have to frequently travel on business, and encouraging vacations and occasional time off for personal reasons such as celebrating an anniversary.

Whether your employer is supportive or not, you as an individual need to take responsibility for maintaining your own marriage so that you can avoid the potentially negative effect a divorce might have on your personal life and your career track. In his book *Don't You Dare Get Married Until You Read This!*, Corey Donaldson says that the majority of issues that cause divorce already exist before the wedding because couples are not willing to ask or answer tough questions: Can physical violence by a mate be justified? What will we do if our child is born with a disability? Are you uncomfortable with women in high-paying jobs? If we both work, can we share the household duties? Daniel Caine, president of a financial planning firm for divorcing couples, says the most common causes for divorce are insecurity, money, communication, clash of values, and insufficient separation from family. He recommends asking such questions as: Are you comfortable with my religious observance? My family? My desire for wealth?[55]

Of course, asking the right premarital questions does not guarantee a healthy relationship. Conflicts will and do occur in even the most solid marriages. Some experts suggest that bickering can be good for relationships. It may be one of the keys to a strong marriage because open conflict improves communication and allows each partner to vent his or her frustrations. But you need to learn how to argue effectively. Dr. Phil McGraw suggests several ways you can make your arguments as constructive as possible.[56]

- Decide what you want before you even start the fight. Avoid simply complaining; ask for what you want.
- Keep it relevant. Focus on what you are arguing about. If you stray, the argument will resurface again until the real issue is addressed.
- Make it possible for your partner to retreat with dignity. Avoid calling each other names that linger beyond the argument. Show your partner courtesy and respect, even if he or she is wrong.
- Know when to say when. If you have to give up too much of your life to maintain the relationship, maybe it's not worth it.

Keep in mind that if your objective in an argument is to win, the other person has to lose. This win/lose mindset will only perpetuate the conflict.[57]

Questions

1. Have any of your coworkers experienced marital conflicts that affected their productivity at work? Did they have any impact on the organization and/or on you? Explain.
2. Have you had a conflict at home that had an effect on your work? Explain.
3. How might the premarital questions suggested in this case impact marital relations? What other questions need to be answered?
4. Recall your most recent conflict with your significant other. Did you follow Dr. Phil's suggestions? What was the outcome?

RESOURCES ON THE WEB

Prepare for Class, Improve Your Grade, and ACE the Test. Student Achievement Series resources include:

ACE and ACE+ Practice Tests	Chapter Glossaries	Audio Glossaries
Audio Chapter Quizzes	Chapter Outlines	Internet Insights
Audio Chapter Reviews	Crossword Puzzles	Self-Assessment Exercises
Learning Objective Reviews	Hangman Games	Additional Closing Cases
Career Snapshots	Flashcards	

To access these learning and study tools, go to **college.hmco.com/pic/reeceSAS**.

HM ManagementSPACE

A Life Plan for Effective Human Relations

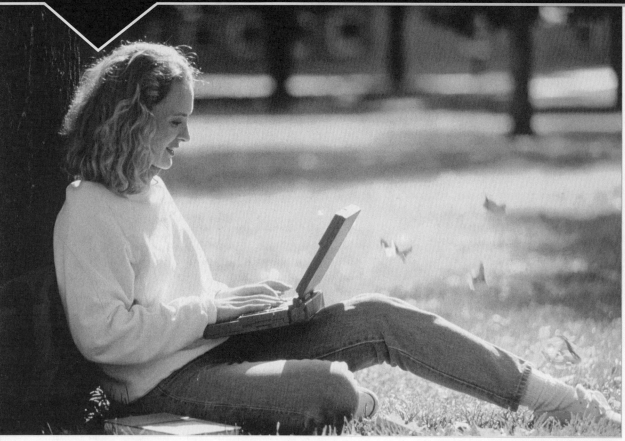

Many people are fortunate to work for a company that encourages telecommuting to balance work/life commitments or simply to allow employees to enjoy things that are important to them. When possible, this employee likes to combine work with an opportunity to enjoy nature.

1. *Define success by standards that are compatible with your needs and values.*
2. *Describe new models for success that provide work/life balance.*
3. *Discuss the meaning of* right livelihood.
4. *Describe four nonfinancial resources that can enrich your life.*

"If you want to be successful, you have to take 100% responsibility for everything that you experience in your life."

—Jack Canfield

Chapter Outline

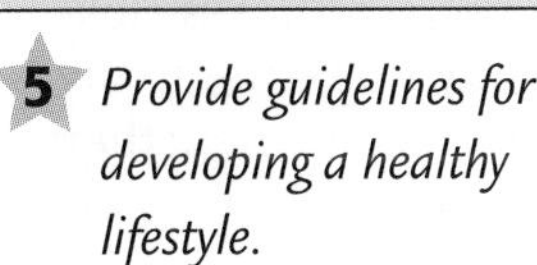

Provide guidelines for developing a healthy lifestyle.

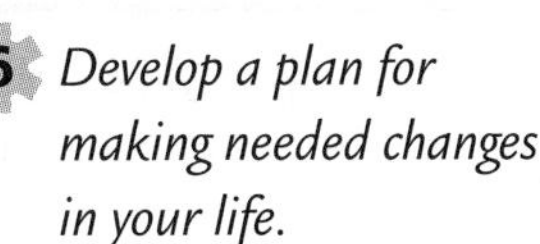

Develop a plan for making needed changes in your life.

Planning for Work/Life Balance

It seems like only yesterday that job seekers were searching for employment with companies that offered the promise of a big paycheck. Job security was not the most important element of the compensation package. Then came September 11, the tech crash, Enron, layoffs, and concerns about Social Security. Now long-term benefits such as health insurance and retirement plans are very important to soon-to-be college graduates. Universum, a research and consulting firm, conducted a survey of 29,046 undergraduates in all fields of study and discovered a changing pattern of job expectations. The CEO of Universum, reflecting on the research findings, said, "This generation is really trying to take their future in their own hands, and do something about it."[1]

This generation is also giving greater attention to work/life balance. In fact, this employer attribute is usually the most important element of the compensation package. Many of today's job seekers have grown up in homes where one or both parents worked long hours and were often cut off from family life. They are questioning a lifestyle that is characterized by long hours at work, infrequent vacations, and loss of leisure time. Many observers of the American scene say you can have a good job or a life, but not both. Maybe this new generation of workers will prove these skeptics wrong.

KEY TERMS

nonfinancial resources *p. 211*
physical fitness *p. 219*
right livelihood *p. 206*
spirituality *p. 214*

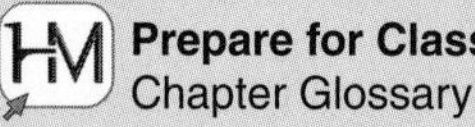

Prepare for Class
Chapter Glossary

Improve Your Grade
Flashcards
Hangman
Crossword Puzzle

In this chapter we help you construct a life plan that will enhance your relationships with people in your personal life and in your work life. This plan will also help you better manage the relationship you have with yourself. We discuss the meaning of success and suggest ways to cope with major disappointments that will surface in your work life. You will learn how to avoid being trapped by a lifestyle that offers financial rewards but little else. This chapter also helps you define your relationship with money and describes four nonfinancial resources that give meaning to life. Finally, you will learn how to develop the mental and physical fitness needed to keep up in today's frantic, fast-paced world.

REDEFINING OUR WORK LIVES

Define success by standards that are compatible with your needs and values.

In Chapter 1 we noted that the labor market has become a place of churning dislocation caused by the heavy volume of mergers, acquisitions, business closings, bankruptcies, and downsizings. General Motors and Ford Motor Company recently added an exclamation point to this dire development when they announced plans to shed 60,000 workers.[2] We also noted that changing work patterns have created new opportunities and new challenges. For example, the demand for temporary workers has increased.

It is important to visualize a future filled with sharp detours and several redefinitions of our work lives. Tom Peters, noted author and consultant, was one of the first observers to recognize that a typical career path is no longer linear and is not always upward. He says, "It's more like a maze, full of hidden turns, zigs and zags that go in all sorts of directions—even backwards sometimes, when that makes sense."[3] The dream of finding job security and knowing that we have "arrived" is obsolete.

Toward a New Definition of Success

Most of us have been conditioned to define success in narrow terms. Too frequently we judge our own success, and the success of others, by what is accomplished at work. Successful people are described as those who have a "good job," "make good money," or have "reached the top" in their field. We sometimes describe the person who has held the same job for many years as successful. We do not stop to consider that such a person may find work boring and completely devoid of personal rewards.

From early childhood on many people are taught to equate success with pay increases and promotions. Too often, unfortunately, people who try to achieve these career goals are forced to give up everything else that gives purpose and meaning to their lives. Po Bronson, author of *What Should I Do with My Life?*, says more people need to search for work they are passionate about. His best-selling book profiles fifty-five people who struggled to find their calling. One of the persons he interviewed was Ann Miyhares, a Cuban American who made her family proud by becoming a senior vice president at a bank, but lost their respect when she exchanged her banking career for that of a social worker.[4]

New Models of Success

2 *Describe new models for success that provide work/life balance.*

In recent years, a growing number of people are angry, disillusioned, and frustrated because they have had to abruptly change their career plans. They gave their best efforts to an employer for ten, fifteen, or twenty years, and then the company eliminated their jobs. For years the firm said, "Take care of business and

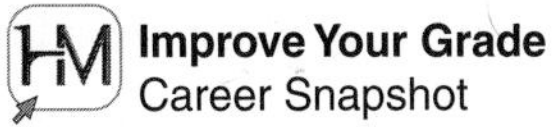

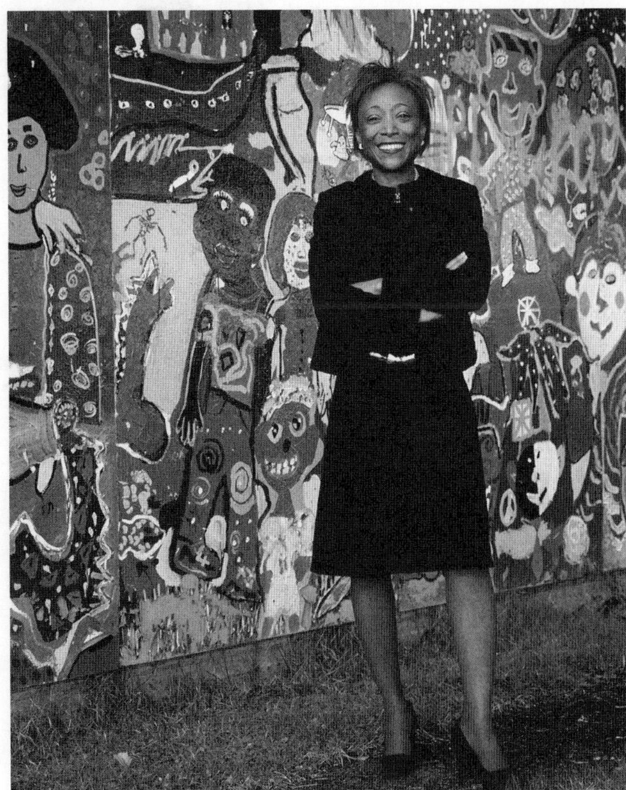

Stella Ogiale is a self-styled socio-capitalist. With a small loan from her sister, a small amount of birthday money, and earnings from a night job at UPS, she founded Chesterfield Health Services. Her company provides home care to mentally or physically disabled patients.

"It's come to my attention, Wycliff, that you're actually planning a life outside the office."

we'll take care of you," but then the situation changed. Under pressure from new global competition, hostile takeovers, and the need to restructure, companies started getting rid of experienced workers. The unwritten and unspoken contract between the company and the employee was broken. Many of the people who lost their jobs during the past decade were once told that if they had ambition and worked tirelessly to achieve their career goals, success would be their reward. But the "reward" for many people has been loss of a job, loss of self-esteem, and increased anxiety about the future.

We should certainly feel sympathy for persons who have lost their jobs and watched their dreams dissolve. But there is another group of people who also merit our concern. These are the persons who still have a job (the survivors), but must work harder and give up leisure time and quality time with friends and family.

It is inspiring to look at a different way of living. When Jeff Soderberg founded Software Technology Group, a technology consulting business based in Salt Lake City, he created a new model of success. His company provides employees with plenty of time to have a life. He doesn't believe there is a correlation between time spent at work and success. He refuses to hire workaholics, and in an industry where 80-hour workweeks are common, he tells new hires, "We expect a 40-hour workweek." Soderberg sets a good example by frequently taking time off during the week to enjoy rock climbing in the nearby canyons.[5]

One-Dimensional Model

The traditional success model defined success almost exclusively in terms of work life. The model emphasized working long hours, reaching work-related goals, and meeting standards often set by others.

The old model of success required us to be "one-dimensional" people for whom work is the single dimension. In the life of such a person, everything that has meaning seems to be connected to the job. When a person defines himself or herself by a job and then loses that job, what does that person have left? Of course, the loss of a job encourages some people to search for meaning beyond their work.

Loss of Leisure Time

Throughout history Americans have burdened themselves with a very demanding work ethic. They spend more time on the job than employees in any other industrialized nation. What's more, downsizing efforts have left fewer people to do the same amount of work, so many people are working even harder. Most of these workers yearn for more leisure time.

TOTAL PERSON INSIGHT

Cheryl Shavers Senior Manager, **Intel Corporation**

"We don't like to think of ourselves as slaves to money, prestige or power, but in fact many only feel worthy by attaining these things. When we allow 'things' to have power over us to the extent that we lose ourselves, our values, our ability to choose, we become slaves."

- U.S. workers not only work long hours, but they spend less time on vacation than do workers in most other industrialized countries. A typical American worker averages about 13 vacation days a year, *including* public holidays.
- By comparison, workers in Germany, France, and Italy take 35 to 40 vacation days each year.[6]
- In addition, American workers, equipped with cell phones, pagers, and Palm Pilots, are often too accessible during their vacations. There is a growing sense, matched by growing reality, that our work is always with us, demanding our attention.[7]

Some of America's best-managed companies realize the negative consequences of long hours on the job and loss of leisure time. The director of human resource strategy and planning for Merck and Company says, "You can't build an effective company on a foundation of broken homes and strained personal relationships." A senior executive at Pricewaterhouse-Coopers says, "We want the people who work for our firm to have lives outside Price Waterhouse—people with real lives are well rounded, and well-rounded people are creative thinkers."[8]

Jack Canfield, author of The Success Principles, *has described 64 fundamentals of success in his best-selling book. These timeless principles have been used by successful men and women throughout history.*

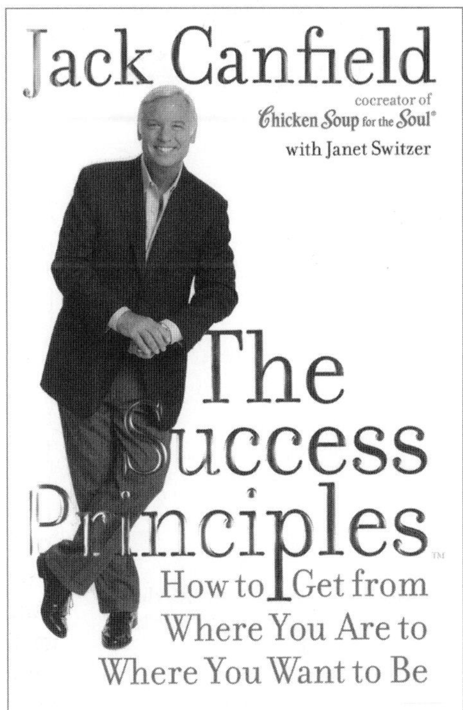

Developing Your Own Life Plan

The goal of this chapter is to help you develop a life plan for effective relationships with yourself and others. The information presented thus far has, we hope, stimulated your thinking about the need for a life plan. We have noted that personal life can seldom be separated from work life. The two are very much intertwined. We have also suggested that it is important for you to develop your own definition of success. Too frequently people allow others (parents, teachers, counselors, a spouse) to define success for them. Finally, as you begin work on your life plan, keep in mind the following advice from Jack Canfield, author of *The Success Principles:*

> If you want to be successful, you have to take 100% responsibility for everything that you experience in your life. This includes the level of your achievements, the results you produce, the quality of your relationships, the state of your health and physical fitness, your income, your debts, your feelings—everything![9]

Because work is such an important part of life, we now move to a discussion of items that will help you in your career planning. We discuss the concept of "right livelihood."

TEST PREPPER 9.1, 9.2

ANSWERS CAN BE FOUND ON P. 237

True or False?

T 1. In a layoff situation, the remaining workers often deal with substantial difficulties.

F 2. A traditional success model is two-dimensional, focusing on both work and personal life successes.

Mutliple Choice

C 3. The organization within which Amy currently works is changing its structure to be "flatter" with less bureaucracy. Amy is an ambitious worker whose career goal is a position in top management. What are the likely implications of the structural change for Amy's career if she stays with this organization?
   a. Amy will be downsized out of her job.
   b. Her career path will be enhanced because she now has a shorter, clearer path to the top of the organization.
   c. Amy's organization will need fewer top managers at the top levels, for which competition from current employees may be intense.
   d. It will take more time for Amy to hit the glass ceiling in a flattened organization.

b 4. For some workers, the "silver lining" (or positive side effect) in the dark cloud of job loss is:
   a. an opportunity to improve job-search skills.
   b. a search for meaning beyond their work.
   c. an opportunity to become a one-dimensional person.
   d. bitterness that permeates all other areas of life.

a 5. Steve is a typical U.S. worker with one year of service at his company. His cousin Hans is a typical German worker, also with one year of service at his company. Which sentence most accurately describes the comparison between Steve's situation and Hans's situation?
   a. Steve receives one-third as much paid vacation as Hans receives.
   b. Hans receives one-third as much paid vacation as Steve receives.
   c. Steve and Hans receive the same number of paid vacation days.
   d. Steve receives one-half as much paid vacation as Hans receives.

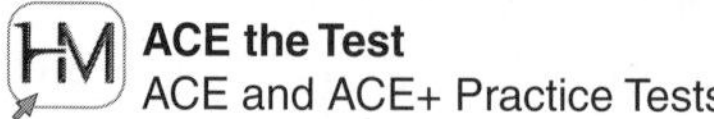

TOWARD RIGHT LIVELIHOOD

3 *Discuss the meaning of* right livelihood.

At age 45 Vera Shanley closed her lucrative medical practice in Atlanta and moved to a small farm near Hillsborough, North Carolina. She had a busy practice and good friends, but she was working 60 to 80 hours a week and thinking about passions that needed to be explored. Now she travels to Third World countries as a volunteer with Interplast, a nonprofit agency that performs free facial reconstructive surgeries on needy people. When she is back home, she works several hours a day as a potter and raises tomatoes and flowers.[10]

right livelihood Work consciously chosen, done with full awareness and care, and leading to enlightenment.

Vera Shanley, like many other people, has been searching for "right livelihood." The concept of right livelihood is described in the core teachings of Buddhism. In recent years, the concept has been described by Michael Phillips in his book *The Seven Laws of Money* and by Marsha Sinetar in her book *Do What You Love . . . The Money Will Follow*. **Right livelihood** is work consciously chosen, done with full awareness and care, and leading to enlightenment. Barbara Sher, contributor to

New Age magazine, says right livelihood means that you wake up in the morning and spend all day working at something you really want to do.[11]

For Stephen Lyons, the search for right livelihood began when he fell on hard times—divorce, unemployment, and bankruptcy. He came from a family of blue-collar tradesmen, none of whom had attended college. He trained as an electrician and had steady work until a recession created large-scale unemployment in the San Francisco area. Finally, he convinced a small college that he could repair their cranky air-conditioning system and ended up with a job and the opportunity to earn a business degree at the school. With more education, he felt confident to start a business installing home solar-power systems. Creating renewable energy has turned out to be a form of right livelihood for Lyons.[12]

There are three characteristics to right livelihood:

1. Choice
2. Emphasis on more than money
3. Personal growth

Dr. Vera Shanley began the search for right livelihood while working long hours at her medical practice in Atlanta. Today she travels the world as a volunteer with Interplast, a nonprofit group that performs free facial reconstructive surgeries on people in Third World countries. When she is home, Shanley works as a potter.

Right Livelihood Is Based on Conscious Choice

Marsha Sinetar says, "When the powerful quality of conscious choice is present in our work, we can be enormously productive."[13] She points out that many people have learned to act on what others say, value, and expect and thus find conscious choice very difficult:

> It takes courage to act on what we value and to willingly accept the consequences of our choices. Being able to choose means not allowing fear to inhibit or control us, even though our choices may require us to act against our fears or against the wishes of those we love and admire.[14]

To make the best choices, you must first figure out what you like to do, as well as what you are good at doing. What you like doing most is often not obvious. It may take some real effort to discover what really motivates you. Students often get help from career counselors or explore a career option during a summer internship. If you are employed, consider joining a temporary project team. A team assignment provides an opportunity to work with persons who perform very different types of duties. You might also consider reassignment within your organization.

Right Livelihood Places Money in a Secondary Position

People who embrace right livelihood accept that money and security are not the primary rewards in life. Michael Phillips explains that "right livelihood has within itself its own rewards; it deepens the person who practices it."[15] For example, people who work in the social services usually do not earn large amounts of money, but many receive a great deal of personal satisfaction from their work. You may need to trade some income for self-expression, mental rewards, or some other form of personal satisfaction. Vera Shanley may not make much money as a potter, but the work provides enormous personal satisfaction.

Many people who once viewed success in terms of wealth, material possessions, and status are realizing that something is missing from their lives. They do not *feel* successful. They once felt pressured to "have it all" but now feel disappointed that their achievements have not brought them real happiness.

Right Livelihood Recognizes That Work Is a Vehicle for Personal Growth

Most of us spend from 40 to 60 hours each week at work. Ideally, we should not have to squelch our real abilities, ignore our personal goals, and forget our need for stimulation and personal growth during the time we spend at work.[16] Most employees know intuitively that work should fulfill their need for self-expression and personal growth, but this message has not been embraced by many leaders. Too few organizations truly empower workers and give them a sense of purpose. When employees feel that the company's success is their own success, they will be more enthusiastic about their work.

The search for right livelihood should begin with a thoughtful review of your values. The values clarification process (see Table 4.1) should be completed *before* you interview for a job. Mark Buzek, a graduate of Ohio State University, decided not to take a job that would require frequent relocation and excessive travel. Although he is not married, he has strong ties with his parents, two sisters, and a brother in Ohio. Staying close to family members is an important value in his life.[17]

When a job fails to fulfill your expectations, consider changing jobs, changing assignments, or changing careers. If the job isn't right for you, your body and your mind will begin sending you messages. When you begin feeling that something is lacking, try to answer these basic questions: What is making me feel this way? What, exactly, about my current position is unpleasant? Choosing a satisfying career and lifestyle requires understanding what contributes to your job satisfaction. Self-exploration and continual evaluation of your needs, goals, and job satisfaction are important. Don't wait for a crisis (layoff) to clear your vision.[18]

Defining Your Relationship with Money

Money is a compelling force in the lives of most people. It often influences the selection of a career and the commitment we make to achieve success in that career. Sometimes we struggle to achieve a certain economic goal only to discover that once we got what we wanted, it didn't fulfill us in the way we had hoped. Money does not create or sustain happiness. Happiness comes from social relationships, enjoyable work, fulfillment, a sense that life has meaning, and membership in civic and other groups.[19]

Many people struggle with money management decisions and seem unable to plan for the future. The personal savings rate in America is at a record low, and the household debt burden is at a record high. After many years of decline, our savings rate is down to about 1 percent of our income, the world's lowest. Many people are ill prepared to cope with the financial drain that comes with loss of one's job or a serious health problem that is not covered by medical insurance. We are also a nation of hyperconsumers, "living way beyond our means and seemingly helpless to save ourselves," according to Geoffrey Colvin, senior editor of *Fortune* magazine.[20]

True Prosperity

The way we choose to earn, save, and spend our money determines, in large measure, the quality of our lives. For example, if you think that having *more* money is going to produce happiness or peace of mind, will you ever earn enough? Shakti Gawain, author of *Creating True Prosperity*, says that more money does not necessarily bring greater freedom, fewer problems, or security. Rather, "Prosperity is the experience of having plenty of what we truly need and want in life, material and otherwise." Gawain says, "The key point to understand is that prosperity is an

HUMAN RELATIONS IN ACTION

Plan to Win the Lottery?

Chances are, you won't win the lottery anytime soon. You can, however, build a large fund with a regular savings plan. A mixture of the following three things can produce amazing results:

- A small amount of money
- An average rate of return
- A period of time for your investment to grow

Steve Moore of the Cato Institute and Tom Kelly of the Savers and Investors Foundation provide a simple illustration of the stunning results that can be achieved. If your parents placed $1,000 in a mutual fund in 1950, and the money was allowed to grow at the stock market's average rate of return, they would now have more than $218,000. This is a reminder that fortunes can be made even by low-wage earners who save regularly during their working years.

internal experience, not an *external* state, and it is an experience that is not tied to having a certain amount of money."[21] Many of us go through life unconscious of our own real needs and desires. We must learn to predict more accurately what will give us lasting pleasure instead of short-term pleasure.[22]

Mature Money Management

Many people do not have a mature relationship with money. They spend everything they earn and more, and then have bouts of financial anxiety. People who are deep in debt often experience symptoms of depression. Money issues continue to be the number one cause of divorce in the United States. Space does not permit a comprehensive examination of money management, but here are some important suggestions from Jonathan Clements, an expert on financial planning.[23]

- *Develop a personal financial plan.* With a financial plan, you are more likely to achieve your financial goals. Without a plan, you are likely to follow a haphazard approach to management of your finances. A key element of your plan is determining where your income is going. With a simple record-keeping system, you can determine how much you spend each month on food, housing, clothing, transportation, and other things. Search for spending patterns you may want to change
- *Spend less than you earn.* Most people who spend more than they earn are buying things they do not really need. They need to get off the earn-and-spend treadmill. One way to spend less than you earn is to establish spending

TOTAL PERSON INSIGHT

Julie Connelly Contributing Editor, ***Fortune***

"Keep in mind that there is no harder work than thinking—really thinking—about who you are and what you want out of life. Figuring out where your goals and your skills match up is a painful, time-consuming process."

guidelines. For example, plan to save at least 10 percent of your pretax income every year for retirement. (Ten percent is the minimum recommended by most financial planners.)

- *Maintain a cash cushion.* If you lost your job today, how long could you live on your current cash reserves? Financial consultants suggest that cash reserves should be equal to the amount you earn during a two- or three-month period.

Many people do not think about financial compatibility before or after marriage. When couples talk about financial issues and problems, the result is usually less conflict and smarter financial decisions. David Bach, author of several books on financial planning, helps couples achieve financial compatibility. He has the partners start by writing down what's most important to each of them—their five top values. They are also instructed to write down what the purpose of money is. He says, "Smart financial planning is more than a matter of numbers; it involves values first and stuff second."[24]

Com-Corp Industries, a manufacturing plant based in Cleveland, Ohio, sees personal money management skills as one key to reducing conflict in the workplace. Employees who cannot live within their means are often under great stress and are more likely to experience interpersonal problems at work and at home. The company provides employees with classes on such subjects as developing a household budget and wise use of credit.[25]

TEST PREPPER 9.3

ANSWERS CAN BE FOUND ON P. 237

Multiple Choice

d 1. In his late 30s, Jerry quits his lucrative career in engineering to attend seminary and become an ordained minister. His ministerial salary is less than half, and his work hours are one-third more, compared to his engineering work. Jerry is happy that he made a conscious, careful career switch that led him to personal fulfillment and enlightenment. Jerry's career change is an example of:
   a. religious awakening.
   b. work repudiation.
   c. conscious enlightenment.
   d. right livelihood.

b 2. Liu is an associate professor at a college that emphasizes teaching over research. Even though Liu will not receive recognition from her employer for her ongoing projects, she continues research in her academic discipline, publishes papers in academic journals, and presents her discoveries at professional conferences. "I love to find evidence of new trends and to share them with my colleagues," Liu says. Which principle of right livelihood does Liu's behavior best exemplify?
   a. Right livelihood is based on career choice.
   b. Work is a vehicle for personal growth.
   c. Right livelihood places money in a secondary position.
   d. Fame is more important than fortune.

b 3. Diego contributes regularly to his IRA account, rewrites his budget for next year as soon as he receives his annual raise, and knows about when he will have accumulated enough savings to afford a down payment on his dream home. Which aspect of prudent money management does Diego's behavior exemplify best?
   a. Determining where income is going
   b. Developing a personal financial plan
   c. Spending beyond one's means
   d. Being cautious about using the services of banks and other financial institutions

c 4. If your parents placed $1,000 in a mutual fund in 1950 and the money was allowed to grow at the stock market's average rate of return, you would have:
   a. $3,000.
   b. $4,500.
   c. over $200,000.
   d. over $100,000.

HM **ACE the Test**
ACE and ACE+ Practice Tests

Defining Your Nonfinancial Resources

4 *Describe four nonfinancial resources that can enrich your life.*

If you become totally focused on your financial resources, then chances are you have ignored your **nonfinancial resources.** And it is often the nonfinancial resources that make the biggest contribution to a happy and fulfilling life. A strong argument can be made that the real wealth in life comes in the form of good health, peace of mind, time spent with family and friends, learning (which develops the mind), and healthy spirituality. Paul Hwoschinsky, author of *True Wealth*, makes this observation about nonfinancial resources: "If you are clear about who you are, and clear about what you want to do, and bring your financial and nonfinancial resources together, it's extraordinary what can happen. I encourage people to really honor their total resources, and magical things happen. New options occur."[26]

nonfinancial resources Resources such as health, peace of mind, time spent with family and friends, learning, and healthy spirituality.

If you focus most or all of your attention on work and you suffer a major work-related disappointment, then the result is likely to be feelings of depression and despair. Thoughts such as "Now I have lost everything" can surface when you fail to get a promotion, find out that you were not selected to be a member of a special project team, or learn that your job has been eliminated. But if you fully understand the power of your nonfinancial resources, then work-related disappointments are easier to cope with. The starting point is to realize that *most* of your resources are nonfinancial. During periods of great uncertainty, it is especially important that you think about your nonfinancial assets and consider ways to enhance them. We briefly discuss four nonfinancial resources that can enrich your life: physical and mental health, education and training (intellectual growth), leisure time (time for family, socializing, recreation), and healthy spirituality (see Figure 9.1).

FIGURE 9.1

Put Balance in Your Life

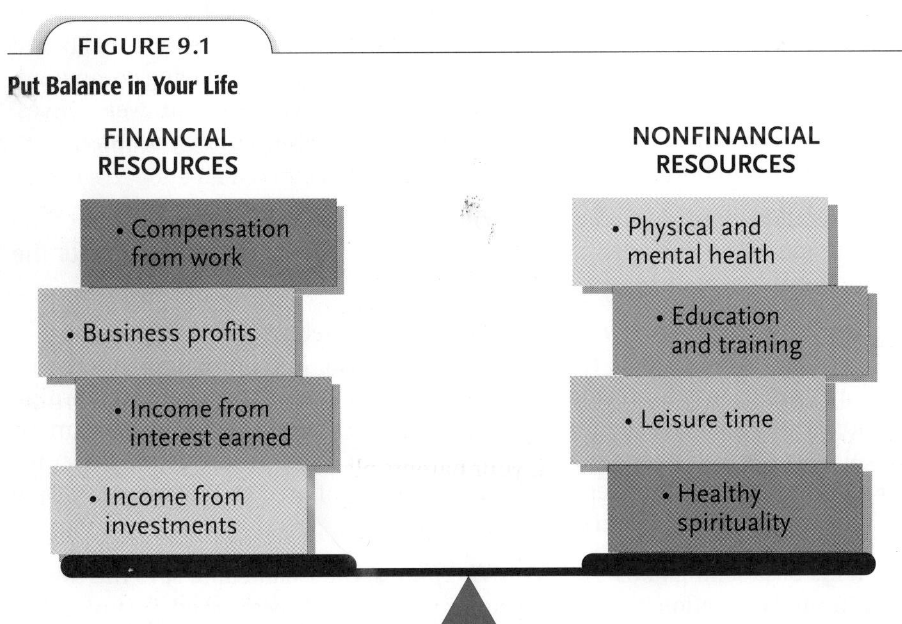

Physical and Mental Health

Is the statement "Health means wealth" just a worn-out cliché, or is this slogan a message of inspiration for people who want to get more out of life? If good health is such an important nonfinancial asset, then why are so many people flirting with self-destruction by eating the wrong foods, drinking too much, exercising too little, and generally choosing unhealthy lifestyles? The answer to the second question may be lack of awareness of the benefits of physical fitness. Here are a few benefits of a modest excercise program.[27]

- There is an interrelationship between health and outlook on life. For example, when the physical body is fit, toned, and strong, this condition has a positive effect on the mind. We are more likely to experience higher levels of self-esteem, feel a greater sense of self-confidence, and have a more positive outlook on life.
- Regular exercise and a healthy diet produce greater mental clarity, a higher energy level, and a more youthful appearance. Even low-intensity exercise such as walking can result in weight loss and reduction in the death rate from coronary artery disease and stroke.

Increasingly, incentives are being used to encourage employee participation in some type of health promotion program. A study conducted by Hewitt Associates found that half of the 960 large companies surveyed believe that employees who make a reasonable effort to manage their health should be rewarded.[28]

Education and Training (Intellectual Growth)

The new economy thrives on a well-educated and well-trained work force. It rewards workers who take personal responsibility for their learning. The need to continually update, train, and develop yourself has never been greater. Here are some tips on how to acquire the skills and abilities you need:

- *Think of yourself as a unique brand.* In Chapter 6 we noted that branding can play a crucial role in your career success. Developing a strong personal brand requires giving attention to several things, one of which is staying competent. To do this you must build your strengths and try to overcome your weaknesses. The authors of *What Every Successful Woman Knows* say, "Build your brand and toot your own horn—a lot."[29]
- *Be selective in what you learn.* Learning often requires large amounts of time and energy, so consider carefully what knowledge or skill will generate the most improvement.
- *Take advantage of various learning pathways.* It helps to think of your job as a learning resource. Take full advantage of instructional programs offered by your employer. Volunteer for team assignments that will provide new learning opportunities. Peter Senge, author of *The Fifth Discipline*, says the fundamental learning unit in any organization is a team.[30] And look outside the company at community college classes or programs offered by Toastmasters, Dale Carnegie, or other organizations.

In his best-selling book *The Art of Happiness*, the Dalai Lama says the role of learning and education in achieving happiness is widely overlooked. He notes that numerous surveys have conclusively found that higher levels of education have a positive correlation with better health and a longer life, and even protect us from feelings of depression.[31]

Leisure Time

Leisure time can provide an opportunity to relax, get rid of work-related stress, get some exercise, spend time with family and friends, or simply read a good book. Many people cherish leisure time, but experience schedule creep. *Schedule creep* is the tendency of work to expand beyond the normal work schedule and replace available leisure time. It often surfaces in small symptoms—an extra hour or two here, a weekend worked there.[32]

If you are working for a workaholic, someone who may have given up all or most of his or her leisure time, you may be pressured to work at the same pace. If your boss is constantly trying to meet impossible deadlines and deal with last-minute rushes, you may feel the need to give up time for recreation or family. If this happens, try to identify the consequences of being overworked. Look at the situation from all points of view. If you refuse to work longer hours, what will be the consequences for your relationship with the boss, your relationship with other employees, your future with the organization?[33] You have choices, but they may be difficult ones. If it looks as though the pressure to work longer hours will never end, you may want to begin searching for another job.

Is it worth taking some risks to protect the leisure time you now have? Should you increase the amount of leisure time available in your life? Consider the following benefits of leisure time:

- As we noted previously in this text, maintaining social connections with friends and family can be good for your health. A growing number of studies show that if you have strong and fulfilling relationships, you may live longer, decrease your chances of becoming sick, and cope more successfully when illness strikes.[34] Time spent with friends and family can be a powerful source of mental and physical renewal.
- One of the best ways to feel satisfied about your work is to get away from it when you begin to feel worn out. People who take time off from work often return with new ideas, a stronger focus, and increased energy. When you discover that end-of-the-week exhaustion is still hanging around Monday morning, it's time to take some vacation or personal days.[35]
- A growing body of research indicates that the American trend toward skipping vacations is hazardous. People who skip vacations have a higher risk of death from heart disease and other serious health problems.[36] You need time away from work to relax, renew your creative powers, and reduce your level of stress.
- Find some quiet time for yourself each day. You might use it to meditate, take the dog for a walk, or just sit quietly. Use this time to nourish yourself and bring balance to your life.

If you want more leisure time, then you must establish your priorities and set your goals. This may mean saying no to endless requests to work overtime or rejecting a promotion. Sometimes you must pull back from the endless demands of work and "get a life."

Healthy Spirituality

A discussion of nonfinancial resources would not be complete without an introduction to healthy spirituality. To become a "whole" or "total" person requires movement beyond the concrete, material aspects of life to the spiritual side of the human experience. Healthy spirituality can bring a higher degree of harmony, wholeness, and meaning to our lives and move us beyond self-centeredness.

spirituality An inner attitude that emphasizes energy, creative choice, and a powerful force for living.

Spirituality can be defined as an inner attitude that emphasizes energy, creative choice, and a powerful force for living. It involves opening our hearts and cultivating our capacity to experience reverence and gratitude. It frees us to become positive, caring human beings.[37]

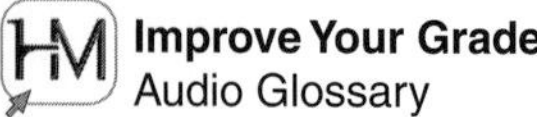

Spirituality encompasses faith, which can be described as what your heart tells you is true when your mind cannot prove it. For some people, faith exists within the framework of a formal religion; for others it rests on a series of personal beliefs such as "Give others the same consideration, regard, kindness, and gentleness that you would like them to accord you."[38] A special report entitled *Spirituality 2005*, published by *Newsweek*, indicates that 24 percent of those polled described themselves as spiritual but not religious; 55 percent described themselves as religious and spiritual.[39]

An understanding of the many aspects of spirituality can give us an expanded vision of what it means to be human. Although spirituality is often associated with religion, it should be viewed in broader terms. Robert Coles, of Harvard Medical School, likes a definition of spirituality given to him by an 11-year-old girl:

> I think you're spiritual if you can escape from yourself a little and think of what's good for everyone, not just you, and if you can reach out and be a good person—I mean live like a good person. You're not spiritual if you just talk spiritual and there's no action. You're a fake if that's what you do.[40]

The words of this young girl remind us that one dimension of spirituality involves showing concern and compassion for others. Thomas Moore, author of the best-selling book *Care of the Soul*, says, "To be spiritual means to mature to a point beyond limited self-interest and anxiety about self."[41] Healthy spirituality involves acts of generosity, sharing, and kindness.

Many companies, large and small, feel that healthy spirituality can enhance the ethical dimensions of the business.

- The philosophy of Worthington Industries is expressed in a single sentence: "We treat our customers, employees, investors and suppliers as we would like to be treated."[42]

TOTAL PERSON INSIGHT

The Dalai Lama Coauthor, ***The Art of Happiness***

"Spirituality I take to be concerned with those qualities of human spirit—such as love and compassion, patience, tolerance, forgiveness, contentment, a sense of responsibility, a sense of harmony—which bring happiness to both self and others."

- Allied Holdings Inc., Herr Foods Inc., and many other companies have hired chaplains to provide needed support and counseling to their employees.[43]
- Lotus Development Corporation formed a "soul" committee to examine the company's management practices and values. The company wants to find ways to make the work environment as humane as possible.[44]

Will the growing interest in healthy spirituality influence education? We are already seeing changes in some professional education programs. More than fifty medical schools across the United States have incorporated spirituality into their coursework. One objective of these programs is to develop medical students' empathy for patients.[45]

Many activities can be considered spiritual. Visiting an art gallery, listening to a concert, or walking near the ocean can stimulate healthy spirituality. Table 9.1 describes some ways to begin your journey to healthy spirituality.

Healthy spirituality can often serve as a stabilizing force in our lives. The various twelve-step programs (Alcoholics Anonymous is one example) emphasize the need for a spiritual connection. "Working the steps" means, among other things, turning life over to a higher power. This spiritual connection seems to give hope to persons who feel a sense of loneliness and isolation.

For many people, a commitment to a specific religion is an important dimension of spirituality. Active membership in a religious group provides an opportunity to clarify spiritual values and achieve spiritual direction. It also provides social connections—an extended family that you can depend on for social support.[46]

TABLE 9.1

Ways to Achieve Healthy Spirituality

As interest in healthy spirituality grows, people are searching for ways to become more spiritual. The following spiritual practices draw our focus away from ourselves and the anxieties in our lives.

- **Meditation** Oprah Winfrey described the powerful influence of meditation this way: "There is no greater source of strength and power for me in my life now than going still, being quiet and recognizing what real power is."
- **Prayer** Dr. Larry Dossey, physician and author of numerous books on the role of spirituality in medicine, says prayer can be a powerful force in our lives. Prayer groups have been established at many organizations.
- **Spiritual Reading** In addition to sacred readings, consider *Healing and the Mind* by Bill Moyers, *The Soul of a Business* by Tom Chappell, and *The Hungry Spirit* by Charles Handy.
- **Time with Nature** Spiritual contemplation during a walk in the woods or a visit to a quiet lake can help us balance mind, body, and spirit.

Sources: David Elkins and Amanda Druckman, "Four Great Ways to Begin Your Spiritual Journey," *Psychology Today*, September/October 1999, p. 46; Larry Dossey, M.D., "Can We Change the World?" *The Inner Edge*, June/July 2000, pp. 22–23.

TEST PREPPER 9.4

ANSWERS CAN BE FOUND ON P. 237

True or False?

T 1. Nonfinancial resources often make the biggest contribution to a fulfilling life.

T 2. People experience schedule creep when their work expands beyond their normal schedule and begins to replace available leisure time.

Multiple Choice

____ 3. Although she has accumulated few assets and earns very little, Sophia's physical and mental health are outstanding; she is a lifelong learner; she uses her leisure time wisely; and she displays healthy spirituality. Sophia is wealthy in terms of:

a. nonfinancial resources.
b. current resources.
c. fiduciary resources.
d. insignificant resources.

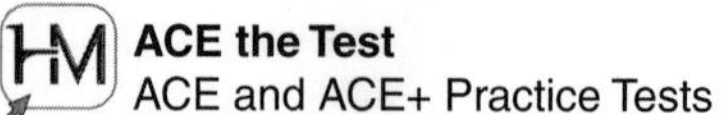

ACE the Test
ACE and ACE+ Practice Tests

____ 4. Walt constantly takes continuing education courses related to his profession so that he can increase his value as a professional. Walt's philosophy best reflects which aspect of intellectual growth?

a. Learning about as wide as possible a range of subjects
b. Taking advantage of various learning pathways
c. Thinking of oneself as a unique brand
d. Viewing one's career as a means to healthy spirituality

____ 5. Dave and Becky spend one Saturday per month helping Habitat for Humanity build homes for poor families in their hometown. Their activity most likely directly enhances their:

a. disposable income.
b. career marketability.
c. spiritual health.
d. intellectual growth.

DEVELOPING A HEALTHY LIFESTYLE

5 *Provide guidelines for developing a healthy lifestyle.*

Earlier in this chapter we noted that a healthy lifestyle can provide a higher energy level, a greater sense of self-confidence, and generally a more positive outlook on life. People who maintain good health usually have more endurance, spend less time feeling tired or ill, and miss less work than persons who are not healthy. Good health is receiving greater attention today because many Americans are investing more time and energy in their work. They are being asked to work longer hours and do more in less time. Good health can help combat stress and tension at work and at home.

The first step toward adopting a healthy lifestyle is to become well informed—to read, study, and learn what can be done to maintain your current level of health or improve your health. In this section we offer guidelines that form the framework for a good diet and a good exercise program.

Guidelines for a Healthy Diet

Eating the right foods can improve your health, boost your energy level, and in some cases extend your life. The link between health and diet is quite clear. We will review several important dietary guidelines.

Maintain a Diet That Is Balanced and Varied

Recently the U.S. Department of Agriculture (USDA) published the MyPyramid, an individualized approach to improving diet and lifestyle (see Figure 9.2). A new USDA website (www.mypyramid.gov) allows consumers to enter their age, sex, and activity level and get back a tailored personal diet. For example, here are the daily recommendations for a 30-year-old female who gets less than 30 minutes of exercise a day:

Grains	6 ounces
Vegetables	2.5 cups
Fruits	1.5 cups
Milk	3 cups
Meat & Beans	5 ounces
Oils	5 teaspoons

This customized plan is based on an estimated requirement of 1,800 calories a day. Everyone should monitor their body weight to determine if they need to adjust calorie intake.[47]

Eating a variety of foods is important because you need more than forty different nutrients for good health: vitamins and minerals, amino acids (from proteins), essential fatty acids (from fats and oils), and sources of energy (calories from carbohydrates, fats, and proteins). The number of servings you need each day depends

FIGURE 9.2

U.S. Department of Agriculture's MyPyramid

Source: United States Department of Agriculture.

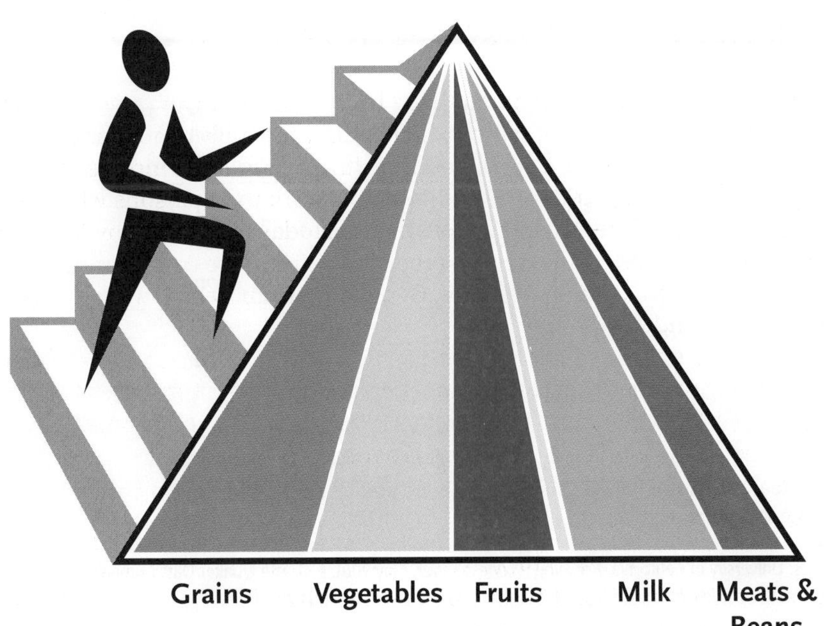

on your total calorie intake. The type of foods you eat is also very important. Whole grains should be substituted for refined grains, and dark greens such as broccoli and kale represent a preferred vegetable food group. These foods help reduce the risk of developing diabetes and heart disease and help with weight maintenance.

Reduce Calorie Intake

Over 65 percent of Americans are overweight, and these added pounds increase the risk of heart disease, cancer, and diabetes. Inactivity combined with diets high in calories, salt, and fats will soon be the number one cause of preventable deaths. Americans are putting on extra pounds much earlier and faster than they did in previous generations. Control of weight is fundamentally simple—*calories in versus calories out*. If you eat 100 more calories a day than you burn, you gain about 1 pound in a month, or about 10 pounds in a year.[48]

Cut Down on Fatty Foods

The foods that are popular with many Americans are relatively high in fat, especially saturated fat, which contributes to high blood cholesterol levels. Many restaurant foods are high in fat because it gives menu items the flavor people often seek when eating out. Heart disease and certain kinds of cancer are byproducts of foods that contain highly saturated fats. Avoid foods that include partially hydrogenated oils—better known as *trans fats*. These artery-clogging fats can be very harmful to your health. Although diet is the most important factor in lowering cholesterol, exercise can help.

Eat Foods with Adequate Starch and Fiber

Foods high in starch, such as breads made with whole grains, dry beans and peas, and potatoes, contain many essential nutrients. Many starches also add dietary

TABLE 9.2

Low-Fat Snack Choices

	Saturated Fat (grams)	Sodium (milligrams)	Calories
Quaker Lightly Salted Rice Cakes	0	15	35
Barbara's Rite Lite Rounds (crackers)	0	200	70
Healthy Choice Microwave Popcorn	1.5	140	100
Mariani Sweetened Dried Cranberries	0	0	100

Note: Read labels carefully. Be sure to notice the portion sizes and be realistic about what you actually consume.

Sources: University of California, *Berkeley Wellness Letter*, May 2001, p. 6; The Quaker Oats Company, Chicago, Ill. Barbara's Bakery, Petaluma, Calif.; Mariani Packing Company, Vacaville, Calif.

fiber to your diet. A growing number of scientists believe that high-fiber diets can help reduce the odds of getting cancer of the colon. Some cereals and most fruits and vegetables are good sources of fiber.

Avoid Too Much Sodium

A common byproduct of excess sodium is high blood pressure. In the United States, where sodium-rich diets are very common, the average person consumes about 5,000 milligrams of sodium each day, more than twice the amount the American Dietetic Association recommends.[49] Table 9.2 includes some examples of foods that are low in sodium and saturated fats.

If You Drink Alcohol, Do So in Moderation

Alcoholic beverages are high in calories and low in nutrients and cause serious health risks when used in excess. Excessive alcohol consumption has been linked to liver damage, certain types of cancer, and high blood pressure.

With the help of these healthy diet guidelines, you can develop your own plan for achieving a healthful diet. Keep in mind that good nutrition is a balancing act. You want to select foods with enough vitamins, minerals, protein, and fiber but avoid too much fat and sodium. You want to consume enough calories to maintain the energy level required in your life but avoid weight gain.

Improving Your Physical Fitness

With regard to exercise, people often choose one of two extreme positions. Some adopt the point of view that only high-intensity activities (running, high-impact aerobics) increase physical fitness. These people believe in the "no-pain, no-gain" fitness approach. The other extreme position is to become a "couch potato" and avoid all forms of exercise. Both positions should be avoided.

Physical fitness can be defined as the ability to perform daily tasks vigorously and have enough energy left over to enjoy leisure activities. It is the ability to endure difficult and stressful experiences and still carry on. Physical fitness, which involves the performance of the lungs, heart, and muscles, can also have a positive influence on mental alertness and emotional stability. Research indicates that even a moderate level of physical activity can have a surprisingly broad array of health benefits on virtually every major organ system in the body.[50] For most people, a program that involves regular physical activity at least three or four times a week and includes sustained physical exertion for 30 to 35 minutes during each activity period is adequate.[51] This modest investment of time and energy will give you a longer and healthier life.

physical fitness The ability to perform daily tasks vigorously and have enough energy left over to enjoy leisure activities.

To achieve lifesaving benefits from exercise, start slowly with an aerobic fitness activity you feel you will enjoy. Walking, swimming, running, low-impact aerobics, and jogging are aerobic exercises. When we engage in aerobic exercise, the body is required to improve its ability to handle oxygen.[52] These exercises strengthen the heart, burn up calories, increase stamina, and help release tension.

If you are younger than 35 and in good health, you probably do not need to see a doctor before beginning an exercise program. If you are older than 35 and have been inactive for several years, consult your doctor before engaging in vigorous exercise.[53]

TEST PREPPER 9.5

ANSWERS CAN BE FOUND ON P. 237

True or False?

____ 1. The best way to improve your physical fitness is through high-intensity activities.

____ 2. People who are physically fit can perform all their regular daily activities and still have enough energy left over for leisure activities.

Multiple Choice

____ 3. Nina reads everything she can find about diet and health. She knows that the first step toward developing a healthy lifestyle involves:
   a. eating a healthy diet.
   b. becoming well informed.
   c. improving physical fitness.
   d. changing habits.

____ 4. Good health can positively impact work life in which of the following ways?
   a. It can help to combat stress and tension.
   b. It can provide a higher energy level.
   c. It can prevent loss of work time due to sick days.
   d. Good health can positively impact work life in all the above ways.

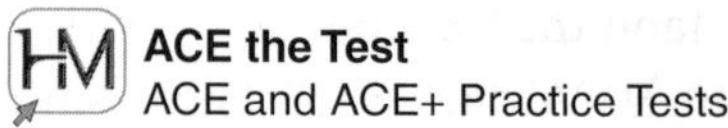

PLANNING FOR CHANGES IN YOUR LIFE

6 *Develop a plan for making needed changes in your life.*

Throughout this book we have emphasized the concept that you can control your own behavior. In fact, during these turbulent times changes in your behavior may be one of the few things under your control. If making changes in your life seems to be a logical course of action at this point, then it is time to do some planning. The starting point is to clearly identify the personal growth goals that can make a difference in your life. What are some behaviors you can adopt (or alter) that will make an important positive change in your life? Once you have identified these behaviors, you can set goals and do what is necessary to achieve them.

The Power of Habits

Before we discuss specific goal-setting methods, let us take a look at the powerful influence of habits. Some habits, like taking a long walk three or four times a week, can have a positive influence on our well-being. Simply saying "Thank you" when someone does a favor or pays a compliment can be a habit. Other habits, such as smoking, never saying no to requests for your time, feeling jealous, or constantly engaging in self-criticism, are negative forces in our lives. Stephen Covey, author of *The Seven Habits of Highly Effective People*, makes this observation: "Habits are powerful factors in our lives. Because they are consistent, often unconscious patterns, they constantly, daily, express our character and produce our effectiveness . . . or ineffectiveness."[54]

Breaking deeply embedded habits, such as impatience, procrastination, or criticism of others, can take a tremendous amount of effort. The influences supporting the habit, the actual root causes, are often repressed in the subconscious mind and forgotten.[55] How do you break a negative habit or form a positive habit? The process involves five steps.

Motivation

Once you are aware of the need to change, you must develop the willingness or desire to change. After making a major commitment to change, you must find ways to maintain your motivation. The key to staying motivated is to develop a mindset powerful enough that you feel compelled to act on your desire to change.

Knowledge

Once you clearly understand the benefits of breaking a habit or forming a new one, you must acquire the knowledge you need to change. Seek information, ask for advice, or learn from the experiences of others. This may involve finding a mentor, joining a group, or gathering sufficient material and teaching yourself.

Practice

Information is only as useful as you make it. This means that to change your behavior you must *practice* what you have learned. If you are a shy person, does this mean you need to volunteer to make a speech in front of several hundred people? The answer is no. Although there is always the rare individual who makes a major change seemingly overnight, most people find that the best and surest way to develop a new behavior is to do so gradually.

Feedback

Whenever you can, seek feedback as you attempt to change a habit. Dieters lose more weight if they attend counseling sessions and weigh-ins. People who want to improve their public speaking skills benefit from practice followed by feedback from a teacher or coach. Everyone has blind spots, particularly when trying something new.

Reinforcement

When you see yourself exhibiting the type of behavior you have been working to develop—or when someone mentions that you have changed—reward yourself! The rewards can be simple, inexpensive ones—treating yourself to a movie, a bouquet of flowers, a favorite meal, or a special event. This type of reinforcement is vital when you are trying to improve old behaviors or develop new ones.

Goals should be an integral part of your plan to break old habits or form new ones. You will need an assortment of goals that address the different needs of your life. Be sure to go to the HM Management Space™ Student Website (**college.hmco.com/pic/reeceSAS**) to find online self-assessments. Each of the items included in these exercises provides an opportunity for goal setting to achieve personal development. After a period of serious reflection, try to narrow the goal-setting possibilities so you will be working on the truly important change you wish to make in your life.

The goal-setting process was described in Chapter 3. The major principles of goal setting are outlined in Table 3.1. These time-tested principles can help you achieve any realistic goal.

TEST PREPPER 9.6

ANSWERS CAN BE FOUND ON P. 237

True or False?

____ 1. Habits can be positive as well as negative.

Multiple Choice

____ 2. As a reward for breaking his smoking habit, Geno has planned a trip to Bermuda next month, on the one-year anniversary of his last cigarette. Which step in breaking a habit does Geno's behavior represent?
   a. Motivation
   b. Knowledge
   c. Feedback
   d. Reinforcement

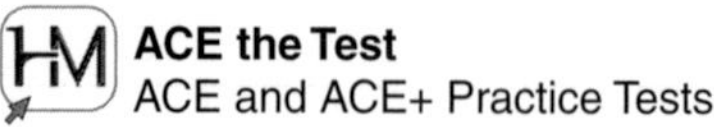

____ 3. Mary has decided she needs to quit smoking for her health and the health of her family. She has spoken with her doctor and has gathered information from the Internet and directly from friends who have quit smoking. What does Mary need to do next?
   a. Reward herself in some way as reinforcement
   b. Get some feedback from friends and family on her progress
   c. Apply the information she has learned and practice the act of quitting smoking
   d. Develop a desire to change her habit

Improve Your Grade
Learning Objectives Review
Audio Chapter Review
Audio Chapter Quiz

LEARNING OBJECTIVES REVIEW

1 *Define success by standards that are compatible with your needs and values.*

- Traditional definitions describe success almost entirely in terms of measurable job achievements leaving out the intangible success to be had in private and professional life.

2 *Describe new models for success that provide work/life balance.*

- The labor market has become a place of great uncertainty due to the heavy volume of mergers, acquisitions, business closings, and downsizing.
- There is increasing pressure to work harder, work longer hours, and give up more leisure time.
- The traditional success model is one-dimensional and defines success almost exclusively in terms of work.

3 *Discuss the meaning of* right livelihood.

- Right livelihood recognizes that work is a vehicle for self-expression, and places money in a secondary position.
- Right livelihood is work consciously chosen and done with full awareness and care that leads to enlightenment.

4 *Describe four nonfinancial resources that can enrich your life.*

- A person's nonfinancial resources often make the biggest contribution to a happy and fulfilling life.
- Each of us has four nonfinancial resources that can enrich our lives:
  - physical and mental health
  - education and training (intellectual growth)
  - leisure time (time for family, socializing, recreation)
  - healthy spirituality

5 *Provide guidelines for developing a healthy lifestyle.*

- Healthy lifestyles can give us a higher energy level, greater sense of self-confidence, and generally a more positive outlook.
- People who maintain good health usually have more endurance, spend less time feeling tired or ill, and miss less work than those who are not physically fit.

6 *Develop a plan for making needed changes in your life.*

- Planning for changes in your life often requires breaking negative habits or forming positive habits.
- The process of breaking habits and forming new ones involves five steps: motivation, knowledge, practice, feedback, and reinforcement.

APPLYING WHAT YOU HAVE LEARNED

Improve Your Grade
Internet Insights

1. In recent years, it has become popular for organizations to develop a mission statement or a statement of values that reflects their philosophy and objectives. Biogen's values statement provides one example (see Chapter 4). Prepare a personal mission statement that reflects your goals and aspirations for a successful life. Your mission statement should cover the roles of financial and nonfinancial resources in your life.
2. Throughout this chapter you were encouraged to take control of your life and establish your own definition of success. This chapter has a strong "all development is self-development" theme. Can we really control our own destinies? Can we always make our own choices? Mike Hernacki, author of the book *The Ultimate Secret of Getting Absolutely Everything You Want,* says yes:

   > To get what you want, you must recognize something that at first may be difficult, even painful to look at. You must recognize that *you alone* are the source of all the conditions and situations in your life. You must recognize that whatever your world looks like right now, you alone have caused it to look that way. The state of your health, your finances, your personal relationships, your professional life—all of it is your doing, yours and no one else's.[56]

   Do you agree with this viewpoint? Take a position in favor of or in opposition to Hernacki's statement. Prepare a short one- or two-paragraph statement that expresses your views.
3. There are many ways to deepen and extend your spirituality. One way is to begin placing a higher value on silence, tranquility, and reflection. If your life is extremely busy, you may not be taking time for thought or reflection. If you are accustomed to living in the presence of noise throughout the day, quiet times may make you feel uncomfortable at first. Over a period of one week, set aside a few minutes each day for your own choice of meditation, prayer, contemplation, or reflection. Try to find a quiet place for this activity. At the end of the week, assess the benefits of this activity, and consider the merits of making it part of your daily routine.[57]

ROLE-PLAY EXERCISE

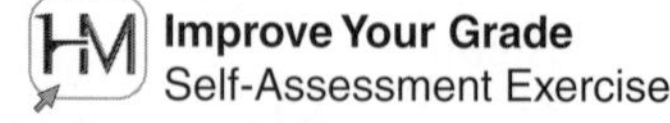

Ambry Waller, one of your closest friends, used to go fishing quite often, and he loved to hike in the mountains. After getting married, his life changed dramatically. He and his wife purchased a new home, and soon they were raising a family. Once the bills started piling up, he abandoned his leisure-time activities and started working long hours at his job. He eagerly volunteered for overtime in order to increase his earnings. As the years passed, Ambry and his wife adopted many trappings of middle-class life: a big house, two cars, a huge flat-screen TV in the family room, and a motorboat that sits idle for most of the year. One afternoon, you meet Ambry for a beer at a local bar. The conversation quickly turns serious as Ambry describes his frustration: "I love my wife and children, but I am so tired of working long hours and worrying about my financial obligations. My credit-card debt is now over $7,000."

In this role-play activity, you will meet with another class member who will assume the role of Ambry Waller. Your goal is to help Ambry identify some ways he can achieve greater work/life balance. Your name for this role play will be Corey Cell.

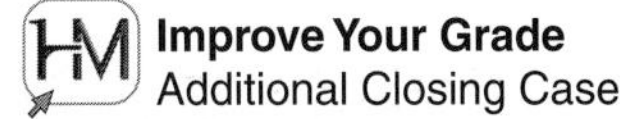

CASE 9.1

Toward Right Livelihood

When Mary Lou Quinlan entered the field of advertising, she set the goal of someday running a major advertising agency. After twenty years of climbing the ladder, she became chief executive officer of N. W. Ayer. Later, she would make a decision that surprised many of her friends and colleagues. Here, in her own words, is what happened:

> In achieving that goal, I became "successful," but I wasn't happy. So I said two words that I had never said before: 'I quit.' Then I took a chance on starting a completely new career.[58]

Quinlan didn't make a hasty decision after leaving her corporate position. She took a five-week sabbatical before deciding to become an entrepreneur. Again, in her own words, here is what happened:

> I got a piece of paper and divided it in half. On the left side, I wrote down what I love to do and what I'm good at, and on the right side, I wrote down what I don't like to do and what I stink at. Unfortunately, what I don't like to do and what I stink at were my job description as CEO.[59]

Quinlan loved to write, she loved public speaking, and she wanted to write a book. She also enjoyed meeting and working with women, and felt they were often neglected as consumers. With these thoughts in mind, she founded Just Ask a Woman, a firm that helps companies market with women, not to them. She based her new company on the premise that women want to be listened to. Quinlan also wrote a book entitled *Just Ask a Woman,* which focuses on what women want and how they make purchases. Just Ask a Woman has become a leading consultancy on women today.[60]

Questions

1. Mary Lou Quinlan says the decision to seek right livelihood should begin with conversations with family members and friends who love you. Ask questions such as "How do you think I'm doing?" and "How do you see me right now?" Do you agree with her advice? Explain.
2. Right livelihood is based on conscious choice, places money in a secondary position, and recognizes that work is a vehicle for personal growth. Which of these three characteristics would be most difficult for you to accept and implement in your life?
3. In your opinion, does the concept of right livelihood seem realistic? Is right livelihood an option for everyone or only a select few? Explain.

RESOURCES ON THE WEB

Prepare for Class, Improve Your Grade, and ACE the Test. Student Achievement Series resources include:

- ACE and ACE+ Practice Tests
- Audio Chapter Quizzes
- Audio Chapter Reviews
- Learning Objective Reviews
- Career Snapshots
- Chapter Glossaries
- Chapter Outlines
- Crossword Puzzles
- Hangman Games
- Flashcards
- Audio Glossaries
- Internet Insights
- Self-Assessment Exercises
- Additional Closing Cases

To access these learning and study tools, go to **college.hmco.com/pic/reeceSAS**.

HM ManagementSPACE

Notes

Chapter 1

1. Jim Carlton, "In Quest for Steady Work, a Man Traces States Decline," *Wall Street Journal,* July 30, 2003, p. A1.
2. Edward M. Hallowell, *Connect* (New York: Pantheon Books, 1999), pp. 1–14.
3. John Seely Brown and Paul Duguid, *The Social Life of Information* (Boston: Harvard Business School Press, 2000), pp. 2–13.
4. Ronald Alsop, "How to Get Hired," *Wall Street Journal,* September 22, 2004; Marshall Goldsmith, "Nice Guys Can Finish First," *Fast Company,* November 2004, p. 123.
5. Joann S. Lublin, "Mergers Often Trigger Anxiety, Lower Morale," *Wall Street Journal,* January 16, 2001, pp. B1, B4; Daniel Roth, "How to Cut Pay, Lay Off 8,000 People, and Still Have Workers Who Love You," *Fortune,* February 4, 2002, pp. 63–68.
6. Sabrina Jones, "How We'll Work," *The News & Observer,* January 2, 2000, p. 3E; Ron Zemke, "Free Agent Nation," *Training,* January 2002, p. 18; Mike Brewster, "The Freelance Conundrum," *Inc.,* December 2004, p. 38.
7. Jeffrey Pfeffer, *The Human Equation* (Boston: Harvard Business School Press, 1998), pp. 293.
8. Chris Lee, "The Death of Civility," *Training,* July 1999, pp. 24–30.
9. Stephen L. Carter, *Civility* (New York: Basic Books, 1998), p. 11.
10. Jeff Pettit, "Team Communication: It's in the Cards," *Training & Development,* January 1997, p. 12.
11. Robert Guy Matthews, "Recovery Bypasses Many Americans," *Wall Street Journal,* August 31, 2005, p. A2.
12. Lauren Storck, "The Rich Make Us Sick," *Psychology Today,* September/October 1999, p. 2; "Helping America's Working Poor," *Business Week,* July 17, 2000, p. 164. "Barely Staying Afloat," *The New York Times,* May 10, 2006, p. A22.
13. Casey Selix, "Employers Push Resilience as a Key Skill for Workers," *San Jose Mercury News,* March 4, 2001, p. 1PC; Harry Wessel, "New Fringe Benefit: Dieting," *The News & Observer,* January 25, 2004, p. 12E.
14. Robert Kreitner, *Management,* 9th ed. (Boston: Houghton Mifflin, 2004), p. 304.
15. Allan A. Kennedy, interview by, in "The Culture Wars," *Inc.,* 20th Anniversary Issue, 1999, pp. 107–108.
16. Anita Raghavan, Kathryn Kranhold, and Alexei Barrionuevo, "How Enron Bosses Created a Culture of Pushing Limits," *Wall Street Journal,* August 26, 2002, p. B1.
17. Suein L. Hwang, "Workers' Slogans Find New Home This Side of the Great Wall," *Wall Street Journal,* October 16, 2002, p. B1.
18. Sue Shellenbarger, "Along with Benefits and Pay, Employees Seek Friends on the Job, "*Wall Street Journal,* February 20, 2002, p. B1.
19. "Great Expectations," *Fast Company,* November 1999, p. 224.
20. Betsy Jacobson and Beverly Kaye, "Balancing Act," *Training & Development,* February 1993, p. 26.
21. Sue Shellenbarger, "Job Candidates Prepare to Sacrifice Some Frills and Balance—For Now," *Wall Street Journal,* November 21, 2001, p. B1; Stephanie Armour, "Workers Put Family First Despite Slow Economy, Jobless Fears," *USA Today,* June 6, 2002, p. 38.
22. Rochelle Sharpe, "Labor Letter," *Wall Street Journal,* September 13, 1994, p. 1.
23. Alan Farnham, "The Man Who Changed Work Forever," *Fortune,* July 21, 1997, p. 114.
24. George F. Will, "A Faster Mousetrap," *New York Times Book Review,* June 15, 1997, p. 8; "Scientific Management," *Training,* December 1999, p. 33.
25. Bradley J. Rieger, "Lessons in Productivity and People," *Training & Development,* October 1995, pp. 56–58.
26. For a detailed examination of the Hawthorne criticisms and the legacy of the Hawthorne research, see David A. Whitsett and Lyle Yorks, *From Management Theory to Business Sense* (New York: American Management Association, 1983).
27. Jim Collins, "The Classics," *Inc.,* December 1996, p. 55.
28. Thomas J. Peters and Robert H. Waterman, Jr., *In Search of Excellence: Lessons from America's Best-Run Companies* (New York: Harper & Row, 1982), p. 14; Tom Peters, "Tom Peters' True Confessions," *Fast Company,* December 2001, p. 80.
29. Stephen R. Covey, *The Seven Habits of Highly Effective People* (New York: Simon & Schuster, 1989), pp. 66–67.
30. Richard Koonce, "Emotional IQ, A New Secret of Success," *Training & Development,* February 1996, p. 19; Cary Cherniss and Daniel Goleman, eds., *The Emotionally Intelligent Workplace* (San Francisco: Jossey-Bass, 2001), pp. 13–26.
31. Denis Waitley, *Empires of the Mind* (New York: Morrow, 1995), p. 133.
32. Michael Crom, "Building Trust in the Workplace," *The Leader,* October 1998, p. 6; Ron Zemke, "Can You Manage Trust?" *Training,* February 2000, pp. 76–83.
33. Harold H. Bloomfield and Robert K. Cooper, *The Power of 5* (Emmaus, Pa.: Rodale Press, 1995), p. 61.
34. Jack Canfield, *The Success Principles* (New York: Harper Collins, 2005), pp. 3–18.
35. Malcolm Flescher, "World Wide Winner—The UPS Story," *Selling Power,* November/December 2001, p. 58.
36. Thomas Petzinger, Jr., "The Front Lines," *Wall Street Journal,* May 21, 1999, p. B1; Robert Kreitner, *Management,* 9th ed. (Boston: Houghton Mifflin, 2004), p. 99.
37. Thomas Petzinger, Jr., "The Front Lines," *Wall Street Journal,* May 21, 1999, p. B1; Lucy McCauley, "Relaunch!" *Fast Company,* July 2000, pp. 97–108; Liz Stevens, "In the Race, America Has the Most Rats," *The News and Observer,* November 21, 1999, p. E3; Julie Gordon, "Teaching Selling Skills to the Financial World," *Denver Business Journal,* November 3, 2000, p. 10B.

Chapter 2

1. Jean P. Fisher, "Surgical Tools Cleaned Improperly," *The News & Observer,* January 7, 2005, p. B1; Jonathan B. Cox and Andrea Weigl, "Health Execs Admit PR Was Inadequate," *The News & Observer,* July 10, 2005, p. A1; Sarah Avery, "Experts' Answers Iffy; Case Has No Parallel," *The News & Observer,* July 10, 2005, p. A1.
2. David Shenk, *Data Smog—Surviving the Information Glut* (San Francisco: Harper Edge, 1997), p. 54.
3. John Stewart and Gary D'Angelo, *Together—Communicating Interpersonally* (New York: Random House, 1988), p. 5.
4. For more information on the components of communication, see Scot Ober, *Contemporary Business Communication,* 5th ed. (Boston: Houghton Mifflin, 2003), pp. 5–9.
5. Suein L. Hwang, "It Was a Wombat for the Meatware, But It Was a Good Sell," *Wall Street Journal,* May 15, 2002, p. B1.
6. "Memos from Hell," *Fortune,* February 3, 1997, p. 120.
7. Cai Shaoyao, "Cyberlingo—A Jargon Not for General Use," *Shanghai Star,* January 6, 2005. [cited 26 October 2005]. Available from http://app1.chinadaily.com.cn/ star/2005/0206/vo2–3.html; INTERNET; Julie Martin, "Cyberlingo! BRB? ROTFL? LOL? It's Greek to Me." [cited 26 October 2005]. Available from www.goodchatting.com/articles/archives/000006.php; INTERNET.
8. Matthew McKay, Martha Davis, and Patrick Fanning, *Messages: The Communication Skills Book* (Oakland, Calif.: New Harbinger, 1995), p. 108.
9. Deborah Tannen, *You Just Don't Understand: Men and Women in Conversation* (New York: Ballantine Books, 1990), pp. 24–25, 85.
10. Peter F. Drucker, quoted by Bill Moyers in *A World of Ideas* (Garden City, N.Y.: Doubleday, 1990).
11. Phyllis Mindell, "The Body Language of Power," *Executive Female,* May/June 1996, p. 48.
12. Don Clark, "Communication and Leadership," July 17, 2005, pp. 9, 10. [cited 27 October 2005]. Available from www.nwlink.com/donclark/leader/leadcom.html; INTERNET.

13. Ibid., p. 7.
14. William B. Gudykunst, Stella Ting-Toomey, Sandra Sudweeks, and Lea Stewart, *Building Bridges: Interpersonal Skills for a Changing World* (Boston: Houghton Mifflin, 1995), pp. 315–316.
15. Clark, "Communication and Leadership," p. 8.
16. "Sssh! Listen Up! *High Gain Inc. Newsletter,* June 2003, p. 3.
17. Ibid., p. 4.
18. Susan Scott, *Fierce Conversations: Achieving Success at Work and in Life, One Conversation at a Time* (New York: Viking, 2002), pp. 156–157.
19. Michael Toms, "Dialogue—the Art of Thinking Together—Sparks Spirit of 'Aliveness' in Organizations," *The Inner Edge,* August/September 1998, p. 462.
20. Stephen R. Covey, *The Seven Habits of Highly Effective People* (New York: Simon & Schuster, 1989), pp. 240–241.
21. C. Glenn Pearce, "Learning How to Listen Empathically," *Supervisory Management,* September 1991, p. 11.
22. Robert Epstein, "Waiting," *Psychology Today,* September/October 2001, p. 5.
23. Martha Beck, "True Confessions," *O The Oprah Magazine,* June 2002, pp. 183–184.
24. Daniel Goleman, "What Makes a Leader?" *Harvard Business Review,* November/December 1998, p. 95.
25. Cary Cherniss and Daniel Goleman, *The Emotionally Intelligent Workplace* (San Francisco: Jossey-Bass, 2001), p. 258.
26. Hendric Weisinger and Norman Lobsenz, *Nobody's Perfect—How to Give Criticism and Get Results* (Los Angeles: Stratford Press, 1981, p. 39.
27. Matthew Boyle, "What We Learned," *Fortune,* December 24, 2001, p. 179.
28. Jonathan B. Cox, "To Blog or Not to Blog," *The News & Observer,* August 21, 2005, p. E1.
29. "Etiquette with Office Gadgets," *Training,* January 1999, p. 24.
30. Marina Krakovsky, "Caveat Sender—The Pitfalls of E-mail," *Psychology Today,* March/April 2004, pp. 15–16.
31. Matthew Holohan, "How to Use E-mail Responsibly at Work." [cited 21 June 2000]. Available from ehow.com/Center/catIndex/o,1004, 1016,00.html; INTERNET.
32. This exercise is based on information taken from Scott, *Fierce Conversations,* pp. 117–118.
33. Jonathan B. Cox and Andrea Weigl, "Duke, Patients Poles Apart over Fluid Mix-up," *The News & Observer,* July 10, 2005, p. A1; Victor J. Dzau, "Learning from the Hydraulic Fluid Incident," *The News & Observer,* July 15, 2005, p. A19; "Report: Surgical Tools at Hospitals Were Washed in Hydraulic Fluid, Not Detergent," *San Diego Tribune,* June 13, 2005. [cited 4 November 2005]. Available from www.symtym .com/index.php/symtym/comments/lube_job; INTERNET; Jean P. Fisher, "Surgical Tools Cleaned Improperly." [cited 4 November 2005]. Available from www.newsobserver.com/new/health_science/ story/2581297p-8376237c.html; INTERNET; Jeff Molter, "Duke Provides Additional Information to Patients Exposed to Hydraulic Fluid," August 4, 2005. [cited 4 November 2005]. Available from www .dukemednews.org/news/article.php?id=9189; INTERNET; Sarah Avery, "New Firm to Track Duke Patients," *The News & Observer,* August 26, 2005, p. B1.
34. Ibid.
35. Ann David, Joseph Pereira, and William M. Bulkeley, "Security Concerns Bring New Focus on Body Language," *Wall Street Journal,* August 15, 2002, p. A1, A6; "The Power of Body Language," Course Archive. [cited 6 January 2003]. Available from www.presentersuni versity.com/courses/show_archive.cfm?RecordID 539; INTERNET.

Chapter 3

1. Shoshana Zuboff, "Only the Brave Surrender," *Fast Company,* October 2004, p. 121.
2. "Struggling with Low Self-Esteem," Go Ask Alice! June 6, 1997. [cited 9 November 2005]. Available from www.goaskalice.columbia. edu/1202.html; INTERNET.
3. David E. Shapiro, "Pumping Up Your Attitude," *Psychology Today,* May/June 1997, p. 14.
4. Douglas A. Bernstein, Louis A. Penner, Alison Clarke-Stewart, and Edward J. Roy, *Psychology,* 6th ed. (Boston: Houghton Mifflin, 2003), pp. 534–535; Richard Laliberte, "Self-Esteem Workshop," *Self,* May 1994, p. 201.
5. Nathaniel Branden, *The Six Pillars of Self-Esteem* (New York: Bantam, 1994), p. 7.
6. Robert Reasoner, "The True Meaning of Self-Esteem," National Association for Self-Esteem, Normal, Il. [cited April 30, 2003]. Available from INTERNET.
7. Phillip C. McGraw, *Self Matters* (New York: Simon & Schuster, 2001), pp. 69–70.
8. Sharon Begley, "Follow Your Intuition: The Unconscious You May Be the Wiser Half," *Wall Street Journal,* August 30, 2002, p. B1; Sharon Begley, "How Do I Love Thee? Let Me Count the Ways—and Other Bad Ideas," *Wall Street Journal,* September 6, 2002, p. B1.
9. Bernstein et al., Psychology, pp. 432–467.
10. Marilyn Elias, "Short Attention Span Linked to TV," *USAToday,* April 5, 2004, p. A1; Lyric Wallwork Winik, "The Toll of Video Violence," *Parade,* July 22, 2004, p. 15.
11. Bernstein et al., *Psychology,* pp. 467–471.
12. Ibid., 471.
13. Emmett Miller, *The Healing Power of Happiness* (Emmaus, Pa.: Rodale Press, 1989), pp. 12–13.
14. Lacey Beckmann, "One More Thing Money Can't Buy," *Psychology Today,* November/December, 2002, p. 16.
15. Amy Saltzman, *Downshifting* (New York: HarperCollins, 1990), pp. 15–16.
16. Miller, *The Healing Power of Happiness,* pp. 12–13.
17. McGraw, *Self Matters,* p. 73.
18. Reasoner, "The True Meaning."
19. Arthur H. Goldsmith, Jonathan R. Veum, and William Darity, Jr., "The Impact of Psychological and Human Capital on Wages," *Economic Inquiry,* October 1997, p. 817.
20. Hyrum W. Smith, *The 10 Natural Laws of Successful Time and Life Management* (New York: Warner Books, 1994), p. 178.
21. Don Miguel Ruiz, *The Four Agreements* (San Rafael, Calif.: Amber-Allen Publishing, 1997), pp. 47–61.
22. James J. Messina and Constance M. Messina, *The SEA's Program Model of Self-Esteem* [cited 9 November 2005]. Available from www .coping.org/selfesteem/model.htm.
23. Branden, *The Six Pillars of Self-Esteem,* p. 33.
24. Matthew McKay and Patrick Fanning, *Self-Esteem,* 2d ed. (Oakland, Calif.: New Harbinger, 1992), p. 42.
25. McGraw, *Self Matters,* pp. 209–212.
26. Arnold A. Lazarus and Clifford N. Lazarus, *The 60-Second Shrink* (San Luis Obispo, Calif.: Impact Publishers, 1997), p. 40.
27. Marcus Buckingham and Donald O. Clifton, *Now, Discover Your Strengths* (New York: Free Press, 2001), p. 8.
28. Ibid., pp. 28–35.
29. Ibid., pp. 28–31.
30. Nanette Byrnes, "Start Search," *Business Week,* October 10, 2005, p. 74.
31. Chip R. Bell, "Making Mentoring a Way of Life," *Training,* October 1996, p. 138; Lin Standke, review of *Managers as Mentors: Building Partnerships for Learning,* by Chip R. Bell, *Training,* April 1997, pp. 64–65.
32. Fiona Haley and Christine Canabou, interviews by, "The Mentors' Mentors," *Fast Company,* October 2003, p. 59.
33. Hal Lancaster, "It's Harder, but You Still Can Rise Up from the Mail Room," *Wall Street Journal,* June 18, 1996, p. B1.
34. Ginger Adams and Tena B. Crews, "Telementoring: A Viable Tool," *Journal of Applied Research for Business Education,* vol. 2, no. 3, 2004, pp. 1–4.
35. Hal Lancaster, "It's Harder, but You Still Can Rise Up from the Mail Room," *Wall Street Journal,* June 18, 1996, p. B1.
36. Gottlieb, "The Radical Road to Self-Esteem,"p. 101.
37. Stan Goldberg, "The 10 Rules of Change," *Psychology Today,* September/October 2002, pp. 38–44.
38. Andrew Weil, "Images of Healing," *Dr. Andrew Weil's Self Healing,* November 2003, p. 3; Amy Dockser Marcus, "Heart Surgeons Try

Using the Power of Suggestion," *Wall Street Journal,* February 20, 2004, p. D1.
39. James Bauman, "The Gold Medal," *Psychology Today,* May/June 2000, pp. 62–68.
40. See McGraw, *Self Matters,* for comprehensive coverage of how internal dialogue influences our self-concept.
41. McKay and Fanning, *Self-Esteem,* p. 42.
42. Julie Morgenstern, "Fire Your Inner Critic," *O The Oprah Magazine,* August 2004, pp. 75–77.
43. Herb Kindler, "Working to Change Old Habits," *Working Smart,* May 1992, p. 8.
44. McGraw, *Self Matters,* pp. 204–205.
45. Roy J. Blitzer, Colleen Petersen, and Linda Rogers, "How to Build Self-Esteem," *Training & Development,* February 1993, pp. 58–60.
46. Messina and Messina, *The SEA's Program Model of Self-Esteem,* p. 9.
47. Haley and Canabou, "The Mentors' Mentors," p. 60.
48. Cheryl Hall, "Mentoring as Critical as Ever, but Companies Are Ignoring It," *San Jose Mercury News,* February 11, 2001, p. PC1.
49. Haley and Canabou, "The Mentors' Mentors," pp. 59–66.
50. Frank Jossi, "Mentoring in Changing Times," *Training,* August 1997, p. 52.
51. Jennifer Reingold, "Want to Grow as a Leader? Get a Mentor!" *Fast Company,* January 2001, p. 58.
52. Dave Longaberger, *Longaberger: An American Success Story* (New York: Harper Business, 2001), p. 8.
53. "David Longaberger Sets the Standard for Success," *Selling,* May 2000, p. 8; Steve Williford and Dave Longaberger, *The Longaberger Story: And How We Did It* (Lincoln-Bradley Publishing, 1991); *Dave Longaberger: An American Success Story* (New York: Harper Business, 2001); P. Kelly Smith, "Entrepreneurial Expert Tami Longaberger: What She Learned from Her Father About Business and Life," April 16, 2001. [cited 8 January 2003]. Available from www.entrepreneur.com/Your_Business/YB_SegArticle/0,4621,288626,00.html; INTERNET.

Chapter 4

1. Troy McMullen, "Private Properties," *Wall Street Journal,* September 23, 2005, p. W10; Cassell Bryuan-Low, "World-Com's Auditors Took Shortcuts," *Wall Street Journal,* July 23, 2003, p. C9.
2. Kees Cools, "Ebbers Rex," *Wall Street Journal,* March 22, 2005, p. A22.
3. Jaren Sandberg, "Office Sticky Fingers Can Turn the Rest of Us into Joe Fridays," *Wall Street Journal,* November 19, 2005, p. B1.
4. David Gergen, "Candidates with Character," *U.S. News & World Report,* September 27, 1999, p. 68.
5. Patrick Smith, "You Have a Job, but How About a Life?" *Business Week,* November 16, 1998, p. 30.
6. Nathaniel Branden, *Self-Esteem at Work* (San Francisco: Jossey-Bass, 1998), p. 35.
7. Stephen R. Covey, *The Seven Habits of Highly Effective People* (New York: Simon & Schuster, 1989), p. 92.
8. Hyrum W. Smith, *The 10 Natural Laws of Successful Time and Life Management* (New York: Warner Books, 1994), pp. 14–15.
9. J. David McCracken and Ana E. Falcon-Emmanuelli, "A Theoretical Basis for Work Values Research in Vocational Education" *Journal of Vocational and Technical Education,* April 1994, p. 4.
10. Sue Shellenbarger, "Some Top Executives Are Finding a Balance Between Job and Home," *Wall Street Journal,* April 23, 1997, p. B1.
11. Katharine Mieszkowski, "FitzGerald Family Values," *Fast Company,* April 1998, p. 194.
12. Rebecca Ganzel, "Book Reviews," *Training,* June 2000, pp. 76–77.
13. Jack Canfield, *The Success Principles* (New York: HarperCollins, 2005), pp. 20–29.
14. Jeffrey Zaslow, "The Latest Generation Gap:Boomers Are Often Unfairly Lumped Together," *Wall Street Journal,* July 8, 2004, p. D1; Shirley Holt, "Generation Gaps in the Workplace," *The Roanoke Times,* March 27, 2005, pp. 1, 3.
15. Katherine Paterson, "Family Values," *New York Times Book Review,* October 15, 1995, p. 32.
16. Toms, "Investing in Character," *The Inner Edge,* June/July 2000, pp. 5–8.
17. Chris Lee and Ron Zemke, "The Search for Spirit in the Workplace," *Training,* June 1993, p. 21.
18. Sonia L. Nazario, "School Teachers Say It's Wrongheaded to Try to Teach Students What's Right," *Wall Street Journal,* April 6, 1990, p. B1; Steve Rosen, "Battle Against Corporate Swindlers Hits the Classroom," *Springfield Newsleader,* January 21, 2003, p. C1.
19. Character Counts! National Office at www.charactercounts.org. [cited 12 January 2003]. Available from www.charactercounts.org; INTERNET.
20. Linda Formichelli, "Programming Behavior," *Psychology Today,* January/February 2001, p. 10.
21. Morris Massey, *The People Puzzle* (Reston, Va.: Reston Publishing, 1979).
22. O. C. Ferrell, John Fraedrich, and Linda Ferrell, *Business Ethics,* 5th ed. (Boston: Houghton Mifflin, 2002), pp. 123–135.
23. Neal Donald Walsch, *Conversations with God, Book 1 Guidebook* (Charlottesville, Va.: Hampton Roads, 1997), p. 71.
24. John Hollon, "Drucker Knew Best," *Workforce Management,* November 21, 2005, p. 58.
25. Sue Shellenbarger, "In Cataclysmic Times, Workers Need Room to Rethink Priorities," *Wall Street Journal,* September 19, 2001, p. B1.
26. Toddi Gutner, "A Balancing Act for GenX Women," *Business Week,* January 21, 2002, p. 82.
27. John Beebe, "Conscience, Integrity and Character," *The Inner Edge,* June/July 2000, pp. 9–11.
28. "Making Sense of Ethics." [cited 13 January 2003]. Available from www.josephsoninstitute.org/MED/MED-1makingsense.htm; INTERNET.
29. "Workers Cut Ethical Corners, Survey Finds," *Wall Street Journal,* March 10, 1995, p. A2.
30. Price Pritchett, *The Ethics of Excellence* (Dallas, Tex: Pritchett & Associates, n.d.), p. 28.
31. "CyberSourceA8 Joins with Association of Certified Fraud Examiners to Support 2002 National Fraud Awareness Week," July 29, 2002. [cited 13 January 2003]. Available from www.cybersource.com/news_and_events/view.xml?page_id5949; INTERNET.
32. "Making Sense of Ethics."
33. Ed Emde, "Employee Values Are Changing Course," *Workforce,* March 1998, p. 84. [cited 18 November 2005]. Available from www.workforce.com/archive/article/21/97/39.php?ht5values%20values; INTERNET.
34. Jerry Useem, "Welcome to the New Company Town," *Fortune,* January 10, 2000, pp. 62–70.
35. Susan Scherreik, "A Conscience Doesn't Have to Make You Poor," *Business Week,* May 1, 2000, pp. 204–206.
36. Andy Pasztor and Jonathan Karp, "How an Air Force Official's Help for a Daughter Led to Disgrace," *Wall Street Journal,* December 9, 2004, p. A1, A10.
37. Ken Belson, "WorldCom's Audacious Failure and Its Toll on an Industry," *New York Times,* January 28, 2005, p. B1.
38. Gregory L. White and Amy Merrick, "Exide Unit Pleads Guilty to Charges over Battery Flaws," *Wall Street Journal,* March 26, 2001, p. B9.
39. Nancy D. Holt, "Workspaces," *Wall Street Journal,* December 2, 2004, p. B4; "Code of Ethics." [cited 27 October 2005]. Available from www.simmons.com; INTERNET.
40. Bob Filipczak, "The Soul of the Hog," *Training,* February 1996, pp. 38–42.
41. Kathryn Cates Moore, "Taking the High Road," *Journal Star,* April 28, 2001, p. B1.
42. Andrew Stark, "What's the Matter with Business Ethics?" *Harvard Business Review,* May/June 1993, p. 38.
43. "Tom Chappell—Minister of Commerce," *Business Ethics,* January/February 1994, p. 17.
44. Ferrell, Fraedrich, and Ferrell, *Business Ethics,* pp. 182–183.
45. Patrick M. Lencioni, "Make Your Values Mean Something," *Harvard Business Review,* July 2002, pp. 5–9.
46. Joshua Hyatt, "How to Hire Employees," *Inc.,* March 1990, p. 2.
47. Anne Fisher, "How Can You Be Sure We're Not Hiring a Bunch of Shady Liars?" *Fortune,* May 26, 2003, p. 180.

48. Jennifer Merritt, "Welcome to Ethics 101," *Business Week,* October 18, 2004, p. 90; Ronald Alsop, "Right and Wrong," *Wall Street Journal,* September 17, 2003, p. R9.
49. Richard Lacayo and Amanda Ripley, "Persons of the Year," *Time,* December 31, 2002, pp. 32–33.
50. Paula Dwyer and Dan Carney, with Amy Borrus and Lorraine Woellert in Washington and Christopher Palmeri in Los Angeles, "Year of the Whistleblower," *Business Week,* December 16, 2002, pp. 107–108; Michael Orey, "WorldCom-Inspired 'Whistle-Blower' Law Has Weaknesses," *Wall Street Journal,* October 1, 2002, p. B1.
51. Dwyer and Carney, "Year of the Whistleblower," p. 108.
52. Sarah Jay, "Corruption Issues: A View from Shanghai," *International Business Ethics Institute,* vol. 1, no. 1, November 1, 1997. [cited 27 November, 2005]. Available from www.business-ethics.org/news detail.asp? newsid531; INTERNET.
53. Chris Hill and Toby Hanlon, "26 Simple Ways to Change How You Feel," *Prevention,* August 1993, p. 126.
54. Sue Shellenbarger, "How and Why We Lie at the Office: From Pilfered Pens to Padded Accounts," *Wall Street Journal,* March 24, 2005, B1; Jared Dandberg, "Hard to Rein in Office Pilfering," *The News & Observer,* November 23, 2003, p. E12; Jared Sandberg, "Office Sticky Fingers Can Turn the Rest of Us into Joe Fridays," *The News & Observer,* November 19, 2003, p. B1.
55. Deborah Solomon, "For Financial Whistle-Blowers, New Shield Is an Imperfect One," *Wall Street Journal,* October 4, 2004, p. A1.
56. "Fraud Busters: Eight Who Made a Difference," Taxpayers Against Fraud, [cited 30 November 2005]. Available from www.taf.org/whistle blowerbios.pdf; INTERNET; "Company to Pay in Kickback Case," *The News & Observer,* July 31, 2004, p. D6; Deborah Solomon and Kara Scannell, "Whistle-Blower Provision Cited," *Wall Street Journal,* November 15, 2004, p. B4; "The False Claims Act/History." [cited 30 November 2005]. Available from www.quitamhelp.com/static/false _claims/history.html; INTERNET; "Qui Tam Basics." [cited 30 November 2005]. Available from www.quitamhelp.com/static/false _claims/history.html; INTERNET; Solomon "For Financial Whistle-Blowers, New Shield Is an Imperfect One."

Chapter 5

1. Rob Walker, "Hook, Line, & Sinker," *Inc.,* August 2002, p. 86.
2. Ibid., p. 88.
3. Ibid., p. 87.
4. Douglas A. Bernstein, Louis A. Penner, Alison Clarke-Stewart, and Edward J. Roy, *Psychology,* 6th ed. (Boston: Houghton Mifflin, 2003), p. 660.
5. Harry E. Chambers, *The Bad Attitude Survival Guide* (Reading, Mass.: Addison-Wesley, 1998), pp. 17–37.
6. John Hollon, "The Cult of Welch," *Workforce Management,* October 10, 2005, p. 74.
7. Daniel H. Pink, *A Whole New Mind* (New York: Riverhead Books, 2005), pp. 48–63.
8. Laura Landro, "Compassion 101: Teaching M.D.s to Be Nicer," *Wall Street Journal,* September 28, 2005, p. D1.
9. Pink, *A Whole New Mind,* p. 154.
10. Jerome Kagan, *Psychology: An Introduction* (New York: Harcourt Brace Jovanovich, 1984), p. 548.
11. William F. Schoell and Joseph P. Guiltinan, *Marketing,* 5th ed. (Boston: Allyn & Bacon, 1992), pp. 166–167; William M. Pride and O. C. Ferrell, *Marketing* (Boston: Houghton Mifflin, 2000), p. 211.
12. Joan Hamilton, "Net Work: At Icarian, It's All Work and Some Play," *Business Week E.BIZ,* April 3, 2000, p. EB116.
13. Nicholas Varchaver, "Who's the King of Delaware?" *Fortune,* May 13, 2002, pp. 124–128.
14. Thomas E. Ricks, "New Marines Illustrate Growing Gap Between Military and Society," *Wall Street Journal,* July 27, 1995, p. A1.
15. Kellye Whitney, "New-Hire Failure Linked to Interpersonal Skills," *Chief Learning Officer Magazine.* [cited 5 October 2005]. Available from www.clomedia.com; INTERNET.
16. Nathaniel Branden, *Self-Esteem at Work* (San Francisco: Jossey-Bass, 1998), pp. 94–97; "Adjusting an Attitude," *San Jose Mercury News,* August 20, 1997, p. G6.
17. His Holiness the Dalai Lama and Howard C. Cutler, *The Art of Happiness* (New York: Riverhead Books, 1998), pp. 16–17.
18. Michael Crom, "Live Enthusiastically and You'll Live Successfully," *Training,* April 1999, p. 6.
19. Dalai Lama and Cutler, *The Art of Happiness,* p. 22.
20. Ibid., p. 23.
21. Patricia Sellers, "Now Bounce Back!" *Fortune,* May 1, 1995, p. 57.
22. Martin Seligman, *Learned Optimism* (New York: Knopf, 2001), p. 4.
23. Redford Williams and Virginia Williams, *Anger Kills* (New York: Harper Perennial, 1993), p. 12.
24. Bob Wall, *Working Relationships* (Palo Alto, Calif.: Davies-Black, 1999), pp. 11–12.
25. Ibid., p. 17.
26. Brian Tracy, *The 100 Absolutely Unbreakable Laws of Business Success* (San Francisco: Berrett-Koehler 2000), pp. 67–70.
27. Branden, *Self-Esteem at Work,* pp. 111–112.
28. Harry E. Chambers, *The Bad Attitude Survival Guide* (Reading, Mass.: Addison-Wesley, 1998), pp. 6–7.
29. Weekly online news from *Workforce Week Management* distributed to subscribers November 29, 2005.
30. Hamilton, "Net Work," p. EB117.
31. Quoted in Nancy W. Collins, Susan K. Gilbert, and Susan Nycum, *Women Leading: Making Tough Choices on the Fast Track* (Lexington, Mass.: Stephen Greene Press, 1988), p. 1.
32. "100 Best Companies to Work For," *Fortune,* January 20, 2003, pp. 128–152.
33. Dave Murphy, "Going to School with 'FISH,' Happy Employees Can Save Companies More than a Few Fins," *San Francisco Chronicle,* April 21, 2002, pp. J1–2; Stephen C. Lundin, Harry Paul, and John Christensen, *Fish!* (Hyperion, 2000); Stephen C. Lundin, John Christensen, Harry Paul, with Philip Strand, *Fish! Tales* (Hyperion, 2001); Walker, "Hook, Line, & Sinker," pp. 85–88.
34. George F. Will, "The Perils of Bad Promises," *The Washington Post,* January 16, 2005 p. B7; Associated Press, "Fed Pension Agency Could See $71 Billion Deficit," June 9, 2005. [cited 9 December 2005]. Available from www.msnbc.msn.com; INTERNET; Associated Press, "Verizon Ends Manager Pension Contributions." [cited 7 December 2005]. Available from www.abcnews.go.com; INTERNET; "Dr. Spencer Johnson." [cited 7 December 2005]. Available from www.spencer johnsonpartners.com; INTERNET; Spencer Johnson, *Who Moved My Cheese?* (New York: G. P. Putnam's Sons), 1998.

Chapter 6

1. Daniel Akst, "Totally Devoted," *Wall Street Journal,* June 16, 2004, p. D8. Michael R. Solomon, Greg W. Marshall, and Elnora W. Stuart, *Marketing,* 4th ed. (Upper Saddle River, N.J.: Prentice Hall, 2006), pp. 275–279.
2. Heather Johnson, "A Brand-New You," *Training,* August 2002, p. 14.
3. Gerry Khermouch, "What Makes a Boffo Brand," *The Business Week,* Spring 2002, p. 20.
4. Stephen R. Covey, *The 7 Habits of Highly Effective People* (New York: Simon & Schuster, 1989), pp. 22, 34.
5. Susan Bixler, *Professional Presence* (New York: G. P. Putnam's Sons, 1991), p. 16.
6. "Author: Success Pivots on First Impressions," *San Jose Mercury News,* November 8, 1992, p. PC2.
7. Douglas A. Bernstein, Alison Clarke-Stewart, Louis A. Pence, Edward J. Roy, and Christopher D. Wickens, *Psychology,* 5th ed. (Boston: Houghton Mifflin, 2000), pp. 226–227.
8. Ann Demarais and Valerie White, *First Impressions* (New York: Bantam Books, 2004), p. 16.
9. Gordon Anders, "Hey, Not So Fast," *Wall Street Journal,* January 11, 2005, p. D9.
10. Danielle Sacks, "The Accidental Guru," *Fast Company,* January 2005, pp. 69–70.
11. Leonard Zunin and Natalie Zunin, *Contact—The First Four Minutes* (New York: Ballantine Books, 1972), p. 17.
12. Demarais and White, *First Impressions,* pp. 22–23.
13. Clyde Haberman, "No Offense," *New York Times Book Review,* February 18, 1996, p. 11.

14. "Disney Restyles Grooming Rules," *San Jose Mercury News,* July 12, 2003, p. B1.
15. Haberman, "No Offense," p. 11.
16. Bixler, *Professional Presence,* p. 141.
17. Suein L. Hwang, "Enterprise Takes Idea of Dressed for Success to a New Extreme," *Wall Street Journal,* November 20, 2002, p. B1.
18. GPA Licensee Certification/Train-the-Trainer," [cited 16 January 2006]. Available from www.globalprotocol.com; INTERNET.
19. Dave Knesel, "Image Consulting—A Well-Dressed Step up the Corporate Ladder," *Pace,* July/August 1981, p. 74.
20. Cora Daniels, "The Man in the Tan Khaki Pants," *Fortune,* May 1, 2000, p. 338.
21. Megan Schnabel and Amy Kane, "Toss the Tie, Lose the Suit—The Casual Look Is In," *The Roanoke Times,* September 5, 1999, pp. B1, B2; Gene Bedell, *3 Steps to Yes* (New York: Crown Business, 2000), p. 143.
22. Anne Fisher, "Ask Annie," *Fortune,* May 15, 2000, p. 504; Frederic M. Biddle, "Work Week," *Wall Street Journal,* February 15, 2000; Mielikki Org, "The Tattooed Executive," *Wall Street Journal,* August 28, 2003, p. D1.
23. Deborah Blum, "Face It!" *Psychology Today,* September/October 1998, pp. 34, 69.
24. Susan Bixler, *The Professional Image* (New York: Perigee Books, 1984), p. 217.
25. Ibid., p. 219.
26. Heather Won Tesoriers, "At Vioxx Trial, Fast Talkers Challenge Court Stenographer," *Wall Street Journal,* October 25, 2005, p. B1.
27. Joann S. Lublin, "To Win Advancement, You Need to Clean Up Any Bad Speech Habits," *Wall Street Journal,* October 5, 2004, p. B1.
28. Ibid.
29. Lydia Ramsey, "You Never Get a 2nd Chance," *Selling,* October 2003, p. 3.
30. Adapted from Zunin and Zunin, *Contact,* pp. 102–108; "Handshake 101," *Training & Development,* November 1995, p. 71.
31. Cynthia Crossen, "Etiquette for Americans Today," *Wall Street Journal,* December 28, 2001, p. W13.
32. Barbara Pachter and Mary Brody, *Complete Business Etiquette Handbook* (Englewood Cliffs, N.J.: Prentice-Hall, 1995), p. 3.
33. Amy Gamerman, "Lunch with Letitia: Our Reporter Minds Her Manners," *Wall Street Journal,* March 3, 1994, p. A14.
34. Ann Marie Sabath, "Meeting Etiquette: Agendas and More," *DECA Dimensions,* January/February 1994, p. 8; "Is Etiquette a Core Value?" *Inc.,* May 2004, p. 22.
35. Leila Jason, "Are There Rules of Etiquette for Cell-phone Use?" *Wall Street Journal,* September 10, 2001, p. R16; Dana May Casperson, "Tactfully Respond to Cell Phone Intrusion," *Selling,* April 2005, p. 5.
36. Dana May Casperson, "Break Those Bad Cell-phone Habits," *Selling,* January 2002, p. 9.
37. Gene Veith, "Curse of the Foul Mouth," *Wall Street Journal,* January 24, 2003, p. D1; Tara Parker-Pope and Kyle Pope, "When #@%&@ Is—and Isn't—Appropriate," *Wall Street Journal Sunday,* featured in *The News & Observer,* January 21, 2001, p. D4.
38. Barbara Moses, *Career Intelligence* (San Francisco: Berrett-Koehler, 1997), p. 175.
39. Nancy K. Austin, "What Do America Online and Dennis Rodman Have in Common?" *Inc.,* July 1997, p. 54.
40. Marilyn Vos Savant, "Ask Marilyn," *Parade,* May 30, 2002, p. 19.
41. Stephanie G. Sherman, *Make Yourself Memorable* (New York: American Management Association, 1996), pp. 3–4; "People in the News," *U.S. News & World Report,* November 8, 1999, p. 12; Ann Landers, "If You've Got Class, Nothing Else Matters," *The News & Observer,* July 11, 1998, p. E2; Carlin Flora, "The Superpowers," *Psychology Today,* May/June 2005, pp. 40–50.
42. David McNally and Karl D. Speak, *Be Your Own Brand* (San Francisco: Berrett-Koehler, 2002), p. 4.
43. Ibid.
44. "The Right Words at the Right Time," *O The Oprah Magazine,* May 2002, p. 202.

Chapter 7

1. Carol Hymowitz, "The New Diversity," *Wall Street Journal,* November 14, 2005, pp. R1–R3.
2. Ibid.
3. Robert Kreitner, *Management,* 9th ed. (Boston: Houghton Mifflin, 2004), pp. 78–79.
4. Marilyn Loden and Judy B. Rosener, *Workforce America!* (Homewood, Ill.: Business One Irwin, 1991), pp. 114–115.
5. Ibid., p. 21.
6. Douglas A. Bernstein, Louis A. Penner, Alison Clarke-Stewart, and Edward J. Roy, *Psychology,* 6th ed. (Boston: Houghton Mifflin, 2003), p. 666.
7. D. Stanley Eitzen and Maxine Baca Zinn, *In Conflict and Order* (Boston: Allyn & Bacon, 2001), p. 237.
8. Ibid.
9. Lewis Brown Griggs and Lente-Louise Louw, *Valuing Diversity* (New York: McGraw-Hill, 1995), pp. 3–4, 150–151.
10. Ibid., p. 151.
11. Yochi J. Dreazen, "U.S. Racial Wealth Gap Remains Huge," *Wall Street Journal,* March 14, 2000, p. A2.
12. Mike Harris, "Newman Going Strong," *The News & Observer,* February 5, 2005, p. C8.
13. Sue Shellenbarger, "Baby Boomers Already Are Getting Agitated over Age-Bias Issues," *Wall Street Journal,* May 30, 2001, p. B1.
14. Anne Fisher, "Finally! A Ray of Hope for Job Seekers over 50," *Fortune,* December 10, 2001, p. 278.
15. Darren Dahl, "A New Wrinkle on Age Bias," *Inc.,* July 2005, p. 36; Kathy Chen, "Age-Discrimination Complaints Rose 8.7% in 2001 amid Overall Increase in Claims," *Wall Street Journal,* February 25, 2002, p. B13.
16. Richard Hadden and Bill Catlette, *Contented Cows Give Better Milk.* [cited 14 November 2005]. Available from www.contentedcows.com; INTERNET.
17. Sue Shellenbarger, "Gray Is Good: Employers Make Efforts to Retain Older, Experienced Workers," *Wall Street Journal,* December 1, 2005 p. D1. Peter Coy, "Surprise! The Graying of the Workforce Is Better News Than You Think," *Business Week,* June 27, 2005, p. 78.
18. Craig Calhoun, Donald Light, and Suzanne Keller, *Sociology,* 6th ed. (New York: McGraw-Hill, 1994), p. 241.
19. Nicholas D. Kristof, "Is Race Real?" *New York Times,* July 11, 2003; Robert S. Boynton, "Color Us Invisible," *New York Times Book Review,* August 17, 1997, p. 13.
20. Stephen Magagini, "A Race Free Consciousness," *The News & Observer,* November 23, 1997, pp. A25–A26.
21. Carol Mukhopadhyay and Rosemary C. Henze, "How Real Is Race? Using Anthropology to Make Sense of Human Diversity," *Phi Delta Kappan,* May 2003, p. 675.
22. John McWhorter, "We're Not Ready to Think Outside the Box on Race," *Wall Street Journal,* March 28, 2002, p. A20; G. Pascal Zachary, "A Mixed Future," *Wall Street Journal,* January 1, 2000, p. R43. A recent book entitled *One Drop of Blood—The American Misadventure of Race* by Scott L. Malcomson provides an excellent review of America's separatist history.
23. Mukhopadhyay and Henze, "How Real Is Race? pp. 673–676.
24. Robert Kreitner, *Management,* 8th ed. (Boston: Houghton Mifflin, 2001), p. 117.
25. Daniel Golden, "A Test of Faith," *Wall Street Journal,* January 7, 2006, p. A1; "Narrow-Minded or Protecting One's Mission?" *Wall Street Journal,* January 16, 2006, p. A15.
26. Kris Maher, "Disabled Face Scarcer Jobs, Data Show," *Wall Street Journal,* October 5, 2005, p. D1.
27. Ibid.
28. Sue Shellenbarger, "A Mid Gay Marriage Debate: Companies Offer More Benefits to Same-Sex Couples," *Wall Street Journal,* March 18, 2004, p. D1; Barbara Rose, "Policies to Accommodate Gays Draw Scrutiny," *The News & Observer,* July 3, 2005, p. E12; Rachel Emma Silverman, "Wall Street, a New Push to Recruit Gay Students," *Wall Street Journal,* February 9, 2000, p. B1.
29. Robert Tomsho, "School & Efforts to Protect Gays Face Opposition," *Wall Street Journal,* February 20, 2003, p. B1.

30. Michael L. Wheeler, *Diversity: Business Rationale and Strategies* (New York: The Conference Board, 1995), p. 9.
31. Chuck Salter, "Diversity Without the Excuses," *Fast Company,* September 2002, p. 44.
32. Jessica Marquez, "Survey Says Diversity Contributes to the Bottom Line," *Workforce Management,* November 18, 2005. [cited 23 February 2006]. Available from www.workforce.com; INTERNET.
33. Fay Hansen, "Microsoft R & D Seeks Global Tech Talent, Not Bargains," *Workforce Management,* July 2005, p. 39; Kreitner, *Management,* p. 80; "Toyota's Charge Toward the Pinnacle of the Sport," *Canadian Grand Prix Program 2002,* p. 54; Robin Townsley Arcus, "World Market," *The Urban Hiker,* October 2000, p. 34.
34. *101 Tools for Tolerance* (Montgomery, Ala.: Southern Poverty Law Center), pp. 4–7.
35. Gail Johnson, "Time to Broaden Diversity," *Training,* September 2004, p. 16; Adapted from Leone E. Wynter, "Do Diversity Programs Make a Difference?" *Wall Street Journal,* December 4, 1996, p. B1.
36 "Time to Diversify," *Sales & Marketing Management,* May 2002, p. 62.
37. Jonathan Hickman, "America's 50 Best Companies for Minorities," *Fortune,* July 8, 2002, pp. 110–120.
38. Ibid., p. 118; Dean Foust, "Coke: Say Good-Bye to the Good Ol' Boy Culture," *Business Week,* May 29, 2000, p. 58.
39. Gail Johnson, "Lockheed Martin Corporation—Focusing on People Development," *Training,* March 2005, pp. 39–40.
40. Kreitner, *Management,* pp. 334–335.
41. Terry Eastland, "Endgame for Affirmative Action," *Wall Street Journal,* March 28, 1996, p. A15; John J. Miller, "Out of One Set of Preferences, Many . . . and Many New Debates," *New York Times Book Review,* March 27, 2002, p. A16; Roger Pilon, "The Complexities of Unfair Discrimination," *Wall Street Journal,* December 13, 2002, p. A17.
42. Miller, "Out of One Set of Preferences," p. A16.
43. Roger O. Crockett, "How to Narrow the Great Divide," *Business Week,* July 14, 2003, p. 104; Sharon S. Brehm, Saul M. Kassin, and Steven Fein, *Social Psychology,* 5th ed. (Boston: Houghton Mifflin, 2002), pp. 478–480.
44. R. Roosevelt Thomas, Jr., "From Affirmative Action to Affirming Diversity," *Harvard Business Review,* March/April 1990, p. 114.
45. "The Court's Social Agenda," *Wall Street Journal,* December 3, 2002, p. A22; Ward Connerly and Edward Blum, "Do the Right Thing," *Wall Street Journal,* December 4, 2002, p. A18; Ronald Dworkin, "Keeping on Course with Affirmative Action," *The News & Observer,* April 22, 2001, p. A31; Robert L. Mathis and John H. Jackson, *Human Resource Management,* 10th ed. (Manson, Ohio: Thomson South-Western, 2003), pp. 144–146; Daniel Golden, "Buying Your Way into College," *Wall Street Journal,* March 12, 2003, p. D1; Adam Wolfsen, "What Makes a Difference," *Wall Street Journal,* February 26, 2003, p. D10.
46. Dworkin, "Keeping on Course with Affirmative Action," p. A31.
47. Elizabeth Schulte, "Can We End Bigotry Through Education?" *Socialist Worker,* July 20, 2001, p. 9; "Bush Marks Black History Month with Call to End Bigotry," [cited 25 February 2006]. Available from www.eyewitnessnewstv.com/global/story; INTERNET; Robert Epstein, "In Her Own Words," *Psychology Today,* May/June 2002, pp. 40–42.

Chapter 8

1. Kevin Allen, "NHL Wiped Out," *USA Today,* February 17, 2005, p. C1; Paul D. Staudohar, "The Hockey Lockout of 2004–05," *Monthly Labor Review,* December 2005, pp. 23–29.
2. Cheryl Shavers, "Some Positive Steps That You Can Take to Resolve Conflicts," *San Jose Mercury News,* March 21, 1999, p. E3.
3. Anne Fisher, "Which One Should I Fire? . . . Is My Voice Mail Monitored? . . . and Other Queries," *Fortune,* November 25, 1996, p. 173.
4. Dudley Weeks, *The Eight Essential Steps to Conflict Resolution* (New York: G. P. Putnam's Sons, 1992), p. 7.
5. Ibid., pp. 7–8.
6. Adam Hanft, "The Joy of Conflict," *Inc.,* August 2005, p. 112; Adam Hanft, "Down with Bossocracy" *Inc.,* April 2004, p. 126.
7. Susan M. Heathfield, "Fight for What's Right: Ten Tips to Encourage Meaningful Conflict." [cited 7 February 2006]. Available from www.about.com; INTERNET.
8. Don Wallace and Scott McMurray, "How to Disagree (Without Being Disagreeable)," *Fast Company,* November 1995, p. 146.
9. Robert Kreitner, *Management,* 9th ed. (Boston: Houghton Mifflin, 2004), pp. 544–546.
10. Ibid., pp. 529–530.
11. David Stiebel, "The Myth of Hidden Harmony," *Training,* March 1997, p. 114.
12. Carol Kleiman, "How to Deal with a Co-worker Who's Getting on Your Nerves," *San Jose Mercury News,* October 3, 1999, p. PC1.
13. "Assertiveness: More Than a Forceful Attitude," *Supervisory Management,* February 1994, p. 3.
14. American Management Association, *Catalog of Seminars* (New York: American Management Association). [cited 1 January 2006]. Available from www.amanet.org; INTERNET.
15. Danny Ertel, "Turning Negotiation into a Corporate Capability." *Harvard Business Review,* May/June 1999, p. 3.
16. Rob Walker, "Take It or Leave It: The Only Guide to Negotiating You Will Ever Need," *Inc.,* August 2003, pp. 65–77.
17. Kurt Salzinger, "Psychology on the Front Lines," *Psychology Today,* May/June 2002, p. 34.
18. David Stiebel, *When Talking Makes Things Worse!* (Dallas: Whitehall & Nolton, 1997), p. 17.
19. Roger Fisher and Alan Sharp, *Getting It Done* (New York: Harper Business, 1998), pp. 81–83.
20. Roger Fisher and William Ury, *Getting to Yes* (New York: Penguin Books, 1981), p. 59.
21. Weeks, *The Eight Essential Steps to Conflict Resolution,* p. 228.
22. Ibid., p. 223.
23. University of North Texas–Dallas: Alternative Dispute Resolution Certificate Brochure, updated 25 March 2002. [cited 22 February 2003]. Available from www.unt.edu/unt-dallas/brochures/adresd.htm; INTERNET.
24. Douglas A. Bernstein, Louis A. Penner, Alison Clarke-Stewart, and Edward J. Roy, *Psychology,* 6th ed. (Boston: Houghton Mifflin, 2003), pp. 412–413.
25. Carol S. Pearson, "The Emotional Side of Workplace Success," *The Inner Edge,* December 1998/January 1999, p. 3.
26. Daniel Goleman, *Emotional Intelligence* (New York: Bantam Books, 1995), p. 34.
27. Robert Kreitner, *Management,* 9th ed. (Boston: Houghton Mifflin, 2004), p. 504.
28. Daniel Goleman, *Working with Emotional Intelligence* (New York: Bantam Books, 1998), pp. 24–28.
29. John Selby, *Conscious Healing* (New York: Bantam Books, 1989), p. 32.
30. Ibid.
31. James Georges, "The Not-So-Stupid Americans," *Training,* July 1994, p. 90.
32. Tim Sanders, *Love Is the Killer App* (New York: Crown Business, 2002), pp. 17–18.
33. Ibid., p. 23.
34. Ron Zemke, "Contact! Training Employees to Meet the Public," *Service Solutions* (Minneapolis: Lakewood Books, 1990), pp. 20–23.
35. Bernstein et al., *Psychology,* p. 454.
36. Ibid.
37. William C. Menninger and Harry Levinson, *Human Understanding in Industry* (Chicago: Science Research Associates, 1956), p. 29.
38. Joan Borysenko, *Guilt Is the Teacher, Love Is the Lesson* (New York: Warner Books, 1990), p. 70.
39. Donella H. Meadows, "We Are, to Our Harm, What We Watch," *Roanoke Times & World-News,* October 16, 1994, p. G3.
40. Bernstein et al., *Psychology,* p. 22.
41. Harold H. Bloomfield and Robert K. Cooper, *The Power of 5* (Emmaus, Pa.: Rodale Press, 1995), p. 334; Redford Williams and Virginia Williams, *Anger Kills* (New York: HarperCollins, 1993), p. 3; Jared Sandberg, "The Upside of Anger: Some Use It as a Shield Against Work, Others," *Wall Street Journal,* October 11, 2005, p. B1; Martha Beck, "Impotent Rage," *O The Oprah Magazine,* October 2004, p. 205.
42. Kimes Gustin, *Anger, Rage, and Resentment* (West Caldwell, N.J.: St. Ives' Press, 1994), p. 1.
43. Art Ulene, *Really Fit Really Fast* (Encino, Calif.: Health-Points, 1996), pp. 170–174.

44. Pemma Chödrön, "The Answer to Anger and Other Strong Emotions," *Shambhala Sun,* March 2005, p. 32.
45. Susan Bixler, *Professional Presence* (New York: G. P. Putnam's Sons, 1991), pp. 190–191.
46. Rolland S. Parker, *Emotional Common Sense* (New York: Barnes & Noble Books, 1973), pp. 80–81.
47. Gustin, *Anger, Rage, and Resentment,* p. 37.
48. Les Giblin, *How to Have Confidence and Power in Dealing with People* (Englewood Cliffs, N.J.: Prentice-Hall 1956), p. 37.
49. Don Miguel Ruiz, *The Four Agreements* (San Rafael, Calif.: Amber-Allen Publishing, 1997), p. 111.
50. Sam Keen, *Fire in the Belly—On Being a Man* (New York: Bantam Books, 1991), p. 242.
51. Arnold A. Lazarus and Clifford N. Lazarus, *The 60-Second Shrink* (San Luis Obispo, Calif.: Impact, 1997), pp. 10–11.
52. Borysenko, *Minding the Body, Mending the Mind,* p. 169.
53. Ellen Safier, "Our Experts Answer Your Questions," *Menninger Letter,* May 1993, p. 8.
54. Leo F. Buscaglia, *Loving Each Other* (Thorofare, N.J.: Slack, 1984), p. 160.
55. Keen, *Fire in the Belly,* p. 242.

Chapter 9

1. Sue Shellenbarger, "Avoiding the Next Enron: Today's Crop of Soon-to-Be Grads Seeks Job Security," *Wall Street Journal,* February 16, 2006, p. D1.
2. Jeffrey McCraken and Joseph B. White, "Ford Will Shed 28% of Workers in North America," *Wall Street Journal,* January 24, 2006, p. A1.
3. Robert M. Strozier, "The Job of Your Dreams," *New Choices,* April 1998, p. 25.
4. Po Bronson, *What Should I Do with My Life?* (New York: Random House, 2002), p. 365; Patricia Kitchen, "Seeking Your Calling," *The Record,* March 9, 2003, p. D1.
5. Ethan Watters, "Come Here, Work, and Get Out of Here, You Don't Live Here. You Live Someplace Else," *Inc.,* October 30, 2001, pp. 56–61.
6. Diane Brady, "Rethinking the Rat Race," *Business Week,* August 26, 2002, pp. 142–143.
7. Jane Bozarth, "In Print," *Training,* August 2001, p. 60. (This article reviews *Dot. Calm—The Search for Sanity in a Wired World,* a book written by Debra A. Dinnocenzo and Richard B. Swegan.)
8. Sue Shellenbarger, "Keeping Your Career a Manageable Part of Your Life," *Wall Street Journal,* April 12, 1995, p. B1; "Career vs. Family: Companies Respond," *Fortune,* April 28, 1997, p. 22.
9. Jack Canfield, *The Success Principles* (New York: Harper Collins, 2005), p. 3.
10. Mary E. Miller, "The Best Use of Her Time," *The News & Observer,* March 9, 2003, p. D1; Susan Broili, "Potter Exchanges Money for Tranquility," *Chapel Hill Herald,* July 23, 2004, p. 1.
11. Yvonne V. Chabrier, "Focus on Work," *New Age,* 1998, p. 95.
12. Bronson, *What Should I Do with My Life?* pp. 68–72.
13. Marsha Sinetar, *Do What You Love . . . The Money Will Follow* (New York: Dell, 1987), p. 11.
14. Ibid., pp. 11–12.
15. Michael Phillips, *The Seven Laws of Money* (Menlo Park, Calif.: Word Wheel and Random House, 1997), p. 9.
16. Sinetar, *Do What You Love,* pp. 14–15.
17. Sue Shellenbarger, "New Job Hunters Ask Recruiters, Is There a Life After Work?" *Wall Street Journal,* January 29, 1997, p. B1.
18. Carole Kanchier, "Dare to Change Your Job and Your Life in 7 Steps," *Psychology Today,* March/April 2000, pp. 64–67.
19. Suze Orman, "The Pursuit of Cold, Hard Happiness," *O The Oprah Magazine,* March 2004, pp. 54–56; Sharon Begley, "Wealth and Happiness Don't Necessarily Go Hand in Hand," *Wall Street Journal,* August 13, 2004, p. B1.
20. Geoffrey Colvin, "We're a Nation Helpless to Save Ourselves," *Fortune,* April 18, 2005, p. 52.
21. Shakti Gawain, *Creating True Prosperity* (Novato, Calif.: New World Library, 1997), p. 7.
22. Carlin Flora, "Happy Hour," *Psychology Today,* January/February 2005, p. 48.
23. Jonathan Clements, "If You Didn't Save 10% of Your Income This Year, You're Spending Too Much," *Wall Street Journal,* December 22, 2004, p. D1; Jonathan Clements, "Rich, Successful—and Miserable: New Research Probes Midlife Angst," *Wall Street Journal,* October 5, 2005, p. D1.
24. Toddi Gutner, "Talk Now, Retire Happily Later," *Business Week,* April 2, 2001, p. 92.
25. Teri Lammers Prior, "If I Were President {3dots}," *Inc.,* April 1995, pp. 56–60.
26. Michael Toms, "Money: The Third Side of the Coin" (interview with Joe Dominguez and Vicki Robin), *New Dimensions,* May/June 1991, p. 7.
27. Susan Smith Jones, "Choose to Be Healthy and Celebrate Life," *New Realities,* September/October 1988, pp. 17–19.
28. Jean P. Fisher, "Healthy Habits Pay Off, Literally," *The News & Observer,* May 16, 2004, p. E1.
29. Toddi Gutner, "A 12-Step Program to Gaining Power," *Business Week,* December 24, 2001, p. 88.
30. Ron Zemke, "Why Organizations Still Aren't Learning," *Training,* September 1999, p. 43.
31. His Holiness the Dalai Lama and Howard C. Cutler, *The Art of Happiness* (New York: Riverhead Books, 1998), pp. 227–228.
32. Sue Shellenbarger, "Working 9 to 2: Taking Steps to Make Part-Time Job Setups More Palatable," *Wall Street Journal,* February 17, 2005, p. D1.
33. Jay T. Knippen, Thad B. Green, and Kurt Sutton, "Asking Not to Be Overworked," *Supervisory Management,* February 1992, p. 6.
34. Art Ulene, *Really Fit Really Fast* (Encino, Calif.: Health-Points, 1996), pp. 198–199.
35. Marilyn Chase, "Weighing the Benefits of Mental-Health Days Against Guilt Feelings," *Wall Street Journal,* September 9, 1996, B1.
36. Sue Shellenbarger, "Slackers, Rejoice: Research Touts the Benefits of Skipping Out on Work," *Wall Street Journal,* March 27, 2003, p. D1.
37. Leo Booth, "When God Becomes a Drug," *Common Boundary,* September/October 1991, p. 30; David N. Elkins, "Spirituality," *Psychology Today,* September/October, 1999, pp. 45–48.
38. Harold H. Bloomfield and Robert K. Cooper, *The Power of 5* (Emmaus, Pa.: Rodale Press, 1995), p. 484.
39. Jerry Adler, "In Search of the Spiritual," *Newsweek,* August 29/September 5, 2005, pp. 47–55.
40. "Making the Spiritual Connection," *Lears,* December 1989, p. 72.
41. Thomas Moore, "Will We Take the Moral Values Challenge?" *Spirituality & Health,* January/February 2005, pp. 10–11.
42. Robert Bolton and Dorothy Grover Bolton, *People Styles at Work* (New York: AMACOM, 1996), pp. 110–111.
43. Rachel Emma Silverman, "More Chaplains Take Ministering into the Workplace," *Wall Street Journal,* November 27, 2001, p. B1.
44. G. Paul Zachary, "The New Search for Meaning in Meaningless Work," *Wall Street Journal,* January 9, 1997, p. B1.
45. Daniel H. Pink, A Whole New Mind (New York: Riverhead Books, 2005), p. 52.
46. Kevin Helliker, "Body and Spirit: Why Attending Religious Services May Benefit Health," *Wall Street Journal,* May 3, 2005, p. D1.
47. Sara Schaefer Munoz, "The Food Pyramid Gets Personalized," *Wall Street Journal,* April 20, 2005, p. D1; "Johanns Reveals USDA's Steps to a Healthier You." [cited 24 February 2006]. Available from www.mypyramid.gov; INTERNET.
48. Paul Raeburn, "Why We're So Fat," *Business Week,* October 21, 2002, pp. 112–114; Sara Schaefer Munoz, "New U.S. Diet Guide Focuses on Calories, Exercise," *Wall Street Journal* January 12, 2005, p. D4; Nancie Hellmich, "Obesity on Track as No. 1 Killer," *USA Today,* March 10, 2004, p. A1.
49. Cassandra Wrightson, "Snacks Worth Their Salt," *Health,* June 2001, p. 52.
50. Ulene, *Really Fit Really Fast,* pp. 20–21; Robert Langreth, "Every Little Bit Helps," *Wall Street Journal,* May 1, 2000, p. R5. Tara Parker-Pope, "Health Matters," *Wall Street Journal,* August 9, 2004, p. R5.
51. John Swartzberg, "Exercise: It's Not Just Physical," *UC Berkeley Wellness Letter,* November 2002, p. 3.
52. Robert A. Gleser, *The Healthmark Program for Life* (New York: McGraw-Hill, 1988), p. 147.

53. *Fitness Fundamentals* (Washington, D.C.: Department of Health and Human Services, 1988), p. 2.
54. Stephen R. Covey, *The Seven Habits of Highly Effective People* (New York: Simon & Schuster, 1989), p. 46.
55. James Fadiman, *Be All That You Are* (Seattle: Westlake Press, 1986), p. 25.
56. Mike Hernacki, *The Ultimate Secret of Getting Absolutely Everything You Want* (New York: Berkley Books, 1988), p. 35.
57. Adapted from Bloomfield and Cooper, *The Power of 5,* pp. 492–493.
58. Mary Lou Quinlan, "Just Ask a Women," *Fast Company,* July 2003, p. 50.
59. Ibid.
60. Just Ask a Woman Brand Consultants, Content Creators, Problem Solvers." [cited on 1 March 2006]. Available from www.justaskawoman .com; INTERNET.

Credits

Chapter 1 p. 2: © Charles Gupton/Corbis; p. 5: Jeff Danziger, Cartoon Arts International/CWS; p. 6: AP IMAGES/Marcio Jose Sanchez; p. 12: Chris Mueller/Redux; p. 20: © Tim Shaffer/Reuters/Corbis.

Chapter 2 p. 26: © Brooks Kraft/Corbis; p. 32: © Money Sharma/Corbis; p. 35: Copyright © 1996 USA Today. Reprinted with permission; p. 41: © Royalty-Free/Corbis; p. 43: © Mike Baldwin/Cornered/www.CartoonStock.com; p. 44: © Steve Chenn/Corbis.

Chapter 3 p. 52: Andersen Ross/Getty Images; p. 57: © The New Yorker Collection 2001 Pat Byrnes from cartoonbank.com. All Rights Reserved; p 58: Time & Life Pictures/Getty Images; p. 63: Courtesy The Gallup Organization; p. 64: © McClatchy-Tribune Information Services. All Rights Reserved. Reprinted with permission.

Chapter 4 p. 74: Adam Rountree/Getty Images; p. 81: © The New Yorker Collection 2002 Alex Gregory from cartoonbank.com. All Rights Reserved; p. 85: Tony Anderson/Getty Images; p. 89: Duke University Photo; p. 90: Time & Life Pictures/Getty Images.

Chapter 5 p. 96: © David Kadlubowski/DIT/Corbis; p. 100: Jacket design by Coudal Partners, copyright © 2005 by Daniel H. Pink, from *A Whole New Mind* by Daniel H. Pink. Used by permission of Riverhead Books, an imprint of Penguin Group (USA) Inc.; p. 102: Time & Life Pictures/Getty Images; p. 105: DENNIS THE MENACE © NORTH AMERICA SYNDICATE; p. 110: Reprinted by permission of the Estate of Reinhold Niebuhr; p. 112: Jeff Greenberg/PhotoEdit.

Chapter 6 p. 118: © Frederic Larson/San Francisco Chronicle/Corbis; p. 121: © M. Thomsen/zefa/Corbis; p. 127: AFP/Getty Images; p. 133: Getty Images.

Chapter 7 p. 140: © AP IMAGES/Manish Swarup; p. 144: © Bob Daemmrich/The Image Works; p. 146: Reprinted by permission of the Southern Poverty Law Center; p. 149: SALLY FORTH © KING FEATURES SYNDICATE; p. 151: Getty Images; p. 153: Courtesy National Sports Center for the Disabled.

Chapter 8 p. 168: © Chris Wattie/Reuters/Corbis; p. 175: From Rich Brinkman and Rick Kirscher, DEALING WITH PEOPLE YOU CAN'T STAND. Copyright © 1994. Reprinted by permission of The McGraw Hill Companies; p. 178: © Timothy Archibald; p. 180: From Team Building, First Edition by Robert B. Maddux. Copyright © 1987. Reprinted with permission of Course Technology, a division of Thomson Learning: www.thomsonrights.com. Fax 800-730-2215; p. 181: SALLY FORTH © KING FEATURES SYNDICATE; p. 183: Courtesy American Arbitration Association; p. 187: © John W. Clark; p. 189: AP IMAGES/Rod Aydelotte.

Chapter 9 p. 200: © Ed Bock/Corbis; p. 203: © Philip Newton; p. 204 © 2006 Leo Cullum from cartoonbank.com. All Rights Reserved; p. 205: Book Cover from THE SUCCESS PRINCIPLES™ by JACK CANFIELD and JANET SWITZER. COPYRIGHT © 2005 BY JACK CANFIELD. Reprinted by permission of HarperCollins Publishers; p. 213: Chris Seward/© The News & Observer.

CREDITS

Answers to Test Preppers

Chapter 1

1.1, 1.2	1. F	2. F	3. a	4. b	5. c
1.3	1. T	2. F	3. c	4. c	5. b
1.4	1. F	2. F	3. a	4. d	5. c
1.5	1. T	2. d	3. a	4. d	5. b

Chapter 2

2.1	1. F	2. T	3. a	4. c	5. c
2.2	1. b	2. a	3. d	4. b	5. a
2.3	1. F	2. b	3. a	4. c	5. d
2.4	1. F	2. F	3. T	4. c	5. a

Chapter 3

3.1	1. T	2. F	3. a	4. a	5. c
3.2, 3.3	1. T	2. F	3. T	4. c	5. a
3.4	1. T	2. c	3. b	4. c	5. a
3.5	1. T	2. F	3. F	4. b	5. a

Chapter 4

4.1, 4.2	1. T	2. T	3. b	4. a	5. b
4.3, 4.4	1. F	2. T	3. T	4. c	5. b
4.5	1. F	2. T	3. T	4. F	

Chapter 5

5.1	1. F	2. d	3. d	4. d	5. a
5.2	1. T	2. F	3. F	4. b	5. c
5.3	1. F	2. c	3. b	4. b	5. d
5.4	1. a	2. c	3. b	4. c	5. c
5.5	1. F	2. c			

Chapter 6

6.1	1. c	2. a	3. b	4. d	5. c
6.2	1. a	2. d	3. d	4. c	
6.3	1. T	2. F	3. b	4. b	
6.4	1. F	2. T	3. c	4. d	
6.5	1. F	2. F	3. c	4. b	5. a

Chapter 7

7.1	1. a	2. c	3. a			
7.2	1. T	2. F	3. F	4. T	5. b	
7.3	1. T	2. F	3. c	4. b	5. d	
7.4, 7.5	1. T	2. c	3. a	4. c	5. d	6. b
7.6	1. F	2. T	3. F	4. c	5. b	

Chapter 8

8.1	1. F	2. T	3. c	4. a	5. a	
8.2	1. F	2. a	3. b	4. a		
8.3	1. T	2. b	3. d	4. b		
8.4	1. F	2. c	3. a	4. b		
8.5	1. T	2. F	3. a	4. d		
8.6, 8.7	1. F	2. F	3. T	4. b	5. d	6. a
8.8	1. T	2. F	3. T	4. b	5. d	

Chapter 9

9.1, 9.2	1. T	2. F	3. c	4. b	5. a
9.3	1. d	2. b	3. b	4. c	
9.4	1. T	2. T	3. a	4. b	5. c
9.5	1. F	2. T	3. b	4. d	
9.6	1. T	2. d	3. c		

Name Index

Subject Index